Metropolis

The post-big-bang city, docklands, racist hooliganism, the new underclass, trade union defeats, the mounting disparities of the north–south divide. . . . These social and political images of late-twentieth-century London seem to mark a decisive break with the past. But as *Metropolis* demonstrates, the spectacle of London in the 1980s is not as novel as might seem. What is striking about London's history since 1800 are the continuities and recurrences which punctuate it.

The fears and hopes of businessmen and socialists, of philanthropists and planners, of locals and immigrants, time and again have converged upon London. These essays focus upon such themes and address important questions about class, nationality, sexual difference, and radical politics within the capital. The book combines the established strengths of social history with more innovatory approaches; it deals as much with the history of representations as with the history of movements and institutions. In doing so it questions received ideas about London's fixed identity and investigates its vast yet elusive presence in the space between neighbourhood and nation.

Gareth Stedman Jones is a Reader in Modern History at the University of Cambridge and a Fellow of King's College, Cambridge.
David Feldman is a Fellow and Lecturer in History at Christ's College, Cambridge.

History Workshop Series
General Editor: Raphael Samuel
Ruskin College, Oxford

For Anarchism
History, theory, and practice
edited by David Goodway

Patriotism
The making and unmaking of British national identity
Raphael Samuel
   Volume 1: History and Politics
   Volume 2: Minorities and Outsiders
   Volume 3: National Fictions

New Views of Co-operation
edited by Stephen Yeo

The Radical Soldier's Tale
John Pearman 1819–1908
Carolyn Steedman

Slavery
And other forms of unfree labour
edited by Leonie Archer

Socialism and the Intelligentsia 1880–1914
edited by Carl Levy

Disciplines of Faith
Studies in religion, politics and patriarchy
edited by Jim Obelkevich et al.

The Enemy Within
Pit villages and the miners' strike of 1984–5
edited by Raphael Samuel et al.

Voices of the People
The politics and life of 'La Sociale' at the end of the Second Empire
Adrian Rifkin and Roger Thomas

Language, Gender and Childhood
edited by Valerie Walkerdine et al.

The Progress of Romance
The politics of popular fiction
edited by Jean Radford

Theatres of the Left 1880–1935
Workers' theatre movements in Britain and America
Raphael Samuel et al.

The Worst Street in North London
Campbell Bunk, Islington, between the Wars
Jerry White

Metropolis · London

Histories and representations
since 1800

Edited by David Feldman

and

Gareth Stedman Jones

Routledge
London and New York

First published 1989
by Routledge
11 New Fetter Lane, London EC4P 4EE
29 West 35th Street, New York, NY 10001

Typeset by Hope Services (Abingdon) Ltd, Abingdon, Oxon.
Printed in Great Britain by T.J. Press (Padstow) Ltd, Padstow, Cornwall.

British Library Cataloguing in Publication Data

Metropolis London: histories
and representations since 1800.—
(History workshop series).
1. London. History
I. Feldman, David, 1957– II. Jones,
Gareth Stedman, 1942– III. Series
942.1

ISBN 0 – 415 – 02515 – X
ISBN 0 – 415 – 02516 – 8 Pbk

Library of Congress Cataloging in Publication Data

Metropolis London: histories and representations
since 1800 / edited by David Feldman and Gareth Stedman
Jones.
p. cm. — (History workshop series)
Bibliography: p.
Includes index.
1. London (England) — Historiography. 2. London (England) —
History. I. Feldman, David. II. Jones, Gareth Stedman.
III. Series.
DA676.85.B48 1989

942.1′0072 — dc19

Contents

Contents

Illustrations

Contributors

Sally Alexander is an editor of *History Workshop Journal* and teaches at North East London Polytechnic. She is writing a book on working women in London between the wars.

Jennifer Davis has taught at the Universities of London and Cambridge. She has published a number of articles on law breaking and law enforcement in nineteenth- and twentieth-century England.

John Davis is a Lecturer at Hertford College, Oxford and the author of *Reforming London: The London Government Problem, 1855–1900*, Oxford University Press, 1988.

David Feldman is a Fellow and Lecturer in History at Christ's College, Cambridge. He is completing a book on Jews, immigrants and the English 1840–1914.

James Gillespie is a Lecturer in Politics at Macquarie University, Sydney. He is writing a book on labour and politics in London in the 1920s and 30s.

Tom Jeffery works in education administration.

Susan Pennybacker is Assistant Professor in History at Trinity College, Hartford, Connecticut. She is completing a book which will be titled *A Vision for London: Everyday Life and the LCC Experiment: 1889–1914*.

Ellen Ross lives in New York City and is an Associate Professor of Women's Studies at Ramapo State College in New Jersey. She has written a number of articles on women, family, and neighbourhood life in pre-First World War London and is completing a book, *Love and Labor in Outcast London. Motherhood 1870–1918* (Oxford).

Gareth Stedman Jones is Reader in Modern History at the University of Cambridge and a Fellow of King's College, Cambridge. He is the author of *Outcast London*.

Deborah Thom is a Fellow of Robinson College, Cambridge and a Senior Research Assistant in the Child Care and Development Group in the Social and Political Sciences Faculty, currently working on the history of child guidance in Britain.

Deborah Weiner teaches architectural history at the University of Davis, California. She is writing a book on the architecture of social reform in late-nineteenth-century London.

Introduction

David Feldman and Gareth Stedman Jones

In the events of the last decade, London has played not just a central but also a spectacular part. It is London which has been the site of the most visible triumphs of a newly unfettered capitalism – the mushrooming of new financial services, the 'big bang', the transformation of the docklands, the dizzying rise of property values, the victory of the Murdoch empire over Fleet Street trade unionism. It is London which leads the figures for wealth per head, as it does in crimes against property. There are also more homeless in London than anywhere else – even when migrants find jobs they can rarely afford to buy or rent housing; hence the coachloads of building workers ferried down the motorways from the north each week and billeted in Portakabins. And it is in inner London that the practice of stacking the homeless in bed-and-breakfast accommodation has reached crisis proportions. London is now the pre-eminent object of interest in everything from fashion to soap opera: the East End, once a highly localized or acquired taste, is now the favoured setting for the national fantasy of everyday life.

It is also London which, to recall a phrase current before 1914, has become once again 'the sphinx of labour'. After decades of apparently stable support, Labour in the elections of 1983 and 1987 has sustained unimaginable losses, and everywhere from Bermondsey to Basildon looks for the moment to be in terminal decline. Angry and exasperated provincial socialists round on London with talk of 'the London phenomenon' and treat it as the citadel of the 'loony left'. Everywhere from Saatchi & Saatchi's gallery to the marinas of the East End, London seems to proclaim the ascendancy of a new Conservative Britain. And yet, it was also London which as recently as the early 1980s mounted the most novel and imaginative challenge to the forward march of the new Conservatism. The Greater London Council (GLC) not only won over a popular consensus in favour of *public* transport, it was also the first authority in the country to attach more than token

1

importance to the battle against racism and sexism and to make discrimination into a political issue.

How urgent it has been to intervene in these areas – and most especially to challenge racist assumptions embedded within culture and patterns of employment – has again been demonstrated in London in particularly dramatic form. Racial hostility against immigrants and their descendants, often violent, and antagonistic policing have been a feature of most of Britain's cities. But it is in London that these antagonisms have found their most extreme expression from the Brixton riots to the battle of Broadwater Farm.

Because of the enormous weight of London in national life both as a centre of power and producer of images, it is not difficult to see that thinking about London and its future is as much a way of thinking about the future of Britain, whether we are thinking about the economy, local government, or the prospects for the unconservative half of the nation. What this future will be is of course unclear. But if we are to speculate intelligently about the directions it might take, we need to be better informed about what London is and how it relates to the nation as a whole.

It is here that historians can make a serious contribution to our understanding. For many of the phenomena of contemporary London, which commentators are apt to imagine as unprecedented, are not quite as novel as they might at first appear. Indeed, after looking at the essays in this book, the reader might come away with a distinct sense of *déjà vu*. It is not that history ever repeats itself in simple or foreseeable ways, but as readers will see there are some striking regularities and recurrences in London's history.

In many ways, for example, the record of the last years of the GLC bears an eerie resemblance to the history of the first London County Council (LCC) during its years of Progressivist predominance – in particular, in the gap between the grandiloquence of its rhetoric, its transformative vision, and the modesty of its real powers. In fact, far from being an unparalleled act of Thatcherite rancour, the abolition of the GLC forms just one more step in the extremely chequered career of municipal government in London ever since the 1830s when London escaped the implementation of the Municipal Corporation's Act. Between that time and this, London government has been reconstructed three times (1855, 1889, 1963), and in each case the reason was narrow political calculation, not larger administrative rationality. Furthermore, on each occasion, the Corporation of the City of London was able to exempt itself from becoming subject to wider metropolitan control. Indeed, by one yardstick the jealous and self-interested particularism of the City goes back at least as far as the 1630s when the corporation refused to take any responsibility for the poor suburbs growing up around its walls.[1]

Similarly, the current experience of 'rate-capping' and the confrontation between local needs and the priorities of central government is not a novelty of the 1980s. In the 1920s the intransigent politics now associated with boroughs like Lambeth was prefigured in the even greater defiance of militant East End councils like Poplar, West Ham, Shoreditch, and Bethnal Green. Nor is there anything especially new about 'the London phenomenon', once we detach it from its current preoccupations. The sectarianism, self-righteousness, and self-importance, as well as the energy and creativity, of metropolitan leftism have a venerable history, as the example of the late-Victorian radical clubs demonstrates.

Even the contemporary withering away of a working-class Labour vote in the East End and the inner southern boroughs looks less astonishing once placed in the context of political behaviour in London over the last hundred years. Before the First World War, political loyalties in the poorer riverside constituencies were mixed; indeed, some remained predominantly Tory. Similarly, during the inter-war period, there was no inexorable forward march of Labour. Between 1919 and 1922 there was a large and novel surge of Labour support, and in 1923 Labour won twenty-two parliamentary seats in London. But in 1931 it was back again to five. Present talk about the need for alliances and cross-class support is now almost one century old. It has always been an essential ingredient in Labour and Progressivist success, right back to Keir Hardie's victory in West Ham in 1892. The cross-class support for Ken Livingstone's GLC had its precedents in Morrison's LCC and before that in the electoral support for the Progressives in the 1890s. Even in supposedly bedrock working-class boroughs like Poplar in the 1920s, the degree of Labour success was far from a simple political ratification of a sociological fact. It turns out on closer inspection to have been built upon a carefully constructed coalition between the employed, various categories of the unemployed, and ratepayers, based upon a skilful manipulation of the loopholes in National Insurance, Poor Law, and local and municipal rating regulations. To the extent that there were Labour strongholds in London – and it was mainly a phenomenon of the 1945–70 period – it was as much bound up with the primacy of Labour conceptions of the nation, or, in a more narrowly material sense, with the distribution and perceived quality of public housing, as it was with more familiar notions of class loyalty.[2]

In the area of social policy and social attitudes, as well, the historian of London cannot escape the sense of witnessing the rerun of old antagonisms and fears, played with new names and a new set of characters. At a popular level, undertones of nativist violence accompanied by the visual and verbal paraphernalia of patriotism had their prefigurations in the late-Victorian agitation about Jewish immigration which resulted in the 1905 Aliens Act – a decisive step in the dismantling of the nineteenth-century liberal state. Similarly, in polite society, contemporary talk about the 'new underclass', and the racial fears which often lie not far beneath it, produces a very similar spectrum of argument to that directed at the nineteenth-century casual poor, with discrete allusions to its 'Irishness' often a whispered accompaniment. With a Conservative housing minister now embarking upon a major reform of housing policy under the acknowledged inspiration of Octavia Hill, the wheel would seem to have come full circle.

Finally, even if we consider the types of economic activity upon which the current prosperity of London is based, and the dynamism of its growth in comparison with that of other regions of the country, what is again most striking is not so much its novelty as its consonance with patterns of wealth creation in the metropolitan area over the last three hundred years. The fact is that ever since the 1840s the growth of the London region has been faster than that of any other area. Between 1841 and 1911 London and the south-east accounted for over half the new jobs created in the period, and in the ensuing decades of the twentieth century, south-eastern predominance has been even more marked. The twentieth-century net gain in employment has been shared almost equally between the south-east and the rest of the country.

As this suggests, there is nothing especially new about the north–south divide. Even in the Victorian period, when Britain was 'the workshop of the world', London accounted for between 38 per cent and 64 per cent of all fortunes of over half a million pounds. By contrast, industrial England never accounted for more than 25 per cent. The picture is much the same among the broader middle class. Already in 1812 more than half of Britain's middle-class income was located in the London region, and comparable figures for 1879–80 suggest a similar pattern of distribution. Regional income data available for the period since 1945 suggest a strong continuity with the Victorian and Georgian period. What the 1980s have witnessed is not the creation of 'a divide' but its sharp accentuation. In 1976 income per head in the south-east was 10 points above that of the north-west; by 1983 the gap had increased to 27 points.

Nor is there anything especially new about the dependence of the London economy upon the expansion of the service sector. Indeed, 66 per cent of the new jobs created between 1841 and 1911 were in the services and transport sector. Although London always had a huge manufacturing sector, it seems probable that the growth of London was never industry-led. On the contrary, much of the manufacturing activity that was – and to a lesser extent still is – concentrated there was stimulated by the consumer needs of a vast and, in significant part, opulent population nurtured by service-led growth.[3]

Yet it would be facile to imply that all these continuities, recurrences, and resemblances are of the same weight or meaning. To recall how different a city London was, one need only think of the remoteness of the economic roles and cultural codes which governed relations between the sexes among the working classes before 1914. Between then and now, the decrease in family size, the expansion of married women's waged work, and successive waves of feminist agitation make the Victorian world less recognizable. Similarly, although there is much poverty and deprivation to be observed in contemporary London, generally they bear little resemblance to what was revealed and anatomized by Booth in the 1880s. The great diminution in the demand for male casual labour in the capital has changed the nature of the problem. More than any other single factor it has been the contraction of the Port of London (its containerization and the displacement of what remains to Tilbury) that has brought about this change – a change which marks the nation's commercial decline and separates the London of 1939 from the city of today. Second, some resemblances may be deceptive. A juxtaposition between the power of the late-Victorian City and the bustle of the post-big-bang City of the 1980s would, for instance, mask the long attrition of the sterling area which occurred in between. Similarly, any analogy between the cult of royalty in the 1890s and the tabloid depiction of royalty today would miss the disappearance of the imperial dimension within which it was originally couched.

Nevertheless, for all the qualifications which a historian might want to make, the continuities and recurrences we have mentioned are neither fortuitous nor specious. As a port and centre of the national transport system London has always attracted large immigrant populations. As the capital city, London's identity has always been straddled between locality and nation, with resulting problems for its municipal government. Service employment – an eternal army of government functionaries, clerks, lawyers, soldiers, financial brokers of every sort, servants, and cleaners – has always been a leading sector in London's development. As a result London has always had a disproportionately large middle-class population and an extraordinarily heterogeneous collection of workers. Finally, as Rasmussen argued fifty years ago, London was the first world city whose growth and shape were determined by the market, and – as anyone observing the Isle of Dogs today could testify – it still is.[4]

These regularities and recurrences suggest threads which bind together London past and present. But the larger questions raised by them highlight the inadequacy of writing about London in a purely local or even regional framework. The space between neighbourhood and nation is precisely the space upon which the social and political history of London has been fought out. In the last 200 years metropolitan conceptions of the nation, the 'underclass', the 'alien', the woman as worker, and socialism had their particular local origins, but their formulation was imprinted upon the nation as a whole. The historian's problem in writing about London is not simply that of studying it as a particular embodiment of national history but, further, of suggesting the formative part played by this particular place in the shaping of national history itself.

The essays to be found in this book are exploratory. They traverse the social, the economic, the institutional, the political, the discursive, but without a settled sense of a hierarchy of determinations by which the material is to be ordered. The ambition to write a total history presented in a previous epoch of historiography has not been abandoned. But the spirit of enquiry is different. It is to capture the fluidity and ambiguity of historical meanings, to explore surfaces and their historical effects, rather than to imagine that, once they are peeled away, an essential core of meaning will stand revealed. Experience, class, or social determination, for example: each of these notions is capable of yielding strong but partial illumination. But they cannot be employed, straightforwardly as organizing principles, in the way in which many historians once believed. For when confronted with new questions, they raise as many problems as they resolve. London poses these questions in acute form. Even the object of enquiry cannot be taken for granted. The city is both the institutional and social fabric of urban life and a set of images, metaphors, and symbols which go beyond it. In attempting to capture the consequences of this conception, the writers in this collection have drawn upon insights derived from sources as diverse as psychoanalysis, discourse theory, social anthropology, and cultural studies. They have built upon the achievements of social history, but gone beyond them, because pre-existing approaches did not provide the means to confront the new questions which the last decade had posed to the historian. It is in this double sense – both of addressing questions raised by the present, and of attempting to open up new ways of writing about history – that the essays to be found in this book have been conceived.

August 1987

Notes

Unless otherwise indicated, throughout this collection, place of publication is London.

1 D. Owen, *The Government of Victorian London, 1855–89; The Metropolitan Board of Works, the Vestries and the City Corporation*, 1982; P. L. Garside and K. Young, *Metropolitan London: Politics and Urban Change 1837–1981*, 1982; P. J. Waller, *Town, City and Nation: England 1850–1914*, Oxford, 1983.
2 F. W. S. Craik, *British Parliamentary Election Results, 1885–1918*, 1974; F. W. S. Craik, *British Parliamentary Election Results, 1918–49*, third edn, Chichester, 1983; H. Pelling, *Social Geography of British Elections, 1885–1910*, 1967; K. Wald, 'The rise of class based voting in London', *Comparative Politics*, January 1977; D. Howell, *British Workers and the Independent Labour Party 1888–1906*, Manchester, 1983.
3 C. H. Lee, 'Regional growth and structural change in Victorian Britain', *Economic History Review*, 2nd series, 33, 1981; C. H. Lee, *The British Economy since 1700*, Cambridge, 1986; Y. Cassis, 'Bankers in English society in the late nineteenth century', *Economic History Review*, 2nd series, 38, 1985; W. D. Rubinstein, 'The Victorian middle classes: wealth, occupation and geography', *Economic History Review*, 2nd series, 30, 1977; W. D. Rubinstein, 'Wealth, elites, and the class structure of modern Britain', *Past and Present*, 76, 1977; P. J. Cain and A. G. Hopkin, 'Gentlemanly capitalism and British expansion overseas, II: the new imperialism, 1850–1945', *Economic History Review*, 2nd series, 40, 1987.
4 S. E. Rasmussen, *London, the Unique City*, 1937.

The social problem

Jennings' Buildings and the Royal Borough
The construction of the underclass in mid-Victorian England

Jennifer Davis

By the second half of the nineteenth century, the distinction between a respectable working-class majority and a far smaller class of demoralized poor was increasingly made in public discourse. In a period of general optimism about the state of class relations, the anxieties of the propertied classes focused on the casual poor who peopled England's inner cities. And it was in London, which housed the largest number of the casual poor, that the worst fears of the propertied classes appeared to have been most dramatically realized. Thus debates about the problem of poverty and proposed solutions came to be shaped to a significant extent by perceptions of the casual poor in London; just as law enforcement strategies during this period came to focus on the casual poor who were popularly believed to bear the major responsibility for crime.

To the mid-Victorians, the pauper and the criminal constituted the 'dangerous classes', drawing their recruitment from the unskilled urban poor.[1] But it was not simply material want that conferred membership in them. In contemporary opinion, what distinguished the dangerous classes from the merely poor was their antisocial values and life-styles.[2] The dangerous classes were perceived as a 'residuum', left behind by the mid-Victorian march of moral and material progress. The values and behaviour attributed to them – violence and licentiousness, thriftlessness and dependence, criminality and political volatility – were those which many believed had now been spurned by the respectable majority of the English nation.[3] The degradation of the residuum and the apparent virtues of the nation as a whole came to offer mutual and self-evident proof of the other's existence.

The notion that such a 'residuum' existed survived profound shifts in the prevailing view of the causes and consequences of poverty over the nineteenth century and beyond. At mid-century, it was commonly believed that demoralized values not only distinguished pauperism but were its cause. Fifty years on, it was widely understood that much of London's poverty derived from the seasonal, overstocked, and underpaid character of the labour market.[4] None the less, the view persisted that there remained a 'residuum' of casual poor, who were distinguished from the rest of society not simply by their apparently marginal relationship to industrial capitalism, but also by the way in which they lived. For this group, it was the experience of poverty itself, in particular the rigours of overcrowded and unhygienic urban living and the uncertainty of low-paid and intermittent labour, which had so demoralized them that neither by their own efforts nor by those of the state were they likely to be absorbed into wider society.[5] They were, depending upon the point of view, seen as unfit, un-English, uncooperative, disreputable, dishonest, lumpen, or lacking any understanding of working-class solidarity.

To a surprising extent, contemporary students of urban poverty have continued to occupy the terrain first mapped out by the mid-Victorians. They too have generally accepted that the casual poor constituted a discrete group, characterized by their marginality to economic and social relations, and by their own strategies for survival, from street selling to theft, which operated outside the primary economy. Their social behaviour has been portrayed in equivalent terms: as unorganized, apolitical, frequently violent, and law-breaking.[6] It has even been suggested that the casual poor shared a 'culture of poverty' which was reproduced over successive generations.[7]

Historians who have presented this view of the nineteenth-century casual poor have frequently taken as their reference twentieth-century sociological and anthropological studies of poverty and culture, often framed within a Marxist tradition. It is all the more remarkable that their descriptions of the casual poor and the cultural assumptions made about them have so seldom transcended those of a century earlier. The notion that the subculture of a certain section of the urban poor, both in the nineteenth century and today, might be juxtaposed with contrasting cultures in the rest of society, be they 'working class', 'respectable', 'English', or a combination of any or all of these, has continued to go largely unchallenged in the existing literature. And this is true even for those who have chosen to represent the 'lumpen-proletariat' sympathetically.[8]

It will be argued here that the category of 'casual poor' which has come to be so widely accepted as a subject for historical analysis was not based on any self-evident material and cultural divisions within the London working class. Rather, the 'casual poor' was an ideological category which was constructed in the 1870s and 1880s as the natural successor to the 'dangerous classes' – the pauper and the criminal – of a decade earlier. But it will also be maintained that once the distinction between the residuum and the 'respectable' working class was accepted in public discourse, it was to have real consequences not only for those deemed to belong to the residuum, but for the rest of society as well. In effect, the social existence of the 'residuum' was as much a consequence of its identification as it was a necessary precondition for it.[9]

Through a study of a Kensington slum and its relationship to the wider community in the third quarter of the century, this chapter will seek to illuminate the process of interaction between image and reality by which the residuum was identified and given concrete existence. This slum, Jennings' Buildings, with its 1,000 or so inhabitants, mainly Irish labourers and their families, was known as a 'rookery' and was, until its demolition in 1873, the focus of local anxieties about the dangerous classes. In the event, a disproportionate number of residents were frequently in trouble with the law; many who lived there were heavily dependent on poor relief; and a great deal of disorder emanated from the Buildings which were filthy and disease-ridden. At first glance, Jennings' Buildings inhabitants appear to typify the 'residuum' which dominated mid-Victorian social anxieties.

But despite their notoriety and widespread unpopularity, Jennings' Buildings and its inhabitants by no means occupied a marginal position in Kensington. They were integral to local structures of power and profit. So much so, that those whose interests lay with the Buildings were able, over a number of years, to defeat attempts by other members of Kensington's political elites to have them removed.

Furthermore, the inhabitants of Jennings' Buildings, far from constituting a homogeneous group, were divided by both material circumstances and social attitudes. They were obviously differentiated by their relative skills, job security, and affluence, and by their relationship to the state, in particular to the police and the Poor Law authorities. They also held widely varying attitudes to work and leisure, to home and family, to religion and the rule of law: attitudes often thought to distinguish the 'respectable' working class during this same period.

Indeed, the economic and social concerns of the Buildings' residents were not simply diverse but often conflicting. As a consequence, what unity there was in Jennings' Buildings was imposed largely from without rather than within. The manner in which the police and the Poor Law authorities interacted with Jennings' Buildings and the representation of this interaction in the local press were crucial to maintaining the popular image of Jennings' Buildings as a rookery and of its inhabitants as a uniformly outcast group. In turn, and perhaps ironically, it was their shared experience of local prejudice, both popular and official, that at times blurred divisions between residents and led them to act together against perceived injustice.

The following section of this essay examines the interconnections between Jennings' Buildings, the economic and social structure of Kensington, and local political initiatives towards the Buildings. The people of Jennings' Buildings will then be considered, especially their often conflicting interests, attitudes, and behaviour. A final section will look at the interaction of the Buildings with the Poor Law authorities and the police, in order to suggest how its public image was constructed and maintained. It will be seen, throughout, that the public image of Jennings' Buildings was to have profound effects on the lives of those whom it purported to represent.

I

Built in the late eighteenth century by a local saddler, Jennings' Buildings stood, until 1873, on the corner of Kensington High Street opposite the parish church of St Mary Abbots and close by Kensington Palace. It was a collection of eighty-three two-storey wooden tenements built around five narrow courts, with a single entrance on to the High Street. By all accounts, the Buildings shared the characteristics of the worst Victorian slums. Its houses were poorly ventilated, without running water or drains. They were immensely overcrowded; the 1,000 or so inhabitants of the Buildings 'all crammed, perhaps, into a place which ought not to contain above a hundred'.[10] There were forty-nine public lavatories for the whole population; and, as a consequence, 'human excreta lie all over the courts, in the dustbins and every corner of the place'.[11] Small wonder that, at mid-century, 'over one half the sickness amongst the poor inhabitants of Kensington occurred in Jennings' Buildings',[12] or that in 1873, despite regular cleaning by vestry workmen, the Buildings' death rate was 33 per 100 compared to 17 per 100 for Kensington as a whole.[13]

The people who lived in the Buildings were mostly Irish Catholics by birth or descent,[14] and were predominantly employed in the poorly paid seasonal trades which dominated west London: market gardening and laundry work for the women, building work for the men.[15] As a result, most of the inhabitants of Jennings' Buildings were poor, and looked it. Local resident Leigh Hunt observed 'the naked feet of the children, and the ragged and dissolute looks of men and women' which, he thought, 'present a painful contrast to the general decency'.[16]

In the middle decades of the nineteenth century, Kensington, which had long been a gathering place for royalty and lesser nobility, was one of London's most affluent and fastest-growing middle-class suburbs. The large aristocratic estates which had dominated this area of west London were, from the 1830s, being broken up by their owners, and the land leased or sold to speculative builders to provide housing for those Londoners 'moving upwards to settle'.[17] The years between 1851 and 1871 saw a peak in this process. Kensington's population grew from 17,869 to 91,645, primarily through immigration from Surrey and Kent, and also from London itself.[18] By this time, the High Street area was Kensington's commercial centre and also boasted some of its finest private residences, housing gentlemen of leisure, members of the professions, successful tradesmen, and some notable intellectuals, including John Stuart Mill and Sir John Simon.[19]

During this same period, while a burgeoning local press helped to entrench the public image of Jennings' Buildings as a rookery, Kensington itself came to be surrounded by a very different mythology. In 1855 Hunt published his guide to Kensington entitled *The Old Court Suburb*. His depiction of Kensington as drawing an early and lasting grandeur from the presence of royalty was a popular one, reinforced by the work of other local writers such as William Thackeray.[20] Others, including Matthew Arnold, propagated the image of Kensington as leafy and bucolic, characteristics encapsulated in the celebrated beauty of Kensington Gardens, a public park since the reign of William IV. A poem by Thomas Tickell, in 1772, had speculated on Kensington's origins in a prehistoric love affair between an 'elfin king', Albion, and his 'fairy love', Kenna, on the site of the Gardens: the myths of rural and royal Kensington united.[21] This myth and its associations were revived and celebrated during the second half of the century.

In 1901 Kensington sought and was granted the title of 'Royal Borough', although, except during the years of Victoria's childhood, the Palace had primarily served as a 'secluded hospital for wayward members of the royal family'.[22] Ironically, too, J. M. Barrie's *Peter Pan in Kensington Gardens*, the apotheosis of the mythological Kensington, appeared in 1906 when the borough's attractions to the London bourgeoisie over fifty years had stripped it of any semblance of its former suburban character.[23] If Jennings' Buildings stood in marked and growing material contrast to wider Kensington, at a representational level, too, it could scarcely have had less in common with its surroundings.

Contemporaries certainly noted and deplored the terrible condition of this tenement compared to 'the noble road' on which it stood. But it was not the Buildings, hideous as it was, which aroused the fear and loathing of the local population. Rather it was those who lived there.

In 1855 the *Kensington Gazette* wrote of the Buildings:

> in the heart of the town there has been an acre long desecrated as the haunt of poverty and disease, dirt and crime. To point out a spot of equal social deformity is difficult – to discover one worse is impossible.[24]

This was a widely held view. To local residents of all classes, Jennings' Buildings was known simply as 'The Rookery'.[25] One working-class woman considered she had grounds for an assault prosecution when a neighbour called her 'only fit to live in Jennings' Buildings'.[26]

Jennings' Buildings was perceived not simply as an isolated pocket of vice, but as one of the many receptacles for the 'dangerous classes' to be found throughout London. The *Kensington Gazette* wrote that 'with the dens of London it holds perfect sympathy, the pulsation of the former being promptly answered by the vibration of the latter'.[27] There was a deep-rooted belief within Kensington that the Buildings was actually populated by refugees from the most notorious 'Irish rookery', St Giles. The *West London Observer* christened Jennings' Buildings 'a second St Giles upon a small scale'.[28]

As early as 1855 Hunt had assumed that Jennings' Buildings would soon go the way of the recently demolished St Giles, 'for one advance brings another, and Kensington has become of late so much handsomer as well as larger, that it will hardly leave the ugly blemish on its beauty'.[29] In the event, Jennings' Buildings was not demolished until 1873, despite the fact that, after the passage of the Metropolitan Local Management Act of 1855, vestries were given increasing powers under various statutes to deal with slums such as Jennings' Buildings.[30] The survival of Jennings' Buildings, well past the peak of Kensington's building book, indicates how firmly embedded it was in local structures of profit and politics.

There were a number of important ways in which Jennings' Buildings and its inhabitants contributed to the local economy.

They helped support local 'tradespeople', for whom they were a useful source of 'ready-money customers'.[31] Local publicans actively competed for the custom of Jennings' Buildings. A number catered almost exclusively to those who lived there; and some, as we shall see, came to play an active role in the social organization of the slum.[32]

For other Kensington residents, ownership of the houses in Jennings' Buildings was a highly profitable proposition. For the most part, these owners did not live in the Buildings, but instead let the houses to tenants, who, in turn, sublet rooms to families and individuals. Overwhelmingly, the tenants and subtenants came from Cork, driven to emigrate by the pressures of famine and poverty at home. Large numbers were members of the same families, relying upon kinship and home-town connections to find shelter in the highly competitive London housing market.[33] The Buildings' tenants provided shelter for both profit and sentiment to those connected to them by blood or community ties. With a captive market, and therefore no need to attract tenants by improving conditions, the Buildings' owners received extremely high returns for almost no outlay.[34]

During the last thirty years of the Buildings' existence, its ownership was consolidated in the hands of the wealthy and influential Bird family.[35] They were not only Kensington's biggest slum landlords – owning large parts of the notorious Potteries as well – but were also the area's largest brickmakers, majority shareholders in the West London Railway, and developers of the prestigious Philmore Estate.[36] It is a measure of the Buildings' profitability that the Birds bought into it when land values in Kensington began their meteoric rise, and refused offers to sell over this period despite disposing of adjoining land at vastly inflated prices.[37]

Finally, the Buildings served as a reservoir of labour, with some tenants also overseeing the recruitment of workers into the local building trade, in which the Birds played a prominent role. When it is also noted that a number of the Birds' businesses were located on the High Street, then the complex web of local economic interests which centred on Jennings' Buildings can be fully appreciated.[38]

Although a variety of individuals, many with considerable local influence, profited from Jennings' Buildings, this alone would not have been sufficient to guarantee its continued existence. Profound divisions within Kensington's governing classes also ensured that, whatever the general fears aroused by the slum, no joint strategy was ever agreed upon to confront its threat.

Before the passage of the Metropolitan Local Management Act, vestry politics in Kensington were dominated by High Street tradesmen, many of whom were connected to the building trade. The Bird family, commanding multiple vestry votes through their numerous local properties and wielding extensive economic influence, were prominent among them.[39] This socially close-knit group also monopolized other key areas of local government, including Poor Law and church administration and numerous local charities connected with the latter.[40] Liberal and pro-reform nationally, they were none the less stout defenders of the local status quo, anxious to cling to the reins of patronage which they had wielded largely on their own behalf for over a quarter of a century. After 1855, although not sitting on the vestry themselves, the Birds continued to maintain close business and political connections with many High Street vestrymen, sometimes acting directly as their patrons.[41]

With the passage of the 1855 Act, the High Street's control of local government was challenged by incoming 'urban gentry', who viewed Kensington as a place to live rather than as a field for economic exploitation. The restricted franchise introduced by the Metropolitan Local Management Act enabled this group, centred in Brompton, to acquire increasing influence on the vestry, which had previously been 'open'.[42] They used their power to centralize local government functions under the vestry and a professional bureaucracy appointed by it. Unlike the High Street oligarchy, whose local power had rested upon a diffuse and informal spread of social and economic influence, the position of these new immigrants to Kensington lay in their ability to dominate the more formal machinery of reformed local government.[43]

The urban gentry sought to use their growing influence in local politics to pursue a more interventionist approach to Kensington's social problems – to shape Kensington's growth in conformity with the gracious suburban image which had been one of its main attractions for them. As a result, they proposed successive vestry initiatives to demolish Jennings' Buildings. These initiatives were successfully blocked, not only by the Buildings' owners, who demanded 'high compensation',[44] but also by opposition from the High Street faction of the vestry. Certainly a wish to protect their economic interests, not least a wish to keep down the rates, was important for some, but so too was an alternative vision of local democracy and the proper role for local government in addressing social problems.

This mixture of motives can be seen in the events surrounding a railway company's bid for the Buildings in 1859, in order to build a station on its site. This plan, as it entailed no public expense, received the enthusiastic support of a majority of the vestry. Successful opposition was raised, however, by a group of philanthropists who in 1857 had opened a non-denominational ragged school in the Buildings supported by public subscription and who now insisted that residents be rehoused by the railway company close enough to continue attendance at the school. In the face of the delay caused by this group's opposition, the railway company moved the station to Gloucester Road.[45] It is not to question their obvious sincerity, but merely to emphasize the complex interconnections within Kensington's ruling elites, to point out that the opponents of the station were all High Street business men, and some had close social and political ties with the Birds.[46]

In the event, it was only the threat of a cholera epidemic in 1867 which finally spurred the vestry to intervene in the affairs of Jennings' Buildings. A decision was taken to 'flush' the Buildings once a day and to provide stand-pipes.[47] But the limited nature of this intervention reveals that the fear of the dangerous classes, no matter how acute in Kensington, did not constitute a sufficient basis for united action against them. In part this was because the dangerous classes and their homes were deeply entrenched within the local economy; but there were also profound divisions of interest and attitude which split the parish's governing classes, of which their differing relationship to Jennings' Buildings was just one touchstone.

The final demolition of Jennings' Buildings owed nothing to the anxieties of local residents nor to attempts by the vestry to have them removed. By 1873 immigration from Ireland had passed its mid-century peak, and the population of the Buildings was falling. Stephen Bird, the founder of the family fortune, had died, and his upwardly mobile heirs may have had less interest in continuing as slum landlords, especially when such a role was increasingly unprofitable.[48] In 1873 they sold the Buildings to the self-styled 'Baron' Albert J. Grant to incorporate into his garden.

II

The residents of Jennings' Buildings were mainly Irish, Catholic, and poor, but, like their social 'betters', they were also deeply divided by economic interest, by social attitudes, and by their behaviour. The use of the descriptive category 'casual poor' to refer to the residents of Jennings' Buildings conceals not only these diversities but also the extent to which, in important respects, residents displayed attitudes and behaved in ways often taken to be characteristic not of the casual poor but of the nineteenth-century working class in general.

While almost all the inhabitants of Jennings' Buildings at times suffered periods of under- or unemployment, a considerable gulf existed beween the precarious position of those who were unable to form connections with either employers or their agents inside the slum, and the relatively secure position of those who could. Some residents maintained regular and often personal relationships with local employers, such as the Birds, which lasted over a number of years. These came to entail mutual obligations, such as an expectation of re-employment after a seasonal lay-off, or the fulfilment of a position of trust at the workplace.[49] Within the casual trades carried on by residents, levels of skill and remuneration could also vary widely. Thus, laundrywomen defined themselves and were paid according to a complex diversity of roles within the labour process.[50]

In other ways, too, the attitudes and behaviour of residents did not fit a simple stereotype of the casual worker. There were a number of social clubs in the Buildings, often centred around the public houses there,[51] and at least one savings club. Its collector did not give receipts, because 'the majority of depositors were very poor people and could not write'.[52] Residents of Jennings' Buildings also played an active role in the London-wide bricklayers' strike of 1859. A local public house, the Marquis of Granby, served as the headquarters for the distribution of pay to striking 'society men'. At a time when picketing was illegal, and in a trade where most labour was unskilled and recruits plentiful, the effectiveness of this strike came to depend not only on the provision of strike pay but also on violence and its threat against potential strike-breakers. Inevitably, it was the violence of the strike, which was vital to its success, and not its organization and discipline, that was noted in the press, so contributing to the prevailing negative stereotype of the Buildings' residents.[53]

Although Jennings' Buildings was known as 'The Rookery', and its inhabitants certainly occupied a great deal of police court time, these people were neither uniformly law-breaking nor opposed to the rule of law. A significant number of criminal charges arising from the Buildings, especially for assault but also for theft, were initiated not by the police but by residents, often against neighbours or family members.[54] Furthermore, whether brought by police or private prosecutors, these criminal charges were not evenly distributed among the Buildings' population, but were concentrated on some two hundred or so individuals, many belonging to the same five families.[55]

For some residents, a run-in with the police was a shameful occurrence, undermining what they explicitly claimed was their 'respectability'.[56] Even those individuals who made frequent court appearances differentiated between activities which did not impugn their self-respect, such as drunkenness or begging, and others such as thieving or sexual licentiousness that did.[57] Indeed, there is almost no evidence of prostitution in the Buildings and little of illegitimacy. A substantial number of residents were married at the local Catholic church, and their children were also commonly baptized there. This was as true for those residents often in trouble with the law as for their apparently more law-abiding neighbours.[58]

None the less, a great deal of violence and law-breaking did appear to emanate from the Buildings if judged by the local press reports. Much of this can be attributed not to a common disreputable culture of the residents but rather to the material conditions of their lives. Given the overcrowded and unsanitary conditions of the Buildings, the High Street served as an important recreational area.[59] And because of the lack of privies in the tenement, the street was also used by some residents 'in true Ottoman fashion'.[60] The public houses which residents frequented – the Marquis of Granby, the Civet Cat, and the notorious Coach and Horses – were crowded and noisy, and nightly customers spilled out on to the pavement. The resulting pressure on the police from the vestry and other concerned individuals to control such behaviour resulted in a high level of charges brought against residents for offences such as obstruction, drunkenness, loitering, and suspicious behaviour. These charges, in turn, not only contributed to the Buildings' reputation as a rookery, but also generated tension between the police and residents which sometimes expressed itself in violence by both sides.[61]

The economic organization of the Buildings also generated disorder and other behaviour easily labelled as law-breaking by those outside. To its respectable owners, Jennings' Buildings represented a source of profit and, for the Birds at least, a field of labour recruitment, but their social and political connections lay with the wider community. They relied upon middlemen and -women living in the Buildings to sublet their property. The power and profit of these men and women derived from their ability to produce rents and labour for the Buildings' owners, on the one hand, and essential services for their fellow residents on the other. They let rooms, lent money, ran beer, grocery, and 'leaving' shops, and recruited labour. One family, headed by the redoubtable John 'Falstaff' Simpson and his wife, Ellen, was engaged in all these activities. Another with similarly wide interests was Edmund Green, a 'grocer'. These Jennings' Buildings entrepreneurs operated in a highly competitive situation. To provide the services that underlay their power they cultivated clients who were often linked to them not only by mutual obligations of services rendered but also by ties of kinship and other connections which had their roots in Cork.

In a number of ways the commercial exploitation of the Buildings contributed to its reputation as a rookery. Some of the business enterprises there, such as the lodging-houses and beer shops, were regulated by parliamentary act and so were always vulnerable to police intervention if they were perceived to fall short of legal standards.[62] There were also numerous points at which attempts to exploit the Buildings and rivalries thus engendered might give rise to violence or to behaviour that might be labelled so by outsiders. Rents and interest had to be collected and penalties for failure to pay enforced. A large number of assault cases arose out of such situations, although the violence involved was often minimal.[63] Indeed, on numerous occasions an assault prosecution served simply as another means by which an entrepreneur might bring pressure to bear on a recalcitrant debtor, even though no violence had occurred at all. For their part, customers could apply similar pressure on their patrons if their expectations of service were not fulfilled. Green had his windows broken by dissatisfied clients.[64] Simpson was accused of assault by disgruntled lodgers.[65] All these diverse activities only added to the Buildings' violent and law-breaking reputation.

Rivalry for lodgers was intense and also led at times to violence or its threat between competing landlords and landladies.[66] But perhaps the greatest rivalry involving the largest number of residents and generating a significant amount of real disorder centred around the provision of jobs. Labour was recruited in the Buildings for local building contractors. Simpson controlled an established recruiting network which originated in Cork. Families might emigrate with the help of relatives and friends, perhaps financed by a loan from Simpson. They could then be lodged by Simpson and his connections and their men fed into the local building trade.

By the 1860s Simpson was facing competition from Green, who had his own source of recruits from Cork. They were referred to as 'Grecians' by Simpson's clients, a word still used by Irish construction workers in England to refer to more recent migrants.[67]

The competition between these groups gave rise to numerous pitched battles which resulted in a large number of prosecutions brought by both the police and participants. These fights, organized along family and home-town connections, paralleled the economic organization of the Buildings themselves and the lines of labour recruitment. In particular, they involved members of five extended families, who had close links with Simpson and Green respectively: the same five families who, as a consequence, faced the bulk of criminal charges at the local police court. As a result, it was not the most marginal or economically deprived residents of Jennings' Buildings who were their most 'criminal' elements, but those most integrated, through the patronage of the Buildings' power-brokers, into the slum's social life and the wider Kensington economy. It was the need of these families to protect the interests of their patrons, and of course their own, which gave rise to behaviour which was sometimes violent and sometimes labelled so by the police and other observers.[68]

Throughout this period, the faction fights of Jennings' Buildings and other immigrant areas were often described as 'Irish rows' as if the first word of this soubriquet explained the second.[69] Historians have continued to portray the faction fights, such as occurred in Jennings' Buildings, as a cultural hangover from the Irish immigrants' rural, pre-industrial past.[70] In fact, these rows were not culturally determined. They and much of the violence of Jennings' Buildings had very precise origins in the operation of its credit, housing, and labour networks, which were in turn shaped by the needs of the 'respectable' residents of Kensington.

The social and economic context in which the Irish poor found themselves upon moving to Jennings' Buildings generated deep divisions which could not always be bridged by a shared nationality, religion, or social class.[71] But the experience of life in the Buildings could also at times forge solidarities. Kinship connections were reinforced and, indeed, at times created by the economic organization of both the tenement and wider Kensington.[72] On a larger scale, the Buildings furnished the support which enabled residents to join the bricklayers' strike. But perhaps the most important common experience of residents was the prejudice of the local law-enforcement agencies, the Poor Law authorities, and the Kensington population in general. This experience led residents not only to define themselves against those outside, but also, at times, to combine in opposition to them. It is to the interaction between the local state agencies and the Buildings that this essay now turns.

III

Jennings' Buildings was not the only slum in Kensington. The Potteries, on Kensington's western border, had a national reputation for insalubrity.[73] But it was the Buildings which served as the particular focus of local anxieties. For one thing, it occupied a central position on one of the parish's busiest streets, and, as a result, passers-by consistently encountered its residents in situations, such as 'obstructing' the pavement, which could only confirm their view of them as the demoralized poor. Prejudice against the Irish was also a crucial factor. Numerous parallels were drawn between residents of the Potteries, of whom only 2 per cent were Irish, and those of Jennings' Buildings, to the latter's disadvantage.[74] The Potteries folk were praised for their 'extraordinary spirit of independence',[75] and the *West London Observer* believed, in 1856, 'that many years had passed since the morality of the Potteries was lower than that of other over-populated districts'.[76] By contrast, the paper referred to the Buildings' inhabitants as the 'lower order of Irish', and believed that although some of them 'might be respectable . . . we can confidently assert that there are a great many who are not'.[77]

This view of Jennings' Buildings' inhabitants as particularly demoralized, and the anti-Irish prejudice it reflected, was shared by those public officials who dealt professionally with the Buildings. In 1873 the Medical Officer reported that the slum's paucity of lavatories was actually 'an advantage, regard being had to the character of residents',[78] while his predecessor noted that those living in the Buildings 'are mostly the lowest Irish', with 'low and disgusting habits'.[79] Mr Edmunds, the Relieving Officer, referred to the Buildings' residents as some 'of the worst characters in Kensington'.[80] Until 1869 the Workhouse Master refused to allow a Catholic priest to visit inmates. His policy was endorsed by the guardians, who threw the priest out when he came before them to complain.[81]

The police and the Hammersmith magistrates also held negative views of the Buildings, reinforced by their anti-Irish prejudice.[82] The Hammersmith magistrate James Ingham, later to become Chief Metropolitan Magistrate, 'said it was very curious that Irishmen directly they saw a row always considered the police to be in the wrong and acted against them'.[83] Inspector Bocking, senior officer at the police station opposite Jennings' Buildings, 'reckoned that it was difficult to find many persons in the Buildings to tell the truth'.[84] A colleague commented: 'We hardly ever take up any of the Pottery people for theft, they are known amongst us to be honest and industrious. Our work lies among the Irish.'[85]

The Irish poor of Jennings' Buildings were generally viewed as being inherently dirty, dependent, and criminal. During the years of Fenian activity in London between 1866 and 1868, the characteristic behaviour attributed to them, which had previously been taken simply as evidence of their general demoralization, was now perceived as a symptom of their 'rebelliousness' as well. In 1866 a High Street business man and vestry member excused the slum's terrible condition, telling the vestry: 'they should remember that the owners have to deal with a rebellious people'.[86] In fact, there is no evidence that residents were active in Irish nationalist politics, but the identification thus made between them and the Fenians arose from and added another edge to popular prejudice.

Circumstances ensured that residents of Jennings' Buildings had frequent dealings with the hostile Poor Law authorities. The number of able-bodied males relieved in Kensington more than tripled in winter when the amount of outdoor work declined.[87] During the rest of the year, unemployment and other misfortunes still drove many to seek relief.

Faced with the hostility of Poor Law officials, the women of Jennings' Buildings often took individual action to achieve what, according to their own lights, was fair treatment from them. The men, who worked together in the stoneyard, sometimes combined for a similar purpose. Over a number of years, Joanna Donovan, an ironer with several convictions for theft, drunkenness, and assault, tenaciously pursued the Poor Law authorities in order to secure the welfare of her children, sitting in at the house of the workhouse surgeon and at the workhouse gates.[88] Taken to court by the Relieving Officer, who had accused her of assault, Donovan claimed: 'It was of no use to go before the Board as the case was settled before admission. Several persons in Kensington who had money in the bank were relieved by Mr Edmunds, but not poor people.'[89]

There were a number of strikes at the stoneyard. During one strike, a Buildings' resident came before the Poor Law Board 'on behalf of himself and others' in the stoneyard to complain about the quantity of bread, 'which was less than it was last winter'.[90] At other times, inmates caused damage or committed assaults in the workhouse in order to have the opportunity to complain of unfair treatment before a magistrate.[91] These individual acts of protest and the stoneyard 'mutinies', which also frequently ended with Poor Law officers making accusations of assault or intimidation against participants, all contributed to the public image of the poor as a violent and outcast group. In fact, far from demonstrating a simple rejection of the state, the disputes of Buildings residents with Poor Law officers reveal the rational and coherent standards by which they judged its conduct. The same point may be made about their interaction with the police.

We have already noted the generally negative attitude of the Kensington police towards the residents of Jennings' Buildings, and how, in addition, they were placed under constant pressure by the public to control its threat. But the Kensington police neither wielded unlimited resources nor sought a day-to-day relationship with the Buildings based on unrelenting and unmitigated hostility. The policing of Jennings' Buildings was thus a far more complex operation than that of the systematic suppression of all those activities of residents which might be defined as criminal either by the police or by the public at large. None the less, as it developed, the pattern of policing of Jennings' Buildings, which was reproduced in slums all over the metropolis, did in crucial ways help to fix the tenement's public image as a rookery.[92]

Lacking the resources to suppress disorder entirely within Jennings' Buildings,[93] the Kensington police sought to contain the slum, allowing clearly law-breaking behaviour such as fights to go on inside which they would have suppressed elsewhere.[94] As a result, the Buildings gained a reputation as a haven of lawlessness, which not only attracted professional law-breakers to lodging-houses such as Simpson's, but was also enhanced by the willingness of the police themselves to direct the homeless poor there.[95]

The police concentrated their resources instead upon controlling residents on the outside streets, where they were easily distinguishable by their ragged appearance and Irish accents. Over the years, residents were consistently arrested for behaviour which if carried on by individuals who did not appear similarly disreputable or if it had occurred in other areas of Kensington would have been seen as harmless or ignored. Most of such arrests were for loitering, drunkenness, and other police-defined offences. In these cases, proof of an offender's residence in Jennings' Buildings was commonly sufficient to obtain a conviction.[96]

By focusing their attention on the Buildings' residents found on the surrounding streets, the local police also ensured that they were more likely to discover them in the course of less ambiguous law-breaking acts such as shoplifting, which if carried on by other members of the population might have remained undiscovered.[97] Furthermore, once residents became known to the police, often at a very early age, they were then more likely to be arrested again. The result of this pattern of policing was not only that, whatever the real incidence of law-breaking in Kensington, it was Buildings residents who were more often arrested, but also that a large part of Kensington's 'criminal class', if defined by their records of repeated convictions, was recruited from them.[98]

Because of the close and constant contact between the police and Buildings residents, it was the police who were relied upon for expert knowledge of them at the police court, by the press, and hence by the population at large. But the police shared the popular image of the Buildings' residents as the demoralized poor, even as, through their activities, they helped to reinforce it. Thus they frequently used violence against residents and sometimes ignored their requests for assistance.[99]

Particularly important to the Buildings' public image were the views of Inspector Bocking, who spent over twenty years at the Kensington police station at a time when few policemen remained on the job for longer than five.[100] Bocking, whose negative views of the Buildings' inhabitants have already been noted, was, according to the local paper, 'always considered an authority on Jennings' Buildings inhabitants'. His opinions were sought by both the press and the judiciary with significant impact.[101] In 1872, when a newly appointed magistrate, Bridges, was trying two residents for assault, Bocking informed him that 'there were about 900 persons of the class of the prisoners and those brought before you yesterday living in the Buildings', thus ensuring that Bridges began his tenure with a suitably unfavourable view of the slum.[102]

None the less, despite the massive concentration of policing on Jennings' Buildings and the hostility this engendered, the relationship between the police and residents should not be seen simply as oppositional. Precisely because of their limited resources, the police could not live on terms of unalleviated hostility with the Buildings. They thus sought to mitigate their potentially explosive relationship with its population in a number of ways. We have already noted how they overlooked law-breaking inside the Buildings which would have been too expensive for them in terms of both manpower and bad feeling to suppress. They also sought a certain amount of collaboration with key individuals there. For instance, they consistently overlooked Simpson's contraventions of lodging-house and licensing laws as well as his more serious involvement in the receivership of stolen property in return for information he supplied about other individuals involved in criminal activities.[103] The police, under the leadership of Bocking, also held out to residents at least the possibility of fair treatment. The inspector, within the limitations of his generally negative view of the Buildings' residents, used his detailed knowledge of them, acquired over twenty years of acquaintance, judiciously. When the Kalibars, father and son, were accused of being drunk and disorderly, Bocking testified to the court that 'the elder prisoner had a good character, but he gave an indifferent account of the behaviour of the son'. As a result, the father was discharged and the son convicted.[104]

For their part, residents were well aware that a testimonial from Bocking might have a decisive effect on their fortunes in court, and at times they sought his intervention on their behalf.[105] But they would scarcely have done so if they had not expected him to behave with a certain scrupulousness towards them. Nor should it be overlooked that, throughout this period, the police were consistently called in by Buildings residents to make arrests, sometimes of neighbours and family members, for offences ranging from assault to theft to, on one occasion, child molestation.[106]

Although the policing of Jennings' Buildings necessarily contained an element of mutual dependency, its overall effect was obviously to generate enormous hostility on both sides. Very often this hostility was expressed in individual or collective acts of violence towards the police by residents. As a result, policemen hesitated to enter the Buildings, especially alone. If forced to do so, often in order to issue summonses brought by inhabitants themselves, they could face jeers and missiles or, more seriously, attempts by large groups of residents to prevent the arrest of their fellows.[107]

When residents combined against the police in ways which were sometimes violent but were just as likely to be perceived as such even when they were not, they were not simply expressing their rejection of the state and its law-enforcement functionaries. The willingness of residents to call in the police to make arrests or to speak up for them in court has already been noted. Residents frequently combined to taunt the police in ways that revealed they had their own firmly held notions of acceptable police behaviour. For a period, policemen who entered the Buildings were followed by shouts of, 'Who stole the mutton? Who stole the goose?' Local police believed that this 'applied to a constable who was in the force some time ago stealing the head of a goose'.[108] This may explain the original provenance of the taunt. But it had also been a popular anti-police chant during the Sunday Trading Riots in Hyde Park two years earlier.[109] When they repeated the chant, residents of Jennings' Buildings, like the working-class protesters in Hyde Park, were thus expressing a more complex critique of contemporary policing than might be encompassed by a simple accusation of police hypocrisy. They were also challenging the moral authority of the police to intervene in their lives, if only at certain moments and in specific areas; and they were drawing upon the knowledge that such sentiments might be more widely shared among the London public.

At particular times and around specific issues, the common experience of residents might lead them to act together. For the most part, however, the economic and social divisions between residents were equally as important in determining their relations to each other as any obvoius similarities such as of religion or birthplace. This point was largely lost upon the surrounding population, who viewed the Buildings' population simply as the 'lower order of Irish', a sub-group of the demoralized poor.

Not surprisingly, residents were well aware of how they were perceived by the local population, whatever their various self-perceptions. This point is nicely summed up in the comment of the then 10-year-old 'urchin' Joseph Simpson to the magistrate Ingham. Accused by the police of throwing a stone at the 'hat of a gentleman' in Jennings' Buildings, Joseph retorted: 'Please, sir, there are not many gentlemen who go down the Buildings for stones to hit.'[110] Indeed, the 'gentlemen' of Kensington preferred to keep their distance from the fever-ridden slum, even as they profited from its existence.

IV

When the definition of the 'residuum' was formulated in the mid-nineteenth century, it was in the context of a number of popular anxieties, which were directly linked to the effects of urban living. These included the discovery of a growing geographical gulf between the well-off and the urban poor, as well as concern about the effects of urban environmental hazards on the poor's well-being. As the century progressed, the conviction grew that the urban environment could actually have an irreversibly negative influence on the physical and moral evolution of poor city dwellers over a number of generations.[111] Underlying these anxieties was the belief of an increasing number of the governing classes that social reform and social policy were failing to effect any substantial transformation in the economic and moral condition of this group, and hence of any diminution in the dangers it was presumed to pose to the social order. This is not to say that all of society constructed these perceptions of the 'residuum' in the same way or for the same reasons in every case. None the less, the belief that such a group existed whose members behaved in identifiably characteristic ways was widely shared.

We have argued here that there was in Victorian London no single group of casual poor who were united by either economic interest or social attitude and behaviour. Individually, the so-called casual poor residuum held attitudes and behaved in ways generally seen as characteristic of the respectable working class, and they were closely integrated into the economic and political structures of the metropolis. But the organization of the London economy also served to create and exacerbate divisions within this group which further belie any attempt to view them as a discrete category or class. And this was true even for those members of the urban poor who shared common roots in Ireland. A wide discrepancy thus existed between the image of the casual poor in London and the material condition of their lives.

But neither did the casual poor exist at two autonomous levels, the one ideological and the other real. Despite their apparent contradictions, 'perception' and 'reality' continuously interacted to shape each other in a number of crucial ways. Thus, the behaviour of the casual poor, conditioned by their economic circumstances, often appeared to substantiate the popular image of them as inherently violent and law-breaking. Overcrowding in Jennings' Buildings led residents to spend time on the streets in numbers which the wider population viewed as threatening. The businesses of the Buildings, labour recruitment, money-lending, and subletting, while they operated in a highly competitive situation, were typically regulated through the exercise of informal sanctions which readily gave rise to behaviour easily labelled as violent and law-breaking by those outside.

But the casual poor did not operate within a separate informal economy, nor did their behaviour arise from the brutalizing effects of poverty or a rejection of respectable values. Rather, as this essay has shown, Jennings' Buildings was an integral part of the wider economy of Kensington. The provision of housing and jobs was determined by the needs of the respectable capitalists outside the Buildings who profited from subletting within and depended upon labour recruiters there to maintain an oversupply of labour for the seasonal trades that dominated Kensington. However, whatever the real sources of disorder in rookeries such as Jennings' Buildings, it helps to explain why theories about the demoralization of the casual poor appeared so convincing to the 'respectable' majority of both Kensington and wider London.

If the popular image of the casual poor depended, in part, upon the manner with which the wider community actually interacted with those deemed to belong to this group, that interaction was, in turn, shaped by popular perceptions about the nature of the casual poor. This interplay between perception and reality is aptly illustrated by the activities of the Metropolitan Police in Kensington, the agency of the state which had the most immediate contact with the casual poor and which also bore direct responsibility for protecting the respectable from the residuum. As this study has shown, the policing of Jennings' Buildings was not only crucial to constituting its inhabitants as a criminal or outcast group, but also itself reflected popular perceptions of the casual poor which the police shared.

The example of the police demonstrates not only the extent to which rhetoric and reality were mutually reinforcing, but also the extent to which they were mutually constraining. Crucial material limitations on policing ensured that, whatever the extent of respectable anxieties, the police could not simply act in response to them but were forced to come to terms with the 'casual poor'. Similarly, while social policy to deal with poverty after mid-century was itself shaped by the prevailing discourse about the casual poor, it was also framed in light of the political and economic costs which the implementation of these policies by central and local government would entail. Certainly, in Kensington this would appear to be the case. Although the poor of Jennings' Buildings were widely viewed as violent and law-breaking, except during the 1866 cholera epidemic, Kensington's political elites were generally unwilling to make even a modest sacrifice of their various economic interests to eradicate that threat. Moreover, because this political elite had differing economic interests, many of which were closely intertwined with the continued existence of Jennings' Buildings, they were hardly likely to be able to settle on a common initiative against the slum.

At the beginning of this essay, it was suggested that over the years the dangerous classes and their successors have been defined by the apparent contrast of their shared culture to those of other social groups: for example, the working class, the respectable, or even the 'English'. But it is possible to go further and argue that the definition of these latter groups itself depends upon the existence of their negative 'other'. We have shown here that the urban poor did not occupy a distinct cultural universe. Placed under similar scrutiny, it is certain that the 'respectable' would prove to be an equally elusive category. As a result, the use of so-called cultural characteristics either to label groups or individuals or to explain their behaviour appears problematic. In the case of England, at least, the evidence suggests that cultural divisions thought to define important social groups, such as religion, ethnic background, or class, have been based on ideological assumptions which actually ignore social, economic, and political factors tending both to fragment these groups and often to reconstitute them across apparent social boundaries.

But even if ideologically based, the belief in such groups has had real social consequences. Throughout the last hundred years, the perceived existence of marginal groups within English society – from Irish immigrants, to Jewish immigrants in the East End at the turn of the century, to racial minorities today – has provided a major justification for the extension of police powers: powers which could, if needed, be deployed more widely against other sections of the population.[112] The experience of popular prejudice, often institutionalized in the activities of the state and local government agencies such as the police, may at times have forged solidarities among groups against which it was directed. But the existence of these outcast groups, even as their threat was variously perceived, has also at times contributed to the making of remarkable political alliances between unlikely bedfellows.[113] Indeed, it is a measure of the power of the image of these outcast groups that such alliances have been more easily constructed with greater significance than any alternative alliances between them and the formally organized labour movement.[114]

Notes

1 This was precisely the point made by the Criminal Recorder in 1859: *Judicial Returns for 1859*, Parliamentary Papers (henceforth PP), vol. XXVI, p. 345.

2 G. Stedman Jones, *Outcast London: A Study in the Relationship between Classes in Victorian Society*, Oxford, 1971, *passim*.

3 According to the *Oxford English Dictionary*, Bright used the word 'residuum' in 1867 to refer to a 'class' of 'almost hopeless poverty and dependence' to be found 'in every constituency'.

4 Stedman Jones, op. cit., pt III.

5 This was Charles Booth's view. See for instance, *Life and Labour of the People of London*, vol. I, *East, Central and South London*, 1892, ch. VI.

6 Very few books in the recent past have sought to recover the lives of the 'casual poor' in the nineteenth and early twentieth centuries. Among the most notable, Stedman Jones, op. cit., and J. White, *The Worst Street in North London: Campbell Bunk, Islington, between the Wars*, 1986, although seeking wider economic and social explanations for the existence of the casual poor, none the less portray that group similarly to nineteenth-century observers – as violent, volatile, politically apathetic, and, indeed, culturally alien to wider English society. See White, ibid., particularly, chs 2 and 3; Stedman Jones, op. cit., pp. 345–9. Various studies of working-class industrial organization

in the nineteenth century have stressed the inability of the casual poor to organize; see, for instance, R. McKibbin, 'Why was there no Marxism in Great Britain?', *English Historical Review*, vol. cccxci, April 1984, pp. 229, 303; and note 53 below. Histories of law-breaking and law enforcement in nineteenth-century England have also generally accepted that the 'casual poor' opposed dominant social values, particularly the rule of law, and were especially prone to law-breaking. For example, see M. Brogden, *The Police: Autonomy and Consent*, 1982, pp. 184–95, or V. A. C. Gatrell, 'The decline of theft and violence in Victorian and Edwardian England', in V. A. C. Gatrell, B. Lenman, and G. Parker (eds), *Crime and the Law: A Social History of Crime in Europe since 1500*, 1980, pp. 238–9.

7 First defined by O. Lewis in the 1950s, see, 'The culture of poverty', *Anthropological Essays*, New York, 1979, pp. 67–80. It has since been widely criticized. For a particularly telling challenge, see C. A. Valentine, *Culture and Poverty: Critique and Counter Proposals*, Chicago, 1968. Recently, this view has attracted support from sections of the British right, offering an explanation for poverty, low educational achievement, and long-term unemployment largely divorced from structural economic causes. For an early example, Sir Keith Joseph, 'The cycle of deprivation', speech given to the Pre-School Playgroups' Association, 29 June 1972, cited in M. Rutter and N. Madge, *Cycles of Disadvantage: A Review of Research*, 1976, p. 4. The concept is still deployed by historians. A recent example is A. Wohl, *Endangered Lives: Public Health in Victorian Britain*, 1983, pp. 43, 61, 77–8, 86–7. G. Himmelfarb has a critique of its general usage without rejecting its validity: *The Idea of Poverty: England in the Early Industrial Age*, 1984, pp. 369–70.

8 An early forerunner was undoubtedly F. Engels on crime: F. Engels, *The Condition of the Working Classes in England*, 1892, reprinted 1969, pp. 157–62. See C. Critcher, 'Sociology, cultural studies and the post-war working class' in J. Clarke, C. Critcher, and R. Johnson (eds), *Working Class Culture: Studies in History and Theory*, 1979, p. 27; R. Johnson, 'Culture and historians', ibid., pp. 45–6, seems to argue for the simple substitution of cultural for the Victorians' moral explanations of working-class behaviour. S. Hall sees the black wageless in England developing a distinct culture which boasts, however, only a 'quasi-political consciousness'; similar political limitations have been ascribed to the casual poor since the nineteenth century. See S. Hall, *et al.*, *Policing the Crisis: Mugging, the State and Law and Order*, 1978, esp. ch. 10 and pp. 395–7; also S. Hall and P. Scranton, 'Law, class and control', in M. Fitzgerald *et al.*, *Crime and Society: Readings in History and Theory*, 1981, pp. 484–5. Most recently, P. Gilroy has argued that the urban poor, particularly blacks, are developing a 'politics of community', resting on shared cultural identities, which contrasts with 'traditional', 'Western' politics, which is class- and institutionally based. Here once more is the assertion of two contrasting political and cultural traditions which appear to

confirm each other's existence: P. Gilroy, *There Ain't No Black in the Union Jack: The Cultural Politics of Race and Nation*, 1987, ch. 5.

9 In this essay, the general term 'residuum' will be used to signify both the dangerous classes of the 1850s and 1860s and the casual poor of the 1880s and 1890s as they were perceived by contemporaries.

10 L. Hunt, *The Old Court Suburb or Memorials of Kensington, Regal, Critical and Anecdotal*, 2 vols, 1855, vol. I, p. 86.

11 F. Goderich Junior, *Medical Officer's Report on the Sanitary Condition of the Parish of St Mary Abbots, Kensington*, 1856, p. 15, Kensington Library (henceforth KL).

12 Ibid., p. 15.

13 T. Orme Dudfield, *Medical Officers' Report, Parish of St Mary Abbots, Kensington*, 1873, KL.

14 In 1861, in an official population of 912, 393 were born in Ireland, and at least 318 were the children of immigrants: *Census*, RG 16, 1861.

15 For a detailed breakdown of occupations, 1851–71, see P. Malcomson, 'Getting a living in the slums of Victorian Kensington', *The London Journal*, vol. 1, no. 1, 1975, p. 52. In 1861, 75.1 per cent of males gave their occupation as labourers and 60 per cent of these as building labourers. Of the women, 59.2 per cent were laundry workers and 13.8 per cent garden workers.

16 Hunt, op. cit., p. 86.

17 F. H. W. Sheppard (ed.), *Survey of London*, vol. XXXVII, *North Kensington*, 1973, p. 4.

18 During these years, 7 per cent of all new buildings in London were in Kensington: ibid., p. 7.

19 Kensington Palace Gardens was known as 'Millionaires' Row': ibid., p. 7.

20 F. H. W. Sheppard (ed.), *Survey of London*, vol. XLII, *Southern Kensington: Kensington Square to Earls Court*, 1986, p. 4.

21 D. Hudson, *Kensington Palace*, 1968, pp. 109–14.

22 Ibid., p. 82.

23 *Survey of London*, vol. XLII, p. 399.

24 *Kensington Gazette*, 6 February 1855.

25 R. W. Brown, *Kenna's Kingdom, A Ramble through Kingly Kensington*, 1881, p. 148; *West London Observer*, 21 January 1865.

26 *West London Observer*, 9 January 1868.

27 *Kensington Gazette*, 21 February 1855.

28 *West London Observer*, 27 November 1858; also Brown, op. cit., p. 149; Hunt, op. cit., p. 87. But in 1851 only 18.6 per cent of heads of household in Jennings' Buildings were born in Middlesex: Malcomson, 'Getting a living', op. cit., p. 52.

29 Hunt, op. cit., p. 87.

30 Stedman Jones, op. cit., pp. 188–90; A. Wohl, *The Eternal Slum: Housing and Social Policy in Victorian London*, 1977, ch. 3.

31 W. C. Hazlitt, *The Hazlitts, Part the Second, A Narrative of the Later Fortunes of the Family with a Survey of the Western and Other Suburbs of London as They Were Sixty Years Since*, Edinburgh, 1912, p. 136.

32 On its opening day, one public house in Jennings' Buildings sold six quarts of beer for a shilling and engaged a band; there ensued 'a great uproar': *West London Observer*, 28 September 1867.

33 For the Irish background to immigration to London, see L. Lees, *Exiles of Erin: Irish Immigrants in Victorian London*, Manchester, 1979, ch. 2.

34 Vestry Minutes, quoted in *West London Observer*, 7 June 1856.

35 By 1870 the Birds owned at least thirty-eight houses; the ex-publican of the Coach and Horses owned five; fifteen were owned by non-Kensington residents; two houses were owner occupied: Kensington Rate Book, 1870, KL.

36 *Survey of London*, vol. XXXVII, p. 71.

37 In 1857 S. Bird sold land in Jennings' Buildings for a ragged school for £930; in 1864 he sold an equivalent piece on Kensington Church Street for £3,500; in 1873 the ragged school was resold for £1,600; ibid., p. 35; E. M. Daniel, *Endowed Charities of Kensington, by Whom Bequeathed and How Administered*, 1891, p. 14.

38 *Post Office London Street Directory*, 1863.

39 See, for instance, Churchwarden Election, Kensington Vestry Minutes, 5 April 1847, KL.

40 For example, *Annual Report*, Kensington Parochial Institute, 1852, KL.

41 Kensington Vestry Minutes, 2 September 1868, KL.

42 A deal with the High Street faction enabled this group to prevent the Kensington Parochial Association, established in 1854, from making serious inroads into the vestry. See *West London Observer*, 10 November 1855.

43 See the struggle for control of the Poor Law administration in 1870, Board of Guardians Minutes, Kensington, KBG 27, pp. 297–375, Greater London Council Record Office (henceforth GLCRO). For a similar example in St Marylebone, D. Owen, *The Government of Victorian London, 1855–1889*, 1982, pp. 276–8.

44 *West London Observer*, 26 July 1856.

45 *West London Observer*, 26 February 1859, 5 March 1859, 26 March 1859.

46 Their leader, Corbett Cresswell, a surveyor, defended Stephen Bird against charges of corruption from anti-High Street vestrymen over his collection of parish dust: *West London Observer*, 26 July 1856.

47 Vestry Minutes, 7 February 1866 and 8 August 1866, KL. This was less radical than the 'unreformed' vestry's response to the 1848 cholera epidemic when regular cleaning and better drainage were introduced: *Report of the Works Committee on Jennings' Buildings, Kensington and Kensington Workhouse*, Metropolitan Sewers Commission, 7 February 1849, GLCRO. Between 1849 and 1856 deaths from cholera in Jennings' Buildings dropped markedly: *Medical Officer's Report*, 1856, p. 9.

48 In the 1860s Augustus Bird built artisans' dwellings in the Potteries: P. E. Malcomson, 'The Kensington Potteries: a study in slum

development in Victorian Kensington', unpublished M.Phil. thesis, University of Leicester, 1970, pp. 30–2.

49 For an example, the assault case against John Daley: *West London Observer*, 22 December 1866.

50 Malcomson, 'Getting a living', op. cit., p. 44.

51 For example, *West London Observer*, 2 March 1871; and *Census*, RG 9–16, 1861.

52 *West London Observer*, 28 November 1857.

53 *West London Observer*, 26 March 1859. To a remarkable extent, historians continue to contrast the violent behaviour of immigrant labour in urban industrial disputes against the more 'mature' trade unionism of the settled English population. E. P. Thompson described the Irish casual labourers as 'pre-industrial'; their virtues, which included 'violent, sometimes good humoured contempt of English authority', and, of course, a willingness to work until they dropped, contrasted with those of the disciplined English artisan who had both 'application and foresight': E. P. Thompson, *The Making of the English Working Class*, 1963, pp. 469–85. More recently D. Geary made a similar observation for the period 1848 to 1939; he believes that groups with 'traditionally low expectations' such as Irish immigrants, rather than organizing, 'protested in individual acts of violence' or drank: D. Geary, *European Labour Protest, 1848–1939*, 1981, p. 6. Lees also draws a dichotomy between traditional forms of protest which the Irish transplanted from their rural homeland and the more sophisticated methods they learned eventually from their English counterparts: Lees, op. cit., pp. 213–19, 249.

54 J. Davis, 'A poor man's system of justice: the London police courts in the second half of the nineteenth century', *Historical Journal*, vol. 27, no. 2, 1984, p. 319.

55 Based on an analysis of 372 reported cases in the *West London Observer* between 1855 and 1873.

56 See the case of Michael Scannell: *West London Observer*, 3 June 1871; see also Davis, 'A poor man's system of justice', op. cit., p. 320.

57 For examples, the case of Margaret Wilkins: *West London Observer*, 24 September 1864; and the case of William Johnson: *West London Observer*, 28 September 1867.

58 On prostitution, see Malcomson, 'Getting a living', op. cit., p. 47. For births and marriages, Baptismal Registers, vol. IV–VI, and Marriage Register, vol. IV, Our Lady of Victories, Kensington.

59 For example, *West London Observer*, 1 October 1864.

60 *West London Observer*, 8 July 1858.

61 See, for example, *West London Observer*, 1 October 1864 and 7 September 1867.

62 *West London Observer*, 24 May 1862.

63 For example, assault case of Mary Handlin: *West London Observer*, 13 June 1868.

64 *West London Observer*, 10 November 1866.

65 *West London Observer*, 27 February 1864.

66 Catherine Welsh assaulted Mary Carter for 'taking a lodger from her': *West London Observer*, 15 August 1868.

67 *West London Observer*, 27 September 1862; D. MacAmblaigh, *An Irish Navvy*, 1976, p. 110; see also E. Partridge, *A Dictionary of Slang and Unconventional English*, ed. P. Beale, 1984.

68 John Swift, 'a fresh arrival' of six weeks, became involved in an ongoing row between the Simpsons and the Sweeneys because he was 'sort of a third cousin' of William Sweeney: *West London Observer*, 27 September 1862.

69 *West London Observer*, 23 June 1866; see also F. Finnegan, *Poverty and Prejudice: A Study of Irish Immigrants to York, 1840–1875*, Cork, 1982, pp. 132–42; R. Swift, ' "Another Stafford Street row": law, order and the Irish presence in mid-Victorian Wolverhampton', in R. Swift and S. Gilley (eds), *The Irish in the Victorian City*, 1985, pp. 179–206.

70 S. Gilley, 'English attitudes to the Irish in England, 1700–1900', in C. Holmes (ed.), *Immigration and Minorities in British Society*, 1978, p. 99; Lees, op. cit., p. 213.

71 In 1872 washerwomen in Kensington struck for 'three shillings a day and no man labour': *West London Observer*, 22 June 1872.

72 At least forty people attended the wake of Bridget Green, wife of Edmund: *West London Observer*, 14 October 1865.

73 In 1854 the average life span in the Potteries was 13 years, in Jennings' Buildings 17 years, and for the 'resident gentry and shopkeepers in Kensington' 48 years: *Medical Officer's Report*, quoted in the *West London Observer*, 2 January 1858; see also Malcomson, 'The Potteries', op. cit., passim.

74 Figures from Malcomson, 'Getting a living', op. cit., p. 54.

75 M. Bayly, *Ragged Homes and How to Mend Them*, 1869, p. 36.

76 *West London Observer*, 20 September 1856.

77 *West London Observer*, 27 November 1858.

78 *Medical Officer's Report*, 1873, quoted in *West London Observer*, 12 April 1873.

79 *Medical Officer's Report*, 1857, p. 15; Board of Guardians Minutes, KBG 19, 24 July 1862, p. 558, GLCRO.

80 *West London Observer*, 2 January 1866.

81 One guardian believed the idea 'was at variance with those protestant principles upon which the institutions of the Parish are based': Board of Guardians Minutes, KBG 19, 14 January 1862, p. 15, GLCRO.

82 See the views of the magistrate Bridges: *West London Observer*, 21 December 1872.

83 *West London Observer*, 2 June 1860. However, Ingham consistently refused parish requests to remove paupers who had been in England some time to Ireland, believing it 'cruel'; he thought the Irish, unlike the English labourer, was 'not accustomed to anything like steady labour': *Select Committee on Poor Removal*, PP, vol. XIII, 1854–5, q. 2255.

84 *West London Observer*, 22 May 1869.

85 Bayly, op. cit., p. 63. On the debate on anti-Irish prejudice in Britain, see Gilley, 'English attitudes', and M. A. G. O'Tuathaigh, 'The Irish in nineteenth-century Britain: problems of integration', in Swift and Gilley, op. cit., pp. 13–36; Finnegan, op. cit., ch. 11.

86 *West London Observer*, 21 April 1866.

87 For example, the number of able-bodied paupers relieved outdoors increased from 197 in July 1869, to 644 in January 1870: *Poor (Metropolis) Accounts and Papers*, PP, vol. LIII, 1868–9, p. 258.

88 *West London Observer*, 20 January 1869.

89 *West London Observer*, 21 November 1868. This claim had some justification; a year later, Edmunds absconded to the United States with several hundred pounds of workhouse funds: *West London Observer*, 27 November 1869.

90 Board of Guardians Minutes, KBG 17, 8 January 1857, p. 148, GLCRO; see also ibid., KBG 27, 6 October 1870, p. 150; and *West London Observer*, 18 February 1871.

91 Davis, 'A poor man's system of justice', op. cit., p. 326.

92 This argument is presented in greater detail in J. Davis, 'Law-breaking and law enforcement: the making of a criminal class in mid-Victorian London', unpublished Ph.D thesis, Boston College, 1985, chs 4 and 6.

93 In 1869 there were 515 men in Kensington (T) division policing 75.39 square miles – the third largest division in London: *Report of the Commissioner of Police of the Metropolis*, PP, vol. XXVIII, 1871, p. 8.

94 This was also true of the Nichol: R. Samuel, *East End Underworld: Chapters in the Life of Arthur Harding*, 1981, pp. 1–2; also O. Gill, *Luke Street: Housing Policy, Conflict and the Creation of a Delinquent Area*, 1977, pp. 59–60.

95 See, for example, *West London Observer*, 1 February 1862 and 9 October 1864.

96 For example, case of Richard Brown: *West London Observer*, 24 May 1862.

97 For example, case of Robert Murphy: *West London Observer*, 9 April 1870.

98 For an example of the criminal career of Dennis Swift, see Davis, 'Law breaking and law enforcement', op. cit., ch. 6.

99 For examples, *West London Observer*, 19 July 1862, 24 July 1865, and 1 January 1870.

100 On Bocking: *West London Observer*, 15 April 1871; on police recruitment: C. Steedman, *Policing the Victorian Community: The Formation of English Provincial Police Forces, 1856–1880*, 1984, pp. 92–105.

101 *West London Observer*, 12 May 1866.

102 *West London Observer*, 21 December 1872.

103 See, for example, *West London Observer*, 25 January 1862; and Davis, 'Law breaking and law enforcement', op. cit., pp. 404–5. Collaboration with beer shopkeepers and publicans was common

police practice: *Report of the Departmental Commissioner Appointed by the Secretary of State for the Home Department to Inquire into the State of Discipline and Organization of the Detective Force of the Metropolitan Police*, 1878, HO45 9442–66692, q. 1644, Public Records Office.

104 *West London Observer*, 12 October 1867.
105 For examples, see cases of Garett Nagle, Edward Foley, and Honora Ryan: *West London Observer*, 16 June 1866, 31 July 1869, and 1 January 1870.
106 Davis, 'A poor man's system of justice', op. cit., pp. 319–20.
107 *West London Observer*, 22 July 1871.
108 *West London Observer*, 19 September 1857.
109 P. T. Smith, *Policing Victorian London: Political Policing, Public Order and the London Metropolitan Police*, 1985, p. 130.
110 *West London Observer*, 8 February 1862.
111 D. Pick, *Faces of Degeneration: A European Disorder, 1848–1988*, Cambridge, 1989.
112 Hall, op. cit., especially ch. 9; J. Davis, 'The London Garotting Panic of 1862: a moral panic and the creation of a criminal class in mid-Victorian England', in Gatrell et al., op. cit., pp. 190–214.
113 See, for example, D. M. Feldman, 'The importance of being English: Jewish immigration and the decay of liberal England', in this volume.
114 This point is powerfully made about the situation of blacks in contemporary Britain by P. Gilroy, op. cit., ch. 2; see also D. M. Feldman, 'Immigrants and workers, Englishmen and Jews: Jewish immigration in the East End of London', unpublished Ph.D. thesis, University of Cambridge, 1986.

2

The People's Palace
An image for East London in the 1880s

Deborah E. B. Weiner

I will give you a house to shelter you and rooms in which to play; you have only to find the rest. Enter in, my friends; forget the squalid past; here are great halls and lovely corridors – they are yours. Fill them with sweet echoes of dropping music; let the girls laugh and the boys be happy within these walls. I will give you the shell, the empty carcase; fill it with the Spirit of Content and Happiness.

In this place you will find, or you will make yourselves, all the things which make the lives of the rich happy. Here you will have music, dancing, singing, acting, painting, reading, games of skill, games of chance, companionship, cheerfulness, light, warmth, comfort – everything.

Walter Besant, *All Sorts and Conditions of Men: An Impossible Story*, 1882[1]

It is not so much relief from actual distress that the people of Mile End and Whitechapel require as some contrast with the grinding monotony of their daily lives.

'A real jubilee offering', *Saturday Review*, 23 April 1887[2]

The Palace has now lost some of its 'entertaining' features, including social (not music-hall) dances, which went off well and has taken to itself more of an educational character. . . . I cannot help feeling somewhat disappointed at the change. It is like the coming of a cloud over Mr Besant's delightful dream and I am jealous of the 'utilitarianism' . . . which has dimmed his vision of enjoyment.

Rev. Harry Jones, *Fifty Years; or, Dead Leaves and Living Seeds*, 1895[3]

In 1886 the architect Edward R. Robson exhibited a design at the Royal Academy for the People's Palace, an institution to be built on Mile End Road in the heart of London's East End (Figure 1). The drawing, 'Oriental in character though the details are Renaissance in feeling', in the words of *The Builder*,[4] presented an elaborately decorated domed building surrounded by a long, ground-storey arcade, recalling the Royal Albert Hall in South Kensington. Replete with minarets capped with gilded cupolas, the building was to have had Portland stone columns, arches, and pediments set off against polychrome brick; its large rotunda was both to have served as an entrance to the Palace and, heated in winter, to have been a playground for the children of the district all year round.[5] In stark contrast to its surroundings, the design was suggestive of an exotic pleasure palace, a far cry from anything hitherto erected in the East End but in keeping with the vision of a 'Palace of Delights' as created by the heroine of Walter Besant's novel, *All Sorts and Conditions of Men: An Impossible Story*, published four years before, the popularity of which played a part in the fund-raising campaign for a centre of recreation in the midst of the East End. The great domed Palace, according to the fund-raising brochures, was to contain a large assembly hall, a library and reading-room, workshops, warm and cold swimming-baths, a gymnasium, rooms for cycling and cricket clubs, social rooms, concert rooms, and a winter garden (Figure 2). It was to be 'a place for social intercourse, and a possibility of escape from the depressing influences of interminable streets'.[6]

The publication of Walter Besant's novel in 1882 corresponded with the availability of funds from a private trust which had as its object the provision of 'Intellectual Improvement and Rational Recreation and Amusement for the people living in the East End of London'.[7] The novel was the outcome of Besant's interest in the East End of London as amateur archaeologist and social investigator.[8] It tells the story of a young heiress recently graduated from Newnham College, Cambridge, determined to see at first hand the way of life of those who toil in the East End, the source of her own personal fortune. Disguised as a poor seamstress, she goes to live and work in Stepney. Her perception of the East End – guided by a well-educated young man whose circumstances have left him to labour in the district – is not that commonly held in the 1880s of horrific poverty and squalor, but rather she is moved by the *tedium* of existence.

Besant's interpretation of the social ills is voiced by his two main characters. The young hero toiling in the East End declares:

What we want here . . . is a little more of the pleasures and grace of life. To begin with, we are not poor and in misery, but for the most part fairly well off. . . . When all our works are in full blast, we make quantities of money. See us on Sundays, we are not a bad-looking lot; healthy, well-dressed, and tolerably rosy. But we have no pleasures.[9]

The answer posited in the novel is the 'Palace of Delights' paid for by the wealthy heiress, an institution which brings grace and pleasure to the East End. The novel concludes:

The Palace is in working order now, and Stepney is already transformed. A new period began on the opening night for all who were present. For the first time they understood that life may be happy: for the first time they resolved that they would find out for themselves the secret of happiness.[10]

The novel, according to one contemporary critic, 'shocked and aroused the conscience of all England'.[11] Another suggested that it had 'probably done more than any other to familiarize the general public with the true character of that dark continent called the East End' (Figure 3).[12] The novel was hugely successful and was influential in shaping the work of the Beaumont Trust: John Barber Beaumont, a Unitarian philanthropist, had shortly before his death in 1841 endowed the Beaumont Philosophical Institution in Beaumont Square, Mile End Road, Stepney, 'for the mental and moral improvement of the inhabitants of the said Square, and the surrounding neighbourhood', leaving £300 a year and a trust of £13,000.[13] Without proper leadership or funding, the Beaumont Institute closed its doors in 1879, the question of the remaining funds left unsettled. In 1882 a new scheme for the Beaumont Trust was drawn up by the Charity Commissioners, and Sir Edmund Currie, the heir to a distillery fortune and an active figure in East End politics, including service on the School Board, was appointed chairman of the Beaumont Trustees. The success of Besant's novel coincided with these events, and Currie set out to build the 'Palace of Delights'. Besant was himself active in getting the project under way. The image of the East End which Besant offered up to readers and to subscribers to the scheme was a relatively comforting one – one which would yield to a practical and seemingly attainable solution, this in contrast to the alarmist vision so often portrayed in the literature of the 1880s.

The initial plans proposed by the Beaumont Trust and launched at the Mansion House in 1884, Professor Thomas Huxley addressing the gathering, were ambitious. The Palace was to encompass both recreation and education. As one fund-raising pamphlet put it:

Members may play or work, as they choose. Whether they resort thither for mental improvement or simply recreation, each will be free to take his own path, though the number be twenty thousand. It is to be a vast club; it is to be a many-sided university; it is to be a playground and college.[14]

Robson was commissioned to design the building, no doubt acquainted with Currie from the London School Board, Robson having served as chief architect to the Board until his resignation in 1884. The first design was used for fund-raising brochures (Figure 4), subsequently replaced by the design of 1886 (Figure 1), as the scheme was more fully worked out.[15]

As the first official gesture of her Jubilee Year, Queen Victoria opened the completed portion of the scheme on 14 May 1887 – the Queen's Hall – and laid the foundation-stone for the Technical School. The Queen's Hall, though standing as an isolated building, was understood to be but the core of a larger complex to be built around it. For the occasion it was decked out with colourful bunting to cover over the bare stock brick of the exterior which awaited its grand palatial façade. The hall, 130 feet by 75 feet and 60 feet high, had been completed (Figure 5). Its sumptuous décor included a stained-glass roof, supported by buff-and-gold Corinthian columns, and a gallery supported by Greek caryatids. The central oval panels of the elaborate ceiling were decorated with the Prince of Wales's feathers, royal arms, royal monograms, and the arms of England, Australia, Canada, India, Wales, and Scotland. Statues of twenty-three queens from history, culminating with a statue of Queen Victoria, lined the walls.[16] The splendour of the hall was noted enthusiastically by the contemporary press, the *Illustrated London News* remarking that

Not the Egyptian Hall, nor the House of Lords, nor even Henry VII's Chapel at Westminster, is nobler in design or more graceful in detail than the Queen's Hall of the People's Palace.[17]

According to *The Times*:

Its marble statues, painted glass, and gilded balconies give an air of splendour and magnificence which is all the more striking for being met with in so unlovely a neighbourhood as that of the East-end of London.[18]

The Queen's Hall is a realization of the great hall described in Besant's novel. The characters in the novel on entering the Palace found themselves in a

lofty and spacious hall. At the end was a kind of throne . . . statues stood on either side: behind them was a great organ:

upon the walls were pictures. Above the pictures were trophies in arms, tapestry carpets, all kinds of beautiful things. Above the entrance was a gallery for musicians.[19]

The fanfare, however, which accompanied the opening of the Palace by Queen Victoria, her highly publicized 'descent into purgatorio',[20] did not, it would seem, represent a consensus of opinion on the part of the founders or the public on the nature of this new institution nor a clear go-ahead for its completion. The building programme continued piecemeal: in Currie's report of 1888 he lamented among other things that

> the difficulty has been the want of full accommodation. The Refreshment Rooms, the Gymnasium, and the Exhibition-buildings have been . . . merely temporary iron buildings, standing only on sufferance of the authorities, and liable at any time to condemnation, while the Winter Garden, the permanent Social Rooms, the rooms for the use of Benefit Clubs, Societies, etc. . . . of the original plans, are not in existence.[21]

Even three years later the Queen's Hall faced Mile End Road bare, the bombastic design of 1886 never having been built. Instead, the exposed stock brick of the structure was acquiring a 'sooty tinge', the building looking 'as dreary and depressing and unattractive as any plot of building land very well could look'.[22] When the building was completed a different image was projected on to Mile End Road: a more subdued neo-classical façade and clock-tower were designed by Robson (Figure 6), closer in style to that of the Beaumont Institution (Figure 7).

In order to understand the changing function and hence the new image of the institution, it is necessary to situate the construction of the People's Palace within a larger historical context. In the 1880s a variety of 'solutions' to the social problems which beset London was offered up. Besant's image of the East End as a place distinguished above all by cultural deprivation found its first expression in a novel he serialized in 1879 with his then partner James Rice, in which he asserted that 'No country town is so dull, none so devoid of society, distraction, and amusement as the East End of London.' It was a place 'destitute of the means of artistic grace', and he suggested to his reader that

> There ought to be a prefect of the East End: he should be one of the royal princes: he should build a palace among the people: there should be regiments of soldiers, theatres, picture-galleries, and schools, to wake them up and make them dismally discontented about their mean surroundings.[23]

Although Besant's scheme for a 'palace' was not elaborated upon until his novel of 1882, or taken on board seriously by public subscription until 1886, it dates in fact to a pre-crisis period, a time when a vision of cultural transformation as a palliative might be offered up as a solution to the social question. Though sparking the imagination of its readers in the alarmist mood of the mid-1880s, it would necessarily compete with a host of other proposals to solve the question of real distress in East London.

The Beaumont Trust employed the image conjured up by Besant's popular novel, the notion of an institution – for Besant that meant a secular institution – which would bring cultural advantages to the East End, thereby alleviating the interminable boredom of the neighbourhood. In their fund-raising and in the design of the building this was one of the themes employed. According to the Palace *Handbook and Guide*, the East End was 'joyless' and 'ugly', while the pleasures of the West 'have been multiplied a hundredfold . . . knowledge, art, skill, have all been used to make happy the lives of those who live in West London',[24] as Besant would have put it.

Further, in architectural terms Besant's notion of bringing West End culture to the East End was realized in *visual* form. The gift-giving relationship, the contribution of West End charity to the East End, the anonymity of which was so lamented in late-nineteenth-century London as a cause of social unrest,[25] was made tangible and visible, as these buildings, with their rooms to accommodate the refined, intellectual tastes of their donors, stood in stark contrast to their surroundings, unlike anything to be found in the East End: the Queen's Hall was a 'drawing-room for those to whom high rents forbid the luxury of a drawing-room'. Ladies' 'social rooms' enabled 'any lady member to hold weekly receptions of her friends in the Palace. A spacious apartment . . . being handsomely furnished . . . replete with every modern convenience'.[26] The Ladies' 'social room' corresponded to the drawing-room provided for the working girls of Stepney by the heroine of Besant's novel. It was there they had tea before their lawn tennis, of which the reader is told they 'are as fond . . . as the students of Newnham'.[27] The evenings were spent in music and dance, the provision of such a place of refinement lifting the girls 'above their neighbours'.[28] Finally, the reading-room made *explicit* the gift of West End culture and intellectual heritage to the East End: the reading-room was modelled self-consciously on that of the British Museum, albeit writ small (Figures 8 and 9).

In the 1880s Besant's version of the solution to the social problem would seem to stand out by the reassuring nature of its claims: the East End did not constitute a frightening mass of humanity threatening the very fabric of society, but rather a population dominated by a respectable working class that suffered from cultural deprivation. It was a version which had appeal, as attested to by the popularity of his novels. In support of the People's Palace the *Saturday Review* offered the observation that

> The 'two nations' which Disraeli described in *Sybil* are, in many respects, two nations still. . . . It is not so much relief from actual distress that the people of Mile End and Whitechapel require as some contrast with the grinding monotony of their daily lives. . . . In 1837 it would have been thought eccentric, and scarcely proper, to treat recreation seriously. Happily it now seems the most natural thing in the world.[29]

The language of 'Rational Recreation', that is of leisure time designed by the middle classes for the working classes, this rhetoric of reform, it has been pointed out, encompassed a wide variety of social criticism of which Besant's pleas are one variant.[30] An examination of the fund-raising campaign – the presence of Thomas Huxley at the launch of the campaign – as well as a look at the larger context in which the institution emerged, suggests that from the beginning, side by side with Besant's pleas for an institution devoted primarily to both recreation and education modelled on West End culture, there were other voices which sought to define the nature of 'Rational Recreation' and the nature of this new institution in terms which were different from those professed by Besant. In the initial plan for the Palace, on either side of the Queen's Hall, the functions were to have been divided, with leisure on one side and education on the other (Figure 10), even if both were to be wrapped in garb more easily associated with a pleasure palace than an educational institution. In the metropolis there were interests fearful of the social situation which sought to shape the new institution on different lines from those seen as crucial by Besant.

Arguments relating directly to the need to educate the working classes in practical vocational skills were made explicit. Drawing on a recent speech by Huxley, Lord Hartington was quoted in the fund-raising pamphlets on the need for scientific training:

> It is impossible in actual hostilities to extemporize effective armaments; 'the possession of scientific knowledge and perfect appliances' is essential in warfare, and the same holds good for industry. In both the prize goes to those who are best prepared to run the race. The comparison is impressive; the consequences are far-reaching.

The advice given is to spend generously in order to protect against aggression:

> to be not niggardly in providing industrial education and diffusing scientific knowledge . . . the drawing, mechanics, mathematics, chemistry, and other sciences or arts which aid the artisan in his daily work may be imparted, and on the spread of such knowledge may depend the continuance of industrial supremacy.[31]

'Rich men, of whom in spite of trade depression, there are still many, with noble balances at their banker', were told of this particularly 'Advantageous investment . . . of most extraordinary and securely profitable description'.[32] Fund-raising literature was written directly to 'Merchants of London'.[33] And fear of foreign competition was used as one inducement to business men to make their contributions; reference was made to the large number of boys coming from Board schools in need of technical training:

> To our regret we see our shops filled with foreign manufactures . . . and we are told that our artizans are not sufficiently trained to use the complicated tools necessary to produce these articles. We turn to America, to Germany, and to France, and we find them well provided with excellent technical schools; whereas London is almost destitute of them. Is this state of things to continue?[34]

The physical fitness of British youth, an issue which was to be high on the agenda of the 'National Efficiency' movement, was also pointed to as needing greater attention if Britain was to be competitive in the struggle for survival. Lord Rosebery, a figure who would be prominent in the movement, contributed £2,500 toward the building of swimming-baths at the Palace.

Lord Rosebery was also to spell out the role which the Palace could play in terms similar to those of the settlement movement:

> We are inside what is called the police radius of London. We have inside that radius two or three populations which would be counted as nations on the Continent of Europe, and the danger is that they should become nations as distinct as any that there are on the Continent of Europe. I hold that it is a great and sacred responsibility, not merely for our statesmen . . . but for all our leading citizens, in whatever capacity it may be given to them to lead, to endeavour to prevent the formation of those distinct nations within our metropolis . . . I believe this People's

Palace may do much, not merely to raise the population of the
East-end of London, but also to prove the sympathy of the
West-end for the East-end.[35]

These sentiments do not contradict those of Besant, but the
various arguments put forward in support of the People's Palace
suggest that it lacked a coherent objective understood and shared
by the public. Contributions fell far below the required amount for
the project. George Bernard Shaw remarked cynically that
middle-class attention – and money – was forthcoming only when
East End poverty was brought to the headlines, through either the
activities of Jack the Ripper or riots, pointing out that the lion's
share of contributions for the People's Palace was received in the
immediate aftermath of the riots of 1886.[36] This is hardly a
testament of faith in Besant's image of a basically docile working-
class population. The novelty of a piece of fiction transformed into
reality seems to have caught the attention of the contemporary
press, but lack of sufficient funding plagued the project.

Criticism of the scheme came from a variety of quarters. There
were claims that the plan was a lavish waste of money; Currie's
position as heir to a distillery fortune was pointed to as having
contributed to the distress of the area he claimed to be helping;
Sabbatarians were concerned about the nature of Sunday gather-
ings at the Palace.[37] Events at the Palace in the early years
included flower shows, donkey shows, an apprentices' exhibition,
a concert of the *Messiah* by the choral society, art shows, debates,
and dances, attended in the first six months by 600,000 visitors.[38]

In the end, however, the financial support necessary came from
a City company, the Drapers' Company, and with it a more
defined role for the institution. From the outset they had helped to
secure the land and to subsidize the building campaign. By 1890
they assumed control over the entire project. Their interest from
the beginning had been in the *educational* side of the Palace,
particularly technical education. In Besant's words on the fate of
his 'Palace of Delights', 'a polytechnic was tacked on to it; the
original idea of a place of recreation was mixed up with a place of
education'.[39] In 1890 the Drapers' Company financed the new
design for the façade of the building, allowing a generous £15,000
for its completion. The clock-tower facing on Mile End Road was
added in 1893. The neo-classical design is far from the quasi-
oriental one exhibited in 1886; rather it is reminiscent of Robson's
design for the Institute of Painters in Water Colours as Piccadilly,
dating from 1882 (Figure 11), and more in keeping with the image
of an educational institution. Out of the Drapers' scheme the East

Figure 1 E. R. Robson's design for the People's Palace, from *The Graphic*, 26 June 1886. (Reproduced by permission of the British Library.)

Figure 2 Promotional pamphlet illustrating the activities of the proposed Palace. (Reproduced by permission of the City Parochial Foundation.)

Figure 3 Cartoon of Walter Besant slaying the dragon of ignorance, misery, and vice from *The Period*, 29 June 1886. (Reproduced by permission of the British Library.)

Figure 4 An early version of the Palace by E. R. Robson, reminiscent of the Crystal Palace, used on the first promotional material for the scheme. (Reproduced by permission of Professor J. Mordaunt Crook.)

Figure 5 The Queen's Hall, opened by Queen Victoria on 14 May 1887. (Reproduced by permission of the Tower Hamlets Local History Library.)

Figure 6 The façade as seen from Mile End Road. (Reproduced by permission of the Greater London Photograph Library.)

Figure 7 The Beaumont Institution. (Reproduced by permission of the Tower Hamlets Local History Library.)

Figure 8 The Palace reading-room, *The Builder*, 7 September 1889. (Reproduced by permission of the Royal Institute of British Architects.)

Figure 9 The reading-room. (Reproduced by permission of the Greater London Photograph Library.)

Figure 10 Ground plan of the Palace, *The Builder*, 26 June 1886. (Reproduced by permission of the Royal Institute of British Architects.)

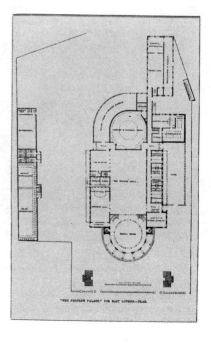

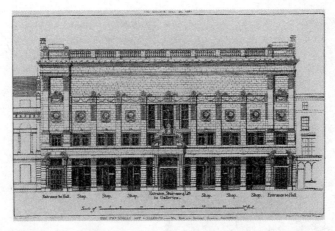

Figure 11 The Piccadilly Art Galleries, designed by E. R. Robson, from *The Builder*, 24 June 1882. (Reproduced by permission of the British Library.)

Figure 12 Toynbee Hall, designed by Elijah Hoole, from *The Builder*, 14 February 1885. (Reproduced by permission of the Royal Institute of British Architects.)

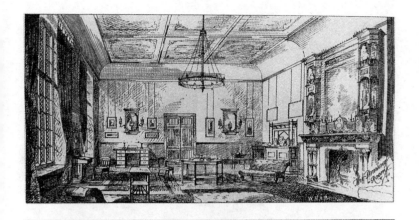

Figure 13 The interior of Toynbee Hall, from *The Architect*, 14 February 1885. (Reproduced by permission of the Royal Institute of British Architects.)

Figure 14 Toynbee Hall. (Reproduced by permission of Tower Hamlets Local History Library.)

London Technical College developed, becoming part of London University in 1907.

The failure of the Palace can certainly be explained by the *naïveté* and simplicity of Besant's vision of what plagued the East End in the 1880s and what was needed to ameliorate its problems; but further, a lack of definition of the role of outsider, the West End gentlemen overseeing the activities of the Palace, contributed to Besant's and Currie's own disillusionment with the project. In Besant's novel, the institution is handed over to the people. The hero and heroine insist that the institution *belongs* to the residents of Stepney: 'I declare the Palace of Delight open, the property of the people, to be administered and governed by them alone, in trust for each other.'[40] But in reality Besant worked overseeing various activities in the Palace, and, indeed, the institution was run by gentlemen from the West End rather than by local residents. Currie admitted that they had felt the need to institute rules and regulations, as well as increased fees in order to exclude undesirable elements.[41] The novelist Arthur Morrison, who had worked at the Palace, employed by the Beaumont Trustees in 1886, was later to write caustically about the institution in his novel *Child of the Jago*. He satirized the work at the Palace:

> The triumphs of the East End Elevation Mission and Panosophical Institute were known and appreciated far from East London, by people who knew less of that part than of Asia Minor. Indeed, they were chiefly appreciated by these. There were kept, perpetually on tap for Wider Humanity . . . specifics for the manufacture of the Superior Person . . . there were classes, and clubs, and newspapers, and games of draughts, and musical evenings, and a brass band, whereby the life of the Hopeless Poor might be coloured, and the Misery of the Submerged alleviated.

But he went on to describe the class of people who partook of these activities: 'The wretches who crowded to these benefits were tradesmen's sons, small shopkeepers and their families, and neat clerks, with here and there a smart artisan of one of the especially respectable trades.'[42]

Central to Besant's social philosophy there is a curious inconsistency: although Besant continually asserts that it is social and economic advantage which divides men and women rather than inherent qualities of birth, his stories repeatedly show the upper class – even when disguised as members of the working class – guiding the poor. This is central to the role of the heroine and hero in *All Sorts and Conditions of Men*. Besant's second novel dealing with the East End, *Children of Gibeon* of 1885, likewise a great success, has among its central characters two young women raised as sisters from birth, one the daughter of a poor washer-woman, the other of noble birth. Not even the women themselves know which is of humble and which is of noble origin. Their appearance is virtually identical, and it is only a birthmark which eventually betrays the secret. Yet even here in a story constructed to illustrate the equality of all, stressing the importance of nurture over nature, it is the woman of noble birth who – like the heroine of his earlier novel – descends to the East End, with her particular wisdom, to instruct the poor. In translating Besant's dream of a 'Palace' into reality, it is this central contradiction which he fails to resolve: while claiming that the members of the Palace must declare never to be 'content until our own bands play our own music; our own journal prints our own literature; our own novelists lie upon our tables; our own critics pronounce our judgements; our own artists paint the picture for our exhibition',[43] Besant and Currie continued to play an active role in the organization of the Palace. Besant edited the *Palace Journal* and directed the literary club and later lamented that no young men of the district emerged as talented writers.[44]

The shift in definition which the institution underwent, and with it the necessity to choose an architectural vocabulary which would convey the appropriate associations to the public, can be compared to another institution of the same period, located near by, Toynbee Hall Settlement House, established in 1884. If the People's Palace lacked a consensus as to the nature of its role, and its founders therefore were uncertain as to the nature of the architecture to convey that role, in contrast Canon Samuel Barnett seems to have possessed a clearer vision of the nature and function of the Settlement House and its role within the community.

Though founded in the 1880s amid growing fear of social unrest, the concept which *underlies* the Settlement House as conceived by Canon Samuel Barnett grew out of ideas current since the 1860s regarding ways in which to bridge the geographical gulf between the rich and poor which was increasingly blamed for social unrest in the capital. Precedents existed for working among the poor, particularly in the work of Christian Socialists, such as J. M. Ludlow, a lawyer and devout churchman, and Frederick Denison Maurice and Charles Kingsley, both clergymen in the Church of England, who after 1848 advocated work among the poor. And the idea of university men and women living and working amidst the poor, participating in the daily life of the community, was inspired by the example of Edward Denison in the 1860s: an

Oxford graduate – son of the Bishop of Salisbury and a member of a wealthy family – he chose to live and work among the people of Stepney in East London. Although his stay was brief and he died young of tuberculosis, the letters he had written of his experiences were to impress another generation.[45]

Barnett was drawing upon this potent image when he proposed that Oxford students 'come into sympathy with the hope, the unnamed hope which is moving the masses', by living and working in Whitechapel in a Settlement House.[46] Barnett had already served for over a decade as vicar of St Jude's in Whitechapel, deeply involved in his role as religious leader as well as in the work of the Charity Organization Society (COS) with its firm stance against 'indiscriminate charity', when he proposed the Settlement idea at Oxford in 1883. In line with the COS attitude towards charity, Denison, too, had expressed the view that 'bodily aid to the poor is a mistake and the real thing is to let things work themselves straight; whereas by giving alms you keep them permanently crooked'.[47] Rather, the well-to-do should 'Build school houses, pay teachers, give prizes, frame workmen's clubs, help them to help themselves, lend them your brains'. What he found so miserable in the East End was

> its uniform mean level, the absence of anything more civilizing than a grinding organ to raise the ideas beyond the daily bread and beer, the utter want of education, the complete indifference of religion, with the fruits of all this, viz., improvidence, dirt, and their secondaries, crime and disease.[48]

Similarly, what Barnett was proposing in the concept of Settlement was the guiding leadership of educated men and women:

> I am afraid that it is long before we can expect the rich and poor again to live as neighbours; for good or evil they have been divided, and other means must, for the present, be found for making common the property of knowledge. One such means is the University Settlement. Men who have knowledge may become friends of the poor and share that knowledge and its fruits as, day to day, they meet in their common rooms for instruction, for music or for play.[49]

The university student, while mingling with the local residents, would remain somewhat aloof, retaining his identity as a social superior. Barnett described the job of the Settlement worker as providing leadership in the community he entered, serving as 'wise counsellors', joining working men's clubs, giving lectures, and even running for office in local elections. Comparing the selfishness and isolation of the well-to-do of his day to a more harmonious past, Barnett described what he termed the 'hospitality' which characterized the feudal relationship he sought to emulate:

> Hospitality was, in the old days, if not the secret, then, to a large extent, the source of power of the chief. The feudal lord entertained his followers and welcomed strangers. The master was the host of his apprentices . . . They thus met, as it were, off their guard. They learnt to know one another's thoughts and manners, they discovered points of likeness, and came into quiet possession of a common inheritance.[50]

A hierarchical relationship was implicit in Barnett's vision: 'Classes', he wrote, 'must exist. A body in which every member is a hand could do no more.'[51] In designing a home for this new institution Barnett was to draw upon an image of a new urban gentry residing as a permanent fixture in Whitechapel, providing guidance to local residents.

In a letter to his brother, Barnett described his plans for the hall as a 'manorial residence in Whitechapel', offering facilities unknown in the community: rooms for sixteen men, a classroom to accommodate three hundred, a dining-room, a conversation room, and a drawing-room.[52] Barnett's manor house was designed by the architect Elijah Hoole in the Elizabethan manner, built in red brick and box stone, reminiscent, it has been suggested, of Oxford and Cambridge (Figures 12, 13, and 14).[53]

Drawing upon an image of an urban squirearchy living among the poor, which had been emerging in London in preceding decades,[54] Barnett's task offered a less problematic question when it came to determining the built form for his institution. The relationship of the institution to its surroundings grew not out of the fantasies of a novelist removed from the East End whose public was responding to the immediate sense of alarm in the 1880s, but out of a long-term commitment and intellectual tradition. Further, rooted in the 1860s, a period characterized by growing social tensions, the solutions offered up by the COS and its followers were developed in response to a less alarming period than that of the 1880s.[55]

Although Besant's 'solution' appears naïve and ill defined, the success of the novel and the ensuing campaign to realize the dream of the Palace – the fund-raising campaign reaching its peak during the crisis winter of 1886 – attest to the sense of alarm and seeming *need* to find a *solution*, however implausible. The inability to find an appropriate face for the People's Palace and the waning support for it were the inevitable outcomes of the panic-ridden situation in which these unlikely plans were made. With the growing focus, however, upon a movement for 'National Efficiency', a movement which rallied the support of a variety of factions concerned with the apparent economic, military, and physical decline of the nation, fears for its inability to compete in .the world's marketplace or in battle, Besant's fantasy of working-class recreation was transformed into a more austere vision of a school for the technical education of the working classes with support from a City company.

Notes

I wish gratefully to acknowledge the support of a J. Paul Getty Postdoctoral Fellowship in Art History and the Humanities held at the time the research for this essay was carried out.

1 Walter Besant, *All Sorts and Conditions of Men: An Impossible Story*, 1882, pp. 138, 330.
2 'A real Jubilee offering', *Saturday Review*, 23 April 1887, p. 574.
3 Rev. Harry Jones, *Fifty Years; or, Dead Leaves and Living Seeds*, New York, 1895, p. 95.
4 'The People's Palace for East London', *The Builder*, 26 June 1886, p. 914.
5 ibid.
6 'A real Jubilee offering'.
7 Bequest of John Thomas Barber Beaumont.
8 Walter Besant, *Autobiography of Walter Besant*, New York, 1902, p. 243.
9 Besant, *All Sorts and Conditions of Men*, p. 50.
10 ibid., p. 331.
11 As quoted by Fred W. Boege, 'Walter Besant: novelist, part I', *Nineteenth Century Fiction*, March 1956, from *Cosmopolitan*, 1891, p. 257.
12 As quoted by Fred W. Boege, *Saturday Review*, 27 November 1886, p. 70.
13 Records of the Beaumont Trust and People's Palace are located at the Greater London Record Office (GLRO); see A/BPP/1/1–4 for reports, letters, accounts, and programmes, etc., relating to the Beaumont Trust and J. T. Barber Beaumont, 1842–73. For reports, letters, accounts, and programmes, etc. relating to the Beaumont Trust and People's Palace, see A/BPP/2/1–3, 1881–91. Additional material, including correspondence between the Beaumont Trust and E. R. Robson, is preserved in the archives of the library of Queen Mary College, University of London, which occupies the site of the People's Palace.
14 Fund-raising brochure reprinting an article from *The Times*, 15 January 1886.
15 The initial design was widely used in promotional literature. *The*

Builder, 29 May 1886, p. 772, questioned 'whether it quite suggests the idea of a people's palace; there is rather a taint of aristocracy about it'.

16 *Handbook and Guide to the People's Palace*, n.d. (1886–7?), Queen Mary College, PP Bundle 3, p. 11.

17 'The Queen's visit to East London', *Illustrated London News*, 21 May 1887, p. 4.

18 'The People's Palace', *The Times*, 14 May 1887, p. 17.

19 As quoted in 'Mr Besant's dream and realization', *Pall Mall Gazette*, 14 May 1887, p. 8.

20 'The hero of the hour', *Pall Mall Gazette*, 14 May 1887, p. 8.

21 Report of E. H. Currie, 1 October 1888, p. 8, GLRO, A/BPP/2.

22 'Additions to the People's Palace', *Daily News*, 14 January 1890, p. 8.

23 (Walter Besant and James Rice), '*The Seamy Side*; a new novel by the authors of *Ready-Money*, *Mortiboy*, etc.', *Time*, II, October 1879, p. 87.

24 *Handbook and Guide*, pp. 6–7.

25 See Gareth Stedman Jones, *Outcast London: A Study in the Relationship between Classes in Victorian Society*, Oxford, 1971, pp. 240–61, for a discussion of the relationship of giver and recipient in late-nineteenth-century London.

26 Announcement of 'Ladies' social', *Palace Journal*, vol. 1, no. 1, 16 November 1887, p. 6.

27 Besant, *All Sorts and Conditions of Men*, p. 101.

28 ibid., p. 105.

29 'A real Jubilee offering'.

30 Chris Waters, 'Socialism and the politics of popular culture in Britain, 1884–1914', unpublished dissertation, Harvard University, 1985, pp. 79–81.

31 Lord Hartington, quoted in fund-raising pamphlet, *Scheme of Training Workshops for Teaching Handicrafts*, including an article from *The Times*, 17 March 1887, on the 'Importance of scientific training for artisans', GLRO, A/BPP/2.

32 Pamphlet reprinting article from *The Times*, 15 January 1886, GLRO, A/BPP/2.

33 Fund-raising appeal dated 27 October 1886, signed E. H. Currie.

34 Pamphlet, *East London Technical and Science Schools, Mile End*, announcement of opening 12 September 1887.

35 Lord Rosebery, quoted at a meeting at the Drapers' Hall convened by the Beaumont Trustees, 19 April 1887.

36 G. Bernard Shaw, 'Blood money to Whitechapel', to the editor of *The Star*, 24 September 1888.

37 The files of Queen Mary College contain the list of subscribers as well as the correspondence of those who refused to contribute.

38 Boege, 'Walter Besant', p. 268.

39 Walter Besant, *East London*, 1901, p. 13.

40 Besant, *All Sorts and Conditions of Men*, p. 327.

41 E. H. Currie, 'The working of "The People's Palace"', February 1890, *The Nineteenth Century*, pp. 346–7.

42 Arthur Morrison, *Child of the Jago*, 1896, 1946, p. 18.
43 As quoted by Peter Keating from the *Palace Journal*, 16 January 1889, p. 850; see Keating, *The Working Class in Victorian Fiction*, 1971, p. 98.
44 Besant, *Autobiography*, p. 242.
45 G. Kitson Clark, *Churchmen and the Condition of England 1832–1885: A Study in the Development of Social Ideas and Practice from the Old Regime to the Modern State*, 1973, pp. 280–2. Clark describes Ruskin's meeting in 1867 with Denison, possibly Rev. Henry Scott, Rev. J. R. Green who was serving at St Philip's, Stepney, and Rev. Brooke Lambert, the vicar of St Mark's, Whitechapel, to discuss what could be done for the poor; Denison and Green suggested the idea of a group of university men living as Denison was doing. The matter went no further, but the concept then of Settlement was discussed as early as 1867.

Besant, too, makes reference to Denison, describing him as 'the pioneer of a great invasion', in *As We Are and As We May Be*, 1903, pp. 246–7, although his own 'solution' does not involve living among the people of the East End.
46 Samuel Barnett, 'University Settlements', first delivered as an address in Oxford in November 1883, in *The Nineteenth Century*, February 1884, and included in *Practicable Socialism: Essays on Social Reform*, 1888, with essays by both Samuel and Henrietta Barnett.
47 As quoted in Karl de Schweinitz, *England's Road to Social Security*, New York, 1943, reprinted Philadelphia, 1961, p. 145.
48 ibid.
49 Barnett, 'University Settlements', p. 107.
50 Samuel Barnett, 'Hospitalities' in *The Universities and the Social Problem*, ed. John M. Knapp, 1895, p. 53.
51 Samuel Barnett, *Towards Social Reform*, 1909, p. 26.
52 As quoted in Henrietta Barnett, *Canon Barnett: His Life, Work, and Friends*, vol. 1, 1918, p. 314.
53 J. A. R. Pimlott, *Toynbee Hall: Fifty Years of Social Progress, 1884–1934*, 1934, p. 37.
54 See Stedman Jones, *Outcast London*, pp. 268–70. The COS represented the viewpoint of the elite of professional London which aspired to form a new urban gentry: while advocating that the poor become independent they also sought to create a hierarchical and deferential urban society. Also see G. Kitson Clark, 'The new politics and the new gentry', ch. VIII in *The Making of Victorian England*, Cambridge, Mass., 1962, pp. 260–74, in which Clark describes the emergence of the liberal professions which were 'forming . . . a new type of aristocracy, a new caste', p. 274.
55 Stedman Jones, *Outcast London*, pp. 281–4.

3

The importance of being English
Jewish immigration and the decay of liberal England

David Feldman

I

The Aliens Act of 1905 was passed for the benefit of London; or, more precisely, for one part of it – the East End. It was designed to reduce the level of Jewish immigration (immigration that happened to be composed of Jews, its supporters insisted).[1] About one-half of the approximately 120,000 East European Jews settling in Britain between 1880 and 1914 made their home in London, 80 per cent of these in the districts of Whitechapel, Bethnal Green, and St George's in the East, just to the east of the City. Charles Booth, surveying in 1902 the changes in St George's since he had first investigated the area in 1887, was struck most by the growth of the Jewish presence. It was to him an inexorable invasion: 'the slow rising of a flood, family follows family, street after street is occupied'.[2] Indeed, by the turn of the century the Jewish population accounted for almost one-half of the population of Whitechapel and St George's in the East. It was little wonder that Whitechapel was known as 'Jew-town', commented the Jewish statistician S. Rosenbaum.[3]

Over the two decades preceding the enactment of the Aliens Bill the immigration question erupted intermittently within debates on social policy. The form of its appearance was subject to alterations, however, changes that reflected the shifting meanings with which London and the East End were endowed. In the first ten years the immigration question was driven by a mixture of apprehension and compassion among the propertied classes in the face of the capital's outcast masses. Some trade unionists also turned anti-alien, particularly in the face of the defeats of new unionism and the breakdown of labour organization among the immigrant workers. Accordingly, Jewish immigrants and their impact upon the surrounding native-born population provided one focus for investigations into public health, sweated labour, and poverty in the capital. As J. A. Hobson pointed out in 1891, the prospects for an Aliens Act depended upon 'the success of other schemes for treating the supply of low-skilled labour'.[4] By contrast, after the turn of the century, when immigration again became a subject for social investigation and political agitation, the emphasis of debate had shifted from the domestic to the imperial consequences of poverty. The arrival of thousands of Russian Jews annually, who were represented as physically enfeebled, without marketable trades, and possessing a 'low standard of life', reacted upon fears of Britain's imminent international decline. The more so since these degraded migrants congregated at the very heart of the empire and were seen to have a deteriorating effect upon the indigenous working classes there.[5] The shape of the anxieties excited by Jewish immigration thus reflected a shift in the fears projected upon London and the East End. The capital ceased to be seen as the most likely site of any breakdown in the body politic. Now it had become the diseased heart of an imperial organism threatened by potential attacks from rival powers.

Hostility to immigration emerged in the context of these debates and the politics of London. Yet historians of the subject continue to approach the anti-immigration movement as an episode in the history of prejudice or anti-Semitism – an unpleasant spectacle of some fascination but of little significance more generally.[6] There is a fundamental problem with this approach which is cast wholly from the experience, not of the putative subjects for study, the opponents of unfettered immigration, but of those whom they threatened – Jews and immigrants. This difficulty is revealed by the vigour with which the immigrant press accused the anti-alien movement of anti-Semitism and irrationality and the insistent manner in which the charges were denied.[7] We have learned little of the intellectual currents, cultural symbols, and political visions which rendered opposition to immigration meaningful for those who took this position.[8] Yet, at the very least, our recognition that the policy of immigration restriction was presented within contexts more widely concerned with the consequences of poverty in London does suggest that we should take serious account of the intellectual foundations of the proposal to restrict immigration and the debate within which it was brought forward.

In looking at the anti-alien movement in its own terms we will be better placed to see the 1905 Aliens Act as one of the turning-points in the decline of liberal England: a revealing response to the creeping transformation of Britain's place in the world. The Act not only prevented the immigration of thousands of Russian Jews and was a source of trepidation for those already settled in Britain, it was also symptomatic of new formulations of the idea of the nation and of a more expansive and coercive state. The Aliens Act of 1905 was a radical innovation, introducing legislation where there had been none. It is a measure of our distance from the nineteenth century that between 1826 and 1905 the ports of Britain were open to all. It is upon the foundation of the 1905 Act that the contemporary edifice of regulation and restriction, inspection and expulsion, has been built.

II

The suggestion that immigration should be restricted first arose as one response to the massive unemployment and riots that marked London winters in the mid-1880s.[9] A belief that immigration caused an increase in the number of unskilled workers in the capital was connected frequently to other interpretations and palliatives which viewed the crisis in terms of gross numbers. Restrictionists presented their arguments as corollaries to schemes for emigration to the colonies and concern with the effects upon the cities of rural depopulation.[10]

Arguments such as these, based upon numbers, became more persuasive if the increase in immigration could be tied to the condition of particular trades. In 1887 John Burnett, the labour correspondent to the Board of Trade, acknowledged that immigration was not the original cause of 'sweating' in the East End but maintained that were it not for the effects of immigration there would have been no demand for an inquiry into the subject.[11] By any definition the sweated trades included those in which Jewish immigrants were most largely occupied: tailoring, boot- and shoemaking, and cabinet-making. In these trades, it was argued, the native artisan was being undercut and displaced by immigrant competitors. By 1890, however, the House of Lords Select Committee on Sweating had come to the conclusion that there was no such thing as a sweating *system*. Its report argued that there were instead a series of symptoms – low wages, long hours, overcrowded conditions – the root causes of which lay in an over-stocked labour market to which immigration did not contribute greatly.[12] Legislation following upon the report, such as the Factory Act of 1891, concentrated upon the symptoms rather than upon the labour market and sought to regulate minimally the conditions in which outworkers laboured.[13] The more radical solutions to the problem went no further in attacking its root cause. Writers such as Beatrice Webb left to one side the intractable problems of the labour market and advocated legislation intended to lead to a transfer of production from workshops to factories. It was assumed that factories themselves would produce trade unionism and decent wages and conditions.[14]

What distinguished advocates of immigration restriction at this time, whether Liberals such as Hobson, Tory democrats such as the Earl of Dunraven, or trade unionists such as Charles Freak of the National Union of Boot and Shoe Operatives, was their insistence upon the labour market as a cause of 'sweating' and the need for policy to be directed towards it.[15] However much they overestimated the effects of immigration, their position addressed a major inconsistency between the analyses and policies of their rivals. They sought to make an intervention in the labour market in one of the few ways available: one which did not involve an unacceptable degree of state intervention in relations of employment.[16] Further, in their insistence that immigrants did compete with native workers in the tailoring and boot and shoe trades, these restrictionists were undoubtedly correct.[17]

All agreed, however, that in any competitive situation the Jewish immigrant had the advantage over the native worker on account of his 'lower standard of comfort'. 'It is undoubtedly true that the foreigner will take less wages than the native worker and owing to his lower standard of existence can maintain himself on what would mean starvation to an Englishman,' wrote Stephen Fox, who had rushed into print to *combat* the restrictionist prescription of Arnold White.[18] This commonplace assumption derived its force from the theory of 'urban degeneration' which pervaded debate in the 1880s. The theory's proponents claimed that the conditions of London life produced a lesser physique and a diminished capacity for work in successive generations. Llewellyn Smith suggested that in consequence provincial migrants dominated the skilled trades and better-paid unskilled occupations in the capital on account of their rude health.[19] The Jewish immigrant was represented as the mirror image of the sturdy countryman; a figure who had adapted so well to the demands of urban life that he was inevitably the victor when competing with the London-born. Booth characterized the situation of the East End worker thus:

> He is met and vanquished by the Jews fresh from Poland or Russia, accustomed to a lower standard of life, and above all of food, than would be possible for one of these Islands; less skilled and perhaps less strong, but in his way more fit, pliant, adaptable, adroit . . . or he is pushed on one side by the physical

strength of the man whose life has hitherto been spent among green fields.[20]

After 1900 the array of arguments brought in favour of an Aliens Act continued to include the undercutting and displacement of native by foreign labour, but it was the effects of the immigrants' presence in the housing market which attracted most comment. Rents for working-class housing rose over the entire country in the 1890s. In London the increase was on average 10 per cent, but in Stepney the figure was closer to 25 per cent. Moreover, in Stepney, the borough containing the districts most densely colonized by Jewish immigrants, the quality of housing, as measured by the level of overcrowding, was in decline. This was a unique tendency in a decade when the level of overcrowding was becoming less severe elsewhere in London's inner districts.[21]

It was widely understood that the need to be close to their place of work kept the working classes confined within overcrowded districts. Among some of the Medical Officers of Health who addressed the Royal Commission on Alien Immigration this realization had produced disenchantment with the effects of enforcing disciplinary legislation against overcrowding and insanitary conditions. D. L. Thomas, the MOH for Stepney, commented: 'if you turn people out of one street they must go into another street; and if the houses in that street are already overcrowded you must accentuate the overcrowding in neighbouring streets; you are bound to because you are doing away with certain houses'.[22] John Foot, the MOH for Bethnal Green, went so far as to call the laws on sanitation and overcrowding a 'dishousing machinery'. He argued cogently: 'what is wanted is much more house accommodation at the lowest possible cost . . . instead of which we have an increased population both home and alien'.[23] In other words, the anti-alien case contained within it a perception that the combined disciplines of the law and the market were not a sufficient response to overcrowding and poor sanitation in working-class housing. By contrast, their opponents advocated fiercer enforcement of the Public Health Act and the by-laws on overcrowding, arguing that 'if the by-laws are steadily and systematically enforced people would find their own accommodation'.[24]

In this second phase of discussion restriction was advocated by enthusiasts of empire and others attracted to the modish pursuit of 'efficiency' and diagnoses of 'deterioration'. Restrictionists were able to align their cause with other reforms emphasizing the need to adjust to a world in which Britain's industrial, commercial, and naval

pre-eminence increasingly was open to question. It was characteristic that uncontrolled immigration to Britain was compared
unfavourably with the restrictive laws enforced by the nation's
competitors.[25] The campaigns for fair trade and immigration
restriction were similar in their appeals to unsentimentality and to
the need to place the nation's own interests first. Indeed, tariff
reformers sought to mobilize working-class support by highlighting
these connections; by collapsing the two issues into the single evil
of unfair 'dumping' – of cheap goods and destitute aliens – by 'the
foreigner'.[26]

By 1887 interest in the subject of immigration had grown to the
extent that one Jewish organization described the year as 'rife to
overflowing with writings on the subject'.[27] Even when it did not
advocate restriction this attention frequently took an unfavourable
view of immigration. The Select Committee of the House of
Commons, which investigated the subject in 1888–9, found
'general agreement that pauper immigration is an evil and should
be checked'. The committee shrunk from proposing legislation
only 'because of the difficulty of carrying such a measure into
effect'. However, a policy of inaction was seen to be feasible in the
short term only, and the committee foresaw the need for legislation to prevent 'the tendency of destitute foreigners to reduce still
lower the social and material condition of our poor'.[28] Some
members did object to this passage, but their opposition should
not be misinterpreted. One of them, Samuel Montagu, the Jewish
Liberal MP for Whitechapel, addressed the first public meeting in
the restrictionist cause. Statutory action was unnecessary, he
argued, not because immigration was a boon or harmless but
because 'leading Jews' had already taken action to regulate it.[29]
Likewise, in the course of the electoral campaign of 1892 Montagu
made clear his opposition to immigration. Complaining that
'Conservatives have had the meanness to spread reports that I was
in favour of the immigration of foreigners', he remonstrated, 'this
is not true. . . . This crowded country is no place for them.' He
claimed to 'have done more to save this country from an invasion
of foreigners than any legislation such as that of the United States
can effect'.[30]

This was not an isolated example of agreement upon the social
and economic effects of immigration between the supporters of an
Aliens Act and their opponents. A similar consensus was apparent
between Lords Salisbury and Rosebery in 1894 when the former
introduced an Aliens Bill into the House of Lords. Rosebery
dismissed Salisbury's claim that Britain was being used to plot

anarchist terror across Europe; but, he conceded, 'with regard to what he said about the exclusion of destitute aliens I am not prepared to offer much objection'.[31]

At the turn of the century, when the issue once again acquired great urgency there was similar breadth of agreement upon the undesirability of immigration. In response to an agitation centred upon the East End, the Conservative government appointed a Royal Commission to investigate the problem of immigration. Its report recommended the exclusion of classes of aliens, among them migrants unable to prove they were capable of supporting themselves or their families. One commissioner, Sir Kenelm Digby, an under-secretary at the Home Office, submitted a memorandum dissenting from the majority conclusion. It was accompanied by a note of support from another commissioner, Lord Rothschild. Their point of disagreement with the majority, however, was concerned not with the effects of immigration but with the best way to deal with these. They allowed that 'the over-crowding in the East End of London in connection with alien immigration should be abated' but believed also that the legislation proposed would be 'impracticable'.[32] Thus in both phases of debate, far from appearing as an exercise in prejudice, the anti-alien case was widely notable for its coherence, its capacity to address weaknesses in the arguments of opponents, and its ability to absorb fashionable themes in social policy. Its proponents were able to command a wide measure of agreement.

III

Further light is thrown on the immigration debate by looking at Jewish responses to the problem. As described by one historian, the Anglo-Jewish elite comprised a group of about one hundred families of 'social prominence and self-conscious patriotism'. At their head were the interrelated banking and broking families of the Rothschilds, Cohens, and Montagus who dominated Jewish communal institutions in the capital on account of their financial support and administrative expertise. Of all the communal institutions it was the Jewish Board of Guardians (JBG) which impinged most immediately upon the life of the immigrant colony. The board was the chief source of relief for the Jewish poor but combined relief with other projects of a more remedial nature focusing upon the deserving poor. Among these were funds providing for programmes of apprenticeship and emigration, and the provision of small loans.[33]

It was in 1886 and 1887, at the same time as the immigration question was being broached more widely, that the JBG expressed its own fear that normally thrifty Jewish families were being driven to seek poor relief on account of the additional numbers thrown into the labour market by immigration. The board's warning that 'the state of our poor already here must not and cannot be ignored' was the restrictionists' watchword writ small and applied to the Jewish population alone.[34] For the JBG this was a problem which could be alleviated by restricting immigration and by repatriating a portion of those applying to it for aid. In 1888 the board's honorary secretary informed the House of Commons Select Committee on Emigration and Immigration: 'it is one of our largest operations sending people back who, having wandered here, prove themselves to be useless or helpless'.[35] Fifteen years later, when the president of the board gave evidence to the Royal Commission on Alien Immigration he argued there was little need for the government to intervene and perform a task which his own organization was undertaking.[36]

Indeed, the efficiency of the JBG's effort is impressive. Between 1881 and 1906 it returned to eastern Europe over 31,000 Jews.[37] The board's representatives made the point that repatriation took place with the consent of those who undertook the journey. But it is apparent from the following explanation of the process that the choices available were determined by poverty and dependence:

> He [the applicant] tells us he cannot succeed without charity. He has been here say nine months. We say: 'if you cannot succeed here and as you had nothing to bring you here you had better go back'. He rather demurs the first time, but the second he agrees and goes.[38]

A rough-and-ready guide to the scale of this operation is that the number repatriated was equal to 56 per cent of the total increase in the number of Jewish immigrants in London between 1881 and 1911.

The Anglo-Jewish elite was notable for its integration within the culture and institutions of the propertied classes in London. Apart from their work among the Jewish poor the communal leaders also participated in charitable activity directed towards the capital's poor in general.[39] Accordingly, the policies of Jewish philanthropic agencies followed with mimetic accuracy, and occasionally pre-figured the principles of, preoccupations and fashions in poor relief more widely current, including those which required the restriction of immigration. In the 1860s the JBG had been a pioneer among those developing policies based upon criticism of the absence of a curative element in the Poor Law; policies which also found an application in the work of the Charity Organization Society.[40] In 1887 the board restated its faith in its founding principles: 'A system of repression of pauperism will continue to be cast aside in favour of guiding the humbler classes to self-helpfulness; aiding them to cope with their difficulties instead of leaving them ruthlessly to overcome them.'[41]

A simultaneous responsibility for the 'undeserving' was in the 1880s a growing obstacle to the thoroughgoing implementation of this formula, particularly in years of depression. The same year, 1887, the board's annual report explained the seeming harshness of some of its actions by pointing out that 'single able-bodied men' had 'more than ever been forced to become independent of charity'.[42] The position became especially contradictory as Russian Jewish refugees were singled out for special treatment, and it was acknowledged that 'they will for some time require careful watching and from time to time assistance'.[43] Yet there were other imperatives at work thwarting the development of an approach to poverty which took account of particular Jewish obligations and the self-evidently respectable status of those classified as refugees. The Russian Jewish poor were assumed to suffer from the same moral failings as the generality, so the administrators of the Russian Jewish fund established especially for them were anxious to discover 'impostors' dissembling among the refugees. These were identified as immigrants who had not come from 'disturbed districts' but who evidently had been attracted to London by the prospect of a large fund being 'generously dispensed'.[44] This sifting was pursued despite a recognition that the definition of who was a refugee was not hard and fast, and in many parts of Russia Jews were not subject to open persecution but yet found it impossible 'to live in peaceful effort to earn their livelihoods'.[45] Even the treatment of those deemed to be genuine refugees was predicated upon a wider view of the social problem. In 1891 the trustees of the fund established for them reported that their constant concern had been 'as far as possible to prevent any increased congestion in the overcrowded districts of London'.[46] This was achieved by a programme of repatriation and emigration.

An examination of responses to the housing crisis at the turn of the century indicates once again that the restrictionists' concern with the social consequences of immigration was shared by Anglo-Jewish opinion. In July 1901 an editorial in the *Jewish Chronicle*, the main communal newspaper, expressed concern that the concentration of immigrants in the East End had 'aggravated the grave overcrowding difficulty'. It went on to suggest that among the native population of the East End many had been displaced when immigrants had occupied new buildings erected after demolitions, and it called for more strenuous efforts to disperse the ghetto.[47] Harry Lewis, a Jewish minister who was a worker both in Toynbee Hall and in communal philanthropy, told an East End meeting that 'the influx of foreign Jews had caused a serious displacement of population which had been very injurious to non-Jews and also to Jews already here'. The immigrants paid higher rents for tenancies by overcrowding their accommodation, something they were able to do on account of their lower standard of life, he explained.[48] Another communal activist, H. H. Gordon, honorary secretary of the Poor Jews' Temporary Shelter and a borough councillor in Stepney, proposed the following resolution at a conference convened to discuss the housing problem in the borough:

> That this conference recognizes and regrets the fact that the overcrowding in East London is largely consequent on the influx of alien immigrants, which has resulted in enormous increases in rents due to the creation of a class of slum landlords, of whose doings this conference wishes to express its utmost disapproval.[49]

The resolution was passed unanimously. A further resolution, also passed unanimously, called upon the Jewish community to prevent further immigration and to promote the diffusion of the immigrants clustered in the East End.

Repatriation was one of the foundations of Anglo-Jewish social policy in these years. Yet some historians have shrunk from suggesting there were any connections between the actions being carried out by the Jewish Board of Guardians, among other communal institutions involved in repatriation, and the measures advocated by the proponents of an Aliens Act.[50] However, it should be apparent that the policies of the Jewish Board of Guardians, in general, did emerge within a context which shared fully the dominant assumptions among the capital's propertied classes over the provision of poor relief and the organization of philanthropy. Their reports were presented in language which both expressed these boundaries to possible action and also engaged in debates within them.

But what role did fear for the reputation of Jews in a gentile society have in forming this policy? Philanthropy was one way in which Jews were able to participate in communal life and to express legitimately their identity as Jews.[51] The existence of a separate Jewish Board of Guardians reflected also the desire of Anglo-Jewry to keep the communal poor off the rates and render them invisible so far as was possible. The interweaving of the 'aliens question' and the 'Jewish question' was a point of continuing concern to English Jews. Criticism of 'aliens' frequently overspilled into commentary upon Jews. William Evans Gordon's volume on 'alien immigration', for example, also included his commentary on the 'Jewish question' and asserted: 'it is a fact that the settlement of large aggregations of Hebrews in a Christian land has never been successful'.[52] English Jews sought to refute claims such as this by promoting the immigrants 'anglicization'. This project concentrated upon education and shaping the recreation of the young but it did also impinge to a degree upon the organization of poor relief.[53] Yet communal reputation did not provide the terms in which the principles of philanthropy and poor relief were generally expressed. Least of all did it provide the justification for the traffic in migrants from west to east. It was the 'problem of poverty' which supplied the principal context in which practices of repatriation were developed.

Evidently, the widespread belief that the immigration of large numbers of east European Jews was not to be welcomed did not lead directly to the opinion that the state should intervene to limit it. Generally, Anglo-Jewish opinion did not support uncontrolled immigration but it also claimed the right to act as the regulating force. It was one thing to repatriate immigrants once they had proved incapable of supporting themselves, argued the *Jewish Chronicle*; it was another to reject them before they had had this opportunity.[54] The argument was not between restriction and unlimited immigration but over whether the state or voluntary bodies should be the agent of regulation. Our recognition that an unfavourable view of Jewish immigration was commonplace and extended beyond the ranks of those who supported the anti-alien agitation should make us question anew why these unexceptional attitudes became the subject of political enthusiasm for some and not for others who by no means welcomed the influx. In other words, why did immigration become a political issue at the turn of the century?

IV

After the Reform Act of 1867 and the redistribution of parliamentary seats in 1885, the Conservative Party was faced with the problem of how it would present itself to the newly enfranchised and empowered urban electorate. The redistribution gave greater representation to London and the south Lancashire towns, areas which provided two strongholds of urban Toryism to the First World War.

The Conservative Party was divided over how to respond to the urban electorate. The most powerful view envisioned the party's future as one defending the ramparts of property, allying the landed and county elites with the burgeoning support to be found among the urban villas. Others, however, who were particularly loud within the party organization and correspondingly weak in the cabinet where priorities were formed, wished the party to conform more to the Disraelian myth of 'Tory democracy'. It was from the project of developing a popular Conservative politics and its coalescence with the more statist preoccupations of Unionism that the immigration question received its political momentum. Sustained support for an Aliens Act came from those within the Conservative Party who hoped it would express a new relationship between their party, the working classes, and the state.[55] It was only after Salisbury's departure that this challenge to his practice of Conservative politics became seriously disruptive; most notably over 'tariff reform'. But whereas the defeat of 'tariff reform' signalled the failure of a radical Conservatism, the Aliens Act represented one of its victories.

After 1885 party politics began a gradual shift away from a concern with the interrelations of privilege, religion, and the pale of the constitution, towards a greater emphasis upon provision for the defenceless needy and the regulation of labour. The aliens question was in the vanguard of this change. The issue was prominent in the 1885 election in Whitechapel but not as a matter of social policy. The Conservative agent objected to the names of 1,800 persons, placed on the electoral register despite their ineligibility as aliens, since the rates they paid had appeared to qualify them for the franchise. For the Conservatives the issue was one which concerned the rule of law, echoing the terms in which Irish 'coercion' was represented, and an opportunity to accuse the Liberal candidate of seeking to turn the constituency into a 'pocket borough'.[56]

In the autumn of 1885 Whitechapel Liberals conducted a vigorous campaign defending the rights of disenfranchised foreigners. Three large and occasionally violent 'indignation meetings' were held. The Conservatives' action was seen to have violated the 'spirit of the times', which was to increase the numbers enfranchised, not the reverse. Naturalization was dismissed as a miserable but expensive technicality. By paying taxes and rates, and by sitting on juries, the aliens had fulfilled all the duties of citizenship and were thus entitled to its rights. As with 'coercion' in Ireland and the restrictions upon political demonstrations in London, radicals felt able to question Conservative interpretations of the rule of law where they seemed to uphold a privileged and unrestrained authority.[57] This was a political argument in which the interests of the 'alien' and the 'working man' were allied. However, as Jewish immigrants were placed within discussions concerned with sweated labour and overcrowding it became possible to place the interests of immigrants in opposition to those of labour. It was a construction which recognized the material effects of immigration in a manner that was beyond a Liberal ideology defined in terms of individual liberty and an attack on privilege.[58]

The first election in which immigration restriction played a part in the East End was that of 1892. In that year almost every Conservative candidate in the East End called for an Aliens Act. However, the manner in which the issue was presented was not uniform. H. H. Marks, the candidate at Bethnal Green NE, attacked the Liberal Party's obsession with Ireland, arguing there were more pressing needs of Englishmen which should come first:

> Chief among these needs he would instance the placing of a restriction upon the alien paupers who were dumped upon the shore and who, by reason of their dire poverty, were compelled to work at starvation wages to the detriment of English workers.[59]

His appeal to the working-class voters was allied to a vision of imperial greatness and, of course, defence of the Union with Ireland. Positive connections were drawn between the domestic and imperial facets of Marks's programme – between immigration restriction, protection, and Ireland: 'These were questions which appealed to every working man, and which demand an early settlement: in a nutshell, the question which they had to decide was whether England shall be little or great.'[60] The construction of labour within an imperial ideology was to be matched insitutionally by the creation of a Labour Department. One value of the immigration issue was that it could be presented in such a way that it might traverse the space between the social relations of the East End electorate and imperial politics. It seized upon a point of immediate experience over which patriotism could determine policy; in which the construction of 'us' as Englishmen became not only a source of visceral pride in imperial achievement but also something which, it was hoped, could fashion an understanding of the local economy.

The significance of Marks's rhetoric can be drawn out by comparing his comments on the aliens question with those of Montagu's opponent in Whitechapel, Colonel Le Poer Trench. Trench directed most of his attention to what he presented as a

Canute-like struggle to prevent aliens from being entered upon the electoral register. Though he too did support immigration restriction, his observations on the economic and social effects of immigration were brief. Embedded within a different conception of Conservative political practice and ideology, Trench remained determinedly patrician and unwilling to champion the working man and to dissolve momentarily social distance in an enthusiastic patriotic unity.[61] Marks, by contrast, had so removed himself from issues of constitutional propriety that he felt able to advocate a swingeing reduction of the naturalization fee to one guinea.[62]

After 1900, as the anti-alien movement attracted thousands of supporters in the East End, the rhetoric of Tory patriotism was matched by one of localism. At the same time the populist current within the agitation became more marked. Anti-alien opinion acquired a leadership within the East End for the first time and was coloured increasingly by local politics. This was given impetus by the creation of the London boroughs in 1899 and encouraged further by the institutions of metropolitan Conservatism. In December 1901 the London Municipal Society, the party's organizing body in the politics of the capital, established municipal associations throughout London. It believed that 'by this means only can the local interest, patriotism and enthusiasm be awakened'.[63] Anti-alienism was one important ingredient in this cocktail, and immigration restriction was one of the few political subjects upon which the society passed a resolution.[64] The London Municipal Society elevated to its executive committee A. T. Williams, the Moderate representative for Stepney on the London County Council, and one of the least temperate of the speakers then addressing anti-alien rallies.

Anti-Jewish as well as anti-alien currents could coexist in this attempt to construct more exclusive local and national identities. At a 'large gathering' of the Whitechapel Primrose League, the Reverend Parry confessed that 'He did not like to be represented in Parliament by a Jew (applause) although he knew Mr Samuel well. He was sure of this, that Whitechapel would gain very much by another representative. (A voice, "an Englishman".)'[65] Within the East End, the attempt to ally the local community with a patriotic unity sometimes achieved a mock-heroic effect, as when Thomas Dewar, MP for St George's in the East, vowed that 'his constant cry would be England for the English and fair play for St George's and Wapping'. But this inadvertent comedy expressed the politically serious attempt to unite traditions of localism with a Conservative, imperial, and democratic patriotism. Dewar's affirmation of purpose had been preceded by a paean to the empire delivered to a lodge of the Ancient Order of Britons. Dewar identified the empire as a people's imperium; its greatness founded upon statesmen such as Joseph Chamberlain who had risen from the 'rank and file'.[66]

There is little evidence to suggest that the hopes placed in the aliens issue by the leaders and representatives of London Toryism were well placed. A reading of the local press suggests that the immigration issue was pressed more widely and vigorously by Conservative candidates in 1892 than in 1895, yet in the former year the Conservatives were routed and in the latter they made good their lost ground.[67] There were exceptions, however, to the general inconsequentiality of the aliens issue. These occurred where Conservatives campaigned strongly on the issue and did well in the face of a Liberal revival. Such was the case with Marks in 1892, and with William Evans Gordon and Claude Hay in Stepney and Hoxton respectively in 1906. But, of course, since the proportions enfranchised in the East End were so low, electoral behaviour was not necessarily a reliable indicator of popular opinion. It is, moreover, quite possible that many Liberals in the East End were anti-alien but yet did not vote Conservative; a suggestion consistent with the considerable anxiety caused to Liberal organizers and candidates by their supporters' opinions on alien immigration.[68]

V

The high points of popular support for an Aliens Act were not marked by electoral contests but by two great public meetings held at the People's Palace in January 1902 and November 1903. The former meeting was held under the auspices of the British Brothers' League (BBL); the latter was organized by the Immigration Reform Association; both attracted enthusiastic audiences in excess of 4,000. Outside of these rallies, in 1902 the BBL claimed a membership of 12,000, mostly concentrated in the East End, and a petition gathered by the BBL amassed 45,000 signatures.[69] The support attracted to the anti-alien cause came from among both the working classes and the shopkeepers and tradesmen of East London.

The voice of propertied anti-alienism was articulated most consistently within the pages of the *Eastern Post*. More generally, the newspaper gave voice to one militant constituency among the small capitalists and property owners of the East End, and it is in this context that opposition to immigration was pursued. In 1902 the newspaper complained that the people of Stepney were 'groaning under their burden of rates and taxes'. Between 1890 and 1906 the level of rates advanced by between 30 and 50 per cent in every London borough. In Stepney the latter figure pertained. The situation was aggravated by the decreasing control over expenditure available to the collecting authority, since growing proportions of the revenue were taken by other bodies. Rates, moreover, were a regressive tax: first, because the rate base was highest where needs were smallest and, second, because the poor spent a higher proportion of their income on rent and rates.[70] The political responses to this situation were varied. Avner Offer has suggested it contributed to the Liberal landslide in 1906. The municipalities felt abandoned by the Conservative government as grants in aid were allowed to agriculture and the church but not to the hard-pressed ratepayers.[71] Another consequence was the revival of ratepayer unions. A less sober response was the right-wing radicalism and local patriotism within which the anti-alien agitation in the East End should be located.

The rates burden was a constant theme of the *Eastern Post*, as was the need for economy in local government. The newspaper was edited by J. L. Silver, who was also, until his death in 1902, the leading advocate on Stepney Borough Council of immigration restriction. The *Eastern Post* advocated radical tax changes in the interest of 'the small tradesman and small professional man', decreasing the burden on these groups and bearing more heavily upon those whose 'income runs into plethora thousands'.[72] It was this group whose businesses stood to suffer from the changing ethnic and social composition of the East End, and who were increasingly isolated among immigrants and the native working class as more of their own number evacuated the district. We can see how immigration restriction could appeal to this constituency as one cheap solution to the problems of overcrowding and rising rents in the East End. Clearly, for this group it was preferable to other solutions being canvassed such as a greatly enlarged sanitary inspectorate or the provision of municipal housing, both of which would be financed out of the rates, or the creation of rent courts, which threatened the rights of property owners. Immigration restriction would be the responsibility of central government and would be funded from that source.

Typically, the first public meeting organized by the BBL was reported to have drawn 'a crowded working class attendance'.[73] The 1902 meeting at the People's Palace was stewarded by 260 'big brawny stalwarts, dock labourers, chemical workers from Bromley, and operatives from Bow, Bethnal Green and Mile End'.[74] The league received its greatest support from Hackney and Bethnal

Green and was comparatively weak in Limehouse and St George's in the East.[75] Yet it was well known that there were few Jews in the south ward of St George's because the largely Irish inhabitants of the neighbourhood would not let them settle. The district may nevertheless have been backward in supporting the league because the language of nation and empire employed by the leaders of organized anti-alienism found little resonance among a population retaining strong links to Ireland and Catholicism.[76]

The BBL blamed immigration for the housing crisis in the East End. Above all, the immigrants were accused of 'displacing' the native population. Used in this way the term 'displacement' pushed the grievances held against the immigrants beyond the economic sphere to encompass the decline of community and an affront to a respectability that seemed peculiarly English. James William Johnson, a Stepney labourer who became chairman of the British Brothers' League executive, demonstrated this tendency to convert economic arguments into cultural ones in his evidence to the Royal Commission on Alien Immigration. Certainly, he blamed immigrants for high rents leading to the 'displacement' of English workers. But their removal from the East End was a moment of cultural disinheritance as well as economic hardship:

> This great influx is driving out the native from hearth and home. . . . Some of us have been born here, others of us have come into it when quite young children, have been brought up here, educated here; some of us have old associations here of such a nature that we feel it a hardship to be compelled to be parted from.[77]

Home and family were prominent also in explanations of the immigrants' success in the labour and housing markets. Their willingness to live beyond the pale of values and practices projected upon the native family played upon ideals and images that crossed class boundaries. A boot and shoe manufacturer complained that 'a respectable and honest man that wants to get an honest living and bring up his family could never compete with them'. An employee of his, a clicker, agreed: 'They work so much cheaper than the native workmen do . . . it affects anyone who wants to live decent, because they could never live decent on the price that these aliens earn for their weekly wage.'[78] Closely connected to this view was one emphasizing the unmanliness of the immigrants, something which was seen to explain their competitive advantage and to mark them out as an inferior type. Whereas the Englishman kept his wife at home, the immigrants sent theirs to work, Johnson claimed, an accusation which reflects more the assumption that being a husband was synonymous with providing support than the pattern of work in the immigrant colony.[79] The immigrants' unmanliness was further marked out by their aversion to heavy manual labour, and their incapacity for trade union organization. James Macdonald of the Amalgamated Society of Tailors described the Polish Jews in his trade as 'a hopeless dejected lot who have not enough backbone to stand up for anything'.[80] A policeman thought the immigrants peaceable because they were 'not men enough to be rough'.[81] It is surely no coincidence that East End anti-alienism was focused by the British *Brothers'* League.

Among middle-class anti-alienists there was the same slippage from an economic to a cultural understanding of the evils of immigration. Apart from the problems of high rents and over-crowding, A. T. Williams complained that another cause of displacement was that the immigrants were not neighbourly; they desecrated the Christian sabbath, stored rags in the yards, and made a noise from homework, and the girls and women among them paraded on the streets in the evenings.[82] The affront to respectability was a recurring theme. 'Every house seems to vomit forth hordes of people,' complained Silver, who attested that 'no decent self-respecting Englishman would live under such conditions'. A haberdasher complained that their habits were 'disgusting', and a midwife averred that 'they were not fit to be among English people'.[83]

By representing the desecration of the home, a fount of middle-class and working-class respectability and of national identity, as the immigrants' offence, the ground was defined upon which a diversity of potentially antagonistic social groups – landlords, shopkeepers, skilled and casual workers – were able to coalesce in the anti-immigrant agitation. The way was also prepared through which to draw powerful connections between housing and patriotism, the East End and the empire. At the first of the great demonstrations at the People's Palace, William Evans Gordon, the Conservative MP for Stepney, represented the meeting as one of 'the English people of East London . . . of all classes, of all creeds, of all shades of political opinion'.[84] This was a patriotism which elided distinctions between property owners and the propertyless, and between political parties: the question was presented as one of home and country – which they all possessed.

Nevertheless, differences of social position and ideological inclination could not be repressed within the anti-alien movement, and its parliamentary leadership was threatened by a form of populism which opposed the will and needs of the people to those of their nominal representatives. This was most clearly articulated by the league's extra-parliamentary and locally based leaders: above all, by Silver, by W. H. Shaw, the founder of the BBL, and in the pages of the *Eastern Post*. Thus when the decision to convene a Royal Commission on the subject of immigration was announced in January 1902, rather than take satisfaction in this step, the *Eastern Post* fulminated against 'Balfour and his place hunters' and those

> who will sooner sit amid the surroundings of the finest club in the world, while our people are being ousted from their work and their homes at the rate of thousands every years, by foreigners for whom our government seems to have more consideration than mere English people.[85]

Here was common ground with the working men in the league who saw the government's failure to legislate as evidence that the 'rich' would look after their own interests only.[86] The political upshot of these attitudes and their potential for conflict with the parliamentary supporters of aliens legislation became clear at the first demonstration at the People's Palace. Here the Hackney MP, H. Robertson, aroused 'loud protests' when he suggested that the Home Secretary should be empowered merely 'to restrain anyone whom he did not think fit from coming into the country' and eventually satisfied the audience by declaring himself in favour of restrictive legislation.[87]

For the MPs it was deeply undesirable that the agitation should be pressed from below and not led from above. One response to the impolitic and potentially disruptive elements in the BBL was to attempt to take it over. A disgruntled William Shaw, having resigned, complained: 'the politicians refused to support me unless I became a tool in their hands'. But for the party leaders this was not enough. He alleged that the East End Conservatives were 'threatened with serious displeasure if they appeared on the British Brothers League platform again'. These pressures led to the formation of the Londoners' League and the Immigration Reform Association, which were to act both as allies and as policemen of the popular agitation.[88]

Throughout 1901 ministers stonewalled in the face of the growing outcry against alien immigration and sought to reassure restrictionist MPs that existing laws gave adequate powers with which to deal with the housing difficulty in East London.[89] At the same time, however, the government was pledged, 'through the mouths of several of its most prominent members', to introduce an Aliens Bill, as Gerald Balfour, the Secretary to the Board of

Trade, reminded the Cabinet in January 1902.[90] It was the popular agitation in East London which made this a pressing contradiction since it gave legitimacy and urgency to the restrictionist enthusiasts in Parliament. As Balfour predicted: 'the question is sure to be raised in the Debate on the Address'.[91] The problem was dramatized at the People's Palace meeting in January 1902. Here, to great acclaim, S. F. Ridley, the Conservative MP for Bethnal Green SW, called upon the government to fulfil the pledges made by Lord Salisbury, Joseph Chamberlain, Charles Ritchie, and other ministers.[92] The government's response to the increasingly embarrassing situation was to announce the appointment of the Royal Commission on Alien Immigration.

This step was largely a consequence of the popular agitation but it was also the way in which the Conservative Party stifled its populist vigour and regained control over a movement which had threatened to outrun its master. While the commission deliberated, the debate inevitably was taken indoors, and links between the East End MPs and the popular discontent were severed. Notably, the next great meeting in the anti-alien cause did not take place until after the commission had reported. A price had to be paid, however, and this was a commission weighted in the restrictionists' favour and which included their leading propagandist, William Evans Gordon. The result was a report that Evans Gordon played a major role in drafting and which recommended legislation to prevent the entry of several classes of alien immigrant.[93]

An Aliens Act offered significant political advantages to Balfour's government in its listless last years. It provided for an item of social legislation which also skirted the two issues most divisive within the Conservative Party – finance and protection. Even before the costly Boer War, Hicks Beach, the Chancellor of the Exchequer, had been concerned that expenditure was out of control.[94] The demand from him and his allies for financial probity was a critical check on any schemes for social reform which would thus be not only expensive but also politically divisive. The great advantage of the Aliens Act, in this respect, was that it was difficult to cost with any precision, but its administration was anticipated to cost as little as £25,000 each year.[95] Further, the Act allowed the government to adopt the language of efficiency and also to offer a measure of protection which at the same time left trade untouched. Contemporaries were well aware that the Act was intended to serve as a piece of 'shop-window' legislation: something for the working classes a little in advance of the election. In this respect, the East End seats which the Conservatives had dominated since 1885 were valuable prizes and worth a little investment. It was generally assumed that the working class was in favour of immigration restriction, and the legislation brought the bonus of Liberal discomfort and disunity as East End candidates and MPs urged the Liberal leader, Campbell Bannerman, not to oppose the Bill.[96]

VI

The Aliens Act was the first legislation to place statutory restrictions upon free entry to Britain following the repeal in 1826 of laws passed during the French Revolution. It was a great success and produced a radical diminution in the rate of Jewish immigration to Britain at a time when Jews were leaving eastern Europe in increasing and unprecedentedly large numbers. It managed this, moreover, with a minimum of expense by acting as a deterrent to potential immigrants and shipping companies. The number of immigrants from Russia declined from 12,481 in 1906 to 4,223 in 1910, yet relatively few were turned away – 4,176 in all between 1906 and 1910.[97]

The most significant requirement of the Act was to demand that adult immigrants demonstrate they were able to support themselves and their dependants 'decently'. Among its other provisions the Act empowered the Home Secretary to expel aliens found wandering without means of subsistence, living in insanitary conditions, or discovered to be in receipt of parochial relief within one year of their arrival in Britain. At the last moment an amendment was allowed by the government which exempted religious as well as political refugees from the Act's provisions, if they were fleeing from 'danger of imprisonment or danger to life and limb'. But it was an addition so vague and narrow as to place great weight upon the Act's interpretation by the new immigration authorities.[98] In 1910 only five immigrants were admitted as refugees.[99] Crucially, the machinery of restriction was set in place according to administrative rather than judicial principles. The burden of proof was placed upon those prevented from landing by an Immigration Officer and a Medical Officer of Health. These migrants were then required to prove their eligibility to land before a board composed of three members and from whose decision there was no appeal.

The anti-alien agitation demonstrates how an invocation of home and nation, family and respectability, was able to mobilize a coalition of diverse interests into a significant political movement. This is of particular interest since the enthusiastic working-class response to the outbreak of war in 1914 has remained opaque in the face of a historiography which portrays that class as caste-like politically and culturally – leading 'a life apart'.[100] The working-class contribution to support for the BBL, albeit local, offers one way of modifying this view by highlighting values and practices crossing class boundaries and which could inform a patriotic political movement.

In this period the working classes were being addressed as part of the nation more insistently than ever before. Nevertheless, it is striking that the electoral returns upon being anti-alien were uncertain and that, moreover, the patriotism of the anti-alien agitation did not prevent it from becoming a site for the expression of political, ideological, and social differences. When popular patriotism is viewed more widely it is notable how discontinuous was its political force. In London, between the aliens agitation and the onset of war it was of little significance. The discontinuity and ambiguity of patriotism within party politics suggest that it should not be conceived of as something to which an individual or a group simply adhered or did not, and the meaning of which can be assumed. Patriotic messages held different meanings for different groups, and the political community they created competed with others for the loyalty of the masses.[101] Not all anti-alien Liberal voters deserted that party for the Conservatives. Some recent historical writing has sought to explain the political and ideological containment of the working classes in this period by pointing to the force of popular patriotism itself, or to patriotism as a vital component within working-class 'deference' or 'traditionalism'.[102] The difficulty of ordering and containing the masses within a community of patriotic sentiment suggests that these interpretations misunderstand the political significance of the rhetoric of national identity. Rather than attempting to read behind patriotism to elicit yet another answer to the riddle of social stability, its greater importance may be its literal one in drawing attention to the various attempts to construct a national community.

In the context of the anti-alien agitation it is notable how attempts to construct a national community were inflected by the growing threat to Britain's imperial predominance. Any idea of a national community inevitably was based upon a series of inclusions and exclusions concerned with who would be contained within the nation and upon what terms. In 1885 radicals had argued for the inclusion of alien voters on the ground that they fulfilled all the requirements of citizenship irrespective of their place of birth. This was a vision of the nation in which its boundaries were porous. In contrast, the antipathetic response to Jewish immigration stigmatized the immigrants for failing to satisfy standards of respectability, masculinity, and home life that were represented as being peculiarly English and, further, sought literally to exclude them from the country. Speaking in support of the Aliens Bill, the Prime Minister, A. J. Balfour, stated his belief that 'we have a right to keep out everybody who does not add to the strength of the community – the industrial, social and intellectual strength of the community'.[103] Subsequently, it became increasingly difficult for Jewish immigrants to become naturalized subjects.[104] The working classes, as we have seen, were allowed a more secure place within this extended community of the imperial nation. But the exclusion of 'aliens' among the 'unfit' signalled, at the same time, the demise of a different vision of the national community. The idea of the nation was thus extended and narrowed in different directions at the same moment.

The Aliens Act was directed against the destitute, the damaged, and the disruptive. This was the principle upon which legislation was introduced by both Conservative and Liberal governments between 1900 and 1914, the aim of which was to segregate, and in this sense 'keep out', other categories of persons also deemed to have a degenerative effect upon the nation's health and efficiency. The category of the 'habitual criminal' was invented, and preventive detention of between five and ten years was sanctioned by the 1908 Prevention of Crime Act for those who had led 'a persistently dishonest life'. The Mental Deficiency Act of 1913 was designed to segregate elements, to prevent them from reproducing and exercising a degenerating influence upon the race, and the Children's Act of 1908 allowed the state to intervene and rescue children from the care of 'unfit' parents.[105] At the same time as it articulated a re-formed vision of the nation, the Aliens Act was one facet of an attempt to extend the state's regulatory and coercive powers upon a broad front and presents a notable example of the connections between these two tendencies.

In response to the relative decline of national power and the fears which this engendered, several national totems were torn down. In foreign affairs and defence both 'splendid isolation' and the *pax Britannica* were swiftly abandoned. Under Conservative and Liberal administrations, European allies were sought, and gun-boats were sacrificed in favour of the home fleet.[106] In the struggle to ensure imperial supremacy the free movement of peoples was a further luxury, a legacy from a period when British power was so secure that such generosity was possible.[107] Significantly, the Liberal and Jewish defence of the alien was fought primarily upon the ground of utility, not of libertarian principle; on the basis of the immigrants' contribution to national and imperial welfare and not upon the principles of asylum and the free movement of peoples. Sir Charles Dilke, a champion of the alien cause who did raise the issue of asylum, spoke also to the fears of national deterioration:

> Miserable as may be their [Russian Jews'] condition when they come here, they are not of a stock inferior to our own. They are of a stock which, when it mixes with our own in the course of years, goes rather to improve than to deteriorate the British race. (Ministerial cries of 'oh'.)[108]

Seen in this perspective, the Aliens Act was not a legislative quirk, brought about by a mixture of opportunism and prejudice, but was at the front of a transformation of the regulatory ambitions of the British state and a reorientation of the idea of the nation. The legacy of liberalism was not overthrown and remained a brake upon the state's coercive capacities. Within narrow boundaries, political and religious refugees were exempted from the Aliens Act, and it remained important for the government to be able to claim that the right of asylum had not been discarded. But even taking into account this qualification, the Aliens Act was a first abrogation of free trade, it drastically attenuated the right of asylum, and it introduced a system of administrative justice. Although a product of the fag-end of a doomed Conservative administration, the Act was not repealed in the following years of Liberal control. It was a landmark in the decline of liberal England.

Notes

I am grateful to Todd Endelman, Margot Finn, and Gareth Stedman Jones for their helpful comments on earlier drafts of this essay.

1 As the Secretary of State to the Board of Trade, Gerald Balfour, observed in 1902: 'though it has never been suggested that restrictions should be confined to these Jews, any measures to be adopted must mainly be considered to their effects on this class of immigrant' – Public Record Office, CAB 37/59/146, 7 January 1902.

2 C. Booth, *Life and Labour of the People of London*, third series, vol. 2, 1902, pp. 1–2.

3 *Jewish Chronicle*, 5 June 1903, p. 13.

4 J. A. Hobson, *Problems of Poverty*, 1892, p. 126.

5 'Foreign undesirables', *Blackwoods Magazine*, February 1901, p. 289; H. Fyffe, 'The aliens and the empire', *The Nineteenth Century and After*, September 1903, pp. 415–19.

6 B. Gainer, *The Alien Invasion: The Origins of the Aliens Act of 1905*, 1972, pp. 26, 44, 79–99, 215; J. A. Garrard, *The English and*

Immigration: A Comparative Study of the Jewish Influx, 1880–1910, 1971, pp. 50–1, 55–6; C. Holmes, *Anti-Semitism in British Society, 1976–1939*, 1979, *passim*.

7 For these accusations, see, for example, *Der Yidisher Ekspres*, 28 September 1900, p. 2; ibid., 22 January 1902, p. 4; and *Jewish Chronicle*, 23 January 1903, p. 20. For one of the many denials of the charge, see *Parliamentary Debates*, fourth series, cxlv, col. 721.

8 C. T. Husbands, 'East End racism, 1900–80: geographical continuities in vigilantist and extreme right-wing political behaviour', *London Journal*, summer 1982, pp. 3–26, suggests that racism was an expression of 'rootless volatility' among 'confused' people with little political sophistication. B. Gainer, *The Alien Invasion*, scrutinizes the debate over Jewish immigration at many levels. Gainer's careful research is undermined by his belief that the opponents of statutory immigration restriction held a monopoly upon good sense, and that opportunism and prejudice characterized the advocates of an Aliens Act. A. Lee, 'Aspects of the working class response to Jewish immigration', in C. Lunn (ed.), *Hosts, Immigrants and Minorities: Historical Responses to Newcomers in British Society*, Folkestone, 1980, pp. 107–33, is a suggestive exception to the usual approach but concludes oddly that the anti-alien movement was a failure and that antipathy to Jews and aliens barely existed. Another exception is B. Williams, 'The anti-Semitism of tolerance: middle-class Manchester and the Jews, 1870–1900', in A. J. Kidd and K. W. Roberts (eds), *City, Class and Culture: Studies in Social Policy and Cultural Production in Victorian Manchester*, Manchester, 1985, which characterizes anti-Semitism reductively as an expression of lower-middle-class anxieties, pp. 83–9.

9 An account of the economic and social crisis in the capital in these years can be found in G. Stedman Jones, *Outcast London*, Oxford, 1971, ch. 16.

10 Hobson, *Problems of Poverty*, p. 57; A. White, 'The invasion of foreign paupers', *The Nineteenth Century*, March 1888, p. 414; Parliamentary Papers (henceforth PP), 1987, LXXXIX, *Report to the Board of Trade on the Sweating System in East London*, p. 18.

11 ibid., p. 4.

12 PP, 1890, XVII, *House of Lords Select Committee on the Sweating System*, fifth report, p. cxxv.

13 The 1891 Act merely extended sanitary inspection to all workshops except domestic ones and required employers to maintain a list of all persons working on and off their premises: B. Hutchins and A. Harrison, *A History of Factory Legislation*, 1903, pp. 216–18.

14 B. Webb, *My Apprenticeship*, Cambridge, 1979, pp. 335–7.

15 Hobson, *Problems of Poverty*, pp. 89–91; Earl of Dunraven, 'The invasion of destitute aliens', *The Nineteenth Century*, June 1892, pp. 990–4; National Union of Boot and Shoe Workers, *Monthly Report*, December 1890, pp. 10–11; ibid., August 1891, p. 10.

16 Hobson's survey of the alternatives listed these as co-operative production, an eight-hour day, public workshops, state business on

uncommercial terms, factory legislation, and trade unionism: Hobson, *Problems of Poverty*, ch. 6.

17 D. M. Feldman, 'Immigrants and workers, Englishmen and Jews; Jewish immigrants to the East End of London, 1880–1906', unpublished doctoral dissertation, Cambridge University, 1986, pp. 83–9.

18 S. Fox, 'The invasion of foreign paupers', *Contemporary Review*, June 1888, p. 859.

19 Stedman Jones, *Outcast London*, ch. 6.

20 Booth, *Life and Labour*, first series, iv, p. 340.

21 A. Offer, *Property and Politics, 1870–1914: Landownership, Law, Ideology, and Urban Development in England*, 1981, p. 268; Stedman Jones, *Outcast London*, p. 325; A. Wohl, *The Eternal Slum: Housing and Social Policy in Victorian London*, 1977, pp. 302–3.

22 PP, 1903, IX, *Royal Commission on Alien Immigration*, q. 5, 755.

23 ibid., q. 6, 602, q. 6, 687.

24 ibid., q. 4, 827.

25 'The alien immigrant', *Blackwoods Magazine*, January 1902, pp. 137, 141.

26 Joseph Chamberlain, for example, asserted he was 'not cosmopolitan enough to wish to see the happiness and prosperity of American workmen secured by the starvation, misery and suffering of British workmen': quoted in B. Semmel, *Imperialism and Social Reform*, 1960, p. 94. For an example of the overlap of immigration restriction and tariff reform, see C. T. Husbands, 'East End racism, 1900–80', p. 12.

27 Jewish Board of Guardians (henceforth JBG), *Annual Report for 1887*, p. 15.

28 PP, 1889, X, *House of Commons Select Committee on Emigration and Immigration (Foreigners)*, p. x.

29 Anglo-Jewish archives, London, AJ/1, *Jewish World*, 22 April 1886.

30 *Eastern Post*, 18 June 1892, p. 6.

31 *Parliamentary Debates*, fourth series, xxvi, cols 1047–55.

32 *Royal Commission on Alien Immigration*, pp. 40–3.

33 I. Finestein, 'The new community', in V. D. Lipman (ed.), *Three Centuries of Anglo-Jewish History*, Cambridge, 1961. On the work of the Jewish Board of Guardians, see V. D. Lipman, *A Century of Social Service, 1859–1959: the Jewish Board of Guardians*, 1959.

34 JBG, *Annual Report for 1886*, p. 12.

35 PP, 1888, XI, *House of Commons Select Committee on Emigration and Immigration (Foreigners)*, q. 3, 553.

36 *Royal Commission on Alien Immigration*, q. 15, 390.

37 These figures are compiled from the JBG annual reports for the years from 1880 to 1906.

38 *Royal Commission on Alien Immigration*, q. 15, 691.

39 Lipman, *A Century of Social Service*, appendix iv.

40 ibid., pp. 27–31.

41 JBG, *Annual Report for 1887*, p. 10.

42 ibid., pp. 16–17.

43 JBG, *Annual Report for 1882*, pp. 62, 65–6.

44 ibid., p. 66.
45 JBG, *Annual Report for 1889*, p. 67.
46 YIVO institute, New York, Mowshowitch Collection, 10804–7. The attempt to develop a set of policies and practices that did take account of the needs of refugees and of the obligations between co-religionists was further hobbled by the parsimony of the Jewish middle classes, the great majority of whom did not contribute to the funds of the JBG: Lipman, *A Century of Social Service*, p. 105.
47 *Jewish Chronicle*, 19 July 1901, p. 15.
48 ibid., 19 September 1902, p. 12.
49 ibid., 1 November 1901, p. 20.
50 A sophisticated but, to this author, uncompelling version of this argument can be found in T. Endelman, 'Native Jews and foreign Jews in London, 1870–1914', in D. Berger (ed.), *The Legacy of Jewish Migration: 1881 and its Impact*, New York, 1983, pp. 113–19.
51 T. Endelman, 'Communal solidarity among the Jewish elite of Victorian London', *Victorian Studies*, spring 1985, pp. 491–526.
52 W. Evans Gordon, *The Alien Immigrant*, 1903, p. 248.
53 D. Feldman, 'Englishmen, Jews and immigrants in London, 1865–1914', in R. Samuel (ed.), *Patriotism and the Making of British National Identities*, forthcoming 1989.
54 *Jewish Chronicle*, 28 April 1905, pp. 7–8.
55 Fair traders such as James Lowther and Henry Vincent were prominent in the anti-alien lobby in the 1890s. On the support from the Unionist camp, see J. Chamberlain, 'The labour question', *The Nineteenth Century*, November 1892, pp. 677–710.
56 *East London Observer*, 5 September 1885, p. 6.
57 ibid., 5 September 1885, p. 6; ibid., 12 September 1885, p. 6; ibid., 19 September 1885, p. 6. On the constellation of radical causes, see John Davis, 'Radical clubs and London politics, 1870–1900', in this volume.
58 The political effects of this are indicated by the path of W. A. Rose. A carpenter and leading member of the Whitechapel Liberal Club, Rose had welcomed Montagu's candidacy in 1885, for the Conservatives had 'spurned both Jews and working man for as long as they were able'. In 1886 Rose emerges again as a supporter of reducing the naturalization fee to ten shillings, but he felt bound to comment upon 'the prejudice existing in many quarters against our neighbours of other nationalities'. In 1902, however, Rose appeared before the Royal Commission on Alien Immigration as a supporter of statutory restriction: ibid., 30 May 1885, p. 6; ibid., 1 May 1886, p. 3; *Royal Commission on Alien Immigration*, q. 9, 178.
59 *East London Observer*, 2 July 1892, p. 7.
60 ibid.
61 ibid., 2 July 1892, p. 6; ibid., 25 June 1892, p. 6
62 ibid., 23 July 1892, p. 7.
63 Guildhall, London, Records of the London Municipal Society, minutes of annual general meetings, 16 December 1901.
64 ibid., 14 December 1903.
65 *East London Observer*, 19 April 1902, p. 5.

66 ibid., 1 March 1902, p. 6.
67 For the fluctuations of the Conservative vote, see H. Pelling, *Social Geography of British Elections, 1885–1910*, 1967, p. 43.
68 British Library, Campbell Bannerman Collection, H. Gladstone to H. Campbell Bannerman, 9 January 1905; ibid., 26 January 1905.
69 *Eastern Post*, 18 January 1902, p. 6; *East London Observer*, 16 August 1902, p. 3; *Jewish Chronicle*, 31 October 1902, p. 9; ibid., 13 November 1903, p. 27.
70 Offer, *Property and Politics*, pp. 283, 288, 291; *Eastern Post*, 25 January 1902, p. 6; ibid., 12 April 1902, p. 4.
71 Offer, *Property and Politics*, chs 14, 15.
72 *Eastern Post*, 19 April 1902, p. 4.
73 *East London Observer*, 11 May 1901, p. 5.
74 ibid., 18 January 1902, p. 2.
75 ibid., 18 August 1902, p. 8.
76 *Royal Commission on Alien Immigration*, q. 2, 122–4, q. 2, 184–6, q. 2, 251–6.
77 *Royal Commission on Alien Immigration*, q. 8, 558.
78 ibid., q. 1, 829, q. 2, 488. On the general point that ideals of family life crossed class boundaries, see Jane Lewis, 'The working-class wife and mother and state intervention, 1870–1918', in Jane Lewis (ed.), *Labour and Love: Women's Experience of Home and Family, 1850–1940*, Oxford, 1986, pp. 102–6.
79 *Royal Commission on Alien Immigration*, q. 8, 859; E. Ross, ' "Fierce questions and taunts": married life in working-class London, 1870–1914', in this volume.
80 Greater London Record Office, London County Council, committee on contracts, presented papers, 12 December 1890, pp. 13, 28.
81 London School of Economics and Political Science, Booth Collection, B 351, p. 151.
82 *Royal Commission on Alien Immigration*, q. 1, 641, q. 1, 724.
83 ibid., q. 2, 627, q. 9, 418.
84 *East London Observer*, 18 January 1902, p. 2.
85 *Eastern Post*, 1 February 1902, pp. 4–5.
86 *Royal Commission on Alien Immigration*, q. 8, 561.
87 *East London Observer*, 18 January 1902, p. 2.
88 *Jewish Chronicle*, 31 October 1902, p. 9; on the Immigration Reform Association and the Londoners' League, see Holmes, *Anti-Semitism in British Society*, pp. 92–4.
89 Gainer, *The Alien Invasion*, p. 181.
90 Public Record Office, Kew, CAB 37/59/146, 7 January 1902.
91 ibid.
92 *East London Observer*, 18 January 1902, p. 2.
93 Herefordshire and Worcester Record Office, Hereford, Papers of Lord James of Hereford, W. Evans Gordon to Lord James of Hereford, 7 June 1903.
94 P. T. Marsh, *The Art of Popular Government: Lord Salisbury's Domestic Statecraft*, Brighton, 1978, p. 268.
95 Public Record Office, Kew, HO 45/10303/117267/51, 4 May 1905.

96 Gainer, *The Alien Invasion*, p. 143.
97 PP, 1911, X, *Fifth Annual Report of the HM Inspector under the Aliens Act*, p. 35.
98 PP, 1905, I, *The Aliens Act, 1905*, pp. 81–3. The difficulty of defining who did come within the provisions of the Act quickly became apparent, the response of the Home Office being that each case had to be dealt with in accord with its particular circumstances. See Public Record Office, Kew, HO 45 10327/132181/11.
99 PP, 1911, X, *Fifth Annual Report of HM Inspector under the Aliens Act*, p. 36.
100 See, for example, E. J. Hobsbawm, 'The making of the working class', in his *Worlds of Labour*, 1984, pp. 194–213; P. Joyce, *Work, Society and Politics: The Culture of the Factory in Later Victorian England*, Brighton, 1980, pp. 332–7; S. Meacham, *A Life Apart: The English Working Class, 1890–1914*, 1974, pp. 190–4.
101 On the different meanings of patriotism, see H. Cunningham, 'The language of patriotism, 1750–1914', *History Workshop Journal*, autumn 1981, pp. 8–33.
102 R. Mckenzie and H. Silver, *Angels in Marble*, 1968, pp. 250–2; A. Lee, 'Conservatism, traditionalism and the British working class, 1880–1918', in D. E. Martin and D. Rubinstein (eds), *Ideology and the Labour Movement: Essays Presented to John Saville*, 1979, pp. 84–5, 95–8; M. Pugh, *The Tories and the People*, Oxford, 1985, pp. 3, 92–3; P. Dodd, 'Englishness and national culture', in P. Dodd and R. Colls (eds), *Englishness: Politics and Culture, 1880–1920*, Beckenham, 1986, pp. 9–11. For a more sceptical view, however, see H. Cunningham, 'The Conservative Party and patriotism', ibid., pp. 283–307.
103 *Parliamentary Debates*, fourth series, cxlv, col. 821.
104 J. Mervyn Jones, *British Nationality Law*, Oxford, 1947, pp. 110, 113; D. Cesarani, 'Anti-alienism in England after the First World War', *Immigrants and Minorities*, March 1987, pp. 16–18.
105 D. Garland, *Punishment and Welfare*, Aldershot, 1985, pp. 219–26; V. A. C. Gatrell, 'Crime, authority and the policeman-state', in F. M. L. Thompson (ed.), *The Cambridge Social History of Britain, 1750–1950*, forthcoming 1989.
106 Paul M. Kennedy, *The Rise and Fall of British Naval Mastery*, 1983, ch. 8. B. Porter, *The Refugee Question in Mid-Victorian Politics*, Cambridge, 1979, p. 219, attributes the introduction of immigration controls to the end of the mid-Victorian boom and the social crisis of the 1880s – an explanation that does not account for the lag of twenty years until the Aliens Act was passed.
107 *Parliamentary Debates*, fourth series, cxix, col. 737, 740; ibid., cxxxiii, col. 1083.
108 ibid., cxxxii, col. 995. See too the evidence of the secretary and solicitor to the Jewish Board of Deputies, C. H. L. Emmanuel, in PP, 1903, IX, *Royal Commission on Alien Immigration*, qq. 16565–765.

4

Free from chains?
The image of women's labour in London, 1900–20

Deborah Thom

Historians of London have been delighted by the wealth of illustrative material that the development of photography brought to the study of urban life. So have historians of women. But while both have argued that great care is needed in interpreting visual imagery ('Who took this picture and why?'), much less has been said about the effects of pictorial representations. The existing genre of photographs of working women had already helped to sustain an image of the working woman. Women had already been objectified and their work turned into both exotica and a species of social problem in the last twenty years of the nineteenth century.[1] Photographs dramatized the sense of discovery characteristic of late-Victorian social investigation. This essay is an attempt to assess the impact of representations of working women created before and during the First World War, an image partly created by photographs of record. It also examines the contribution of London to this image. London dominated social commentary in the early twentieth century. It was the period in which mass national newspapers began to exploit photography in the interests of campaigns for social reform and in which technical change made portable cameras usable in all sorts of lighting conditions.

Ideas about working women in this period shifted, and visual and verbal representations of the working woman changed. The image was no longer that a proportion of women worked because they were poor or unsupported. It was now one in which all women's labour was that of the weak and defenceless. The woman worker was, paradigmatically, the sweated worker. This became the frozen image of working women perpetuated through the changes of the First World War and beyond. The persistence of this image had profound consequences for social policy, trade union organization, and working women's own understanding. From it followed important assumptions about wages, collective organization, and family life; assumptions which were built into legislation and practice. But before examining the production and effects of these images, the context in which they were produced must be set out by looking at the social investigations and the organizations of working women from which they came. The essay will discuss the situation of woman workers, the groups who represented them, and the two campaigning issues on which they focused: sweating and motherhood. Then the actions and representations themselves will be described and the whole drawn together around the changes of the First World War.

In the years after 1900 there developed a new form of representation of working women. They were no longer an interesting survival of the old days. They were becoming a symbol of the unacceptable present, a new cause for concern; and the most photographed objects of such concern were to be found in the capital. It was the conditions of London working women that were increasingly used as a metonym for the condition of the female working class, ignoring all local variations and considerations of the labour market. Of course imagery of the working woman was not only photographic. Although the great governmental analyses of female labour lay some time in the past, the demand for women's exclusion from certain trades which had prompted them remained a live issue.[2] Women continued to work with dangerous chemicals and to suffer gynaecological problems seen as arising from their employment and to excite the concern of reformers as a result.[3] The new factor in the discussion in the 1900s was the growth of women's own organizations which had begun to base themselves in London. These organizations campaigned primarily on issues of general social need to do with women as social beings, mothers, and daughters, rather than upon the specific interests of workers in certain trades who happened to be women. Even in the most powerful image most people have of London women organizing at the end of the nineteenth century – the match-girls at Bryant & May and their strike in 1888 – the pictorial theme that most caught the public imagination was their piteous poverty, meagre dress, and sheer need.[4] Here was a damning indictment of an industrial system that left women physically unprotected against lethal industrial disease and exploitation. Working women represented forces which, if magnified or accelerated, would produce social damage. This strike remained a fairly isolated image of the potential power of working women until organizations representing the woman worker came together ten or twenty years later, but it set the agenda for later struggles to organize women in industry.

The Fabian Women's Group was the best organized of these

groups. It was small, and primarily a forum for discussion and presentation of research findings. Its members appear to have seen themselves as a propaganda body, and were, almost to a woman, London-based. They were not among the Fabian Society's small working-class membership. They were supported either by family money, as wives or daughters, or by those few middle-class professions like journalism that enabled independence from family.[5] Other groups included the Women's Industrial Council, which had some members in common with the Fabians and produced as many reports as did the FWG, as well as a campaigning journal, the *Women's Industrial News*.[6] The women's trade union organizations – the Women's Trade Union League and the National Federation of Women Workers – both located themselves in London (in 1903 and 1906) in the same offices and with the same administrative staff. The WTUL had been in existence for many years but had been revitalized by the appointment, as general secretary, of Mary Macarthur, a shop-owner's daughter who had gone into trade union work for the Shop Assistants' Union in Scotland. She was lured south by Margaret Bondfield (of the Shop Assistants) and Gertrude Tuckwell (president of the WTUL) to help revive women's unionism. The WTUL was supposed to encourage unionism among women in general; the NFWW was set up in 1906 by the WTUL to provide a trade union where there was no suitable union in existence, or where the existing unions did not admit women, so this was to be a general union based on sex. They too ran journals: the *Women's Trades' Union Review* (from 1891 until 1919) and the *Woman Worker* (from 1907 to 1911 and 1915 to 1920).[7] The location in London and the concentration on London's workers were not accidental. Among legislators, an increased interest in social reform was noticeable, and women workers were seen as an essential locus of that reform. Among women's organizations the move towards parliamentary lobbying was well under way. It was particularly aimed at sympathetic MPs capable of proposing and drafting reforms of interest to working women. These London-based organizations concentrated on legislative change more than organization at the point of production.[8]

There were two preoccupations shared by all these organizations. The first was the campaign against sweating; the second the organization of working women in their own defence. Sweating is best defined loosely as contemporaries defined it. It was work that did *not* take place in factories, that was not protected by government agencies or trade union representation, that did not provide a living wage. It was done not only by women, nor was all women's work sweated.[9] Sweating had been identified as an evil by a variety of pressure groups in the 1880s, and the House of Lords Select Committee on Sweating had concluded that certain labour conditions usually associated with the term should be eradicated by registering outworkers and subjecting their workplaces to sanitary inspection.[10] This was ineffective because workers were not well enough organized to enforce supervision. It was thus the agitation of the industrial women's organizations that began the process of rescuing these occupations from the vicious circle of low wages and the absence of union organization. The membership of these organizations was small, but their representatives allied with Liberal reformers and some male trade unionists to form the Anti-Sweating League. This was the major force agitating for a minimum wage, which would remove such trades from their marginal position. Its main effect was to bring the issue of low wages, especially women's low wages, before the general public.[11]

The ASL shared premises in Mecklenburgh Square with the Women's Trade Union League and the NFWW, beneath the apartment of Mary Macarthur, its main organizer.[12] Macarthur had a valuable link with the editor of the Liberal *Daily News*, and it was this newspaper's sponsorship of the exhibition against sweating in 1906 that led to the forming of the league.[13] The exhibition was organized by George Shann, a paid organizer of the Workers' Union which was beginning to organize widely among sweated workers mainly in the government sector.[14] The exhibition handbook, written by Richard Mudie-Smith, and the reprinting of photos of exhibits in the *Daily News*, shocked polite society. Macarthur's most notable propaganda coup was a piece of detective work tracing the line of sweated workers who participated in the manufacture of baby clothes. She nearly lost her own life when one of the sweatshops turned out to be infested with diphtheria, and the baby clothes by implication were thereby dangerous even to the privileged children who wore them. This piece of exposure carried ambiguous benefits for working women. It turned them into disease, something that could be catching, as well as a social problem to be deplored.[15] Other issues which were raised by the anti-sweaters tended the same way. Workers in luxury goods – tennis balls, artificial flowers, millinery, embroidery, toys – were all featured in issues of the *Women's Industrial News* as subject to sweating. Their work was attacked not only because it produced inessentials but because it damaged the women's health – and the health of society – because of the toll taken on both motherhood and on men by the lowering of male wages. Concerns over employment were often used to express wider anxieties about social health.[16] Barmaids presented one case where the state was urged to use powers of general regulation to deal with matters of sexuality arising from work, because barmaids were felt either to be in especial moral danger or to cause it because they were in regular contact with the temptations of both men and drink. The Women's Industrial Council devoted considerable space to a discussion on barmaids in 1910–11; it seems reasonable to surmise that some of the discussion reflected a particular concern about women whose work involved the entertainment of men. Finally, the state was called in to deal with danger to motherhood, both because of the effects of working conditions on physical health and because it affected these women's ability to look after children; women were at work, often in their own homes, when they should have been mothering.[17]

As a result of this emphasis on sweating by organizations representing women workers, sweating became a synonym for women's work. Such an equation is clear in the work of Edward Cadbury – one of his books about sweating was called *Women's Work and Wages* – but it was also implicit in the books by B. L. Hutchins and Clementina Black, *Women in Modern Industry* and *Married Women's Work*. Thus the type of investigation into women's employment that became prominent at this time implied that such employment was problematic, that it should, if possible, be altered in major structural ways, but that such changes were beyond the capacities of the sweated worker herself. Sweated workers were defenceless workers and therefore could play little part in the eradication of the sweating system. One of the major structural changes envisaged by commentators and reformers was that the state should intervene to end sweating, by taking an active role in controlling women's work in general. This intervention was not seen as necessary for male workers, who were deemed capable of effective organization. Gender was therefore being turned into the prime division distinguishing different groups of workers in agitation over working conditions, and to a lesser extent over maintenance of wages levels.

What part did photographs play in this emphasis upon the weakness of the sweated woman worker to resist exploitation? Arguably, their role was central because of their association with the growing power of the national press. Newspapers as well as social reform organizations were based in London. Fleet Street was taking over from the provincial press as moulders of opinion as the press proprietors began to extend centralization. Even quite impoverished journals of the left began to use illustrative evidence. A new tie-up between journalism and the exhibition reinforced the power of photographs to underline social commentary. In a novel way, women's working lives became an exhibit, and an exhibit based almost exclusively on the experience of work in London. This was a marked feature of the catalogue of the 1906 exhibition. Novel shots of interiors dramatized a notion of revelation of the previously hidden.

The first trade boards were set up in 1909 mainly as a result of this agitation and the campaigning in Parliament of the two MPs, Sir Charles Dilke and J. J. Mallon. The trades they covered were not as exclusively London-based as the exhibition photographs and the 'sweating' literature had been; but those that were, were mostly trades involving women – the paper-box trade, shirt and tailoring operations.[18] Government workers were also covered by the Fair Wages scheme of 1906, primarily those making uniforms in Pimlico (Westminster).[19] The other large groups affected by these new pieces of legislation were women chain-makers in Birmingham and others engaged in metalwork or pottery work around the Black Country.

Increasingly social reform organizations resorted to mass action to dramatize their campaign demands. Women were at the forefront of this process. One of the national demonstrations of 1908 was that for the first International Women's Day. The campaigners for the vote had learned from their Independent Labour Party tradition to use the press, in particular by highlighting the drama of demonstrations. Women had added a touch of pageantry to many of their processions by wearing historic costume or massed 'colours', by carrying banners specially embroidered or painted for the occasion, or by singing special songs. The use of spectacle was not new, but the political emphasis on it was. Many political actions were designed solely to gain the attention of the press. The first event of this sort, the great suffrage demonstration of 1906, marked the relocation of suffrage organizations in London.[20] Industrial women participated in these events in tiny numbers and were usually represented by Annie Kenney for the Women's Social and Political Union or by anonymous mill-girls in the National Union of Women's Suffrage Societies. In London, where they were a token presence, they were always represented by 'respectable' working girls, not the impoverished, married worker about whom the suffrage organizations were often ambiguous, frequently arguing that the vote would eradicate both married women's work and sweating.

On the other hand, trade unionists and anti-sweating organizations did parade sweated workers. The great impact of the chainmakers' agitation derived from a street demonstration of women, who forged chain by hand, carrying their chains draped about their persons. It was a profoundly disturbing image and it was backed up by photographs of their homes and workplaces; in one of these photos was to be seen an infant's cradle, the only clue that the burly figures, lit from underneath by the light of their forges, were in fact female. The campaign struck at the heart of the ambiguity inherent in these depictions. Were these women heroines or victims? As far as trade unionists were concerned they were of course both, but the impact of their chains was one which could not lightly be overridden in trying to portray women workers as equal partners in the social and political order. The chain-makers' own arguments about their case rested upon the claim that their work needed both skill and strength and that it was underpaid. But their representatives argued the case for a minimum rate of payment with appeals to the needs of society, the demands of social justice, and the deservingness of the women concerned. The most effective images were probably those of the sweated worker as victim.[21]

Such an emphasis continued in the period of industrial unrest and sex war, even though it was challenged by imagery of a more threatening character. In 1911–12 the East End of London was both the major area of union organization and the major source of propaganda. The NFWW increased its membership and its public visibility in a series of strikes among jam-makers, clothing workers, biscuit packers, and other workers of the East End. Mary Macarthur used her considerable speaking powers to the limits of her strength in turning these strikers into union members.[22] By some definitions they were not strictly speaking sweated workers at all because they worked in factories. They were unrespectable by comparison with the previous group representations of organized women workers, because they were working class, mothers, and militant. The imagery derived from this agitation was of the growth of the notion of female masses, women as members of a working class. It was helped along by the newsreel and brilliant manipulation of the public sphere by other women's organizations, the WSPU in particular. In the process class tended to be emphasized. But this representation was at odds with the dominant one, and was soon to be dropped again, once war began.

Such imagery was, in any case, qualified by the renewed interest of reformers in the protection of motherhood. This interest in working mothers has been characterized as 'social imperialism' and has led to much debate among historians about, in particular, the interests of reformers in improving the 'condition of the race'.[23] But it is clear that there was no necessary contradiction between the interests of the imperial nation and those of working women, and that women could often exploit official concern to get what they wanted. Woman's social role was increasingly defined by her potential or actual motherhood. This was especially the case for working women. The inspiration of empire was manifest in the notion of the working women of 'Darkest England',[24] a newly explored set of social images derived from an analogy to the exploration of 'Darkest Africa'. They became an object of attention in a new way. The exhibition, photographs, and reportage were all used to render them visible, to bring the hidden to light. This sort of exploration was not new in London, but the concentration on women was. The women on whom this attention focused were those who were particularly defenceless, not only because of their work in sweated trades, but also because motherhood, rather than waged work, was seen as their vocation.

This preoccupation coincided with a ferment of self-organization, in which women struggled to achieve representation in the state *and* within the trade union movement. Trade unionists were particularly active in campaigns to protect gynaecological health; the campaign against lead was organized by the WTUL, and the interest extended to other potteries' poisons.[25] Again, the emphasis was placed upon the workers' need to rely on external protection by the extension of factory inspection and/or union organization; both would be achieved from outside the workplace and outside the worker's social circle: indeed, for women workers, often outside their social range altogether, as the lightly fictionalized account of union organization by Kathleen Woodward in *Jipping Street* makes clear: 'the women in the factory continued stonily to eye the preachers of revolt, the liberators who descended on us from unknown worlds of competence and comfort, too palpably unblemished by the experience that was ours'.[26]

The first months of war reinforced this picture of defenceless women and imperilled motherhood as a result of severe unemployment in women's trades, concern over war babies, and the sacking of domestic servants. Tiny numbers of women were aided by the Queen's Work for Women Fund set up by Queen Mary with the aid of Mary Macarthur. Macarthur railed against the extent of unpaid patriotic labour, which she called 'sister Susies sewing shirts for soldiers'.[27] Most of the women who helped here were London based, as were many of the trades whose functions the workrooms took over. The far greater numbers of textile workers and domestic servants were unrecognized in the propaganda about female unemployment. The pictures of the unemployed typically show a small workroom environment, and this was replicated in

Figure 15 Chain-maker in a widely-circulated photograph, 1912.
(Reproduced by permission of the Gertrude Tuckwell Collection.)

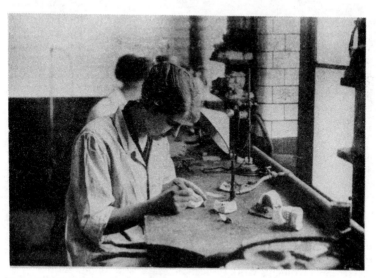

Figure 16 Dentists: not new work, but described in those terms.
(Women's Work Collection, Ministry of Munitions 1916. Reproduced by
permission of the University Library, Cambridge.)

Figure 17 Gauging shells, 1915: a dilution picture. (Women's Work Collection, Ministry of Munitions 1916. Reproduced by permission of the University Library, Cambridge.)

Figure 18 Women mechanics: another dilution photograph, 1915, before regulation. (Women's Work Collection, Ministry of Munitions 1916. Reproduced by permission of the University Library, Cambridge.)

Figure 19 Shipyard – working on a propeller: the heroic woman dilutee, 1915. (Women's Work Collection, Ministry of Munitions 1916. Reproduced by permission of the University Library, Cambridge.)

Figure 20 A woman stoker at the furnaces of a large South London factory: the exotic image of women in trousers, 1915. (Women's Work Collection, Ministry of Munitions 1916. Reproduced by permission of the University Library, Cambridge.)

Figure 21 A record of what women did: 1918–19, brewery work.
(Women's Work Collection, Imperial War Museum. Reproduced by
permission of the Trustees of the IWM.)

Figure 22 Group of silica workers, 1918–19. (Women's Work Collection, Imperial War Museum. Reproduced by permission of the Trustees of the IWM.)

Figure 23 London brewery workers, 1918–19. (Women's Work Collection, Imperial War Museum. Reproduced by permission of the Trustees of the IWM.)

the fund's centres. The work done in many of the workrooms was to replace previously imported goods based on luxury trades, for example, the German toy industry, artificial flowers, and fur.[28] This was one way in which the war accentuated the prevailing imagery of women's employment; the other was even more influential, and more visual.

Mrs Pankhurst and Lloyd George were both shrewd users of the mass media, successful demagogues and stagers of events. Together they organized a demonstration that was part of his campaign for the leadership of the Liberal Party and hers for the vote. It was originally called the 'Women's Right to Work' march and became the 'Right to Serve' march. Records in the Ministry of Munitions archive at the Public Record Office show that it was designed to attract public attention and that it was extremely expensive to mount.[29] The aim of this unusual event was to publicize the Women's War Register, and it was extremely successful, with both major newsreels featuring it in their shows. The main impression was of an entire gender made militant, this time in pursuit of an acceptable patriotic end rather than of the interests of their sex alone. Joan of Arc and other historical figures were more prominent in the demonstration than existing women workers.[30] The intention was to emphasize the novelty and heroism of women's war service, not its continuity. The register itself was based on these notions. Women were not to be conscripted but they were to register as all men did briefly at the beginning of the war. They were to become one vast pool of labour power. They were all to sign on for war work, in order to make good labour shortages, particularly in engineering. They were not enrolled by skill or experience, and no commitment was given on their rate of pay, hours, or conditions of work. In the eyes of trade unionists, as the 1915 TUC discussion shows, all these women were seen as potentially sweated workers.[31] Either they were already sweated workers or, as domestic workers and housewives, they would know nothing about trade unionism or industrial life. The common factor of their gender was seen as inherently likely to allow them to be sweated. The demonstration accentuated this by emphasizing women's detachment from industrial work as a positive qualification for such service rather than a barrier to it.

The government's pursuit of new workers to make armaments meant that the photograph came into its own as an adjunct in campaigns to convince both employers and workers that women were capable of filling the gaps in the economy. The organization of dilution, the replacement of skilled men by semi- or unskilled workers, was particularly dependent upon photographs. The War

Office commissioned photographers to survey new work done by women and published two booklets using selections of these photographs over Christmas 1915.[32] These photographs were deposited in the Imperial War Museum, in the Women's Work Collection. Some categories were not represented in the booklets. Chosen images included a larger proportion of single figures than might be expected from the overall total. Two aspects seem to be stressed in the selection: the novelty of the task (mending or making false teeth, gauging instruments, working lathes, making howitzers); or the socially unusual (getting dirty or wearing trousers). The capacity of women to undertake such work in wartime was described as though it was novel or unnatural. Although Horace Nicholls (the best of these photographers) took some striking group photographs, formal and informal, they were not reproduced in these booklets. Nor have they been much used by historians to illustrate arguments about woman's work in wartime. Historians have tended to prefer the greater drama and visual effect of individuals or small groups. It was not in the government's interest to remind employers that women were already workers, with workers' inconvenient attitudes and divisions. Women were thus pictorially characterized as novices, heroic workers motivated solely by patriotism. (Mixed in with this simple propaganda aim was also the general drama and sex appeal of young women engaged in vigorous physical activity – bound to appeal to professional image-makers at the time and particularly appealing to historians since.)[33] The 'Replace a man for the front' poster campaign similarly reduced women to units of labour, and emphasized the novelty of war work by portraying all replacement workers as directly concerned in war production, wearing uniform.[34] All these images of working women tended to assume that work, like gender, was homogeneous. The only category noticeably excluded from the booklets were those shots in which the women looked regional or disorderly. The London brewery workers, for example, were represented by three young, comely barrel-cleaners in trousers rather than the much larger number of skirted cockneys, arms akimbo, whom Nicholls photographed in the brewery yard.

In fact, war work was not like that at all. Not all war work was munitions work, but the effect of the organization of dilution was to make it seem that way. Each dilution officer carried a handbook with photographs of women doing new tasks; exhibitions in each major town showed women doing these new tasks.[35] The impression conveyed to contemporaries was of a much larger amount of replacement of men than took place and a much larger number of women new to the work-force. The focus on London added to this distortion. The paraphernalia of royal visits and of officially sanctioned journalism all focused on London munition workers. For example, Gilbert Stone's book *Women War Workers* includes only one large group of manual workers – Arsenal girls; Hall Caine's *Our Girls* had several pages of text on the same group and was published complete with a special page for a message 'From one of our girls to one of our boys'; in the Topical Budget newsreel films on women's war work it was munitions work that represented working-class women, but statistics show otherwise.[36] Women war workers were as likely to be doing women's work as men's, and women workers were more likely to be doing work that women in general had done before. The biggest expansion was in commercial work or in industries which had already employed women. Women did go into larger workplaces in larger numbers than before – but the photographs did not show the larger workplaces, they showed individual workers within them. (The exception here was in munitions, but this was necessarily seen as 'for the duration of war' only and therefore emphasized the differences, rather than the continuity, of factory labour for women.) The image of women workers in wartime, then and now, is of a frail girl wrestling alone with a machine, working heroically and against her nature for the duration of war only. This added to the impression of novelty and difference that government and employers wished to emphasize in the reports on women's labour at the end of the war, designed as they were to vindicate the effectual failure of equal pay in wartime. Working women were seen as unable to organize in their own defence and to accept unequal pay. This was partly implicit in the response of their own organizations – which was to increase the number of unpaid organizers on the same assumption. All women were treated like the sweated workers of the great unrest of 1910 to 1911 in the East End.

What were the effects of this potent image of the working woman on women themselves? They did not imagine their own work that way. They do not keep the heroic war pictures at all – they keep the group portraits, the souvenir programmes from the concerts, the war worker's badge. They stayed in London as workers and retained the distinctions with which they went into the factories.[37] But legislation and regulation had absorbed these images. The two major official documents discussing women's work, the War Cabinet Committee on Women in Industry and the Hills Committee of the Ministry of Reconstruction,[38] retained the presumption of deficiency in experience and priority of motherhood from the pre-war period. It was these assumptions that they read into the war experience rather than more specific points, for example, the formidable physical strength of women railroad navvies, the technical skill of women arc welders, or the engineering capacities of lathe workers. The London labour market had been read on to the social map of women's work with extremely important social implications. The continuation of the older paradigm of women's organization – outside organizers appealing on social grounds to a wider public interest – resulted in an ignorance about important changes that had taken place. Thus the 'new trades' of outer London which were increasing at the expense of the sweated work of the old female labour market went unnoticed.[39] In this process photographs had been extremely influential because they had determined the visual image of the 'working woman' in public discourse. Far from the novelty of wartime superseding the old picture, photographs implied either that the novelty was due to war and therefore reversible, or else that there was no novelty. War workers were doing what came naturally to women; they were more women than workers, workers only during wartime.

Images influence people. The coincidence of the exploration of women's work by social investigators using the pictorial to accentuate their points with the development of concern particularly for the welfare of Londoners was to distort legislation by government and organization by labour. Women were turned into objects of public concern in ways that had profound consequences for the organization of production. A new concentration on the needs and problems of London arising in part from the centralization of women's own organizations added to this distortion and increased the power of the image. It has also greatly affected the view of historians. The concentration on London for suffrage has been much criticized, and quite rightly; it overemphasizes certain groups and certain strategies. A similar concentration on the woman worker in London also needs criticism. For she is as much an ideological construct as the suffragette. Large numbers of women did work in sweatshops; they did find it hard to be mothers and workers in a society which gave them little support in that process; but the emphasis of the photographs distorts historical interpretation by implying that changes in the lives of working women came solely from outside. What they erase are all those changes for the better achieved by working women at the beginning of the Welfare State as the result of their own activities: the unheroic, undepicted struggles over tea-breaks, premium bonus systems, excessive discipline at work, milk depots, and health visitors' clinics – dependent on government and social reformers, but not created by them alone.

Notes

1 Changes within photography have been very thoroughly analysed by, among others, J. Dyos and Wolff (ed.), *The Victorian City*, 1973; M. Hiley, *Seeing through Photographs*, 1983; and S. Braden, *Committing Photography*, 1983. I am very grateful too to Angela John, whose work on pit-brow women first helped me to see photographs in a new light (*By the Sweat of their Brow*, 1980), and whose conversation has been of great benefit. I would also like to thank Nigel Wheale, who discussed the issues. Since writing this essay the book based on the photographic collections of the Imperial War Museum and elsewhere by D. Condell and J. Liddiard, *Working for Victory? Images of Women in the First World War*, 1987, has been published, some of which bears out my arguments, and some of which I find myself arguing against.
2 J. Lewis, *Women in England*, Brighton, 1984; and the bibliography of contemporary sources in M. Vicinus (ed.), *Suffer and Be Still*, Bloomington, Ind., 1973, pp. 193–4.
3 H. A. Mess, *Factory Legislation*, 1923, B. L. Hutchins, *Women's Work in Modern Industry*, 1915; A. Anderson, *Women in the Factory*, 1922; all describe the need for government intervention; S. Lewenhak, *Women in Trade Unions*, 1977.
4 A. Stafford, *A Match to Fire the Thames*, 1961; it was partly publicized so well because the match-workers brought their case to Fleet Street itself to enlist the support of Annie Besant, and were taken up by campaigning newspapers.
5 The introduction by S. Alexander to a reprint of one of their pamphlets provides a good brief guide to the group: M. Pember Reeves, *Round About a Pound a Week*, 1979 (first published 1911).
6 E. Mappen, *Helping Women at Work*, 1985.
7 M. A. Hamilton, *Mary Macarthur: A Biographical Sketch*, 1925; M. Bondfield, *A Life's Work*, 1951.
8 Although Mary Macarthur described herself as a Tolstoyan (K. Woodward, *Queen Mary*, 1927, p. 190) she did not share any of the syndicalist politics that the description might imply, and her 'left' politics were far more concerned with welfare than with industrial militancy. See D. Thom, 'The bundle of sticks', in A. John (ed.), *Unequal Opportunities*, Oxford, 1986. See also C. Webb, *The Woman with a Basket*, 1927. The only national organization for working-class women not based in London was the Women's Co-operative Guild. But the guild's main interest was in the organization of the working-class housewife.
9 There is an extensive discussion of sweating in J. Schmiechen, *Sweated Industries and Sweated Labor*, 1984; J. Morris, 'The characteristics of

sweating: late-nineteenth-century London and the tailoring trade', and E. Mappen, 'Strategists for change: social feminist approaches to women's work', in John (ed.), op. cit.

10 Schmiechen, op. cit., p. 140.

11 D. M. Sells, *The British Trade Board System*, 1923.

12 See note 5.

13 Schmiechen, op. cit., p. 180.

14 R. Hyman, *The Workers' Union*, Oxford, 1971.

15 M. Cole, *Women of Today*, 1938, pp. 109–10; Hamilton, op. cit., p. 66; 'The cry of the woman worker', *Penny Pictorial*, cited in ibid., pp. 109–10.

16 P. N. Stearns, 'Victorian working women' in Vicinus (ed.), op. cit.; J. Lewis, *Women in England*, Brighton, 1984. For example, the Board of Trade inquiry into wages of 1906 and the Royal Commission on Outwork of 1907 both looked far more at women than similar inquiries of the past.

17 J. Lewis, 'The working-class mother and state intervention', in J. Lewis (ed.), *Labour and Love*, Oxford, 1986, pp. 99–120.

18 Sells, op. cit., ch. 1.

19 E. Colston Shepherd, *The Fixing of Wages in Government Employment*, 1923, pp. 1–2.

20 J. Liddington and J. Norris, *One Hand Tied behind Us*, 1978, has a good short account of differences between suffrage campaigners in the introduction; L. Garner, *Stepping Stones to Liberty*, 1984, also outlines the differences; M. Mackenzie, *Shoulder to Shoulder*, 1975, contains examples of the demonstration and other representations of the political cause.

21 S. Boston, BBC television, 1977 programme about the chain-makers of Cradley Heath first alerted me to the powerful imagery of this strike. and her book added to this; Hamilton, op. cit., p. 87.

22 Hamilton, op. cit., pp. 101–7; S. Rowbotham, *Hidden from History*, 1968, cites this and first directed me to the centrality of women's unionism and Mary Macarthur to the 'new' working women of the pre-war period.

23 The debate is summarized and criticized by D. Dwork, *War Is Good for Babies and Other Children*, 1986, in which she attacks Anna Davin, Jane Lewis, and Carol Dyhouse for not seeing the benevolence of reformers, and the worthwhile effects of their endeavours; it does not seem to me, as I state in the text, that there is any necessary contradiction here.

24 G. Stedman Jones, *Outcast London*, 1971; P. Keating, *Into Unknown England*, Manchester, 1976.

25 See D. Thom and A. Ineson, 'Women munition workers and their poisoning', in P. Weindling (ed.), *A Social History of Occupational Health*, 1984.

26 K. Woodward, *Jipping Street*, 1928, pp. 120–1.

27 *Daily Sketch*, 8 November 1915, in the Gertrude Tuckwell Collection at the Trades Union Congress.

28 Parliamentary Papers, 1914–16, xxxvi, *Interim Report of the Central Committee for Women's Employment*, Cd 7848, Imperial War Museum Women's Work Collection. E. S. Pankhurst, *The Home Front*, 1932, p. 202, has descriptions of her dispute with Macarthur over the workrooms.
29 Public Record Office, MUN 5.70.26, Records of the Ministry of Munitions, 11 August, 28 August 1915.
30 Topical Budget newsreel, BFI 2140A.
31 D. Thom, 'Women's employment in wartime Britain', in J. Winter and R. Wall (eds), *The Upheaval of War*, Cambridge, forthcoming. G. Braybon, *Women Workers in the First World War*, 1981, ch. 6, deals with the public image of women workers.
32 War Office, *Women's Work on Munitions and Women's Work in Non-Munitions Industries*, 1916.
33 A. Marwick, *Women at War*, 1976.
34 Poster, Imperial War Museum.
35 Dilution officer's handbook in my possession.
36 D. Thom, 'The ideology of women's work in Britain, 1914–1924, with special reference to the NFWW and other trade unions', unpublished Ph.D. dissertation for the CNAA at Thames Polytechnic, 1982, appendix 1.
37 This assertion is based on interviews with women war workers carried out over 1976–81.
38 Parliamentary Papers, 1919, xxxi, *Report of the War Cabinet Committee on Women in Industry*, Cmd 135; 1918, xiv, *Report of the Hills Committee* (the central committee on women's employment).
39 M. Glucksman, 'In a class of their own, women workers in inter-war Britain', *Feminist Review*, 24, autumn 1986.

Politics:
visions and practices

5

Radical clubs and London politics, 1870–1900

John Davis

Late-Victorian London contained a large and discrete working class but lacked a firmly founded labour movement. Though the metropolis was the setting for much of the emergent social politics of the 1880s, London's contribution to early labour politics was limited, and the London Labour Party was not formed until 1914. The claim of Liberal Progressivism to the metropolitan working-class vote was not effectively challenged until after the First World War.

The problem posed by this paradox is, if anything, emphasized by the approach adopted in the classic political study of London labour's emergence. Paul Thompson is actually more anxious to show 'why the Liberal Party failed to hold the allegiance of the working-class voter'[1] in the long run than why it took so long to lose it; but the almost messianic role given to the manifestly weak Independent Labour Party and Social Democratic Federation raises obliquely the question of their inadequacy. Ten years after Thompson, Gareth Stedman Jones portrayed the political attitude of the London working class as the product of a developing class culture.[2] Commercialization of the central area from the 1870s entailed the destruction of traditional artisan centres. The highly political work-centred culture of mid-century artisans consequently gave way to a culture based upon the 'depoliticized haven' of the working-class home. Social outlets like the pub and the music-hall – apolitical if not Tory in tone – became central to a substitute 'culture of consolation'.[3]

The argument is extended to explain the general conformism of the British working class before 1914. I do not wish to question the assertion that British labour recognized 'the existing social order as the inevitable framework of action'.[4] I am more concerned with the model presented of London's particular depoliticization, and the reasons why 'after 1870 London pioneered music-hall, while coal, cotton and ship-building areas in the north generated the most solid advances in trade unionism'.[5] I believe that while the emphasis upon class culture has given London labour history a vital dimension absent in Thompson's more traditional approach, it carries an inherent risk of exaggerating any apparent political decline. I will argue that the political weakness of the London working class derived more from institutional than from cultural forces.

London's Radical working men's clubs invite study because they encapsulate the changing nature of London labour politics.[6] On the face of it they embody precisely Stedman Jones's model of the displacement of politics by leisure. Until the mid-1880s they provided 'a lively focus for working class political enthusiasm'.[7] Thereafter they became increasingly devoted to the provision of professional entertainment, to the distress of their political founders and the contempt of the ascetics in the SDF.[8] Until the mid-1880s the social appeal of club life had appeared to answer the problem of working-class political mobilization, compensating in part for the organizational superiority of the established middle-class parties. By 1900, however, club politicians concluded that the clubs' social attractions had sapped their members' political commitment. The transformation raises the question of the relationship between the social and political interests of the London working class.

In 1875 there were 77 clubs in the metropolitan area affiliated to the Working Men's Club and Institute Union, with perhaps 16,000 members.[9] By 1900 153 metropolitan clubs were affiliated, with an estimated 45,000 members.[10] This rapid growth brought changes in the nature of the clubs themselves. The early clubs had often developed from a nucleus of artisans from a single trade or even a single workshop. Some, like the Alliance Cabinetmakers' Club or the Cigarmakers' Club, were directly linked to craft unions; others, like the shoemaker-dominated United Radical Club in Hackney, were largely composed of men in the same trade. Club expansion, however, giving the largest clubs four-figure membership totals by the end of the century,[11] worked to erode both the links between clubs and particular industries and workshops and the artisan predominance in the movement as a whole. Though the clubman of 1900 had still to have a sufficient disposable income to take advantage of the entertainment and refreshments available, and though he was still very likely to be a trade unionist, his club would probably have evolved into much more than a social outlet for a localized craft.

The early club had provided a craft forum, offering 'a conversazione on labour, work and wages, and where to find it'[12] in a city where industry was characteristically scattered and small scale. George Howell depicted the club as a platform for 'certain craftsmen who prided themselves upon their skill at their particular crafts':

> Thither these 'dons', as they were termed in some trades, would congregate to discuss politics and parade their ability as workmen; and thither, also, would go the youthful aspirant, anxious to pick up scraps of information as to 'tricks in trade'.[13]

Howell took for granted the conjunction of trade and political discussion in this *ad hoc* education. F. W. Galton, apprenticed as an engraver in Holborn in 1880, recalled that his 'early interest in politics was assured by the continual discussion going on in the workshops for no word on such subjects was ever heard at home'.[14] The political atmosphere of the small workshop and the political awareness of the London artisan need no fresh emphasis, and the political commitment of the clubs produced by this culture is unsurprising. Many of the clubs prominent at the peak of club Radicalism in the 1880s could claim political ancestry. The Eleusis in the King's Road and the Borough of Hackney Club evolved from branches of the Reform League, the Patriotic Club on Clerkenwell Green from a group of Finsbury republicans.[15] The Tower Hamlets Radical Club was formed by 'about a score of old and resolute Radicals . . . driven from tavern to tavern by police espionage and presumptive officialism'.[16] The United Radical Club in Kay Street, Hackney, was the product of a politically inspired secession from Lady Clifden's institute in Goldsmith's Row,[17] and the desire for unfettered political discussion frequently inspired opposition to middle-class philanthropic control of clubs. Around half the London clubs affiliated to the Club Union advertised their political commitment in their titles; many others claimed a political role.

The metropolitan club politician of the 1870s and 1880s subscribed to the values of post-Chartist artisan Radicalism. The Chartist legacy included a self-conscious labourism and the conviction that working-class progress depended upon constitutional reform, as 'those who were not voters were practically the slaves of those who were'.[18] It included also a belief in the mass protest as a political weapon, drawing upon memories of Kennington Common in 1848 and Hyde Park in 1866. Much of the directness of Chartism and the Reform League had been lost, energy being dissipated in the conventional Radical pursuit of sinister interests - the royal family, the House of Lords, the established church, ground landlords, the City Corporation – but there survived a sense of class identity and a faith in direct action. Associational politics in the clubs reinforced both, and was taken by club politicians to give their organizations a basis of legitimacy lacking in the official Liberal caucuses.

The Birmingham-model caucus adopted in all the London boroughs from the late 1870s was stigmatized by club Radicals as 'a mutual admiration society', 'an anti-democratic institution – a mere conscienceless party machine', seeking 'the substitution of local discipline for popular force'.[19] In London's enormous pre-1885 parliamentary boroughs the caucus had provided a means of resolving – or suppressing – tension between suburban Whig and inner-city Radical through the discipline of the machine. The charge that 'caucuses never, or very rarely, publish a programme or statement of objects and . . . have never been known to remonstrate with the party leaders for the most flagrant violations of Liberal principles',[20] had some substance as the demands of party unity placed loyalty before ideology. The franchise extension of 1867 and the liberal registration of tenement occupiers in London from the early 1880s was also creating a working-class Radical constituency inadequately represented by the borough associations. This 'vast body of latent Radicalism that only wanted the opportunity to assert itself'[21] found its outlets not in the borough Liberal associations so much as in the various single-issue pressure groups which proliferated in that decade, in the political action of some craft unions or the London Trades Council, and in the activities of the Radical clubs.

Systematic political activity by Radical clubs began in Chelsea in the mid-1870s. There the Eleusis had promoted working-class electoral registration and, with the three other components of the borough's Combined Political Committee of Radical Clubs, had involved itself in the selection of parliamentary candidates.[22] The Combined Political Committee pre-dated the Chelsea caucus and was later said to dominate it.[23] It encouraged imitative club federations in Westminster, Finsbury, Hackney, Marylebone, and Tower Hamlets.[24] By 1884 the Hackney Radical Federation, with 3,600 members and 'militant to a degree', could be seen as the dominant political force in the borough.[25] In the following year the Marylebone Radical Club pronounced its ostentatious hostility to official Liberalism and called for 'the establishment of the independent Radical Party'.[26]

As the divisions within London Liberalism grew in the mid-1880s, club dissidence contributed to the party's discomfiture. In the mêlée of the 1885 general election no fewer than fourteen of the fifty-eight new London seats were threatened with Liberal splits.[27]

Some were caused by the intransigence of sitting MPs, who had never acknowledged the prerogative of the caucus, let alone that claimed by the clubs, but others were prompted by Radicals 'in open revolt against the Whig candidates brought forward by the local wirepullers'.[28] Many seats saw open club opposition to caucus candidates – Lorne in Hampstead, Hozier in Woolwich, Knight in West Marylebone, Holms in Central Hackney.[29] In Bethnal Green NE George Howell's successful labour candidature was promoted by the United Radical Club and the Hackney Radical Federation.[30] In Haggerston another successful labour candidate, W. R. Cremer, was foisted upon the Liberal Association with the support of local clubs and unions, displacing the Manchester businessman and temperance advocate who could have expected the Liberal nomination in quieter times.[31]

Club Radicalism displayed a growing confidence in the mid-1880s. Seventy-eight new London clubs were founded in the five years 1884–8,[32] an expansion which appeared to emphasize the weak popular foundations of official Liberalism. Sidney Webb, writing in 1890, believed these 'spontaneous democratic organizations of the metropolitan artisans' to be 'the most important part of the fighting strength of London Liberalism', controlling at least a fifth of the Liberal vote.[33] The period saw a steady increase in the number of political demonstrations, a form of populist protest much favoured by the clubs. These rallies lent apparent plausibility to the clubs' repeated claim that their associational politics gave them a strength which could not be attained by the party machines. The Liberal managers, conscious that the clubs represented a vein of enthusiasm not well tapped by the party, and sensitive to any indication that franchise extension and the Corrupt Practices Act had made London politics more 'popular', responded with a cautious sponsorship of political demonstrations. Although the presence of Cabinet ministers at such rallies was discouraged, as this 'would rob them of their spontaneous character',[34] the massive demonstration against the Lords' obstruction of the franchise Bill in 1884 was co-ordinated from the National Liberal Club,[35] and answered Gladstone's call for protests of 'dignity and weight . . . [as] at the time of the first Reform Bill'.[36] The next largest demonstration of the decade, the 1887 rally against Irish coercion, was organized by James Stuart and the London Liberal MPs.[37] With the party then out of office, the *Weekly Dispatch* argued that 'the only substitute for a general election is public demonstrations on a vast and imposing scale'.[38]

More tangible evidence of the party's new interest in association-alism came with the reorganization of the London constituency parties in 1886–7.[39] In many areas new political clubs were founded in conjunction with the reformed associations, and with party support. 'Ever since the upsetting of the old metropolitan constituencies by the Redistribution Act', explained the *Weekly Dispatch*:

> political organizers have been coming round to the opinion that the electoral battles of the future, as far as London is regarded, will really be decided in the clubs and other institutions where the voters congregate together at times when they have the leisure and inclination to talk things over . . . Better than any threats or wheedling from the candidate, his agent or his committee is the public feeling in a good club.[40]

For a few years Liberal organizers in London saw associationalism as the most promising means of nursing an urban working-class electorate. The new clubs were designed, in the frank and apposite terms used of the Newington Reform Club:

> with a view of 'spreading the light' of advanced political thought among the many of whom it was felt that a Political Association, pure and simple, appealed in vain – to provide a means, in fact, by which the earnest thinker and the indifferent voter could be brought into direct and constant personal contact, and the latter through quiet conversation and friendly argument be induced to take an intelligent interest in his country's affairs.[41]

The political club, 'essential to the well-being of every association',[42] was called upon to dispel the image of exclusive elitism that had tainted the party machinery.

By the late 1880s, then, London Radicalism had emerged as the most 'advanced' sector of British Liberalism, led by spontaneous and genuinely working-class organizations in the clubs. The Liberal Party had been induced to encourage mass demonstrations and had sponsored associational politics as part of its own reorganizations. By the end of the decade, policy had also moved to the left, with the formulation of the 'London Programme' by the small band of London Liberals who had survived the 1886 election, the blessing of this programme by the leadership at Clerkenwell and Limehouse,[43] and the development of municipal collectivism by the London County Council Progressives. The political awakening of the working class had pulled Liberalism further to the left in London than anywhere else in Britain, making all the more pointed the subsequent political failure of London labour.

The modern charge of a retreat into apoliticism is also to be found in the contemporary club press. Frequent laments were published for the lost activism of clubland, sacrificed to 'the desire for comic dramas, burlesques and spectacle that require no demand upon the intellectual faculties'.[44] The old Chartist Ben Lucraft, interviewed in 1895, was 'convinced that clubs are not political enough', and contrasted 'the earnest work of the old reformers' with the 'milk-and-watery debates and resolutions of the present leaders of men'.[45] James Morden, septuagenarian treasurer of the Borough of Bethnal Green Club, lectured on old Chartists in the late 1890s in the hope of correcting 'the lamentable ignorance of working men of the career of those who gained for us the free speech and the cheap newspapers we have today'. His belief that members now saw their clubs as 'places where cheap refreshment can be obtained, and where they can take their case without paying much for it', was widely held.[46] Rising real earnings were taken to have seduced clubmen into an apolitical hedonism, causing them to forget that 'it was by political agitation they had gained many of their dearest privileges'.[47]

Traditional club politics fell victim to the commercialization of leisure.[48] The tension between political and commercial ends was implicit in club life from the start, though it was only in the 1890s that it became clear that the balance had tilted irreversibly against the politicians. The early departure of clubs from pub rooms, itself often a reflection of the greater commercial pressure upon landlords, had launched them upon an unabating quest for solvency. Profits from entertainments and the bar proved more reliable than subscriptions and more capable of expansion. While the clubs were still dominated by their political founders it was possible for political activism to ride upon expanding profits; in the 1880s the Tower Hamlets Radical Association could still maintain that 'the bar is subordinate to more important departments' and the Deptford Liberal Club followed 'a consistent policy of subordinating the merely social side of associated life to the more important consideration of political utility'.[49] Some clubs imposed on new applicants a membership test of adhesion to specified Radical tenets.[50] Others were 'extremely careful as to the men whom they admit to membership'.[51]

This sort of exclusiveness at a time of growing demand for leisure facilities was at best quixotic. At worst it brought bankruptcy. For some time the purest political clubs attempted to ignore the implications of their inevitable competition with pubs, music-halls, and other clubs. One Eleusis trustee told the club's 1880 annual dinner that 'there was of course a debt resting on the club, and he hoped there always would be, as that was a sign of life'.[52] Ten years later the president, Aeneas Smith, told the twenty-second annual dinner of the Eleusis's 'awkward financial position', but assured members that 'the Club had never been in any other condition, and that they aimed rather at political usefulness and success than at making money'.[53] Such bravado was muted, however, by the wave of crises which ran through the leading political clubs with the downturn in the London economy in the early 1890s. On top of the troubles at the Eleusis, the Patriotic was said to be 'in dire straits' in 1892; the United Radical only just escaped bankruptcy in April 1891, and the Tower Hamlets Radical folded in the same year.[54]

One obituarist of the THRC attributed death to the loss of political integrity that had followed its move to larger premises in 1881: 'the enlargement of premises and extension of membership very often means much less political usefulness and activity'.[55] Five years later Henry Mundy, political stalwart of the Central Finsbury Radical, called for 'smaller clubs and earnest men. If men want all social amusements then they should join social clubs.'[56] But in practice it was hard to steer a middle course between competitive expansion and rapid decline. Affiliation of almost all Radical clubs to the Club Union meant that members of one affiliated club could gain admission to any other. This and the tendency of clubs to cluster – with forty-three in an area two miles square to the east of the City by the early 1890s[57] – allowed a high degree of consumer discrimination. Clubmen had 'got beyond the wooden form and beer barrel stage, and look for as much comfort at least as they would obtain at an average public house'.[58] Audiences at club entertainments were 'the most critical – I might say hypercritical – and amateurish acting and out of date pieces will not be swallowed by them'.[59] Bigger clubs could afford better facilities and better performers; smaller ones made do with dingy halls and 'old-time actors who used to strut and fret their hour upon the stage of the Boro' of Hackney'.[60] Failure to expand could bring not just stagnation but the sort of precipitate decline experienced by the Tower Hamlets Radical, which saw membership fall from 600 to 100 just before its death.[61]

The early clubs had achieved an easy balance between political discussion and entertainment. Club poets like J. B. Leno and Richard Gaston were also political lecturers. The first president of the Borough of Hackney Club, James Lowe, had aimed 'to unite intellectual training with amusement, and combine in one a club and a college'.[62] Club expansion was based, though, upon the recruitment by recreational incentives of men who would not have joined through political motivation. This was always likely to shift the balance between politics and entertainment towards the latter. It provided an ironic vindication of the club democracy for which the political stalwarts had always fought. Emancipation from middle-class philanthropists and 'parson-powered psalm-smiters' had been justified by the claim that democratically-run clubs took 'men as they are, and start from that point, instead of simply telling them what they ought to be'.[63] If the rank and file preferred entertainments to political lectures, there was nothing in the club ethic to deny them. It should be remembered that if there ever was a golden age of 'standing room only' for lectures on the plight of the Bulgars or the appropriation of charitable endowments, it was an age of small club memberships and small club houses. It is unlikely that the ordinary political lecture was ever more than a minority pursuit. Topical subjects or impressive lecturers could pull crowds, but this remained true in the 1890s: 'a really first-class man is generally sure of a good audience; it is the third-raters who grumble at the small audiences'.[64]

But how far was the decline of the political lecture symptomatic of a general decline of political interest? All that can legitimately be inferred is the decay of a particular form of political activity, a traditional form whose decline was duly lamented by traditionalists. Mid-century artisan politics had rested upon the transmission of political wisdom by the self-consciously literate autodidacts produced by the London working class in such impressive numbers – the political equivalent of the transmission of craft skills described by Howell in the passage quoted earlier. At a time of limited literacy and few cheap newspapers it was sustained by rank-and-file deference to the expertise of the self-taught: 'It often occurs', wrote J. B. Leno in his autobiography, 'that when one of the toiling class exhibits superior speaking or argumentative powers to his fellows, he is chosen to be their advocate.'[65] The artisan politician in the workshop or the club enjoyed for some years a near monopoly of political influence.

This rather elitist system had its advantages and its drawbacks. The ability of the elite to set the political agenda and to rely upon the fairly uncritical support of their followers made the early clubs into crudely effective political instruments without the constitutional paraphernalia of the caucus. The workshop and the club were admittedly restricted platforms, and the club politicians were often generals without an army, but when a downturn in the London economy created broader discontent among the London working class they found that they could mobilize mass movements behind the least demotic of causes – republicanism in the late 1860s and early 1870s, the more esoteric elements of secularism in the mid-1880s. On the other hand, the monopoly position enjoyed by these opinion-formers fostered a rigidity which impaired ideological development. They tended to adopt militant positions within a traditional political framework, and the absence of informed criticism prevented their intellectual evolution. Thus while artisan Radicalism had appeared advanced in the Chartist period, it presented an ironically conservative face in the 1880s. Belfort Bax's complaint that the clubs showed 'little or no political initiative or influence of ideas outside the range of current political questions and party politics' in the 1870s and early 1880s[66] and Sidney Webb's criticism of the 'harsh, secular Radicalism' prevailing in the clubs at this time[67] both reflect socialist impatience at this narrowness of view. The club lecturer Frederick Rogers found that he had 'long ago seen through the fallacies of popular Radicalism without knowing it', and 'proclaimed from many a club platform that if Throne, Church and Peerage were swept away at once the working classes would benefit as little by the change as they did by the destruction of the monasteries at the Reformation'. His reward was declining audiences.[68] Though the clubs generally sympathized with the social movements which changed the face of London politics in the 1880s, they were not prominent in their promotion. The housing furore of 1883–4 was of middle-class philanthropic instigation, the unemployment demonstrations of the mid-1880s were organized by the SDF, and the strikes of the late 1880s were led by New Unionists like Burns and Mann who remained sceptical of the club movement. The Eleusis programme of 1886, issued in the midst of the unemployment protests and two years after the housing crisis, was unaffected by these movements, calling instead for the four unattained points of the Charter, the abolition of hereditary privileges, the separation of church and state, free secular education, and land nationalization.[69] Other club programmes showed similar preoccupations.

The perpetuation of this brand of politics depended upon club audiences remaining convinced that abolition of the House of Lords, disestablishment, or the reform of London municipal government would improve their quality of life. Their continued insulation from the more material elements of labour politics depended upon club lecturers retaining their effective monopoly of political education. But from the mid-1880s the club lecturer was challenged not only by entertainments but also by the spread of cheap popular newspapers, particularly after the introduction of the earnestly Radical *Star* in January 1888. 'The halfpenny newspaper is the educator in place of the aforetime lecture,' declared *Club World*.[70] 'Who wants to be bored with Home Rule or London reform when he can read all about the subjects in the *Star*?' asked a North London Club member in the *Club Journal*.[71] The decline of traditional political didacticism therefore reflected not only the admission of new members who had not joined to hear political lecturers and did not intend to be corralled into doing so, but also a belief on the part of many who were not hostile to politics that the lecture was an outmoded form. There was a quaintness about the convictions and obsessions of the older generation of club politicians that bordered on absurdity once they could no longer command respect for their unique political wisdom. W. S. Sanders's vignette of the old Chartist in the Battersea SDF – a vestry roadsweeper who had learned at the feet of Bronterre O'Brien that the root of all social evil lay in the currency system – depicted a figure whose equivalent could be found in most clubs. He commanded 'a certain measure of awe and reverence', but he was a curio by the 1890s.[72] That decade provided much evidence of the diminishing ability of club politicians to sell the totems of traditional Radicalism to their members. The lack of response to the Armenian massacres in 1896 contrasted pointedly with the clubs' reaction to the Bulgarian atrocities twenty years earlier.[73] The 1897 jubilee confirmed the death of London republicanism, still vigorous ten years earlier.[74] The Jameson Raid and Fashoda roused the Metropolitan Radical Federation but caused little stir in the clubs.[75] Above all, the 'present insane enthusiasm displayed over the Transvaal War'[76] in 1899 disturbed the club politicians who had assumed clubmen to be 'superior to the emotions of patriotism'.[77]

The decline of didacticism and the erosion of the respect once commanded by a self-appointed political elite are, though, as consistent with a process of evolution in labour politics as with one of decay. No doubt they were consequences of 'the undermining of the distinctiveness and cohesion of the old artisan culture in London',[78] but the real problem lies not so much in accounting for this development as in explaining why artisan politics did not give way to a more advanced form of labour organization. In the industrial north the working class had dispensed with artisan leadership a generation or more earlier without this curbing their political development; why should London differ?

It is obviously attractive to seek an explanation in the process of metropolitan growth that accounts for most of London's distinctive features. There is no doubt that the commercialization of the central area destroyed many traditional artisan centres, but it is less clear that it prompted the mass migration of the skilled

113

working class to the suburbs and the submergence of their political aspirations in an apolitical domesticity.[79] The image of domestic introversion would appear most appropriate to the outer suburbs, but migration to these areas was an overwhelmingly middle-class pursuit except where artificially encouraged by such devices as workmen's trains. The unusually successful artisan might have moved to these areas, but the removal of artisans from the central area was far more often the consequence of commercial demand for central land than of upward mobility of this sort. Artisans cleared from the centre were more likely to land in areas not generally described as suburban, forming the inner ring of working-class districts around London's commercial core. The most obvious effect of metropolitan development was not the dispersal of the working class but its concentration in areas such as these. While the working-class identity of former artisan centres in the central area – Chelsea, Holborn, Soho – was destroyed, that of Bethnal Green, south Hackney, Shoreditch, and the parts of Finsbury and Clerkenwell untouched by the commercial expansion of the City was reinforced. Working-class domesticity was, it appears, itself increasing in this period,[80] but not to the detriment of those social institutions – like the clubs – which owed their growth in part to the increasing spatial concentration of the working class. Any political implications of this concentration are likely to have been worked out in these social centres.

The transition from a work-centred form of politics to one based on neighbourhood and community was part of the evolution of London labour politics. The workplace atmosphere fostered an intense political commitment in those touched by it, but in a city with so diverse and fragmented an industrial base its influence was necessarily limited. The hostility of new unionist leaders to stalwarts of the old labour politics like George Howell – 'this Capitalist hack' to Burns[81] – derived largely from their belief that the craft basis of traditional labour politics had given it an innate sectionalism which inhibited expansion. The emancipatory impact of new unionism in 1888–92, mobilizing the unskilled more effectively than ever before, indicated the narrowness of the old politics. In December 1889 the *North London Press* carried a perceptive survey of London labour's *annus mirabilis*, which described the contagious effect of the gas workers' strike, galvanizing 'the whole unskilled labour army of East and South London':

It did so more easily because unskilled workers in different employments mix with one another more freely than do skilled

114

men. For instance, a compositor is always a compositor, and a movement amongst the engineers does not affect him much. But labourers in gas works may be coal porters or dockers next week; the uncertainty of employments shifts them about, and makes them one mass of intermingling men, and action amongst one section fires the other.[82]

While circumstances permitted, the new unionism exercised a politicizing influence which was probably little less intense than that of the workshop and considerably more extensive. But it remained vulnerable to movements in the London economy. The clubs and other institutions which derived their strength and identity from the increasing social homogeneity of working-class areas rested on a firmer base. They did not stretch so far into the ranks of casual labour, but expanding membership totals in the 1890s imply that their influence was none the less spreading rapidly.

Casting the net wider entailed some dilution of political intensity. Just as the replacement of 'the trade pub near the workplace' by the 'local' some distance from it meant that 'conversation was less likely to concern trade matters, more likely to reflect common interests, politics to a certain extent, but more often sport and entertainment',[83] so the expansion of the clubs led to the displacement of political lectures by entertainment. But at the same time it became clear that questions which had an obvious bearing upon the class concerns of the working man continued to arouse a general interest. 'The best-attended meetings are those at which Labour is discussed,' commented the *Club Journal* in 1891.[84] The eight-hour-day agitation of the same year prompted widespread discussion in the clubs.[85] Each of the major industrial disputes of the 1890s generated interest and, often, substantial financial support for the unions involved. The Finsbury clubs claimed to have raised £150 for the dockers in 1889,[86] and support for the engineers in 1897 was considerable, reflecting concern among club unionists that 'the aristocracy of labour is attacked, and in spite of the many thousands stored up, there is a chance of being beaten'.[87] The transition from the club politics of the early 1880s to the club politics of the late 1890s was a move from a universalist Radicalism to a more selective 'labourism'. The former, though intensely ideological, was narrowly dependent upon the proselytizing of an artisan elite. The latter, though more pragmatic and frequently dormant, was more broadly founded upon the common experiences of different branches of labour, brought together in social centres.

This was also the basis of the increasing electoral activity of the clubs in the 1890s – a phenomenon hard to square with any analysis of declining political commitment. During the 1892 general election the *Club Journal* commented that 'if we were to print half the election matter we have received we should be accused of making the journal a political organ', and observed with some relief that 'all the working men are not lovers of sing-songs, but are serious-minded when the occasion demands'.[88] Ben Troke, of the North Camberwell Radical Club, acknowledged that

> in a big club a considerable proportion join for the social enjoyments to be obtained, but when these members see the good work being done by the more serious minded ones, they want to have a finger in the pie, and so we gain a strong body of workers – and voters also. At election times I have, I must confess, been rather astonished to witness the zeal displayed by many members whom I had previously thought to have no inclinations outside the billiard room.[89]

'We don't talk much about politics', wrote the Gladstone Radical Club reporter after the Progressive victory in the 1898 LCC elections, 'but when the time comes to use our votes we make our power felt.'[90] Even in the overtly social Carlyle Club 'the influence of the club was quite as strong at the election times as if it was called a Liberal or Radical one. Votes on the right side were given when the time arrived.'[91] More and more clubmen sought election to local authorities during the 1890s; the volume of the clubs' electoral activity increased in rough proportion to complaints of their neglect of politics. The 87 metropolitan clubs providing statistics in 1898 accounted for 532 seats on local bodies.[92] In 1899 the Borough of Bethnal Green Club had 18 members on local boards.[93] The Borough of Shoreditch claimed to have carried 14 seats in the vestry elections, the Bermondsey Gladstone Club 12 and the St George's and Wapping Reform Club to have elected 15 out of 18 candidates to the vestry and 17 out of 18 to the guardians.[94]

The sort of intense but occasional commitment required by election work was better suited to club life in the 1890s than the regular asceticism demanded by political lectures. It could draw upon partisanship and 'clubability' without requiring political erudition or sophistication. It could involve the growing number of club members whose primary commitment to their clubs was not political. C. B. Grossmith's 'great experience of men joining as social members and turning out good political workers' dissuaded him from applying political tests in the Paddington Radical Club.[95] Arguably this form of uncoercive mobilization represented a purer form of associational politics than the didactic approach favoured by the traditionalists. The strength of associationalism – the ability of social loyalties to generate a shared political partisanship – remained. What had been lost was the power of old-style club politicians to lead an uncritical rank and file in directions of their own choosing. Even this was qualified; club politicians might no longer be able to drive their members down the ethical byways of secularism or Cobdenite internationalism, but associational politics still required opinion-formers, and it is likely that their expertise and articulacy gave them a greater influence than they often acknowledged. It is striking that the clubs' essential commitment to Radicalism remained unimpaired, in a city where consistent Unionist electoral success implies a substantial amount of working-class conservatism.

Club Tories surfaced occasionally: after the 1895 general election the Bermondsey Gladstone Club reporter told *Club World* that 'some of our members were to be found working for the Conservative candidate', but the warning that 'conduct such as this will be dealt with by the committee' suggests that it was considered deviant.[96] For all the repetitious complaints of clubmen lapsing into political apathy, for all the concern over their susceptibility to jingoism and other base emotions, they were never accused of defection to Toryism. Except for occasional labour campaigns, club election activity was entirely devoted to Liberal and Progressive candidatures. No doubt the stratum of the working class from which clubmen were largely drawn was inclined to Radicalism, and no doubt Tory partisans avoided joining Radical clubs even when they were noted more for their beer than their politics. Nevertheless, the 1890s saw so rapid an expansion of club membership that the new intake cannot have consisted exclusively of committed Radicals. It is impressive testimony to the clubs' capacity for political socialization that their Radical allegiance survived the loss of membership tests, the decline of political lectures, and the recruitment of a new type of clubman drawn primarily by recreational facilities.

Such socialization would appear to have outweighed, amongst those affected, the more obvious but ephemeral influences characteristic of popular politics in late-Victorian London – the largess of parliamentary candidates, the covert propaganda of the music-hall, and the overt propaganda of the populist Tory press. It is arguable that the political influence of the clubs was more extensive in the 1890s than in the 1880s, though it took a different form, with direct propaganda of usually limited appeal giving way to an indirect influence touching larger numbers.

The real problem for working-class politicians lay in giving this influence any organizational potency. The challenge to official Liberalism in the mid-1880s had indicated the need for the party to pay more attention to the working-class electorate, but had not made the case for a separate labour organization if the Liberals responded. There was no significant ideological difference between most club Radicals and the Radical wing of the Liberal Party. Clubmen had generally been unsympathetic to the anti-Gladstonian stance of Hyndman's Democratic Federation,[97] and most clubs severed their links with the organization when it transformed itself into the Social Democratic Federation, with an explicit socialist commitment, in 1884.[98] Before 1885 the case for a separate working-class Radical organization had been strengthened by the intransigence and 'Whiggery' of much of the Liberal elite, but the home rule split, the party reorganization, and the leftward shift in policy after 1885–6 changed the position. Clubmen still justified their independent stance by continuing to invoke the advantages of working-class associationalism over the middle-class caucus, but the battle was steadily coming to be fought on the narrow ground of organizational efficiency, where the clubs proved weak.

Several attempts to create a durable club federation culminated in the formation of the Metropolitan Radical Federation in 1886.[99] Thirty-two clubs were represented in proportion to subscribing membership; an executive was elected annually by ballot. James Tims, secretary of the new organization, considered it 'a contrast in representative principles to some other political organizations in existence',[100] but relations with official Liberalism involved more than representational purity. The MRF's formation coincided with the overhaul of the constituency Liberal associations, which were generally re-established without compulsory subscriptions, in the hope of inducing 'the working man to join and give himself a full voice in [their] deliberations'.[101] The reorganization ended with the creation of another federal body in the London Liberal and Radical Union. The unanimous decision of the MRF executive not to join the new union was predictable, and the reasons given familiar – that 'the power of this new union is concentrated in few hands' and that reform could be advanced 'better by ourselves than if we submerged our programme in the sea of weak-kneed Liberalism'[102] – but the federation was left with the duty of justifying its continued independence.

Its preferred justification lay in the power of the public demonstrations. Tims believed the MRF to be 'perhaps the only organization in London which in a few hours could put 50,000 men into the streets of London'.[103] This claim carried some force at the time of the successful reform and coercion demonstrations, but within a few years it had been seriously weakened. There were always doubts about the cost-effectiveness of the demonstration as a form of political action. Mobilizing a crowd for a routine protest required the payment of stewards and, often, the protesters themselves, and costs escalated when opponents used similar tactics.[104] Squeezing money from the clubs was often difficult: a successful eight-hour-day rally was mounted for £123 11s 0d in May 1890, but only £60 of this had been raised by mid-June.[105] Monster meetings could give better value for money but were more expensive. A six-figure crowd was assembled to frighten the peers in 1884 for just over £1,000.[106] Doubtless 'Lord Salisbury and his party would be only too willing to pay £20,000 if they could get a meeting like it', but there was still 'some difficulty in raising the necessary funds',[107] and it is likely that even this pinnacle of demotic protest had to be subsidized by wealthy Liberals.

Liberal support was seldom unequivocal, and misgivings increased with the emergence of the public order question. Like the Chartists, Radical demonstrators walked the slender line between moral and physical force. The 1884 Reform Demonstration Committee had calmly minuted its intention to protest 'in such overwhelming numbers as to convince the Lords of the futility of further opposition to this measure of justice'.[108] The rally turned out more carnival than uprising, and its promoters could not have managed a riot had one occurred, but the hint of suppressed power remained essential to this form of protest. Such subtlety was invalidated by the Pall Mall rioting of February 1886, when the Carlton Club windows were smashed by an uncontrolled crowd.[109] The episode developed from a clash between Fair Trade and SDF contingents and did not involve the MRF or the clubs, but the consequent prohibition of Trafalgar Square meetings and the militarization of the Metropolitan Police under Sir Charles Warren[110] made the protest march a dangerous pastime. Several clubs were involved in 'Bloody Sunday' in November 1887, when 'a large body of police, with batons drawn . . . charged furiously into us, beating and kicking the people in the most cowardly and brutal manner'.[111] The lesson was later driven home by assaults on temperance demonstrations and even a Salvation Army march.[112] 'Depend upon it,' wrote the secularist and MRF executive member G. W. Foote to the *Star*, 'the police will not waste their time in arresting; they will simply crack skulls and ride their horses over fallen men.'[113] The London Liberal MPs understandably showed little enthusiasm for this sort of engagement. Having failed in the Commons to induce the House Secretary to curb Warren or rescind the Trafalgar Square prohibition, they declined to front an MRF free speech meeting in April 1888.[14]

'The doors of all the great halls are closed against us,' complained the *Star*, 'most of the great open spaces can only be available for our use by special permission of the Metropolitan Board, and only the parks are left.'[115] The parks in fact hosted several demonstrations in the late 1880s, though most were small SDF unemployment rallies.[116] Free speech could never be suppressed entirely; what was lost was the confidence, derived from the demonstrations of 1866 and 1884, that an orderly mass protest could bring direct results. During 1888 London Liberal leaders stressed the primacy of organizational work over ostentatious public demonstrations.[117] Lack of party sanction in turn made the MRF less ready to confront the police. Fear of 'a second Bloody Sunday' led B. T. Hall to urge the federation's council not to attempt a free speech demonstration in Hyde Park in 1890: 'was it wise to run such a risk, seeing the apathy shown by the front Opposition bench?'[118] The MRF gradually accepted defeat on the free speech issue, which became the virtual monopoly of the SDF, and the demonstration drifted to the margin of Liberal political activity.

If organizational criteria were paramount, though, it was hard to see the clubs as more than ancillaries to the constituency associations. 'The club might do the educational work, but the association did the political part,' J. R. Seager, architect of the Liberal constituency reform, told the Holborn Liberal and Radical Association.[119] Clubs could perhaps provide the Liberal associations with 'a perfect body of canvassers who know every hole and corner of the division'[120] and might secure the registration of potential voters who could not have been reached by other means,[121] but they were far from indispensable. The MRF, arguably little more than a club caucus, also faced the charge that it was 'merely an appendage to the skirts of an official party'.[122] It responded occasionally with schemes to recreate club associationalism on a metropolitan scale,[123] more often with ostentatious militancy when the opportunity arose. Falling among Fabians in the early 1890s, it produced an ambitious programme of municipalization for the second LCC election in 1892.[124] After a quiescent spell in the mid-1890s, it resurfaced to voice an outspoken anti-jingoism during the Boer War. Usually, though, it was ineffective. It faced continually the problem afflicting both pressure groups and the organizers of demonstrations – the inadequacy of financial support from the clubs, which, 'spending hundreds per annum in "booze" grumble at the miserable sum of a guinea or two the federation requires to carry on its work'.[125] While the London Liberal and Radical Union had an income of over £2,000 per annum in the late 1880s,[126] the MRF was perennially impoverished. Its £20 annual income by the late 1890s[127] compared badly even with the sums devoted by component clubs to their own political work[128] and would do little to mobilize a city of five millions.

The price of the clubs' success in helping drive London Liberalism to the left in the 1880s was the creation of a radicalized Liberal Party, courting working-class support and practising social reform in the municipal arena, which blocked the way to independent labour politics in London for a generation. For nearly twenty years the London working class derived greater benefits from municipal Liberalism than it could have expected from any nascent Labour organization. The Progressive Party on the London County Council – preponderantly Liberal/Radical in composition, supported by a client 'labour bench' of trade unionists – implemented a social programme which included slum clearance and rehousing schemes, the municipalization of most of the tramway network, the provision and protection of parks and open spaces, direct labour for council projects, and a wages policy designed to prevent 'sweating' by the council itself or its contractors. Liberal success in these directions, though, retarded the growth of independent labour politics in London, with the result that metropolitan labour activists were unable to develop the kind of organizational strength that would enable the national party to withstand the challenge of Liberal welfarism after 1906.

The explanation lay in the failure of associational politics to provide labour politicians in the clubs and the MRF with an organizational base from which they could challenge the established parties. Associationalism had appealed to them as a means of involving a class which had still to develop habits of political action. It carried the obvious danger that its social appeal would obscure its political purpose, but the picture of a metropolitan working class distracted from its political duties by recreational hedonism needs to be qualified. Club expansion destroyed the intensely political atmosphere of the early days, when dissent or abstention had been embarrassingly conspicuous, but it also allowed a more muted form of political enthusiasm to embrace larger numbers. Club politicians found that the most epicurean social member could be won to a generalized political partisanship and induced to canvass for friends. Clubmen could be elected in

121

growing numbers to local boards, and clubs could provide impressive support for strikers. The problem lay in making systematic use of this commitment. Early club Radicals had deployed quite successfully 'a band of artisan politicians . . . who will cheerfully give their time and labour for the cause they have at heart'[129] but they failed to develop any more regular political machinery. Clubs' expansion increased their influence but dissipated their power. They proved less effective at caucus politics than the caucuses, and their claim to wield the force of populist mass protest was soon devalued.

The established parties soon found that associationalism, though a useful adjunct to their conventional activity, was essentially peripheral to it. The crises of the mid-1880s had led the Liberals both to radicalize policy and to flirt with associationalism, but the policy shift alone proved enough to stop the rot and obviate any need to incorporate the clubs in party processes. There are obvious temptations in the argument that associationalism was central to the democratic modernization of political parties, making 'political loyalty an integral part of the lives of a large number of people', impinging upon 'much more than political man', creating 'a party of social integration' in place of the caucus.[130] Victorian party managers undoubtedly hoped to recruit support by means of political propaganda 'cleverly disguised with a coating of popular entertainment'.[131] The London evidence suggests, however, reasons why this proved a late-Victorian blind alley, why the Primrose League dwindled after 1900, and why twentieth-century parties have not depended upon their ability to provide recreational *douceurs* for the masses.

The period after 1890 saw the specialization of both recreation and political organization to the point where it became very difficult to combine the two. In an increasingly competitive leisure market, entertainment had to be provided whole-heartedly if at all, and not as a vehicle for political indoctrination. Meanwhile, the caucus emerged as the best means of managing a large urban electorate. Democracy pointed not to associational incorporation but to the continual refinement of the party machine. This did not prevent the clubs from effecting a good deal of political socialization but it did limit their value as surrogate political organizations. This development fed upon itself as the clubs' increasingly apolitical image reduced their appeal to the younger generation of labour activists whose provincial equivalents helped turn the unions away from Liberalism in the 1900s. The hope that the club movement could stand at the head of independent labour politics in London died with the 1880s generation.

The final lesson is unsurprising – the importance of trade unionism in the rise of labour and the significance of the absence of mature industrial unionism in London. Unionism elsewhere did what the London clubs could not do: it combined the power of political socialization on the shop-floor with the efficiency of a centralized leadership and bureaucracy. Union leaders were spared the conflict between political and recreational objectives that beset the London clubs; the 'employers' counter-attack' and the series of judicial reverses culminating in Taff Vale made political action appear a pre-condition for union survival and the realization of all union aims. Union leaders were able to nurture their own political party at a time when London's club politicians were losing deference, status, and power.

It was the want of this institutional force or an effective substitute for it which inhibited London labour. A working class cohesive enough to create and sustain its own cultural facilities and environment remained retarded in its political development. Labour's emergence in London came to depend less upon the exertions of the metropolitan working class than upon the displacement of the Liberal Party nationally, and a predominantly middle-class Liberal Progressivism spoke for London labour down to the First World War.

Notes

I am grateful to Nicky Allen, Jose Harris, Jeremy Maule, John Rowett, Philip Waller, and of course the editors and fellow contributors for their helpful advice.

1 P. Thompson, *Socialists, Liberals and Labour*, 1967, p. 86.
2 G. Stedman Jones, 'Working-class culture and working-class politics in London, 1870–1900: notes on the remaking of a working class', *Journal of Social History*, 7, 4 (Summer 1974), reprinted in his *Languages of Class*, 1983. All references here are to the reprint.
3 ibid., pp. 217 ff., 237.
4 ibid., p. 237.
5 ibid., p. 236.
6 For existing studies, see J. Taylor, *From Self-Help to Glamour: The Working Men's Club, 1860–1972*, History Workshop Pamphlet no. 7, 1972; P. Bailey, *Leisure and Class in Victorian England*, 1978, ch. 5; L. Marlow, 'The working men's club movement, 1862–1912: a study of the evolution of a working-class institution', unpublished Ph.D. thesis, Warwick University, 1980; T. G. Ashplant, 'London working men's clubs, 1875–1914', in Eileen and Stephen Yeo (eds), *Popular Culture and Class Conflict 1590–1914*, 1981; S. Shipley, *Club Life and Socialism in Mid-Victorian London*, History Workshop Pamphlet no. 5, 1971.

7 Thompson, op. cit., p. 93.
8 See the correspondence 'Should Social Democrats join Radical clubs?', *Justice*, 11 June, 18 June, 2 July 1892.
9 *Workmen's Club-Journal*, 27 November 1875.
10 B. T. Hall, *Our Fifty Years. The Story of the Working Men's Club and Institute Union*, 1912, p. 112; *Club Life*, 7 January 1899.
11 Mildmay Club membership rose from 1,000 in February 1896 to 2,400 in January 1899. The North Camberwell Radical Club was admitting 40 new members a week after taking new premises in 1892. Central Finsbury Radical Club membership rose from 250 to over 1,000 in eighteen months after the club's move to Goswell Road. See *Club World*, 15 February 1896, 20 August 1898; *Club Life*, 28 January 1899; *South London Press*, 29 October 1892.
12 Letter from 'Committee man' (Dulwich WMC), *South London Chronicle*, 26 November 1892.
13 G. Howell, 'Club rooms at public houses', *Social Notes*, 10 July 1880.
14 F. W. Galton, MS Autobiography, p. 41 (British Library of Political and Economic Science).
15 For the Eleusis and the Borough of Hackney, see *Radical Leader*, 4 August, 11 August 1888; *Echo*, 12 February, 20 February 1884; B. Burke and K. Worpole, *Hackney Propaganda: Working Club Life and Politics in Hackney, 1870–1900*, 1980, p. 8. For the Patriotic, A. Rothstein, *A House On Clerkenwell Green*, 1966, pp. 41–2.
16 *Club and Institute Journal* (henceforth *CIJ*), 26 September 1884; *Echo*, 24 April 1884.
17 *CIJ*, 5 September 1884; *Radical Leader*, 25 August 1888.
18 Letter from Fletcher Pape, New Commonwealth Club, *Weekly Dispatch*, 15 February 1885.
19 *Radical*, 18 December 1880; J. Morrison Davison, 'Demands of the new democracy', *Democrat*, 20 February 1886; G. Howell, 'The caucus system and the Liberal Party', *New Quarterly Magazine*, X, 1878, p. 583.
20 Morrison Davison, op. cit.
21 Mr Stearn, at a meeting of Marylebone Clubs, *Marylebone Independent*, 15 August 1885.
22 *Chelsea News*, 21 August 1875, 26 February, 11 March 1876.
23 *Echo*, 20 February 1884.
24 *Westminster and Chelsea News*, 7 October 1882; *Islington Gazette*, 11 April, 8 May 1884; *Eastern Argus*, 19 June 1884; *CIJ*, 30 January 1885; *Democrat*, 14 February 1885; *Weekly Dispatch*, 15 February, 13 September 1885; *Echo*, 24 April 1884; Thompson, op. cit., p. 93.
25 *Eastern Argus*, 19 July 1884; *Democrat*, 15 November 1884.
26 *Marylebone Independent*, 1 August 1885.
27 Letter from 'MP' on 'Duplicate Liberal candidatures', *Daily News*, 15 September 1885.
28 *Democrat*, 25 July 1885.
29 ibid.; *Marylebone Independent*, 7 November 1885; *Democrat*, 19 September 1885; *Weekly Dispatch*, 20 September 1885.

30 Though it was agreed to 'submit our claims to the Liberal Association and agree to abide by their decision, whatever it might be' – G. Howell, MS Autobiography, vol. I (1), Howell Papers (Bishopgate Institute). See also F. M. Leventhal, *Respectable Radical: George Howell and Victorian Working-Class Politics*, 1971, p. 205.
31 H. Evans, *Sir Randal Cremer: His Life and Work*, 1909, pp. 116–18; *Borough of Hackney Express* 18 April, 2 May, 16 May, 23 May 1885.
32 S. Webb, *Socialism in England*, 1890, p. 123.
33 ibid., p. 123.
34 Gladstone's view, quoted by Dilke to the Victoria Park Demonstration Committee in 1884. Cf. Rosebery's reply to the same effect, *Eastern Argus*, 6 September 1884.
35 Reform Demonstration Committee minutes survive in the George Howell Papers.
36 Quoted by A. Jones, *The Politics of Reform, 1884*, 1972, p. 162.
37 *Weekly Dispatch*, 3 April 1887.
38 ibid., 10 April 1887.
39 For the reorganization, see J. H. Davis, 'The problem of London local government reform, 1880–1900', unpublished D.Phil. thesis, Oxford University, 1983, pp. 164–6.
40 *Weekly Dispatch*, 4 April 1886.
41 Advertisement in West Newington Liberal and Radical Association, *Fourth Annual Report, 1889–90* (Southwark Archives).
42 Letter from W. J. Smith, *Holborn Guardian*, 14 May 1887.
43 M. Barker, *Gladstone and Radicalism*, 1975, p. 138.
44 *Club World*, 16 November 1895.
45 ibid., 20 June 1896.
46 *Club Life*, 15 July 1899.
47 Trowbridge at the Borough of Shoreditch Club, *CIJ*, 2 January 1892.
48 The process is well analysed in Ashplant, op. cit., pp. 249–59.
49 *Radical*, 5 February 1881; *Radical Leader*, 29 September 1888.
50 e.g. Eleusis (*Radical Leader*, 4 August 1888), Hammersmith (ibid., 17 November 1888).
51 ibid., 3 November 1888 (Shoreditch Liberal and Radical Club).
52 *Westminster and Chelsea News*, 4 December 1880.
53 *West London Press*, 22 November 1890.
54 *CIJ*, 22 October 1892, 18 April, 5 September 1891. The THRC resurfaced as the Tower Hamlets Reform Club a year later, with popular concerts two or three times a week: *East London Observer*, 10 September 1892.
55 H. A. Fuller, Patriotic Club, *CIJ*, 19 September 1891.
56 *Club World*, 26 December 1896.
57 W. Pett Ridge, 'Club life in East London', *National Review*, 18, 1891–2, p. 135.
58 *Club World*, 9 November 1895.
59 'Prompter', ibid., 6 November 1897.
60 URC report in *CIJ*, 21 October 1893.
61 ibid., 5 September 1891.

62 F. Rogers, *Labour, Life and Literature*, 1913, p. 67.
63 Article on West Southwark Radical Club, *Sun*, 24 November 1889.
64 Letter from 'A social man', *Club World*, 30 November 1895.
65 J. B. Leno, *The Aftermath: With Autobiography of the Author*, 1892, p. 53.
66 E. Belfort Bax, *Reminiscences and Reflexions*, 1918, p. 73.
67 Webb, op. cit., pp. 123–4.
68 Rogers, op. cit., p. 115.
69 *Radical Leader*, 4 August 1888.
70 Editorial, *Club World*, 16 November 1895.
71 Letter from 'A daily reader', *CIJ*, 4 March 1893.
72 W. S. Sanders, *Early Socialist Days*, 1927, p. 21.
73 *Club World*, 19 September 1896.
74 'Would Jubilieve it? That some of our members are walking about with a Jubilee band round their hats, and a Queen's purple tie, and yet they are members of a Radical club!' – Bermondsey Gladstone Club reporter, *Club World*, 19 June 1897.
75 ibid., 11 January 1896, 26 November 1898.
76 Cynicus, Borough of Hackney Club reporter, *Club Life*, 2 December 1899.
77 T. S. Peppin, *Club-land of the Toiler*, 1895, p. 68. The Holborn Gladstone Club passed a resolution that 'the British were entitled to equality with the Boers in the Transvaal' despite the opposition of its secretary, and imperialist feeling was said to dominate the Gladstone Radical. The Millfields Radical Club reporter complained of 'democracy having given way to so-called patriotism' (all *Club Life* 28 October 1899). Richard Price's assertion in *An Imperial War and the British Working Class*, 1972, p. 70, that 'the most impressive feature of the clubs during the period of the war was the absolute lack of jingoistic excitement' is based upon a selective reading of the club press.
78 Stedman Jones, op. cit., p. 215.
79 ibid., p. 218.
80 See M. J. Daunton, *House and Home in the Victorian City*, 1983, ch. 11.
81 John Burns's Journal, 19 March 1891 (British Library Add. MS 46311).
82 *North London Press*, 28 December 1889.
83 Stedman Jones, op. cit., p. 220.
84 *CIJ*, 25 April 1891.
85 'The near approach of the big Eight Hours Demonstration in Hyde Park has caused quite an awakening among the political drybones – the "dead-uns" who . . . have now suddenly recollected that they belong to a political club' – North Camberwell Radical Club report, *CIJ*, 11 April 1891. See also ibid., 31 January, 18 April, 2 May 1891.
86 *The (Islington) Londoner*, 12 March 1897.
87 *Club World*, 6 November 1897; also 13 November, 4 December 1897. For the Patriotic Club's support of the Silvertown strikers, see *North London Press*, 23 November 1889; and for the Boro' of Bethnal Green Club's support of the bookbinders, *CIJ*, 9 July 1892.

88 *CIJ*, 9 July 1892.
89 *Club World*, 17 September 1898.
90 ibid., 12 March 1898.
91 *Club Life*, 20 May 1899.
92 *36th Annual Report of the Working Man's Club and Institute Union, 1898*, table VII, p. 27. The total declines after the replacement of the vestries by the smaller borough councils in 1900.
93 Interview with James Morden, *Club Life*, 15 July 1899.
94 ibid., 11 March, 20 May, 10 June 1899.
95 Interview in *Club World*, 10 September 1898.
96 *Club World*, 27 July 1895.
97 See Pape's letter to *Weekly Dispatch*, 11 June 1882.
98 Shipley, op. cit., p. 4.
99 *Radical*, April 1886; *Hackney and Kingsland Gazette*, 20 January, 29 March 1886.
100 Letter in *Weekly Dispatch*, 16 January 1887.
101 James Rowlands, at the inaugural meeting of the Holborn Liberal and Radical Association, *Holborn Guardian*, 26 March 1887.
102 Letters from M. M. Dilke and James Lenn, both MRF delegates to the LLRU inaugural conference, *Weekly Dispatch*, 16 January, 23 January 1887.
103 *Star*, 8 February 1888.
104 See the description of the tactics employed by both sides in the London government debate, Select Committee on the Corporation of London (Charges of Malversation), Parliamentary Papers, 1887, X; and Davis, op. cit., pp. 119–21.
105 *People's Press*, 26 July 1890.
106 Details of expenditure, though not receipts, are in the George Howell Papers.
107 E. H. Pickersgill, quoted *Eastern Argus*, 23 August 1884.
108 Reform Demonstration Committee Minutes, 4 July 1884, George Howell Papers.
109 Report of the Committee on the Origin and Character of the Disturbances in the Metropolis on Monday, 8 February, Parliamentary Papers, 1886, XXXIV.
110 V. Bailey, 'The Metropolitan Police, the Home Office and the threat of outcast London', in V. Bailey (ed.), *Policing and Punishment in Nineteenth-Century Britain*, 1981, pp. 106–7.
111 J. N. Lee, West Southwark Liberal and Radical Club, in *Weekly Dispatch*, 20 November 1887.
112 'Police-made-riots', *Sun*, 30 June 1889; *People's Press*, 14 June 1890.
113 *Star*, 20 April 1888.
114 *Weekly Dispatch*, 22 April 1888.
115 *Star*, 2 March 1888.
116 Police orders were issued for over eighty political meetings between April 1885 and December 1890, listed in the return in PRO MEPO/2/248.
117 See, e.g., Lawson at St Pancras, *Weekly Dispatch*, 22 April 1888; Seager at Holborn, *Holborn Guardian*, 16 June 1888.

118 *People's Press*, 14 June 1890.
119 *Holborn Guardian*, 23 June 1888.
120 *Sun*, 24 November 1889, on West Southwark Radical Club.
121 At the 1883 Bethnal Green revision court 'Richard Bayne came to court stating that he "had received no paper nor nothing", but had given his name in at the Commonwealth club' – *Eastern Argus*, 6 October 1883.
122 *Club World*, 12 January 1895.
123 e.g. Tims's letter 'Radical organization', *Star*, 5 March 1888; and the proposals for a new political union to combine 'social advantages' with politics, *CIJ*, 17 January 1891.
124 A. M. McBriar, *Fabian Socialism and English Politics, 1884–1918*, 1962, p. 239.
125 Letter from 'Ino', *South London Chronicle*, 5 November 1892. Annie Besant criticized the clubs for their parsimony towards the Law and Liberty League (*Star*, 23 April 1888). Of the £60 raised for the eight-hour-day demonstration in 1890 only £4 1s 6d came from clubs (*People's Press*, 26 July 1890). See also the comments at the MRF seventh anniversary dinner, *CIJ*, 16 December 1893.
126 *L&R. Liberal and Radical*, 10 March 1888.
127 *Club Life*, 24 June 1899.
128 The Central Finsbury Radical Club allowed its political committee £44 in 1892–3 – *Daily News*, 28 March 1893.
129 *Echo*, 24 February 1884, on the Eleusis.
130 M. Pugh, *The Tories and the People, 1880–1935*, 1985, p. 42; J. Garrard, 'Parties, voters and members after 1867: a local study', *Historical Journal*, 1977, pp. 163, 145, for these and similar claims for the power of political associationalism.
131 Janet H. Robb, *The Primrose League*, 1942, p. 89.

6

'The millennium by return of post'

Reconsidering London Progressivism, 1889–1907

Susan Pennybacker

The 'failure of London socialism' has often been explained by reference to a unique metropolitan tradition of popular conservatism, nursed in an urban environment hostile to the development of any unified proletarian movement. That the socialist intelligentsia found the capital a desirable headquarters has never been disputed; equally, however, it is usually assumed that, by its very nature, London was intrinsically incapable of fostering or sustaining a mass movement for radical social change – a meteoric 'new unionism' and the sect-like SDF proved rather than challenged the rule. The political attitudes of Londoners have been distinguished from their provincial counterparts by reference to the absence of a factory proletariat, a surfeit of acquisitive middle-class suburbanites, the rapid and seductive commercialization of leisure, the proximity of Parliament and Crown, and the vastness of the conurbation. Accordingly, to glance at the map of London was to perceive the cause of the dissipation of radical movements – the anomie of urbanness coupled with the riches so tantalizingly close at hand militated against both the left's organizational potential and perhaps even its credibility. Posed against the stereotypical portrait of a more stable and incremental growth of labour and socialist currents in other parts of Britain, such a profile has been invoked in order to help account for the putative 'backwardness' of London labourism.[1]

Because this essay has as its subject a failed movement of populist and radical intent, one of the foremost examples of 'municipal socialism' of its day, it too seeks explanations for the historic forms of anti-socialism, anti-statism, and significant popular conservatism in the seat of empire. In doing so, however, no a priori assumption is made that Londoners could not embrace a popular socialist and radical creed, or that urban structures prevented them from participating in a rich metropolitan political life. Instead, the very engagement of the populace with the

London County Council, the programmes and platforms offered by politicians, and the internal contradictions of the movement itself are seen here as providing the keys to the dynamic of Progressive success and failure. In seeking to define that dynamic, the essay examines several strategic areas of controversy for Progressives and their opponents, paying close attention to certain aspects of rhetoric, appeals to special groups within the populace, and the practical image that the LCC conveyed in carrying out some of its policies. The Progressive experiment, it is suggested, engendered enthusiasm and spawned disillusionment because of the ways in which it was articulated – both to the electorate and to those many inhabitants of London who knew it best through the medium of institutional intervention. In discarding the notion that the roots of anti-statism or anti-socialism lie in the deficient characteristics of the electors or in the problem of an aberrant social environment, here it is assumed, instead, that attitudes emerged and developed over time, and only in the face of the Progressives' attempts to carry out a highly contradictory vision of the reform of metropolitan life. The Progressive vision first appeared palatable to many, and yet could not sustain a claim to its own distinctiveness, on the one hand, or to the capability of realizing its ambitions, on the other.[2]

As the seat of the largest municipal authority in the world, the London County Council, late-nineteenth-century London was the scene of a sweeping movement for local government reform. This movement sought to bring Londoners into a more inclusive municipal politics symbolized by the LCC's creation in 1888, a victory somewhat marred by the fact that council powers had in each instance to be mandated by Parliament. Nevertheless, the LCC was the first popularly elected authority after the London School Board and was led in the early years by the party whose name signified its intended legacy – the Progressives.[3]

The creation of the LCC was a catharsis in the government reform struggles of the century – a brilliant opportunity to practise democracy in this new form. Despite the limited franchise, this was the first time that any large number of the inhabitants of the city had chosen a central civic leadership. By the mid-1880s the embarrassing state of municipal government had seemed unworthy of the world's greatest city. A change following on the collapse of the Metropolitan Board of Works was long overdue – the MBW had earned its nickname, the 'Board of Perks'. As one Bethnal Green candidate put it: 'Many things want doing to take away the reproach against London of being the worst governed city in civilization'.[4] Persons of all political callings wished to try their hands at governing London. The first LCC election came on the heels of the Great Dock Strike and witnessed veterans of the 'new union' drives and the 1887 unemployment demonstration competing for the Progressive mantle with staid Gladstonians and New Liberals. W. W. Bartlett, an avowed socialist running in South St Pancras, proudly displayed his scar from the most recent 'battle of Trafalgar' on the hustings.[5]

John Burns, London's most renowned socialist and leader of the dock strike, easily won the LCC seat for Battersea and remained in the forefront of Progressivism after his appointment in 1906 to the Cabinet. While Burns enjoyed a massive public following, and figures like Ben Tillett, Harry Quelch, Will Crooks, Will Steadman, and Sidney Webb also represented Progressivism in its early days, the party (as it was called only after 1892) was initially dominated by official Liberalism, with Liberal Unionist defectors occasionally entering its ranks. John Benn, publisher, Liberal MP, teetotaller, social reformer, and ardent Nonconformist, was one of the most representative figures of the Progressive majority. He served terms both as party leader and as LCC chairman:

> let us peep over this fragment of the old City wall and see how the trustees of the wealth left by our fathers, the old craftsmen of London, are getting on. Ah, the City turtle is on its back, the knees of Gog and Magog are shaking, the Griffin is rocking on his pedestal. Another blast from the slums, and, like Jericho, the walls will fall, and a greater, a brighter, and a better London will be ours.[6]

The term 'progressivism', especially familiar as the name for the United States movement that aimed at ousting city 'machines' like Tammany Hall, appeared in other Liberal contexts; J. A. Hobson and W. Clarke edited a *Progressive Review*.[7] Progressivism was initially successful in uniting a broadly based constituency comprised of Liberal association members, trade unionists, Nonconformists and social reformers, Fabian fellow travellers, the rank and file of the working men's clubs, and even supporters of the Liberal Imperialists, boasting Rosebery as the first LCC chairman. Rate rises, expensive experiments in 'dubious' forms of municipalization, fissures and fractures amongst its own supporters, and the organizational revitalization of municipal Conservatism all signalled Progressivism's dissipation. In 1895, the year of the third triennial LCC election, their majority was only held through appointed aldermanic posts. They were able to restabilize in the elections of 1898, 1901, and 1903, only to be trounced from office in 1907.

The Conservative triumph in 1907 was realized in the largest single electoral poll in London's county municipal history. From 1900 the LCC franchise was the same as the parliamentary franchise with the addition of between 80,000 and 100,000 women voters.[8] By 1907 rate rises *had been* extensive, especially following on the Education Act of 1902, and adverse Conservative publicity was extreme and provocative. The 'middle-class ratepayer element' voted Conservative in large numbers in 1907; though the Progressives did not tend to lose great numbers of their working-class supporters, they failed to garner a larger electoral constituency over time, losing most new voters to the Conservatives in elections in which there were persistent and high rates of abstentionism.[9]

London's burgeoning 'lower middle class', the fastest-growing sector of its population at the turn of the century, played a crucial role both in offering some support to Progressivism and in filling out the ranks of Conservative voters in 1907. The economic uncertainty faced by this stratum offers a tempting case for the rates, pure and simple, being the cause of Progressivism's decline. But the rates are never pure and simple – what were they to be spent upon? For what reasons did anyone defend paying them, and how were they made to appear particularly unjustified over time? Economic uncertainty was always a factor for *most* voters – it does not explain the fierce contention of the 1907 campaign, nor its antecedents. To conclude that the 1907 defeat was simply based in the objection of electors to rate rises (as previous accounts have done), or even that an experimentalist regime threatened propertied interests, is to point only to the most obvious features of any moment in municipal history. Here instead the task is to unravel some of the threads that tied its supporters to Progressivism, to suggest what might have been attractive about its detractors, and to ask how, for some, its appeal was eventually uninviting. Without this, we cannot account either for Progressivism's initial failure or, viewed in the light of Morrison's London victory in 1934 or the 1945 Labour victory, for its ultimate historic appeal.[10]

I

The 1889 election was fought by candidates portraying themselves as 'non-political'. Municipal politics was presented as resting on a commitment to serve London, not on the ties of party *per se*. Indeed, no candidate contested office under banners employed in parliamentary campaigns, the Conservatives adopting the name of the 'Moderates' and later, significantly, that of the 'Municipal Reform Party'. T. P. O'Connor of Bethnal Green explicitly approached 'women and men of no politics' in his campaign.[11] It was thought that those who normally did not participate in elections might be wooed to do so in a contest in which their more immediate needs were at stake. This implied that there were special responsibilities to be carried out by the successful candidate. As the *Star* put it:

> The great necessity is to elect men who would run the Council on proper lines, court publicity for all its meetings and proceedings, and be the sworn foes of rings and cliques. That, and not the attainment of any party object whatsoever, has been our motive throughout.[12]

The participation of members of the House of Lords gave greater status to the race, and many of those who won the first contests as well as many of their successors eventually arrived at the House of Commons. The LCC was in effect a nursery for Parliament. While the LCC would attempt to influence the parliamentary activities of the parties, and in turn be looked to as an arena influencing parliamentary votes, in the first election the Progressives stressed the distinctive character of the municipal tasks. Lord Rosebery explained:

> We have not gone for a pure political issue on Imperialist lines. The great work of the Council is a sanitary work. Its primary task will be the better housing of the poor. That is politics in the municipal rather than the Imperial sense.[13]

The vital issues for candidates, as enumerated in 1889 in the *Star* would remain at the heart of the LCC contests before the First World War: the taxation of ground rents, control of the police, equalization of rates, the question of open spaces, the abolition of coal and wine dues, the municipal control of gas and water, of markets, and of cabs, the licensing of places of public entertainment, 'the question of City endowments and of general municipal reform'.[14]

Competing visions of London life and a variety of strategies with which to attack these problems soon fostered controversy, despite the Progressives' wide electoral margin in 1889. At the time of the next election in 1892, T. George Fardell, leader of the Moderate Party, Conservative MP, and LCC councillor, as well as a great ground landlord, surmised: 'there is now . . . in existence a municipal policy with an ardent body of supporters and an equally ardent body of opponents, a policy embracing finance, public-houses, labour, improvements'.[15]

John Burns, vocal and charismatic advocate of a socialist vision for London, called for the creation of municipal workshops and stores, free transport to work, farm colonies for the unemployed, municipal clothing factories to relieve sweated labour, and an Imperial Labour Bureau for all of Great Britain. He researched the history of public works during the 1840s and cited precedents for his schemes in British policy in India, Ireland, and other colonies. He demanded that the unemployed be absorbed into the labour force through the promulgation of shorter hours for all and the elimination of labouring women from factory occupations, a step that would be justified by the payment of higher wages for their husbands. Following upon this initial reorganization of labour would come the municipalization of industry and, ultimately, the nationalization of monopolies.[16]

If this vision did not come to fruition, the propertied, Burns contended, had much to fear. It was 'regulation or riot, reduction or revolution'.[17] In the dock strike Burns had demonstrated his skill in motivating and leading crowds. His approach to the LCC had continuity with the positions he had taken during the strike. He saw a socialist strategy as capable of dividing the working class into its most deserving and least deserving elements, separating, through public works departments, the 'labouring sheep . . . from the loafing goats', just as the docker's tanner was meant to decasualize dock labour.[18] The regulation of labour on a vast scale, the promise of trade union wages and conditions, would attract the 'quality workmen' of the metropolis to the LCC. Socialism to him meant not only the eradication of poverty but the disaggregation of the working class, its categorization according to skill and fortitude, its absorption into a system of municipal and state employment – all of which Burns hoped would lead to the 'industrial reorganization of society'.[19] In the spirit of the Victorian charity tradition he assigned a special role to the respectable worker, now, of course, also an elector:

> On you, the aristocracy of labour, who are here tonight, the greater burden of responsibility for altering this must rest. Your immunity from these conditions ought to be the measure of your duty to help those who clamour for your aid.[20]

This mode of thinking and of speaking echoed a Fabian literature, which had persistently called for the municipalization of London's utilities.[21] Historians have given little attention to the Fabian insistence on linking these proposals to a special role for the working class. The municipalization of the docks would create a permanent dock labour force in its wake; they called for the dock labourer to become as regular an employee as the rail porter. The municipalization of the gas supply would involve the gas worker in collectivism. The unearned increment seized from the ground landlord would help to rehouse the people, and all would be undertaken under the banner of what Shaw termed the 'Disestablishment and Disendowment of Idleness'.[22]

Just as Burns emphasized the divisions in the working class in order to appeal to certain strata of it, so the Fabians emphasized the absence of political commitment amongst the lower echelons of the working class. Shaw even declared that 'every working man was a political pauper'. No party, he contended, could win without a base in the more reliable middle class. And the middle class could not be recruited to follow a party that taxed them heavily in order to end unemployment. It was with an eye to this dilemma that he defended the call for the taxation of ground rents, not as a revitalization of the 'old Whig cry for the conversion of indirect into direct taxation', but as the connection between what he termed 'Municipal Socialism' and 'Radical Finance'.[23]

The attack on the ground landlord formed the centrepiece of all London municipal socialism, and was supported by many non-socialists as well. It afforded its adherents a means with which to articulate an inclusive strategy of mobilization aimed at the richest and most parasitic of London property owners.[24] The Fabians, like Burns, wanted to thrust themselves into the pivotal position of administering the municipality for the benefit of the producers and the consumers, and they tended to work harder than many other Progressives and to be more highly visible. Demands like 'communism in water' were part of a programme that also sought to assist in 'organizing the demoralized dock labourers and so heal the spreading social ulcer of the East End'.[25] The Fabians and the labour wing of Progressivism offered a strategy not far removed from that of their Liberal colleagues – but they were not alone in offering a visionary municipal programme.

The opponents of Progressivism were assisted by their own camp's internal diversity. There were conservatives in London who supported the taxation of ground rents. In a paper read before the Society of Arts, Dixon Henry Davies spoke of the 'legitimate forms of communal adventure'. He supported government possession of the water supply, the harbours, and the cemeteries but he thought that trams, the electric supply, housing, and the gas supply were best left in private hands. He attacked 'municipal traders' for their hypocrisy, 'masquerading in the ermine of impartial authority', arguing that self-interest actually motivated them, as it did all persons in commerce.[26] Like the Municipal Reform Party, he claimed to be speaking in London's best interest, emphasizing the necessity of preserving industry which would otherwise flee under the pressure of aggressive property taxation. The municipally minded conservative proudly stood for 'freedom of contract', anathema to socialists, and defended such measures as in the interest of the working class.[27]

The Liberty and Property Defence League, a short-lived bulwark of London anti-municipalism, protested against the charge that they represented the ground landlord:

> Confusion of the League and ground landlordism in one common misrepresentation for the time served its purpose. The working-class voters were misled by the prospect of living rent free as soon as the ground landlord should have been eradicated by the LCC . . . as for the League itself, it had never made the defence of ground landlords *qua* ground landlords a special feature of its programme.[28]

The league claimed a greater interest in the 'labour question' and in the preservation of freedom of contract. The league understood itself as explicitly committed to the principles advocated by the *Edinburgh Review* in its heyday and saw itself as perpetuating that tradition, supporting limited public ownership while opposing, for instance, the municipalization of gas and water. It opposed a trade union monopoly and the institution of trade union wage rates by the municipality, warning that strict wage rates would prevent bargaining up, as well as labour mobility.[29]

The logic of the league was not easy to dismiss. As W. A. Crofts, a league speaker, recounted it, Liberals, Levellers, Chartists, and anarchists had all been against state interference.[30] The league saw 'personal liberty' and the "natural right" to freedom' as the creeds of the working men of the Chartist days, now betrayed by the modern labour movement.[31] Davies similarly accused the building trades of trying to create *ateliers nationaux* at the LCC, while accusing the Progressives of cynically feigning a non-partisan stance: 'Apparently the assumption is that the municipal body is the sole repository of civic virtue. All this is ridiculous nonsense. It is very much the same spirit as the attack which was made upon the Corn Law reformers.'[32]

Essential to this critique was the reconstruction of a working-class English past, of an age when *laissez-faire* principles had been shared by all the nation, in which the workers had benefited from capitalism's triumph. Now an age of darkness had descended, and the league, like Belloc and other critics of collectivism, warned against the inevitability of state socialism, promising that 'the deadening effect of which on all branches of industry and originality the working classes will be the first to feel'.[33]

The London Municipal Society, bastion of Conservative strategy and strength within the municipal movement, was, like the league, contemptuous of the crass characterizations of its members as greedy and uncommitted to civic life. And like the league, the LMS attempted to establish a distinctive philosophical progeny. The necessary municipal feats of the period could hardly be carried out, in their estimation, by those influenced by Marx. His predictions of inevitable capitalist decline had proven wrong in their view, and this in and of itself ought to warn the public of socialism's erroneous first premisses.[34]

At the Parisian International Exhibition, league municipal activists met with others of like mind; they were proud of their prolific links with the rightists of the Parisian *conseil municipal*. Asserting the need for wider organization in England, they hailed the formation of a ratepayers' defence league. Populist groupings of this sort were already active in London's neighbourhoods and gained strength upon the Conservative victory represented by the creation of the London boroughs in 1899. A new spirit of localism, portrayed as popular democracy against the centralism of the LCC, characterized the activities of many of these bodies, not all of which were partisan. These groups tended to express a concerted desire for improving London, a willingness to support limited municipal enterprise through forms of taxation which would not threaten their members' budgets.[35]

II

Meanwhile the majority who had brought Progressivism to power now awaited its practical results, and increasingly the party's relationship to London trade unionism attracted interest. Even the Liberty and Property Defence League had pronounced on the death of Parnell: 'the "labour question" is now given a first place on all authorised programmes'.[36] The Progressives hardly disagreed. Even as they waged protracted and ultimately unsuccessful struggles to achieve control of gas, electricity, and water, the business of accomplishing a quick victory in the fight against rising unemployment loomed large.

The TUC had called for trade union wages and the promulgation of 'direct labour' programmes by all local and national authorities, and indeed by 1894 thirty-eight London boroughs had endorsed fair wage clauses in municipal contracts.[37] The London Society of Compositors had established the precedent with the London School Board, and now the LCC followed suit. When the council established its 'direct labour' Works Department in 1892 under

Burns's leadership, the trade union movement was delighted. From this moment onwards, all municipal parties shared a common receptacle of hope and grievance. The department employed over 3,000 workers a week at the peak of operation. It was independent of outside contractors from London's building industry and in its heyday was responsible for the construction of many of London's schools, housing estates, and civil engineering efforts.[38]

The Works Department violated the Conservative belief in freedom of contract while nominally fulfilling Progressivism's pledge to provide employment for London's workers. But when the department was proposed, the *Spectator* warned:

> It would compel the Council to establish an industrial army of its own, would create a desire in the administrative committee for needless grandeur in all the works attempted and would compel them to keep their forces employed even when there was no work urgently requiring to be done.[39]

Unionized workers were the targets of the Conservatives; the Works Department was 'not democracy or philanthropy . . . only socialism badly applied for the benefit of a single class in the community, certainly not the most oppressed class, at the expense of the remainder'.[40] The unemployed would ultimately suffer if all wages rose. And the Conservatives began to single out the 'labour members' of the Progressives as most responsible, just as the trade union movement was doing.

No sooner had the Works Department begun than a series of scandals erupted, which were precipitated by dubious accounting practices, part of a scheme by the staff to cover up for discrepancies in cost. Despite a judgement by Price Waterhouse that the department was solvent, the rhetorical use of the department's internal corruption enhanced the credibility of Conservative criticisms. On this issue, none could be satisfied. Especially in the wake of the scandal, many Progressives were sceptical of the significance of preserving the department. They were not themselves dependent on a trade union constituency in the way that councillors and alderman whose wages were paid by London Trades Council collections were. Hence a split within the Progressive camp widened. Trade unionists were dissatisfied with the absence of a closed shop on the building sites; those not in the unions who were residents of areas where works were being carried out found themselves wanting for work even when mammoth undertakings like the Blackwall Tunnel and the Boundary Street estate were under construction next door.[41]

While Benn advocated 'local work for local men', Burns stated that he felt that all those employed ought to be trade unionists. He and alderman Will Steadman of the Bargebuilders voiced this opinion in a public inquiry that filled the old County Hall in Spring Gardens, off Trafalgar Square, to overflowing, reportedly exciting more popular interest than any other nineteenth-century London government controversy.[42]

There were many discrepancies in the views expressed in defence of the Works Department. Burns called it the 'first scientific step yet taken for the unemployed question'. Other councillors could defend it only on grounds of 'cost-efficiency'; some projects had obviously proven more cost efficient than others. A further crack in the edifice of support was widened when the question of what actually determined 'efficiency' was raised. It could only really be defined with reference to market forces in the private sector. There were no checks on council estimates – these could be offered by the architect's department and accepted without competing offers. In fact, the absence of competition, and its elimination, had been the original purpose of the department in the minds of the Progressive left wing.[43]

While Progressive opinion on the Works Department divided, the self-righteousness of the Tories was unabated. Here they had an example of what a socialist economy would look like. In the pre-1917 world, this was an anomaly. All the Conservatives' worst suspicions were confirmed, and the supporters of the department could offer the Progressives little consolation. For them, far from providing a sinecure for the unemployed, the department had managed neither to preserve enough jobs, nor to preserve trade union exclusivity. Though the department at first survived the scandal, it was 'starved out' by continual limits imposed on its capital expenditures, and figured prominently in the bitter electoral feuds of 1907. The fewer the contracts awarded it, the fewer the chances to effect the economies of scale on which its marginal 'profitability' rested. The Municipal Reform conservative majority of 1907 closed down the department in 1909.

Meanwhile, Moderates and later Municipal Reformers had not hesitated in offering their own programme for the workers. They claimed a record of support for trade union rates and hours, after the Progressives had been trounced from office. They preached in favour of the sole use of British firms giving preference to London workmen, and for 'British work to British workmen' – claiming that the 3,000 dismissed Works Department employees were actually busying themselves on other LCC contracts given out to firms in the private sector under the new regime. One tract issued, entitled *Progressives vs Workers: How the Progressives Killed the Building Trades*, promised workers garden cities, pleading: 'Vote solid for Municipal Reform. Fair Hours and Wages and the Policy that will give the London Working Man the work that is his by right.'[44] Of special pride was the presence on the LCC of conservative alderman H. R. Taylor of the bricklayers' union; his name appeared alongside a list of Municipal Reform measures ostensibly in aid of working-class Londoners. The Works Department episode had opened up a floodgate of anti-Progressivism. But it was not in and of itself the party's undoing.

III

Rosebery's original notion that the Progressives could relegate their municipal work to the articulation and promotion of a 'sanitary policy' had obviously proved short-sighted. Mafeking shook the metropolis while the Progressives were in power, recalled by some as a more vibrant series of celebrations than those marking the close of either of the world wars.[45] The LCC parties attempted to outdo each other in constructing a rhetorical link between the municipality and the fate of empire and race, often sharing the national perspectives of the parliamentray parties in the proximate general elections.

John Burns's appeals were rife with such references: 'A world Empire engages your attention, and should secure your devoted energies and thought. All your sobriety, courage, self-sacrifice is needed for London's sake and Britain's future.' He posed the struggle to provide the poor with housing in terms of 'the interests of physique, of morals, of industrial efficiency and municipal health'.[46] There was no need to force the connection – the Progressive programme, including the version stressed by 'Labour' members, could hardly have been construed as disloyal to king and country. The elimination of the poorest conditions and the poorest sections of the working class could only make London and nation more fit.

Another patriotic version of municipalism, skilfully incorporating an advertisement for Irish independence, was the Fabian and ILP call for 'Home Rule for London'. The City Corporation would be suppressed, together with the existing district and vestry boards. LCC powers would be expanded and the administration of the Poor Laws centralized – a classic component of the radical strategy for solving the unsolved problem of London government, and a counterpoint to the Conservative cry for devolution, itself dubbed 'tenefication' by the Progressives.[47]

The Progressives criticized the Moderates' 'misuse' of the imperial notion, accusing their opponents of luring Londoners away from an honest appraisal of the inadequacy of municipal provision. At the same time, the Progressives continued to use imperial imagery to boost their own electoral campaigns. The sticky controversies that caught the Liberal Party nationally in polemic at the time of the Boer conflict illustrate an additional side of Progressivism's instability. In the context of the movement's general appeal to the imperially minded, it still had to reckon with the national Liberal Party issuing pamphlet series like that entitled 'London's Imperial Politics', which sought to distance Liberalism from the particular locus of national imperial rhetoric at that moment. The series included *London and the War*, which nakedly exhibited the internal strife in the party, undermining the unanimity of the imperial appeal. The hostility towards the tone of public celebration was unmitigated:

> Even the working classes themselves, whose motto should always be 'True Imperialism begins at home', had neither eyes nor ears for anything but the South African war. Housing, London education, the taxation of London's fabulous site values – these, and a hundred other questions of pressing communal importance, could barely be mentioned without obvious impatience.[48]

Yet when the Progressives themselves thought back upon their first and only period of power, a sense of imperial mission coloured their memories. In 1924, telling the story of the early LCC, they were quick to proclaim that 'the men who came to the work of London government were kindled by enthusiasm and a belief in the high destinies of London as the Centre of Empire'.[49] It was not surprising that the Municipal Reformers made use of the contradictions. By 1909 they chimed with Rosebery: 'Socialism is the end of all, the negation of faith, of family, of property, of monarchy and of Empire.' They thanked themselves for inaugurating Empire Day in the London schools – the Municipal Reformers could add to the list of gains accruing to London's working class under their steady hand.[50]

In launching aggressive appeals to the prospective women electors, all sides attempted to demonstrate their unique commitments just as they had on imperial issues. But both sides chose the same tack – couching their rhetoric in terms of the special nature of women's knowledge of municipal affairs and the necessity of municipal government becoming the 'housekeeper of the nation'.[51] Thus Mrs Charles Mallet of the Women's Local Government

Society, while acknowledging that men and women share 'indissoluble interests', wrote that county councils might be 'more important and far-reaching over the lives of women than over the lives of men':

> Does it need exhaustive logic to prove that domestic matters . . . are scarcely likely to be understood by the country squire, the busy merchant, the men engrossed with the fluctuations of the Exchange, or the Market, than by those persons who, alike by nature, by tradition, by the practice of many centuries, have become experts in domestic management?[52]

While the Progressives explained that 'women from the mere fact of their sex and their motherhood are usually more sympathetic and more unselfish than men',[53] Municipal Reformers urged women electors

> to bring their shrewd common sense to bear upon practical matters which are far more important to them in their everyday life than imperial affairs . . . if you have no vote persuade your husbands to vote the right ticket and so do something to reduce your household expenses, and to help provide work for the unemployed.[54]

The Progressives coupled their appeal to women as different from men with an admonishment to improve family life and to honour the sanctity of the home by a vote to either party. Municipal life would be culturally uplifting, as Burns explained, speaking of his working-class constituency:

> Many of them know the geneaology of every racehorse since Eclipse. That with them is first; their wives and children and the rest are nowhere . . . to each married man I make this appeal – when you have a spare hour take the missus and children to theatres, music halls, parks, libraries, museums and the number of places of healthy diversion and recreation that the LCC and the State, by Collective effort, have secured for the musical, artistic and recreative enjoyment of all.[55]

The contradictions were rife. A woman was the appendage to her husband, but uniquely equipped to handle municipal affairs. And while each party wooed women voters, who by definition were often unmarried, women's actual representation in the council remained circumscribed by law. Only two Progressive women councillors attempted to take their seats before the 1907 Qualification of Women Act. These were then unseated by the action of Moderate members, though they continued to serve in committee work without the right to hold office. After the 1907 defeat of Progressivism, the Fabian Women's Group and other societies continued the struggle to elect women candidates as Progressives.[56] In 1913 Susan Lawrence was elected as a Labour councillor for Poplar. All parties defended the claim of the LCC as a model employer, exemplified, they argued, by its commitment to hiring women.

LCC hiring patterns and employment practices failed to bring most working-class women into positions of authority in municipal government, though women were visible in the LCC staff in a series of lower-middle-class and professional capacities. They served as typists, attendants in the asylums, teachers, doctors, inspectors of welfare facilities, and charwomen and cleaners. Each job assigned them was perceived as gender-related, and all were governed by a marriage bar that forbade employment beyond the date of matrimony, a stipulation only amended for schoolteachers and upheld until the 1930s. Decision-making roles for women were consistently limited to those related to the tasks of ministering to London's poorer inhabitants (and especially to women and children), or carrying out the assignments set by male colleagues of superior station within the LCC bureaucracy.[57]

IV

A principally middle-class group of women, LCC employees as well as volunteers in agencies like the Child Care Committees in the schools, replicated many aspects of the social relations common to the Victorian charity tradition in their work. With the authority of the law and the ostentatious power of the LCC behind them, these women encountered complaints and criticisms of council intrusion into the daily lives of Londoners, on the one hand, and the charge of inadequate facilities and care, on the other. As the duties of the council expanded to reach deeper and deeper into London's neighbourhoods, men and especially women, who had not confronted the state in this form before, became objects of LCC policy.

The Public Control and Public Health departments of the council were pivotal to the task of the regulation of everyday London life. Though hamstrung by limits on their powers and the failure of many efforts at municipalization, these committees, with their growing inspectorates, attempted to carry out systematic reform of the habits and practices of the public in many spheres. They were very often assisted by neighbours who reported on neighbours or by shop-owners who notified the council of the infringements of their competitors.

The unsanitary conditions of life prevailing in much of the metropolis prompted council scrutiny. The maintenance of drainage and sewage facilities often preoccupied an inspectorate besieged with reports of persons of bad character using passages as urinals, of defective WCs, of blocked drains, or of cats, pigeons, pigs, and illegal cowsheds prompting fear of disease. There were complaints of unsanitary basement workrooms where kitchens and WCs sat side by side (one restaurant beneath the Strand had a pony stable in the kitchen), and of workers often sleeping near the sewage drainpipes of an entire house, in unventilated rooms. A typical complaint from residents of New Bond Street alleged the 'overcrowded condition of a workroom occupied by foreign Jews' and the 'nuisance of dogs in one of the rooms and the absence of adequate wc's in the workshop'.[58] Organizations like the Ladies' Sanitary Association assisted the LCC in ferreting out offenders.

Smoke and river pollution led the council to prosecute some industrial firms, but much of it came from the one million chimneys in use daily across London; regulating these clearly involved the vigilance of neighbours who objected to the smoke and assisted in the notification of individual householders. Without door-to-door surveys and massive public expenditure much went undone in the cause of sanitation. *The Times* taunted: 'So we have bands in the parks, "steam yachts" as Sir J. W. Benn has happily called them on the river, empty trams on the Embankment and sewage in the basement . . . purity in the music hall and sewage in the home.'[59]

The parks and open spaces of London were under LCC control, and here vagrants and persons engaging in unlawful acts were singled out by the constabulary. Forbidden were 'brawling, fighting, quarrelling, cursing, swearing or using indecent or improper language, or holding or taking part in any running, boxing, wrestling or walking match. Being intoxicated, gambling, playing at any game of cards or dice'; the list of offences is lengthy.[60] In the markets, the council sought not only to gain municipal control in the long run, but to force the hands of costers who sold surplus vegetables at a lower price than the operators of covered stalls and to clear the streets of barrows blocking the businesses of more respectable grocers.[61]

With the passage of the Shop Hours Act of 1892, between 20,000 and 25,000 shops of all description came under council purview. Shopkeepers were forced to display notices acknowledging the illegality of employing under-age children for excessive hours.

It was estimated that 50,000 schoolchildren worked out of school hours in London. By 1900, 113,000 shops had been investigated. A Seats Act of 1899, partly the result of trade union lobbying, further protected employees and made shop-owners more vulnerable to fines.[62] Outworkers were also investigated by the council, and WC facilities were forced upon employers who had often failed to provide separate toilets for men and women. Bread now had to be weighed before being sold. Publicans had to use official glass measures, 35,000 of which were checked in 1894–5 alone. Carmen who worked for coal merchants were followed through the London streets by inspectors who watched as they sold quantities of coal on the side before making their appointed deliveries. An elaborate illicit market in coal was unearthed and to a great extent obliterated.[63]

The preoccupation of the LCC with the fate of women and children, signalling its involvement in a national debate on provision, informed much of the regulatory legislation.[64] Employment agencies specializing in work for governesses and domestic servants were often covers for prostitution rings and were assailed by the council. Laundries, barbers, hairdressers, and massage parlours were licensed, with careful attention to the sleeping areas for women located on the premises of such businesses.[65]

The traffic in children and the concerns prompted by infant mortality rates resulted in part in the Acts governing midwifery, infant life protection, and children. After March 1905 a woman could not practise as a midwife without registering and being periodically inspected. Her home, medical paraphernalia, and her person were checked. This led to prosecutions of midwives who bartered in babies or were intoxicated or unclean while assisting deliveries or when under inspection. Similarly, the Infant Life Protection Act of 1897 stipulated that children under 5 in paid care for more than forty-eight hours be registered with the police; it was estimated that 90 per cent of the infants in registered houses were illegitimate. Again the LCC uncovered a network, used not simply by working women whose children were watched by others, but by families who were seeking to keep scandalous pregnancies and unwanted children off the public record.[66] These and other dimensions of LCC work often raised ethical and moral conflicts for the staff, who for this particular work 'were in touch with police, poor law officers, registrars of births and deaths and other officials whose duties were likely to bring them in contact with infants kept apart from their mothers'.[67]

Lodging-houses were inspected for VD cases and provided the LCC with a base to watch for outbreaks of contagious diseases, especially those thought to be 'tramp-borne'. Again, without house-to-house inspection the council found its results limited. In lodging-houses frequented by the very poor (and the council was careful to make such categorizations), residents often did not bake or wash their clothes for months. In the early 1900s the LCC established its own municipal lodging-houses while advocating the closure of shelters and food-halls for 29,000 London vagrants, insisting that such charity facilities were a stimulus to idleness. In its view, the more respectable of the homeless ought to have been sent to labour colonies. These proposals reflect LCC hostility to the prevailing charity organizations, many of which enjoyed special exemption from municipal regulation.[68]

Finally, in their last years of power, the Progressives began to administer the highly controversial 1902 Education Act, and through the medium of the schools made further inroads into the domestic lives of Londoners. The schools were in many ways the principal institutions of LCC regulation in its most refined and comprehensive mode. Curriculum, files and records of families and children, cleansing and haircutting, attendance officers – all these provided links between the LCC and a wide spectrum of London's inhabitants.[69]

The council began to see its educational work as

eugenic work . . . for the healthy development of the mass of normal children; the special and industrial schools branch . . . makes the best of what is recognized as human debris . . . the council is attempting to touch, as far as it can, the cause of the child's ill-health, malnutrition or neglect – not in the school but in the home.[70]

As early as 1897, before becoming the school authority, under the Cleansing of Persons Act the LCC had gained the right to purify, strip, or even destroy homes in which contagious diseases were found or reported. If such were not reported, the household faced fines. As a school authority, the LCC acquired further rights. Parents who repeatedly failed to assist in improving their children's health were also subject to prosecution; and towards the end of the period, molestation and child abuse cases were seen as new areas of work.[71]

V

Such legislation, initiated under the Progressives, was largely upheld by their Conservative rivals after 1907. While Municipal Reform failed to seize control of vital public utilities because of its principled opposition to state ownership and its own vested business interests, it did persist in the quest for greater regulation of everyday life even as the Progressives had done.

But it was the Progressives who had inaugurated many of the policies and bore the stigma (when it had to be borne), of greatest association; this was notoriously so in the case of their music-hall purification campaign. If a single characterization was linked with the Progressives in the minds of Londoners even more than the grand proposals for municipalization, it was the charge of 'municipal puritanism' – the prudish, 'Paul Pry' reputation earned in their attempts to pursue a harsher licensing policy; 'faddists, pharisees and prowling prudes' were the charges one Progressive recalled.[72]

The responsibility for licensing many kinds of places of public entertainment had devolved on to the LCC from the justices. Yet the council's role under the Progressives was not that of censoring lyrics and cancelling performances because of lascivious sexual allusion. The council's central concern, as in all other matters, was the political task of obtaining wider powers from Parliament, in this instance the right to oversee all of London's theatres. This was an effort that failed to win the support of the national Liberal Party leadership, who clearly had no desire to alienate those of the London *rentier bourgeoisie* who would have been more heavily taxed under the Progressive proposals.[73]

Although the LCC Theatres and Music Halls Committee members acknowledged privately (and indeed to Asquith, Home Secretary) that they had not used their fledgling inspectorate to assist in closing down halls because of the nature of performances, the contrary impression left among Londoners was indelible – the Progressives were never to shrug it off. Their alcohol policy, which forbade consumption in any newly opened halls, and the attack on prostitution so dominant in the Empire Music Hall campaign, contributed to a divided response to LCC policy. Temperance groups, ratepayer associations, and religious bodies petitioned the council in support of its campaign; some trade unions and citizen groups from a variety of London neighbourhoods opposed it. Thousands of Londoners participated in the music-halls campaigns by lending their names and voices to one of the opposing sides.[74]

The net result of Progressive policy in the halls was to circumscribe performance nominally rather than to effect a fundamental change in preoccupation or sentiment. Proprietors did submit lyrics to the committee on occasion, while inspectors made notes of objectionable verses and scenes, but the principal decisions taken by the committee in the licensing sessions were made on the basis of faulty structures, unsafe gangways, and substandard dressing and lavatory facilities. Halls were rarely closed down. Music-hall programmes maintained their fidelity to the caricature of domestic life (the slavery of marriage, the insipidness of the respectable workman, the cuckold husband, the conniving wife) and of the aristocrat and politician as buffoon, and paid homage to Crown and empire. What did change was the growing tendency to characterize the Progressives as the *Financial News* had done, as 'prudish, pious linen-drapers and buttermen'.[75]

But we should not be content with a description of the Progressives as killjoys, puritan intruders into an authentically populist mode of everyday life; the purveyors of a stultifying moral vision in the face of genuinely proletarian forms of leisure. For Londoners tended to participate in a diverse metropolitan culture, as influenced by the presence of the imperial and national capital as by the inherited pleasures more indigenous to the poorer haunts of the East End. The Progressives could easily have convinced themselves of their mission – the eradication of poverty and the furtherance of a cultural code of conduct in keeping with the preferences of one of their prime constituencies: the anti-aristocratic, modestly educated 'lower-middle-class' Nonconformist. Creating a civic culture, at once humane for the deserving and punitive for the corrupt or dissolute, still seemed a worthy endeavour to many in the metropolis. One striking case reveals the complex nature of state intervention in general in the years before the First World War.

The Olympia Theatre offered a show in 1900 featuring African 'natives' performing in military scenes of the Boer War. These Africans were forced to reside in unkempt huts equipped with only the most minimal hygienic facilities – a basement trough served as a toilet. The surrounding neighbourhood of Earls Court became the scene of an Edwardian moral panic when black performers purportedly behaved aggressively towards white women in the vicinity of the hall. The LCC was besieged with requests to act, much as it was by music-hall vigilantes. In this instance, however, Progressive moral fervour was not unleashed upon prostitutes, pub owners, or lecherous and 'indecent' music-hall performers, but on the Barnum & Bailey London representative, who was summarily accused of inhuman treatment of 'the natives'. They were shipped back to Africa after the LCC refused to continue to license the Olympia.[76]

Those Londoners who had toured the 'native encampment', observing the Africans cooking, eating, and sleeping in their 'natural environment', or had felt the exotic and fearsome presence of Africans with pay-packets in their pockets drifting through what must have seemed the very foreign soil of Earls Court, witnessed this act of intervention on behalf of an exploited minority of near-slave labourers. The case did not perhaps appear different in kind from those involving the supervision of neighbourhood facilities or the halls where white performers worked. But it does offer a distinct and provocative example of an incident that will have made the Progressives feel especially self-righteous. They had satisfied those advocating charity towards performers who were seen as racial inferiors, the religious lobby advocating the abolition of inhumane conditions, and the panicked residents of Earls Court, who wished to repossess their streets. In this instance, the convolution of racial fear, moral mandate, and state prerogative provided a platform for the Progressive quest. Cases like that of the Olympia kept alive the fires ignited in the musichall controversies, no doubt contributing to Progressive myopia. The demonstration of their power to regulate and to satisfy one grumbling group of protesters only served to underline the potential abuse of Progressive powers for others.

The regulation of areas of everyday life forced the Progressives to confront a multiplicity of political forces and groups in London, even apart from the election periods, and this was a task for which the movement was ill suited. The Progressives' stance on public morality left them especially vulnerable; not surprisingly, defection occurred within their own ranks. Radical Anglican cleric and Progressive LCC councillor Stewart Headlam wrote polemics condemning 'municipal puritanism', while the Metropolitan Radical Federation (purveyor of local government reform and a bastion of the clubs' movement and nineteenth-century trade unionism) ratified a motion in solidarity with one of Headlam's ripostes: 'We welcome and will accord our support to any effort to infuse a more liberal spirit into the administration of our music halls, theatres, parks and open spaces.'[77]

Headlam wrote of the LCC 'damaging' the cause of socialism by association, and of his own party's reprehensible 'appetite for managing other people's lives'.[78] Mark Judge's Entertainment Reform League and the Puritan League for the Defence of the People's Pleasure also formed to oppose Progressive policies, as if to warn that there was not a winning basis of unity to be had in the cultivation of a priggish and intrusive reputation.[79]

Hardly an entrepôt of devout church-goers, hegemonic temperance movements, or the 'stable family life' stereotypically associated with the northern and Midlands industrial towns, London fostered its own diverse and unique cultural life. Dens of hedonism, pockets of atheism and feminism, swarms of those whom Hugh McLeod identified as 'lapsed chapel-goers, young men and women with a sense of commitment and capacity for reading that the chapel demanded, freed from compromises with the establishment' – these thrived in the metropolis.[80] One in ten employed males was a clerk. Such pleasure-seeking bed-sitter lodgers, along with many women from provincial areas, came to serve the new commercial and financial establishments of the empire city, swelling the 'lower-middle-class' work-force at the century's end with a ready music-hall audience. Young men and women, whose chief desire was for a place to live more central than the boring and pedestrian suburban villadom to which they found themselves consigned, shared lodgings and rented houses together.[81]

Despite the assumptions of the movement's leadership, the undynamic and puritanical aspects of Progressivism may well have been as unappealing to London's newest and fastest-growing sector of the population as it was to the trade union supporters of 'Sunday evenings for the people'.[82] Though there were many vocal advocates of vigilance and purity, in elections numbers counted for more than shrill voices. It is arguably the case that no new votes accrued to the Progressives as a result of their moral policy. Instead, in consonance with other areas of doubt about them, this aspect of Progressivism offered grounds for political alienation and even disloyalty.

VI

The most notorious propaganda of the early LCC campaigns accompanied the contest of 1907. Avner Offer, Kenneth Young, and others have described the aggressive and hostile anti-socialist posters and broadsheets whose creators followed the lead provided by the lengthy critique of municipal socialism published in *The Times* in 1902. The election witnessed the first assault on an ostensible left by the Northcliffe press, opening a new and seemingly permanent chapter in party-political diatribe. The Conservatives had a field-day with the Works Department, the unremunerative Thames steamboat scheme, the rising rates. The beleaguered onlooker and potential elector was the object of continuous attempts at persuasion, shock, and exposé – all directed at convincing him of the corruption, scandal, and misuse of funds proffered by an embattled Progressivism. One infamous Trafalgar Square rally, staged by the Municipal Reformers, was the scene of a major riot provoked by groups of supporters attacking each other and suppressed only by police intervention.[83]

Significantly, the labour question occupied a central place in the campaign. The Municipal Reformers had moved closer to the Progressive rhetorical stance on labour issues, arguing that their opponents had engaged in dubious experimentation at the expense (quite literally) of their labour constituency. Quality workmanship, they said, had suffered. 'Trade union wages' was the battle-cry of the mediocre, opportunist workman; they, Municipal Reform, had upheld the cry for 'fair wages' instead. The casual labourers and tradesmen of the building industry (certainly a majority of building workers) had been neglected by the Progressives. Given Conservative support for many 'working-class reforms', Progressive claims far outstripped their accomplishments. Poverty and unemployment, the Municipal Reformers noted, lingered even as the rates increased.[84]

The London Trades Council, voice of the skilled and organized sectors of London's work-force, provided a forum for the incremental labour defection from the Progressive fold. Some few independent labour candidates had always run in LCC elections, and others had sat on the Progressive 'labour bench'. The LTC had controlled aldermanic posts and kept certain councillors on wages raised by the unions through shop-floor collections. But, as time wore on, the loose electoral commitment to Progressivism faced vocal challenges in the LTC as candidates were vetted more closely for their stances on labour issues.[85] A majority of LTC representatives, who stood for 60,000 trade union members in London, began to voice disenchantment with a broad range of Progressive policies and especially with the LCC's treatment of its own work-force. This excerpt from the *Trades and Labour Gazette*, organ of the LTC, captures the bitterness felt in labour circles over the Progressive housing policy. It was issued on the morning of the party's 1907 defeat:

The Progressives have been routed at the County Council elections and they are surprised. Why they should be surprised is hard to imagine, for what, in the name of goodness, have they ever done to stir up the enthusiasm of the worker to whom they look for support?

They are supposed to take up a Collectivist policy and to municipalize all the services, but they have attempted this in such a fainthearted way that they have actually estranged those who gave them a vote thinking that they would pursue a vigorous policy to establish municipalization. When he turns to the housing policy of the Progressives he finds that they will provide him with a rabbit-hutch in a back street at a higher rental than the capitalist. The Tories know well sooner or later the Liberal party will be divided into two camps, one favouring individualism and the other collectivism. The Progressives are really between two stools and are bound to come to grief. Having had an opportunity to justify their existence and neglected it, we see no reason to pity them.[86]

In the election, the LTC endorsed only certain Progressives. Their own programme called for direct labour, for the creation of a labour exchange and work for the unemployed, and for metropolitan-wide wage standards in municipal employment. They often petitioned for municipal workshops, especially for the production of clothing, as an antidote to sweating, and called for the creation of a variety of public institutions from a 'municipal theatre for the working man' to fair-rent courts.[87] While the failure of Progressivism to maintain the fidelity of the LTC *per se* did not cost the party the election, it cost it the opportunity for building up a wider constituency amongst those who might have offered it greatest support – the enfranchised working class.[88]

As some trade unionists moved away from the Progressives towards independent candidates, the London Labour Party took its earliest organizing steps for the purpose of participating in the 1913 LCC election. Other voices hounded Progressivism from right and left. The Archbishop of Canterbury thought that the LCC had not been hard enough on the music-hall owners; the Free Trade in Amusements lobby criticized the council for placing a damper on artistic freedom. The Women's Industrial Council wanted more facilities for working women. The LCC Staff Association demanded fairer conditions and higher pay for LCC clerks, while the manual grades – asylum workers, the men who managed the sludge vessels, the parks attendants – and the schoolteachers formed the core groups of the Municipal Employees' Association, the National Union of Public Employees, and the National Union of Teachers branches that would grow throughout the vast service.[89] Besieged on all fronts, the Progressives went down in ignominious defeat. In the aftermath lingered the talk of socialism, the municipal cants, the forgotten creeds of LCC collectivism, and home rule for London.

Conclusion

In 1902 John Burns responded to the charge that the Progressives had not succeeded in rehousing the very poor of London:

These are objections not against the Council, but are due to causes that are economic, personal or industrial. If the LCC rents are too high it would be a mistake to lower the rent by reducing the standard of tenements and degrading the character of accommodation. This would defeat the real end of housing, which is better, cleaner and larger homes. Better that wages should follow rent than that rent be adapted to wages. Then cheap house rent at the community expense would be grant in aid to lower wages, which must be enormously raised if industry, efficiency and hygienic comfort are to be maintained.[90]

And after the 1907 defeat of his party, John Benn said of the early Progressive administrations that all had been done, 'not as a first step to the end of all things', but for the express purpose of giving private enterprise increased opportunity. Sidney Webb had defended the Works Department in 1894 as a chance for the best contractors in the private sector to thrive at the expense of the worst – the LCC would set a competitive standard with which to drive the jerry-builders to ruin.[91]

It is a hallmark of the period that the various socialisms and social reformist currents were informed by theories of meritocracy and the competitive ethos of Social Darwinism and positivism. Benn, Burns, and Webb all shared these influences, and the municipal socialism at the root of the Progressivist consensus displayed them. Exemplary housing, exemplary business acumen, exemplary tenants, exemplary builders – these were to act as beacons for the lower forms of metropolitan life. Tipping their hats to the wealthier contractors who would pay trade union wages, asking the poor to postpone their aspirations in favour of Burns's 'labour aristocracy', allowing time for the Webbian bureaucrats to permeate further, all rested upon the belief in the inevitable triumph of London democracy, to be realized in the popular electoral mandate of a greatly socialized London economy. The fledgling steps taken in that direction formed the Progressive 'accomplishment', from the Boundary Street estate to the Blackwall Tunnel. But the vision did not prove palatable to enough Londoners to allow the Progressives to keep on winning elections.[92]

The Progressives rallied their defective trade union allies to fight unsuccessfully in the two remaining pre-war contests. R. C. K. Ensor, Susan Lawrence (a former Conservative), and Will Crooks formed the new Labour bench, refusing to bind themselves to the Progressive rump. By 1913 only Lawrence was left, and she and others had run for office independently, shedding the Progressive stigma. In 1913 the remaining Progressives concentrated their rhetorical attack upon the greedy – a line of least resistance. Out of office, they picked up on a strand of municipalism evident in pre-1907 conservative talk, claiming that they were the best cultivators of viable ground for business. But the claim did not convince; the tide had turned, and Municipal Reform would hold office until 1934.[93]

On the eve of the First World War, then, Londoners inhabited a civic realm of a very different order than that of the late nineteenth century. But to understand the changes in the dynamic of London politics as determined by the rising costs of municipal improvement (as reflected in the rates) or the party-political alignments at the national level is, in a sense, to turn the argument on its head. Perceptions of popular political attitudes in London had a great deal to do with motivating politicians both to demand or to criticize rate rises and to expand county party organization. Further, we cannot explain Progressivism's failure as a failure of Liberalism *per se*. The Liberals carried London overwhelmingly in the 1906 general election just one year before the LCC débâcle; to be sure, Conservative fears of a conspiracy in national and municipal policy fuelled their fighting spirit and their desperate tactics in 1907. But the earlier Liberal administrations had been loath to extend powers to the Progressives in many instances – and the Londoner had often voted differentially in national and local elections without party fidelity. The Progressives had consciously weakened their ties to the National Liberal Federation after 1902 in a bid to placate Liberal Unionists and labour supporters. The hostility to the Conservative Education Act of that same year, which greatly assisted the Liberal 1906 victories in London, played the opposite role in 1907; there was sufficient discord over Progressive willingness to carry out the Act to alienate some of the party's Nonconformist supporters. It was no coincidence that the expenses that came with the absorption of the school board forced the greatest rate rises of the Progressive period. Contention over this issue explains some of the disjunction between the 1906 and 1907 results, but it hardly serves to account for Conservative strength as a whole.[94] Nor was the 1907 defeat of Progressivism simply a precursor of Liberal decline nationally. Those who voted for Municipal Reform, or who did not bother to go and vote for the Progressives, were not necessarily doing so out of support for the Conservative Party or out of antipathy towards official Liberalism.

The deeper forces addressed in this essay are those that will have challenged Londoners to ask, over and over, what are the rates paying *for*? Thus popular political programmes and their extensions in policy were themselves inspired by judgements about the predilections of Londoners. The prospects and hopes for the metropolis conjured up by the politicians for those who in turn had to live with the realities of LCC accomplishments were calculated to meet the perceived practical needs of the elector, to cultivate his or her cultural and moral sensibilities. No candidate or party leader wanted to be seen as a pickpocket at best. Ironically, Progressivism, artificially created to offer an image of a 'party above politics', fundamentally misjudged both the flexibility of capital and the receptivity of labour. Its assault on the private sector, however quixotic, raised fears of state socialism, while some of its social policies invited its critics to call for a defence of their civil liberties. While the middle-class electorate decided the final electoral result in 1907, by dividing its affections at best, it was not without elaborate attempts on the part of all participants, throughout the Progressive years, to curry favour with a working class – some of whose members became bitterly disillusioned. Just as initial Progressive success constituted a limited left victory, so this disillusionment with them lay at the heart of the 'failure of London socialism', of which we need to know much more.[95]

Thus far, many interpretations of the origins of anti-statism and anti-socialism have identified a nineteenth-century legacy of working-class suspicion of social welfare measures, often assigning significance to the defensive creation of a separate working-class culture, which in London in particular is thought to have been apolitical and socially conservative. This essay presents other ways of accounting for the variety of anti-statist expressions that have occurred since the days of London Progressivism. The significant popular appeal of ameliorative interventionist proposals is undeniable. At first, many, many Londoners wanted to see the promulgation of measures that would create a higher standard of living, even as they did in 1945. The character of their contact with the local state, *not their distance from it*, seems to have highlighted the contradictions so apparent in the electoral propaganda of the municipal parties. For many, the LCC was not the authoritarian state – it was the niggling state, the bureaucrat always there when you do not need him, never there when you do; the champion of lost causes whose real day-to-day workings were just as likely to annoy as to console. The enthusiasm for radical change and the ultimate abandonment of a leading party is hardly peculiar to London at the turn of the century. Recent British history is characterized by the repeated alienation of the populace from state practices which were initially eagerly awaited. The Progressive moment was an early signpost in a process which is still unfolding and deserves our attention.

Notes

I am grateful to Gareth Stedman Jones, Jennifer Davis, and especially David Feldman for their comments on this essay, and to those who discussed an earlier version of it in the Social History Seminar, King's College, Cambridge, in May 1987. I thank John Mason for his assistance in its final preparation. The essay draws upon research originally funded by Girton College, Cambridge. I received further support from the NEH Summer Stipend Program, 1985, and from Trinity College, Hartford, Connecticut. Archival entries from the holdings of the Greater London Record Office are abbreviated below; entries refer to the papers of the public health (PH), public control (PC), works (WKS), and education (EO) committees of the LCC as well as other documents.

With regard to the quotation in the title of this essay, John Benn, cited in A. G. Gardiner, *John Benn and the Progressive Movement*, 1925, p. 98 (*Daily Telegraph*, 28 January 1920), recalled the LCC's first meeting in 1889: 'The Progressives outnumbered the Moderates by a majority of two to one, and were already full of great schemes, mostly framed to secure a millennium for London by return of post.'

1 See, e.g., parts of the argument of P. Thompson, *Socialists, Liberals and Labour*, 1967, pp. 2, 294–5; G. Stedman Jones, 'Working-class culture and working-class politics in London', in G. Stedman Jones, *Languages of Class*, Cambridge, 1983. For important revisions of the provincial case, see P. Clarke, *Lancashire and the New Liberalism*, Cambridge, 1971; P. Joyce, *Work, Society and Politics*, Brighton, 1980.

2 For arguments concerning forms of popular anti-socialism and anti-statism, see H. Pelling, 'The working class and the welfare state', in H. Pelling, *Popular Politics and Society in Late Victorian Britain*, Cambridge, 1968; Stedman Jones, op. cit.; Norman McCord, 'Rate-payers and social policy', in P. Thane (ed.), *The Origins of British Social Policy*, 1978; P. Thane, 'The working class and state "welfare" in Britain, 1880–1914', *Historical Journal*, 27, 4, 1984; Jane Lewis, 'The working-class wife and mother and state intervention, 1870–1918', in J. Lewis (ed.), *Labour and Love*, Oxford, 1986.

3 For the history of London government and the LCC, see: Thompson, op. cit.; D. Owen, *The Government of Victorian London*, Cambridge, Mass., 1982; J. Davis, *Reforming London*, Oxford, 1988; G. Gibbon and R. W. Bell, *History of the London County Council*, 1939; K. Young, *Local Politics and the Rise of Party*, Leicester, 1975; J. R. Kellett, 'Municipal socialism, enterprise and trading in the Victorian city', in *Urban History Yearbook*, 1978, pp. 36–45; A. Offer, *Property and Politics*, Cambridge, 1981; S. D. Pennybacker, 'The "labour question" and the London County Council, 1889–1919', unpublished Ph.D. thesis, Cambridge University, 1984. On Progressivism, see: Gardiner, op. cit.; P. Clarke, 'The Progressive movement in England', *Transactions of the Royal Historical Society*, 5th series, vol.

24, 1974; Michael Freeden, *The New Liberalism*, Oxford, 1978, ch. II;
P. Garside and K. Young, *Metropolitan London*, 1982, chs III–V.

4 *Star*, 3 January 1889, p. 2 (Massingham's pro-Progressive newspaper).
5 ibid., 9 January 1889, p. 2.
6 Gardiner, op. cit., p. 132.
7 See P. Clarke. 'The Progressive movement', op. cit.; Freeden, op. cit.
8 For aggregate electoral data, see Garside and Young, op. cit., p. 343.
No greater percentage of electors voted in an LCC election nor in any
Greater London Council election (the LCC's successor). In 1889 the
Progressives and Liberals won 73 seats, the Moderates 45; 500,000
voted in a 50 per cent poll. In 1907 Municipal Reform (former
Moderates) won 79 seats, the Progressives 37 (two seats went to Labour
and an Independent); 840,730 voted in a 55.5 per cent poll (ibid.). On
the franchise, see Thompson, op. cit., pp. 70, 80; Young, op. cit., p. 96.
Lodgers were briefly in the electorate during the 1907 contest and helped
it swell to its greatest pre-1914 strength; over a half million tended to
vote. Yet the potential electorate may only have been slightly larger
than Thompson's estimates of the parliamentary electorate: one-fifth
of residents of middle-class districts, one-tenth of residents of inner-
London working-class districts. P. Hollis, *Ladies Elect*, Oxford, 1987,
discusses women and the LCC franchise.
9 On rate rises, see Davis, *Reforming*, op. cit., pp. 141–75, appendix III,
pp. 264–75; Gibbon and Bell, op. cit., pp. 100–1. John Mason has
assisted in establishing an estimate of Progressive gains and losses in
1907, comparing data from *The Times* and the *East End Observer* with
categories established by Charles Booth and employed by P. Thompson
(see Thompson, op. cit., appendix A, p. 304). The abstention rate was
often at 50 per cent; the Municipal Reformers received 240,846 votes
in 1907, the Progressives 195,558 (S. Knott, *The Electoral Crucible:
The Politics of London, 1900–14*, 1977, p. 97).
10 The explanation of 1907 as an affirmation of a pre-existing Conservative
voting pattern, or even in terms of Unionist fears of official
Liberalism, becomes a tautology in the light of this essay's concerns;
e.g. Young, op. cit., pp. 93–7, which concludes: 'The Municipal
Reform victory of 1907 was, then, no aberration; the passage of time
which elapsed before it was achieved is more surprising than the
eventual result.'
11 *Star*, 12 January 1889, p. 2.
12 ibid., 7 January 1889, p. 1.
13 ibid., 8 January 1889, p. 2.
14 ibid., 14 January 1889, p. 1.
15 *Spectator*, 26 March 1892, p. 426; Fardell chaired the metropolitan
division of the National Union, 1896–1912 (Young, op. cit., p. 14).
16 See, e.g., *The Unemployed*, Fabian Society Tract no. 47, 1893.
17 ibid., p. 18; 'reduction' refers to reducing the numbers of unemployed.
18 ibid., p. 13; S. Pennybacker, 'New unionism and socialism . . .',
University of Pennsylvania, 1977, author's possession.

19 *The Unemployed*, op. cit., p. 5.
20 *The Straight Tip to Workers: Brains Better Than Bets or Beer*, Clarion Pamphlet no. 36, 1902, p. 5.
21 e.g. *Municipalisation of the Gas Supply*, Fabian Municipal Programme no. 32, 3rd edn, 1896.
22 *The Fabian Election Manifesto, for the General Election, 1892*, 1892.
23 ibid.
24 See the brilliant discussion of the London property question in Offer, op. cit.
25 Fabian Society tracts: *London's Water Tribute*, no. 34, p. 216; *The Municipalisation of the London Docks*, no. 35, p. 219.
26 Society of Arts, *The Cost of Municipal Trading*, 1903, pp. 2, 6.
27 For another cautious approach to municipalization, see Emil Garcke, 'The limitations of municipal enterprise', paper read before the National Liberal Club Political and Economic Circle, 24 October 1900.
28 *Annual Report, 1892–93*, p. 18; E. Bristow, 'The Liberty and Property Defence League and individualism', *Historical Journal*, XVIII, 1975, pp. 761–89.
29 *Report of the Proceedings at the First Annual Dinner of the LPDL, July 12, 1888*, 1888; *Second Annual Dinner, 1889, Report of Proceedings and Speeches*, 1889; and ibid.; The *ER*'s editor attended the second dinner, calling the LPDL's principles those of the early *ER*; for an analysis of the latter, see B. Fontana, *Rethinking the Politics of Commercial Society: The Edinburgh Review, 1802–32*, Cambridge, 1985, p. 183; Freeden sees the LPDL as Spencerian, op. cit., p. 33.
30 'Municipal socialism', 1892.
31 *Annual Report 1892–93*, op. cit., p. 11.
32 ibid., pp. 10, 16.
33 *First Annual Dinner*, op. cit., p. 37.
34 LMS, *Socialism and the Progress of the Working Classes . . .*, n.d.
35 LPDL, *Second Annual Dinner*, op. cit., p. 36; H. T. Muggeridge (ILP), *The Anti-Municipal Conspiracy Exposed*, 1903; McCord, op. cit.
36 LPDL, *Annual Report, 1893–94*, p. 11.
37 Pennybacker, 'The "labour question"', op. cit., ch. II.
38 ibid., chs II, III.
39 'The latest socialist scheme', *Spectator*, 17 December 1892, p. 880.
40 ibid.
41 Pennybacker, 'The "labour question"', op. cit., ch. III; WKS/GEN/1/1.
42 ibid.; *The Times*, statement by Sir Arthur Arnold, 26 May 1897, p. 1.
43 Burns, 'The unemployed', op. cit., p. 13; WKS/GEN/1/1; Pennybacker, 'The "labour question"', op. cit., ch. III.
44 See, e.g., the London Municipal Reform leaflets: *Municipal Reform vs Progressive Socialism*, n.d., post-1910; and *Progressives vs Workers*, n.d., pre-1907.
45 Ada Reeves, *Take It for a Fact*, 1954, p. 89.
46 *The Straight Tip to Workers*, op. cit.

47 e.g. *Questions for LCC Councillors*, Fabian Society Tract no. 26, 1893; 'tenefication' was derived from an early proposal to form ten corporations from the existing parliamentary boroughs (Young, op. cit., p. 54, fn. 77).

48 London Liberal Federation, *London's Place in Imperial Politics*, no. 6: Dr Macnamara, MP, '*London and the South African War – an Indictment of the Cabinet*, n.d., post-1903, pp. 11–12.

49 Nettie Adler (London Progressive Association), *London Women and the LCC*, 1924, p. 5.

50 London Municipal Reform Leaflet no. 103, *Labour and Municipal Reform*, 1908. Rosebery's speech of 9 September 1909 is cited in Municipal Reform, *Municipal Reform vs Progressive Socialism*, op. cit., p. 3.

51 Mrs Charles Mallett, Women's Local Government Society, *Shall Women Be Eligible to Serve on County Councils?*, 1895, p. 3. See Hollis, op. cit., chs 6, 7, 10.

52 ibid., p. 3.

53 Ursula M. Bright, *To the Electors of the LCC: An Appeal*, Progressive Leaflet no. 10, n.d., p. 1.

54 London Municipal Reform leaflet, *Appeal to Women Voters*, 1903.

55 *The Straight Tip to Workers*, op. cit.

56 Hollis, op. cit., ch. 6; Fabian Women's Group, *Three Years' Work, 1908–11*, 1911; Pennybacker, 'The "labour question"', op. cit., appendix; Fabian Women's Group, Minutes, vol. I, 1908–10, offers evidence of FWG electoral work with the Progressives in the years just before the war.

57 Pennybacker, 'The "labour question"', op. cit., chs I, IV, V; 'Topics of the day, the employment of married women', *Daily Graphic*, 8 April 1914, and 'Is your charwoman married?', *Daily Sketch*, 10 April 1914; D. Copelman, 'A new comradeship between men and women: family, marriage and London's women teachers, 1870–1914', in Lewis (ed.), op. cit.; M. Zemmick, 'Jobs for girls: the expansion of clerical work for women, 1850–1914', in A. John (ed.), *Unequal Opportunities: Women's Employment in England, 1800–1918*, 1986.

58 For a general account, see Anthony S. Wohl, *Endangered Lives: Public Health in Victorian Britain*, 1983. See PC/GEN/1/8; PH/REG/5/2; LCC/MIN/10,025; PH/GEN/2/19; LCC/MIN/9642; New Bond Street citation appears in PH/REG/5/2, no. 64.

59 See PC/GEN/1/8, which specifically responds to the Interdepartmental Committee on Physical Degeneration; PC/GEN/1/4; PC/GEN/1/34; 'Story of the LCC', *The Times*, 21 January 1907.

60 LCC Parks and Open Spaces, vol. I, 1903, 'Parks Staff Regulations', p. 96; see also LCC/MIN/8823.

61 See PC/GEN/1/8; PC/SHO/3/6; PC/GEN/2/18; PC/SHO/3/8; PC/GEN/1/4, 1894–5, e.g. 10 June 1902, comments on Commercial Road, Stepney: 'the Jews have attempted to establish a market in these streets, but at present time only barrows are used and the police keep the costers moving'; LCC, Minutes, 19 November 1901, indicate that

Sir Samuel Montagu pressured the LCC to take control of the markets in 1893 and 1894.

62 PC/GEN/2/18, p. 17; PC/SHO/3/7; PC/SHO/3/9, 25 April 1912.

63 PH/GEN/2/19; PC/WM/3/15; PC/GEN/1/4, annual report 1893–4; PC/ GEN/2/18, annual report 1892–3; PC/WM/3/4; LCC/MIN/9667.

64 See J. Lewis, *The Politics of Motherhood*, 1980; Deborah Dwork, *War Is Good for Babies and Other Young Children*, 1987; Deborah Thom, 'The ideology of women's work, 1914–24 . . .'. unpublished Ph.D. thesis, Thames Polytechnic, 1982; PC/GEN/1/4, annual reports 1892– 3, 1903–4; PC/MASS/2/1; PC/EMP/3/1.

65 PH/GEN/1/2; PC/GEN/1/4, reports for 1893–7; LCC Public Control Committee, 'Misc. repts of James Ollis, chief officer, on infant life protection'; LCC/MIN/8670; PH/GEN/1/2.

66 PH/GEN/1/2, 26 November 1897, 9 November 1908. See also PC/GEN/1/4, 1896–7.

67 Citation from PC/GEN/1/4 for 1893–4. The contradictions in adminis- tering policy appear, e.g., in Public Control Committee, 'Misc. repts of James Ollis', op. cit.; PH/GEN/1/2, op. cit.; House of Commons, proof of evidence, James Ollis, 10 March 1908, p. 8, discusses 'attempts to break down the barriers of this secrecy', referring to the role that nurse-mothers played in upholding the discretion of families. Foster-mothers threatened to give up infants if they were subject to inspection.

68 PH/REG/1/24; PH/GEN/2/21: the committee surmised 'that the evidence given before us points irresistibly to the conclusion that both free food and free shelters are demoralising to the recipients and a source of danger to the community'; PH/GEN/1/1; Letitia Fairfield Papers, 'Public assistance in relation to venereal disease', 5 March 1936.

69 PH/GEN/2/21; PH/SHS/3/16; PH/SHS/1/14; Pennybacker, 'The "labour question"', ch. IV; EO/WEL/1/1.

70 EO/WEL/1/1: 'Need for a social welfare branch in the education department', memo to Blair from Turner, 16 November 1909. Blair was appointed chief education officer under the Progressives. The second part of the citation is from 'Further points', 11 January 1910, summarizing the clerk's views.

71 PH/GEN/2/15; PH/GEN/1/1; PH/GEN/2/21; PH/GEN/2/18; PH/SHS/ 3/6; PH/GEN/2/15; EO/WEL/1/1.

72 See S. D. Pennybacker, ' "It was not what she said but the way in which she said it": the LCC and the music halls', in Peter Bailey (ed.), *Victorian Music Halls. Volume I: The Business of Pleasure*, Milton Keynes, 1986; PC/ENT/2/17.

73 ibid., pp. 124–6 and fns 32, 33. The LCC proposed a 'terminable annuity' which would have required more financial obligation on the part of ground landlords who owned land on which the halls were erected, a notion scoffed at by Asquith, then Home Secretary.

74 ibid., pp. 132–3 and fns 75, 76.

75 21 November 1893.

76 LCC Theatres and Music Halls Committee, presented papers, 'Olympia, Hammersmith, 1896–1905'; Ben Shepard, 'Showbiz imperialism: the case of Peter Lobengula', in John M. Mackenzie (ed.), *Imperialism and Popular Culture*, Manchester, 1986.

77 Stewart Headlam, *On the Dangers of Municipal Puritanism*, 1905.

78 ibid., p. 13.

79 *The Anti-Puritan League for the Defence of the People's Pleasure*, n.d., signed by Hubert Bland, G. K. Chesterton, Walter Crane, Headlam, and G. S. Street amongst others.

80 'White collar values and the role of religion', in G. Crossick (ed.), *The Lower Middle Class in Britain 1870–1914*, 1977, p. 78.

81 See Pennybacker, 'The "labour question"', op. cit., ch. I.

82 LCC Theatres and Music Halls Committee, presented papers, 25 January 1893, 'Sunday entertainments, 1893–1909'.

83 See Thompson, op. cit., chs IV, XI; Offer, op. cit., ch. 18; Young, op. cit., ch. III; *The Times*, 21 January 1907, 25 February 1907.

84 Municipal Reform leaflets: *Municipal Reform vs Progressive Socialism*, op. cit.; *Labour and Municipal Reform: Better Labour Conditions for LCC Workmen*, n.d., after mid-1907; *The Progressive Policy Is the Same As the Socialist Policy*, leaflet K, n.d.

85 Progressive Minute Book, 1895–6, held in the Greater London Record Office; AC/1632/1, Progressive Minute Book, vol. II, 1890–8. For early and continuous labour activity on behalf of selected 'labour candidates', see, e.g., London Trades Council, Minutes, 11 February 1892, 10 March 1892, 12 May 1892, 7 February 1907; annual report, 1898. See Thompson, op. cit., appendices C and D, for an overview of labour representation; Pennybacker, 'The "labour question"', op. cit., pp. 205–6, 212.

86 'Reflections on the LCC election', *Trades and Labour Gazette*, March 1907, p. 1.

87 LTC, Minutes, 1 November 1891, 12 November 1891, 2 June 1892, 13 October 1892, 22 July 1897, 9 August 1900, 12 September 1901, 10 October 1901.

88 See note 8 above. See comments by Benn in Gardiner, op. cit., p. 344, in which he faults the ILP for hindering Progressivism, and p. 361 on the 1907 election: 'The Labour opposition in the constituencies had lost the Progressives six seats, but even if there had been no split, the Moderates would still have had an overwhelming victory.' Progressive turn-out was lower in certain East End areas in 1907 than it had been in 1904, e.g. Stepney (−25.3 per cent) and Limehouse (−20.2 per cent) (Knott, op. cit., p. 98). Seats were lost by the Progressives in Mile End, Hoxton, and St George's in the East. But the great accretion of strength to the Municipal Reformers was in the middle-class areas. This conforms to a pattern for the 1910 general election described by Neal Blewett, *The Peers, the Parties and the People*, 1972, esp. p. 481, where he corrects Thompson's figures for the percentage of the total electorate voting Liberal in 1910, finding Liberal strength most seriously in decline in the middle-class areas. He emphasizes

throughout the disenchantment with Liberalism, rather than Unionist appeal *per se*, additionally arguing that the Conservatives never recovered their traditional base (of 1886–1906) in London's working-class areas.

89 LTC, Minutes, 12 November 1908: 'The trades council ventures to express the hope that the labour members [of the LCC] will continue to assert themselves on behalf of the workers, independently of whatever party may be in power'; PC/ENT/2/17; Pennybacker, 'The "labour question"', op. cit., chs I, V; Bernard Dix and Stephen Williams, *Serving the Public, Building the Union: The History of NUPE*, 1987.

90 *The Straight Tip to Workers*, op. cit.

91 Benn, *London Municipal Notes*, February 1913; Webb, 'The economic heresies of the LCC', *London*, 16 August 1894.

92 For an overview of Progressive accomplishments, see Gibbon and Bell, op. cit., chs 11–23; and Gardiner, op. cit.; Progressive Party, *Manifesto by Labour Leaders to All Trade Unionists: Workmen, Defeat These Attacks on your Rights, Whatever May Be your Politics!*, 1910, signed by Sidney Webb and several national trade union leaders; Benn, *Moderate Rates and Who Pays*, 1911; Benn, *Exploited London – a Demand for the Restitution of Citizenship Rights*, 1912.

93 On later progressivism, see J. Bush, *Behind the Lines*, 1984; J. Gillespie, 'Economic and political change in the East End of London during the 1920s', unpublished Ph.D. thesis, Cambridge University, 1984, ch. 8.

94 On changing Progressive ties to the Liberal associations, see Garside and Young, op. cit., p. 98; Thompson, op. cit., p. 107. On the debate and discord elicited by the 1902 Education Act, see David Bebbington, *The Nonconformist Conscience*, 1982, ch. VII; Gibbon and Bell, op. cit., pp. 253–7; Gardiner, op. cit., p. 320; Norman and Jeanne MacKenzie (eds), *Diary of Beatrice Webb*, 1983, pp. 229–32, 268, 272, 277, 280–5, especially for trade union alienation from the supporters of the Bill. Gardiner quotes Benn: 'The London public had differentiated between their corporate interests and their general political affiliations' – op. cit., p. 320; London Reform Union, *To Conservatives and Liberal Unionists*, 1898, is indicative of Progressive approaches to a constituency wider than that of official Liberalism.

95 The issues raised in this essay are explored in Pennybacker, *A Vision for London: Labour, Everyday Life and the LCC Experiment, 1889–1914*, in progress.

7

Poplarism and proletarianism
Unemployment and Labour politics in London, 1918–34

James Gillespie

'Poplarism', the use of local government by the labour movement as a base to defend working-class standards of living and resist central government control, has been celebrated as the high point of post-war London radicalism, as an example of a radical movement apparently capable of transcending the barriers of ethnic, occupational, and gender conflicts which had long served to stultify the London socialist movement. Most of the studies have confined attention to the dramatic confrontations between Labour-controlled local authorities and Whitehall during the early 1920s. The retreat of radicalism at a local level after 1925, the shift of the priorities of Labour's left from 'the local road to socialism' with a concentration on reform from the centre, has been treated as part of the accommodation of Labour to capitalism.[1] Historians with more limited sympathy for the radicalism of Poplar have stressed the importance of the construction of the electoral and organizational machine of the London Labour Party, under the firm hand of Herbert Morrison, seeing the defiance of the law by East London borough councils as an irrational obstruction to Labour's prospects of winning the middle-class vote. Despite this difference in political sympathies, both approaches have rarely strayed from the analysis of politics purely as a matter of leadership, organization, and ideology, with little attention to the relationship of local social and labour market structures and class formation.[2]

These failings have not been unique to the historical analysis of the labour movement in London. Recent studies of the early development of the Labour Party have used a similar abstraction of organization and leadership from economic and social structures. McKibbin's assertion that Labour advances were 'the political mobilization of an already existing industrial class consciousness: in practice it concentrated more on the extension of organization than upon the perfection of policy' are based on this essentially passive relationship of Labour and its members and supporters.[3] By examining an area of London marked by the lack of rapid structural change in its dominant industrial and labour market structures, this essay suggests a more productive direction in which research should proceed. Instead of assuming that the Labour Party was merely 'a vehicle for working-class representation', an expression of class unity and consciousness of corporate identity, any analysis should start from the complex set of shifting alliances which constituted the party at a local as well as national level. Increased state intervention in the local economy before and during the First World War combined with an opening of local political institutions to working-class control with the extension of the franchise in 1918 to establish a new relationship between politics and the local economy. It was this changed framework which made possible both Poplarism and the new strength of Labour in East London. The politics of social class which dominated the East End of the 1920s was founded on a series of alliances between groups sharing a common political interest in the control of the institutions of local government. The use of borough councils and boards of guardians to advance the interests of Labour's constituency provided the basis of political unity, not any sense of class unity engendered by the workplace. Throughout the political conflicts of the early 1920s this sense of local political identity, although frequently expressed in the language of inter-national socialism, provided the basis for Labour's strength in the face of attacks from the London County Council and Whitehall.[4]

Before the First World War the response of East London's working class to all forms of party politics, Tory, Liberal, and Labour, was notorious for its crushing apathy. Trade union militancy, despite the dramatic upheavals of the dock strikes of 1889, 1911, and 1912, remained confined to isolated pockets of the work-force for most of the period. This attenuated growth of Labour politics in pre-war London has been taken as the political expression of a more profound backwardness of development of the East End working class, with the apparent indifference of the East End to any recognizable 'modern' working-class politics a symptom of the peculiar industrial history of the region. A massive casual labour market, founded upon a chronic oversupply of labour and exacerbated by the instability of the demand for dock workers, combined with the small scale of London's industries, based on workshop production and outworking rather than steam technologies and the factory, to produce a fragmented and impoverished working class.[5]

This analysis has relied upon an implicit model of the structural pre-conditions of London politics as the political representation of a coherent class interest. The success of an independent working-class politics is dependent upon the development of large-scale forms of production, concentrating the labour force in factories and creating the conditions of mutual sympathy which enabled the extension of bonds of class interest beyond the point of production. Paul Thompson's study of pre-war politics in London relies heavily on a contrast between London's disorganization, the 'lack of neighbourliness and co-operation among working class Londoners', and the 'closely knit' communities of the north of England where workplace and chapel combined to nurture an organic, oppositional working-class culture.[6] Political allegiances are merely one aspect of a deeper culture based on workplace, trade union, co-operative, and chapel. In this view London has been an anomaly, its exceptional development in the pre-war decades the result of deeper aberrations of social and industrial structure.

If the retarded growth of trade unionism and mass working-class politics in London before the First World War stemmed from a pre-industrial labour market, it has been frequently suggested that the principal cause of the political transformation of the capital originated in a fundamental restructuring of the labour market. Tomlinson has summarized this standard view of the development of London politics:

> the growth of factory industry and its social effects [was] one of the conditions of existence of a mass socialist movement in London, which emerges for the first time only after 1918. In the nineteenth century the diversity of working class conditions had been one major obstacle to the development of a socialist political movement so that, although they proliferated in London, socialist political groups remained on the whole marginal political forces.[7]

In her account of East London during the First World War, Julia Bush has stressed the appearance of more stable patterns of employment, a shift towards factory-based production, and a consequent strengthening of trade union organization amongst the unskilled. In this increasingly favourable environment trades councils developed a mass constituency, with campaigns against profiteering, housing shortages, and conscription. This new class-based mobilization provided the basis for Labour's sweeping successes at the 1919 local elections, when every metropolitan borough council in the East End was won for Labour. London's exceptionalism was finally overcome by the development of forms of class organization common to the rest of working-class Britain.[8]

This approach to the political history of Labour in London has been based on several fundamental misunderstandings of the economic and political history of the capital. It was the main strongholds of casual labour and sweating that gave Labour its most spectacular advances in the post-war years. The centres of 'new industry', light engineering, and factory-based consumer goods in west and north-east London gave Labour weak support until the late 1930s. In new industrial areas such as Acton and Willesden the core of Labour support was drawn from pockets of railwaymen and bus workers, not from semi-skilled factory workers. Similarly, trade unions found the new factories difficult to organize. It was in the transport industries – the docks and the operations of the London Transport Combine – and the inner-city workshops of the clothing and cabinet-making trades where trade unionism achieved a greater foothold, not in the larger factories of outer London.[9] These errors have been compounded by the assumption that a unionized working class was the condition of existence for mass Labour politics. Even where unionization made progress, the expected equation of trade union strength and support for Labour was reversed. In the East End trade unionism remained dependent on political intervention for its success, whether the labour market regulatory measures of dock labour registration, or the enforcement of minimum wage levels by trade boards in the clothing trades.

Politics and industry in East London, 1918–39

Far from sweeping away the old conditions of casual labour and workshop production, the impact of the factory in the East End of the 1920s was limited and developed within existing labour market structures of casual hiring and outworking.[10] Trade unionism remained a fragile growth in the old inner industrial perimeter of East London comprising the boroughs of Poplar, Shoreditch, Stepney, Bethnal Green, and south Hackney. The rapid growth of the new mass unions of the unskilled, such as the Workers' Union, during the First World War was soon dissipated in the combination of post-war slump and readjustment to peacetime conditions. Equally, the organization of the workshop trades which continued to dominate the East End economy – cabinet-making, tailoring, and the former 'sweated trades' – was fitful. Strike waves at the end of the war were followed in each case by a retreat into a few protected enclaves of key workers or workshops and factories dependent upon fair wage clauses in central and local government contracts. To the extent that trade unionism became more firmly established in these areas of London during the inter-war years, it was a by-product of political intervention. Trade boards used the fiat of the Ministry of Labour to enforce agreements between employers and trade unions in otherwise unorganized sectors of industry. Similarly, Labour Party control of local authorities and pressure on the central government could bring political pressure to bear on recalcitrant employers. A brief examination of the most important areas of employment – the docks, casual labour, and the clothing trades – illustrates this point.

Wartime conditions had enabled a decisive advance of labour organization on the London docks, and with the peacetime boom in port work conditions seemed ripe for a thoroughgoing decasualization of dock labour, traditionally the heart of the East London casual labour market. Despite earnest attempts by officials from the Ministry of Labour, neither dockers nor their employers were prepared to make the sacrifice of their freedom of action that decasualization and permanency would entail. The limited scheme which was implemented from 1919 achieved a reduction of the numbers competing for work on the docks, restricting appearance at twice-daily calls to those who could demonstrate a continuing involvement in dock labour. Within this protected enclave the numbers of registered dockers still greatly outnumbered the work available, providing employers with a large reserve of labour and reproducing the insecurity of casual labour. At the same time intervention by Whitehall faced deep suspicion and resistance from its supposed beneficiaries, contributing to the frequent breakaway movements from the Transport and General Workers' Union by sectional groups hostile to Bevin's policy of compromise with employers and state. However, while far from the decasualization reformers had demanded for more than three decades, this new arrangement stabilized conditions of dock labour. A Toynbee Hall survey examined the effects of registration during the postwar depression, noting that it had blocked

> the influx of labour from other trades. If no registration schemes had existed, enormous numbers of men from other trades in East London would have sought employment in the Port during the present trade depression, and it is improbable that the Unions of the Port could have succeeded in protecting the interests of their members. The result would have been that the employment of genuine dock labourers would have been even worse than it is at present.[11]

Within the loose shield of registration, however, competition for work on the docks remained as fierce. Its victims increasingly turned towards political action to alleviate their conditions.

Although paternalist regulation by Whitehall had failed to achieve a thoroughgoing decasualization it encouraged a belief in political remedies for the alarming social consequences of the disorganized casual labour market. In the endemic underemployment of the docks, intervention by local authorities to provide generous relief to the families of strikers and to the unemployed, and preferential access to relief works, had a more direct effect on the living conditions of casual dockers. Labour-controlled local authorities intervened in the local economy, directing employment policies to raise wage rates and encourage decasualization of the labour market. Fair wage and trade union clauses in local authority contracts were rigorously enforced, and resources were thrown into support for industrial action; the East London boards of guardians provided vital underpinning during the unofficial dock strike of 1923 and the General Strike of 1926. The steady transfer of powers from recalcitrant local councils and guardians to the Conservative London County Council during the 1920s emphasized the new importance of local government as an actor and stake in industrial conflict.[12] In the political discussions which followed Labour's unexpected victories at the borough council elections in 1919 George Lansbury set out the fundamental principles which would govern Labour's employment policies:

> long years ago the Labour movement decided that whenever it got into power the conditions of municipal labour should be such as to attract the best people, and to set an example to other employers. There can be no possible doubt about the effect of this policy. Every step forward taken by organized Labour in its fight for better conditions has been preceeded by a struggle, and in many cases a victory, for a higher standard of work and wages under municipal and other authorities.[13]

While pre-war Progressives had also espoused similar policies, particularly at the LCC, Labour's approach was both more thoroughgoing and more closely linked to the encouragement of trade unionism and reform of the casual labour market. Over the next three years Labour-controlled councils intervened extensively in the working of casual labour markets by improving the conditions of direct employees, implementing drastic changes in the treatment of the unemployed, and enforcing as far as possible these changes on the work-forces of other employers. Municipal workers employed permanently or casually on direct works, often funded by the central government under unemployment relief or public housing schemes but administered locally under very loose guidelines, received high minimum wages and generous conditions.

The Labour Metropolitan Councils of Bethnal Green, Shoreditch, Stepney, and Poplar all introduced minimum wages of £4 per week for male employees; Poplar extended this to its female workers. At the same time casual staffs were granted holiday- and sick-pay. Fair wages clauses extended these conditions and trade unionism to firms supplying local government contracts.[14] Although these actions were supported by local branches of municipal trade unions, many of whom formed a significant block within local Labour parties, the initiative usually came from a more political level. The East End borough councils defied both the advice of the London Labour Party and the requests of Ernest Bevin to confine their awards to those negotiated by the local authorities' Joint Industrial Council, and granted wages and conditions considerably higher than those negotiated by municipal unions elsewhere in London.[15]

This approach to local politics was a distinctive element of a Labour politics formulated within local government in the 1920s. While owing a deep debt to pre-war municipal socialism, it shared little of the concern for extending the strained local tax base which marked its Progressive predecessors.[16] Local government was to be the prime political instrument for political and economic progress and the victory of socialism. Theodore Rothstein, a British Socialist Party (and founding Communist Party) member, put a view common on Labour's left after the local government victories of November 1919, demanding that 'We must turn the local councils into so many forts from which to assail the Capitalist order.' This heroic politics of local government was not limited to the left. John Raphael, elected with the backing of Whitechapel's costers to Stepney's new Labour-controlled council, described the shift in power in local government:

> It has been said at this Council meeting that in the good time coming the local Soviet will meet in this very Chamber at the Town Hall. But is not the Soviet already installed, installed under the national constitution and by law sanctioned? It is undoubtedly a council of Workers who know their legal power and use it. They would wish greater scope. But they do frame their own policy within the limitations which chafe many of them.[17]

Clement Attlee, the first Labour Mayor of Stepney and one of the Stepney councillors who voted to support Poplar's stand against the central government, argued that 'municipal work is part of the means of changing the basis of society from profit-making to Life'; while Lansbury described his fellow councillors at Poplar as 'all clear class-conscious socialists working together, using the whole machinery of local government and Parliament for the transformation of Capitalist Society into Socialism'.[18]

Despite these rhetorical assertions of the political priority of local government in the march for socialism, however, there were few attempts to elaborate a justification for this policy. At best, Labour's municipal leaders made a connection between their policies at local level and the wider conflict between capital and labour. Replying to threats of surcharge by the district auditor for paying council manual workers a minimum wage greatly in excess of the going labour market rate, Sam Elsbury, a clothing trade union official and deputy leader of the Communist–Labour alliance which dominated Bethnal Green Borough Council from 1919 to 1928, argued that

> Behind this move [to reduce wages] there is the same class struggle. Behind this move are individuals who are adopting this method of attempting to badger the Councils and to compel them to reduce wages for the purpose of using it as a lever to reduce wages in their private workshops, factories, mines and railways. You must realize, as we all realize, what is happening today. You cannot look at a newspaper without you find that Labour is defending its standpoint all along the line. We say that we are simply defending it in the same manner here.[19]

Hence, Labour-controlled councils awarded minimum wages considerably in excess of trade union rates, with little or no consultation through the formal negotiating structures of the Whitley councils approved by the national leaderships of municipal trade unions. Council employment was used as a political weapon to reward supporters and strengthen sympathetic organizations. In Bethnal Green and Shoreditch membership of the National Unemployed Workers' Movement or a trade union was a prerequisite for employment on council-administered relief works or on its regular work-force. Poplar and Stepney required trade union membership by all council workers and employees of council contractors. These latter provisions were in line with TUC and Labour Party policy at a national level, although opposed by the London Labour Party. A ministry survey in 1926 found that, of twelve councils in England which enforced these policies rigorously, ten were in greater London; all the metropolitan boroughs in East London were amongst the offenders.[20]

Relief works for the unemployed provided a point of intersection between Labour-controlled local authorities' attempts to ameliorate the condition of the unemployed and to modify the more general conditions of the casual labour market. Although relief works to meet sudden unemployment crises had become a standard practice before the war, the East End borough councils quickly developed programmes on a far larger scale. Using grants and low interest loans from the central government, during the winter of 1920 to 1921 Bethnal Green employed over 2,000 men for periods of between 8 and 13 weeks, and Shoreditch employed over 1,000 men for 4-week periods on relief works. Despite periodic promises that suitable work would be found for unemployed women, this work was solely for unskilled males; snow clearing, road mending, and repairs on council properties were typical activities.[21] These relief projects dovetailed with seasonal downturns on casual trades, especially those outdoor employments most affected both by the national economic slump and a normal slump in winter. In Stepney from 1922 to 1923 over one-third of all council relief workers were dockers, and this proportion was even higher in riverside wards.[22]

Although centrally funded relief works were intended to meet short-term cyclical downturns, they quickly became a prop for the casual labour market. In Stepney, as in other Labour-controlled boroughs, the council directed that all relief works be spread, with beneficiaries selected on a basis of need, giving all those eligible a periodic spell of labour. An investigator found that in Stepney in the late 1920s men came to the employment exchange year by year and reminded officials that 'Next month's my month on the relief'. By the late 1930s there was a 10 per cent variation in Stepney's council work-force each winter as public works policy became integrated with the cycle of demand for unskilled casual labour.[23]

The workshop trades were also subject to intervention by central and local government. The clothing trades, the classic location of homeworking and the 'sweating system' in the late nineteenth century, saw rapid structural changes after the introduction of minimum wages under the Trades Board Acts of 1909 and 1918. Despite the hopes of the anti-sweating campaigners, the trade boards did not usher in the disappearance of the small workshop. They did introduce a new means of regulation of wages and conditions within an industry which remained largely unorganized. Although homeworking became less important in the East End clothing trades, the typical industrial unit remained small. When a substantial factory sector emerged in the 1920s it remained dependent on complicated chains of subcontracting with the workshop sector. Far from being an archaic survival, the small workshop played a dynamic role in the reorientation of the industry from the export-based 'slop clothing', where the worst examples of sweating had occurred, to share the prosperity of new consumer markets at home.[24]

As with the docks and other centres of casual labour, the restructuring of the labour market supplying the workshop trades was achieved through a new relationship between the state and industry. Instead of the 'moralization' of economic relationships that its advocates hoped would result from bringing workers and employers together under the benign chairmanship of the state, the trade boards in the tailoring trades quickly became a means by which the small organized sectors of the industry were able to enforce their interests on their unorganized competitors.[25] Despite attempts to weaken the boards in the mid-1920s, the Ministry of Labour became the guarantor of industrial agreements made by parties unable to control more than limited enclaves of the trade. Trade union energies increasingly turned towards the indirect enforcement of improved wages through the trades boards, or by influencing the buying policies of Labour-controlled local councils.[26]

Consequently, although casual labour and unemployment re-mained central to the local economy of East London, their political context had been radically transformed. Not only were trade union strategies increasingly articulated around state inter-vention at local and national levels, but a new political constituency created electoral pressures encouraging interventionist policies by local authorities. The Representation of the People Act of 1918 widened parliamentary and local government franchise, admitting the bulk of the working class to the electorate and making recipients of relief eligible to vote for the first time in elections for boards of guardians. At the same time, the full employment and high wages of the war years helped to undermine the already tattered basis of the pre-war administration of the Poor Law, the old distinction between the 'deserving' and 'undeserving'. The resulting crisis of Poor Law administration went far beyond the confines of Poplar and other Labour-controlled boards. A survey of unemployment in the East End made by Toynbee Hall residents summed up this change:

a question to which pre-war enquiries gave much attention was the genuineness of the unemployed. Were they really unemploy-able, and would they really work if they had the chance? It has not been thought necessary in the present investigation to consider this question in any detail because the figures speak for themselves . . . the great majority of those who were unemployed last winter were in work before the depression in trade began and were out of work only because trade is slack throughout the country.[27]

The post-war crisis and the politics of unemployment

As the second winter of mass unemployment ended, the *East End Observer* complained that

a distinct change has come in the attitude of people to the Poor Law, whose machinery has been utilized to the full by the so-called 'Organized Unemployed'. Not only have the old prejudice and disinclination to take State charity disappeared, but on the part of Authority itself there are entirely new ideas as to the extent to which relief should be given.[28]

A contemporary anti-Labour publicist, George Drage, charged that

In the East End not only is the offer of outdoor relief made to all and sundry, lodgers, friends and relatives, but rewards are given to active and zealous agents in the way of appointments. Promises are made to give exceptional wages and conditions to persons employed by the Guardians, while the incomes of provision dealers are trebled through relief tickets. . . . None but administrators from outside the local area can hope to obviate the very real intimidation now exercised on relieving officers, guardians, social workers and local shopkeepers who do not fall in with the popular view as to outdoor relief.[29]

For many East End councillors these charges were accepted with pride. Lansbury's son Edgar, a Poplar councillor, defended the relief policies of the riverside boards of guardians during the dock strike of 1923: 'for the first time of which he had any recollection in a dispute between employers and workmen, the latter, at all events in Poplar, Bermondsey and West Ham, had been able to stand up to the employers with a full belly'.[30] John Scurr, the Mayor of Poplar, argued that Labour's policies of high local expenditure were a means of improving the conditions of Labour's supporters. A 'saving' on rates was really a deduction from the real wages of the workers, while opponents of local expenditure were really attempting to reverse this redistribution of income. He argued that the widespread reverses Labour experienced in the 1922 borough elections were due to a failure to defend this record of high rates and expenditure. Instead:

Certain sections of the Labour Party recognizing this psychology have tried to stem the tide of Labour defeats by endeavouring to prove that Labour saved the rates and would, and could, reduce them. Wherever such an attempt was made it ended in disaster. The electorate either frankly disbelieved them, or else felt that the opponents would do the job better. Labour lost because it allowed its opponents to choose the ground and the weapons of battle.[31]

This identification of socialist politics with the high-rating and -spending policies of the local authorities of the East End was sharply challenged by the leadership of the London Labour Party. Herbert Morrison, the LLP's secretary and dominant figure throughout the inter-war years, repeatedly attacked the East End Labour boroughs for concentrating on purely local solutions to national problems and threatening attempts to build electoral support in more middle-class areas of the metropolis.[32] This attack on Poplarism was echoed by the Webbs in the final volume of their history of the Poor Law. They suggested that the term 'proletarianism' provided a more apt characterization of narrow sectionalism, the politics of Poplar and its sympathizers. Proletarianism was one aspect of the more general movement to guarantee a minimum standard of life for the working class without reference to labour tests and the indignities of the Poor Law. However, by taking the institutions of local government as the terrain of battle, they argued, Labour was unable to move beyond the expression of a sectional class interest inimical to the national politics on which socialism must be based. The politicization of poor relief through boards of guardians dominated by the votes of the recipients of relief would inevitably lead to the pauperization of the population, creating a further obstacle to the abandonment of the remnants of the Poor Law.[33]

Despite their hostility, the Webbs' account of 'proletarianism' captured several of the main features of Labour control of local government in the East End. A concentration on the more 'progressive' or explicitly socialist elements which distinguished Poplar's policies, such as equal pay for women employees, has often obsured the extent to which it shared a common approach with its less confrontational neighbours in the East End. This proletarianism had little in common, apart from rhetoric, with socialist strategies and more with meeting the immediate needs of a local economy dominated by casual labour.[34] The Labour-controlled councils reworked the demands of pre-war ratepayer Radicalism, the demand for rate equalization and the rating of land values, and tied this to the economic crisis of mass unemployment on predominantly working-class communities. The otherwise contradictory interests of ratepayers, both working-class tenants and small business owners, and the recipients of (rate-financed) unemployment relief could be reconciled in a politics which focused its demands on the transfer of rate revenues from the wealthier boroughs of West London. Labour policy was defensive; the interests of the working class were identified with those of the local community, and only rhetorical attempts were made to link policies, which Lansbury admitted offered little more than a 'bandage', to more general socialist objectives. The class struggle of Labour rhetoric was displaced into a demand for a redistribution of financial resources between urban areas.[35]

As with political intervention in the casual labour market and the workshop trades, local action to relieve unemployment occurred within a framework set by Whitehall. In the early 1920s unemployment relief was provided through a system of contributory unemployment insurance, largely financed by the Exchequer, and through the Poor Law, funded from local rates. This dual system created sharp divisions between the unemployed according to the source of their relief or benefits.

The extension of unemployment insurance to the majority of the work-force under the Unemployment Insurance Act of 1919 committed governments to a shift from local financing of unemployment relief. Its timing, at the onset of a major depression, prevented the scheme from being established on a self-financing basis, and prevented a thoroughgoing reform of the Poor Law. The non-contributory out-of-work donation, a temporary measure introduced to smooth demobilization at the end of the war, set a precedent for tampering with the contributory actuarial basis of unemployment insurance. It also established a relatively high standard of benefit: 29 shillings a week for men, 24 shillings for women, and dependent allowances of 6 shillings for the first and 3 shillings for each subsequent child. Both these provisions rebounded on the government as levels of unemployment rose. Unemployment insurance was extended to the majority of workers in November 1920, giving benefits to all manual workers in non-agricultural trades, with an income limit of £250 per annum. For the following decade governments tampered with the mix of local and central control and financing and reduced the level and duration of benefits, but in the absence of thoroughgoing reform from Whitehall the Labour-controlled boards of guardians in areas such as the East End could win considerable autonomy.[36]

This reliance on the Poor Law increased as the pressure of rising costs of unemployment insurance payments led to tightening of insurance benefits. The Ministry of Labour implemented severe cuts in benefits. The 1920 Act reduced benefits to a maximum of 15 shillings for adult men and 12 shillings for adult women, and in November 1921 dependant allowances became 1 shilling for each dependent child and 5 shillings for a dependent spouse. Faced with the political dangers of removing a large proportion of the unemployed from insurance benefits, the coalition government moved to extend 'uncovenanted' benefits, not linked to past contributions, to cover those whose entitlements had expired.

The combination of capitulation to political pressure, the effective abandonment of the contributory principle, and the reduction of levels of benefit provided an explosive mixture. Treasury-inspired attempts to reinstate the link between contributions and insurance entitlements created a major political split within the ranks of the unemployed between those who received insurance payments and those who had exhausted their entitlement to these benefits and relied upon the Poor Law. Moves to place insurance on a sound actuarial footing by restoration of the link between contribution and benefit forced more of the unemployed to depend upon the guardians for relief. At the same time, recipients of insurance benefits contributed to the costs of the Poor Law through the local rates as under the Rent Restriction Act landlords were prevented from raising rents but could pass on rate increases to their unemployed tenants. Expenditure from the rates by boards of guardians in predominantly working-class areas resulted in a transfer of income between administrative categories of the unemployed.

These differences between the unemployed according to type of benefit received had contradictory political potential as administrative categories were not hard and fast. Gaps at the end of periods of entitlement to insurance benefits made insured workers temporarily dependent on the Poor Law. The generous policies followed by boards in areas such as the East End meant that many insured unemployed supplemented their incomes by turning to the boards of guardians for emergency relief.[37] The beginning of each gap period saw a large fall in the numbers of unemployment insurance books lodged at the exchanges. During the first gap period, starting in August 1921, the national figure reached over 200,000. T. J. MacNamara, the Minister of Health, warned Lloyd George that 'the unemployed and the people who have exhausted benefit are, in the main, congregated in comparatively few centres', where they were subject to the appeals of ' "Unemployed Committees" organized on communistic lines' and agitations such as that of Poplar. Unfortunately there is little statistical information from the early 1920s on the overlap between relief under the Poor

Law and insurance benefits. One study in 1923 claimed that one-third of insurance recipients had their benefits supplemented through the Poor Law, while many others either were refused poor relief or were too proud to apply, despite their obvious need. A Birmingham study in January 1923 found that more than 17 per cent of those unemployed were receiving benefit from both systems. In other areas where the Poor Law was administered more generously, as in the East End, this proportion was undoubtedly higher.[38]

The gap and the low level of benefits meant the temporary abandonment of the attempt to remove all but the unemployable from the jurisdiction of the Poor Law. It is clear that the Ministry of Labour pushed a permissive attitude towards the generous policies of boards of guardians during the early 1920s, treating the local treatment of the unemployed as a safety-valve preventing the collapse of the shaky unemployment insurance system. Ministry officials 'regarded Poor Law relief as a useful way out and supplement to the unemployment benefit and were anxious that it should not be made impossible by the imposition of too strict conditions'.[39] This approach outlived the immediate crisis. Advising that a blind eye be turned to illegalities in the administration of one East London board in 1928, officials warned that there would 'almost certainly be an exhaustive discussion in the Divisional Court of the law and practice of the Guardians and of all the anomalies in the present position of which we are all too well aware'.[40] During the 1920s the Ministry of Health generally followed this advice, relying on the indirect sanctions of the district auditor and administrative action against individual boards rather than a tightening of the entire system. Strong action was postponed until the entire Poor Law system was replaced; in the meantime, ministry intervention was haphazard, a response to immediate crises such as the use of relief to support strikers on the coalfields in 1926. Great crises, such as the imprisonment of the Poplar councillors, were more likely to be embarrassments outside its control (in this case contempt of court arising from a dispute between the borough council and the LCC) than a result of direct intervention from Whitehall.

This relative autonomy of the Poor Law created a political dilemma for each of the local Labour parties in the East End. The advice from the London Labour Party was uncompromising. Herbert Morrison argued that Labour guardians should take a firm and paternalistic attitude towards the unemployed, counterposing 'thoughtful action' to 'mere ignorant appeals to the baser kind of mob passion'.[41] Local Labour parties were to work closely with the unemployed, but with the aim of bringing them under party tutelage. The potential conflict of interests between local rate-payers and recipients of relief was to be resolved in favour of the former, as

> We must continue to insist that the problem is a national one. Both the Government and our municipal opponents will be delighted if we make unemployment a *local* charge upon the rates. And when the unemployed, no less than the employed, are called upon to pay extra rents because of the extra rates, our opponents will be on the alert to saddle the Labour Party with the blame. Any statements which lead the unemployed to think that our Borough Councils can provide any material solution of the problem will constitute a mere side-tracking of the agitation, will be playing into the hands of the Government and our political opponents and creating bitter disappointment for the unemployed whose sufferings are hard enough already. Let the Government do the right thing and Labour boroughs will cordially co-operate.[42]

In late 1920 organizations of the unemployed appeared in many parts of London. These were at first on a very local and non-political basis for social activities and begging expeditions through the West End.[43] The first major attempt to add a political dimension to these organizations was initiated by the new Labour-controlled borough councils of the East End. In Bethnal Green, Stepney, Shoreditch, and Poplar mass meetings were held in late October demanding work or maintenance for the unemployed and an immediate programme of relief works. The campaign culminated in a march to Downing Street led by the mayors and broken up violently by police as it entered Whitehall. In response, a meeting of twelve of the unemployed organizations elected a London District Council of the Unemployed, led by three unemployed engineers with experience of the wartime shop stewards' move-ment. The organized unemployed took a prominent part in local politics in all of the East End boroughs, using direct action, occupations, and demonstrations to push recalcitrant boards of guardians into increasing relief scales and liberalizing workhouse regimes. Opposed by the official labour movement and raising the particular ire of the leadership of the London Labour Party, the National Unemployed Workers' Movement, as it was renamed in 1921, moved into an often uneasy but close relationship with the Communist Party at a national level, but retained its place in the complex set of alliances which made up the labour movement in the East End.[44] The success of local Labour parties in the East

End in the early 1920s was a function of their ability to bridge the gap between different categories of the unemployed and those potential supporters still in the work-force. The unemployed became a significant component of Labour's organizational base throughout East London. However, where the party appeared to subsume its interests with those of the organized unemployed, this provided a recipe for electoral defeat.

Poplar provides the clearest example of the advantages of posing the political problems of unemployment as a financial burden on the entire local community, rather than attempting to provide direct representation of the immediate interests of the unemployed. With a mass membership and a record of success at both local and parliamentary elections unequalled in London, Poplar provided the model of a stable and broadly based local Labour organization, dominating both the board of guardians and the borough council from 1919. The politics of unemployment always played a central role in the construction of this political support. However, despite Lansbury's formative role in the *Daily Herald*'s 'Go to the Guardians' campaign in December 1920, encouraging the militancy of local committees of the unemployed, the Poplar Labour Party always maintained a distance between itself and unemployed organizations in the borough. In contrast to Bethnal Green, members of the NUWM were not accorded the same preference in council employment and on relief works as trade unionists. Instead, the Poplar guardians justified their generous rates of relief and abandonment of principles of less eligibility in terms of a politics of redistribution of the financial burden of unemployment, forcing the collapse of the Poor Law system, as

> If society cannot organize its economic affairs so as to provide work for all its able-bodied members, then society as a whole should provide them with adequate maintenance from national funds, obtained under existing conditions by increased taxation upon the large and superfluous incomes of those whose social position is maintained only as a result of 'preying on the poor'.[45]

It has been argued that political co-operation between working-class ratepayers, employed and unemployed, and those receiving poor relief was undermined by transfers between these groups through local taxation. The achievement of the Poplar councillors was to transcend these local divisions by attacking the inequities of local government finance within London as a whole, calling for the burden of local unemployment to be borne on a national, or at least metropolitan, level. The adequate maintenance of the unemployed was shifted from financial transfers within a community already struck by economic disaster, into a demand for a more equitable transfer of resources between areas of London. Political unity was constructed, not at the level of class or position in (or out) of the work-force, but on the basis of local government finance. Rate equalization was an issue with resonance on all sides of politics in the East End; hence both Conservative and Liberal councillors either abstained or supported the crucial resolution that Poplar withhold its precepts from the London County Council.

This political representation of the maintenance of the unemployed as a question of inequitable municipal finances provided part of the basis for Labour's strength in Poplar, its ability to forge links between groups which aligned with Municipal Reform or Progressives in neighbouring boroughs. In the years from 1913 to 1914 around 63 per cent of net expenditure by guardians within the LCC area had been borne by the Common Poor Fund. In the wake of the successful campaign by Poplar and other East End boroughs this had increased to 85 per cent in 1922 to 1923.[46] Consequently, Labour in Poplar was able to avoid a close identification with the organized unemployed. An otherwise critical report to the Ministry of Health found that the organized unemployed in Poplar were never in great favour with the guardians, who preferred to deal with them as individuals rather than as a collective interest. In contrast to other areas of the East End, in Poplar the organized unemployed committees remained small and isolated from the mainstream of the labour movement and fell under the sway of ultra-leftist groups such as Sylvia Pankhurst's Workers' Socialist Federation.[47]

In other areas of the East End Labour's stability and strength were in inverse proportion to its dependence on the organizations of the unemployed. In Bethnal Green, lacking Poplar's strong pre-war organizational infrastructure, the Labour Party depended on the support of loosely affiliated campaigning organizations. In the 1919 elections branches of the National Federation of Discharged and Demobilized Sailors and Soldiers carried out this function, providing candidates and canvassers. From late 1920 the committees of the organized unemployed, later to become the National Unemployed Workers' Movement, were Labour's mainstay. Defying repeated directives from Whitehall, Bethnal Green co-opted members of unemployed committees to the council committees which allocated relief work, and made membership of the organized unemployed a prerequisite for employment.[48]

A major consequence of this close identification with the unemployed was Labour's conspicuous lack of success at board of guardians elections in Bethnal Green. Despite Labour majorities in the borough council from 1919 to 1928 (when disaffiliation by the London Labour Party finally destroyed the stormy Communist–Labour alliance which had dominated council politics), Labour never won more than a handful of seats on the board. Its opponents, never able to unite in council elections, were able to campaign on a broad-based economy ticket of 'people's candidates', appealing successfully to the divisions between working-class ratepayers and the unemployed and exploiting the heavily masculine appeals of the unemployed organizations, which concentrated heavily on the interests of young, able-bodied unemployed men.[49]

In contrast, Shoreditch, with a similar industrial and employment structure to Bethnal Green, adopted a more hostile attitude towards the organized unemployed. Labour organization in the borough was dominated by a group of municipal trade unionists, opposed to the Communist influence on the organized unemployed. At the height of unemployed militancy in 1920 the borough council and board of guardians succumbed reluctantly to pressure to give members of the Shoreditch Unemployed Organization preference on relief works, but declined to follow Poplar's lead in refusing to pay LCC precepts and removed preference in early 1922. While rejecting the militancy of the NUWM, Labour in Shoreditch was no less committed to a conception of the use of the Poor Law to defend the living conditions of its constituents.[50]

The proletarianism of the East End Labour parties, their concentration on the defence of local interests and neglect of the broader alliances necessary to political power at a metropolitan or national level, had severe consequences as political power shifted from the borough level. After the General Strike the Conservative government moved from a reliance on the indirect controls of district auditor and local ratepayers. The Guardians Disqualification Act of 1926, used to dismiss the West Ham board in 1927, helped push other Labour-controlled boards into retreat, reducing rates of benefit and tightening eligibility. Similarly, direct grants from Whitehall for relief works were withdrawn from East London councils in late 1926, while a series of adverse court rulings limited councils' autonomy in setting wage rates.[51] Whereas Morrison and the London Labour Party had been marginal to the conflicts over the policies pursued by local authorities in the early 1920s, the local parties increasingly turned to the centre for leadership. In these circumstances, Morrison's calls for moderation and a thoroughgoing purge of communists from the local Labour parties met a more receptive audience, as he warned that 'those responsible for the organization of the working class movement here have had to concentrate on preserving intact the political and industrial structure of our movement in readiness for better times and a more aggressive democratic spirit'.[52]

The final blow came with the transfer of Poor Law functions to county councils in 1929. The immediate result of this shift of responsibility to the new LCC Public Assistance Committee (PAC) was a change in political control. Local relief committees represented the distribution of political parties within the LCC; in the East End this meant Conservative majorities for the first time since the First World War. The second major change resulted from the rule that no member of a local PAC was to be resident or hold political office in the area under its jurisdiction, a prohibition strengthened by requiring the appointment of relieving officers from outside the area. The direct link between Poor Law relief and local politics was severed.

The Labour Party, at a metropolitan and national level, supported both these developments. In 1934, after its victory at the LCC elections, Labour endorsed the view that, since the transfer from the boards of guardians, 'The functioning of district sub-committees has thus become semi-judicial. The trend of poor law relief administration has consistently been from the personal to the judicial.'[53] Morrison's horror at the entanglement of local politics in unemployment relief appeared vindicated, and the borough parties were left with little audience for their complaints at the eclipse of local democracy. When the London Labour Party formulated its response to the new rigorous approach to unemployment relief adopted by the PAC the old insistence on the link between the reorganization of the local economy and relief of unemployment was absent. While dissenting sharply over immediate issues of administration, the LLP saw the unemployed as damaged individuals needing treatment, rather than active members of the labour movement. After distancing itself from the Municipal Reform Party's punitive notion of test work, an LLP report in 1930 continued:

> The view is urged in some quarters that outdoor relief should be given universally free of conditions. We share the objection to test work as such, but in our judgment it is of importance in lengthy cases of unemployment that suitable training and education should be afforded to able-bodied men in order that they shall be assisted to retain the best possible morale and spirit and that they may not become partially unfitted for the resumption of industrial life when work is available.[54]

Enlarging on this analysis, the LLP executive accepted a limited use of punitive work tests, as

> The individual who is believed to be evading his social and domestic obligations . . . cannot justly complain of harshness if test work, as ordinarily understood, is imposed . . . clearly, if the individual is a hopeless 'wrong 'un', he must not be allowed to think that he can live indefinitely upon the rates.[55]

These views met with some opposition from trade unionists. Thomas Naylor, of the London Society of Compositors and the chairman of the LLP, argued that test work should be retained only for punitive purposes, when the PAC was convinced an applicant was deliberately shirking work. As a training measure it was worse than useless in a time of mass unemployment, a waste of money and energy. What was most marked, however, was the shift from the notion of the unemployed as a necessary element in any Labour alliance to the status of passive objects of social policy. The sole advocate of the attitudes of the early 1920s came from the ILP representative on the executive, Wyndham Albery, who supported calls for industrial training but argued against any form of punitive test work which treated poverty as a crime.[56] The combination of financial constraints on borough councils and the shift of political functions to the county level had destroyed the political basis for the alliance of casual labourers, skilled workers in the workshop trades, and the unemployed which had provided the strength of the borough parties in the early 1920s. A form of proletarianism continued to mark the policies of Labour-controlled councils in the East End, but in an increasingly debased form, exemplified in the declaration of John Sullivan, who dominated Stepney's Irish Catholic Labour machine from the mid-1920s, that 'if there is a chance of giving a Labour man a job, of course we will put him in, yes, and get value for our money'.[57]

The successes of Labour in the East End during the 1920s did not stem from a fundamental shift in relationships of production but were the result of a more complex interplay between a framework of intervention in local labour markets initiated by Whitehall and the tensions within the hybrid system of unemployment relief. This political conjuncture, lasting for a decade, established politics at the borough level as the prime locus for Labour advance in London, and the source of a politics which appeared to offer a fundamental contradiction to the dominant forces of British society. One consequence was a tendency for the left wing of the London labour movement to leave national and metropolitan political issues in the hands of their opponents, such as Morrison, and concentrate on local issues. The shift of the politics of unemployment relief to a national level, combined with a more concentrated onslaught on the remaining 'Poplarist' councils by the Ministry of Health, meant that the left wing of the Labour Party was bereft of much of its political base and forced to move on to a political terrain which its opponents had already made their own.[58]

Notes

1 N. Branson, *Poplarism*, 1979; K. Bassett, 'Labour, socialism and local democracy', in M. Boddy and C. Fudge (eds), *Local Socialism*, 1984, pp. 82–90.
2 B. Donoughue and G. W. Jones, *Herbert Morrison: Portrait of a Politician*, 1973, ch. 6; G. W. Jones, 'Herbert Morrison and Poplarism', *Public Law*, 1973, pp. 11–31; B. Keith-Lucas, 'Poplarism', ibid., 1962, pp. 52–80.
3 R. McKibbin, *The Evolution of the Labour Party 1910–1924*, Oxford, 1974, p. 240; see also K. D. Brown, 'The Edwardian Labour Party', in *The First Labour Party 1906–14*, 1985; and C. Howard, 'Expectations born to death: local Labour Party expansion in the 1920s', in J. M. Winter (ed.), *The Working Class in Modern British History*, Cambridge, 1983, p. 77. Unfortunately, recent attempts to redress this balance by explaining political change in terms of transformations of the labour process and class relations at the workplace have been even less successful. The history of the Labour Party is reduced to a mere reflex of industrial relations in a few key (almost entirely male-dominated) heavy industries – R. Price, *Labour in British Society*, 1986.
4 Brown, op. cit., p. 9; on the need to analyse Labour as 'a perpetually shifting fulcrum between contending and initially extra-party pressures from left and right', see R. Samuel and G. Stedman Jones, 'The Labour Party and social democracy', in *Culture, Ideology and Politics*, 1982, p. 327.
5 G. Stedman Jones, *Outcast London*, Oxford, 1971, pp. 337–49; 'Working-class culture and working-class politics in London, 1870–1900: notes on the remaking of a working class', in *Languages of Class: Studies in English Working Class History 1832–1982*, 1983; P. Thompson, *Socialists, Liberals and Labour: The Struggle for London 1885–1914*, 1967, *passim*; on the weakness of working-class Toryism in East London, see M. Pugh, *The Tories and the People*, Oxford, 1985, pp. 105–7.
6 Thompson, op. cit., pp. 13, 39.
7 J. Tomlinson, *Problems of British Economic Policy 1870–1945*, 1981, pp. 68–9.
8 J. Bush, *Behind the Lines: East London Labour 1914–1919*, 1984, ch. 7.

9 R. Parker, 'Trade unionism in new industrial areas', in G. D. H. Cole (ed.), *British Trade Unionism Today*, 1939.

10 The following paragraphs are a summary of the detailed argument presented in J. A. Gillespie, 'Industrial and political change in the East End of London during the 1920s', unpublished Ph.D. thesis, Cambridge University, 1984.

11 *Unemployment in East London: A Survey from Toynbee Hall*, 1922, p. 38; G. Phillips and N. Whiteside, *Casual Labour: The Unemployment Question in the Port Industry 1880–1970*, Oxford, 1985, ch. vi.

12 Gillespie, op. cit., p. 168; P. Ryan, 'The Poor Law in 1926', in M. Morris (ed.), *The General Strike*, Harmondsworth, 1976, pp. 358–78.

13 G. Lansbury, 'Labour in local affairs', *Daily Herald*, 13 December 1919.

14 *Eastern Post*, 5 June 1920, 17 June 1922; *East London Observer*, 24 January 1920, 17 June 1922.

15 See the criticisms expressed by Bevin and others in London Labour Party, *Report of the Executive Committee for 1925–26*, p. 25.

16 On the more fiscal motives of 'municipal socialism', see A. Offer, *Property and Politics 1870–1914*, Cambridge, 1981, ch. 18; J. Harris, 'The transition to high politics in English social policy 1880–1914', in M. Bentley and J. Stevenson (eds), *High and Low Politics in Modern Britain*, 1983, pp. 72–3.

17 'John Bryan' (Theodore Rothstein), *The Call*, November 1919; J.R. (Raphael), 'Revolution complete: a Labour borough council', *New Commonwealth*, October 1920.

18 C. R. Attlee, 'Labour and the municipal elections', *New Leader*, 13 October 1922; G. Lansbury, 'Foreword' to C. W. Key, *Red Poplar: Six Years of Socialist Rule*, 1925, p. 3.

19 Metropolitan Borough of Bethnal Green, 'Notes of meeting with district auditor', 26 January 1926.

20 W. Citrine and J. S. Middleton, circular letter, November 1926; letter, Herbert Morrison to J. S. Middleton, 16 November 1926, Labour Party Archives, JSM/WAG/81 and 82; Public Record Office (henceforth PRO), HLG 68/16.

21 Metropolitan Borough of Bethnal Green, *Annual Report, 1921*; Metropolitan Borough of Shoreditch, Minutes, 27 October 1921.

22 E. C. P. Lascelles and S. S. Bullock, *Dock Labour and Decasualization*, 1924, p. 57.

23 R. C. Davison, *The Unemployed: Old Policies and New*, 1929, p. 50; H. Clay, *The Post-War Employment Problem*, 1929, p. 18; D. L. Munby, *Industry and Planning in Stepney*, Oxford, 1951, p. 335.

24 Gillespie, op. cit., pp. 193–5.

25 R. H. Tawney, in League of Nations Union, *Towards Industrial Peace: Conference at the London School of Economics, 1 to 4 February, 1927*, p. 18; Gillespie, op. cit., ch. 6.

26 For examples of the lengths to which councils went to enforce trade union clauses in municipal contracts, see Metropolitan Borough of

Bethnal Green, Works and Stores Committee, Minutes, 8 December 1925, 14 September 1926, 11 January 1927; London Labour Party, 'Municipalities and clothing contracts', *Municipal Circular*, no. 170, 7 May 1930.

27 The changes in the working-class franchise were particularly striking in East London, an area with one of the lowest enrolments before the First World War – H. C. G. Mathew, R. I. McKibbin, and J. A. Kay, 'The franchise factor in the rise of the Labour Party', *English Historical Review*, xci, 1976, pp. 723–52; cf. P. F. Clarke, 'Liberal, Labour and the franchise', *English Historical Review*, xcii, 1977, pp. 582–9; *Unemployment in East London*, op. cit., pp. 6–7.

28 *East London Observer*, 4 March 1922.

29 Quoted by Rev. H. J. Marshall, *Socialism and the Poor Law*, London Municipal Society Pamphlet no. 29, 1927, pp. 19–20.

30 *East London Observer*, 25 August 1923.

31 J. Scurr, *Labour and the Rates: A Policy for Labour Councillors*, Labour Research Department, 1923, p. 5; for similar defences, see Key, op. cit.; J. Abrahams, 'The guardians' elections', *Shoreditch Echo*, February 1928; G. Lansbury, 'Poplar and the Labour Party: a defence of Poplarism', *Labour Monthly*, June 1922, pp. 383–91.

32 For Morrison's views, see 'Unemployment and the rates', London Labour Party Papers, 7 September 1921, folio 713; and *Report of the Executive Committee 1920–21*, paras 46–56.

33 S. and B. Webb, *English Poor Law History. Part II: The Last Hundred Years*, ii, 1929, pp. 850–1.

34 Branson, op. cit.; A. Deacon and E. Briggs, 'Local democracy and the issue of pauper votes in the 1920s', *Policy and Politics*, ii, 1979–80.

35 Sir John Benn, *London Rates and London Industries: The Grievance and the Remedy*, London Reform Union, 1912; G. Lansbury, 'Foreword' to Key, op. cit. The 'little Moscows' of Scotland and South Wales present other examples of the construction of a political common interest in defence of communities overwhelmed by mass unemployment – S. Macintyre, *Little Moscows: Communism and Working-Class Militancy in Inter-War Britain*, 1980, p. 14.

36 On the administration of unemployment benefits, see A. Deacon, *In Search of the Scrounger*, 1976; R. Lowe, *Adjusting to Democracy: The Role of the Ministry of Labour in British Politics, 1916 to 1939*, Oxford, 1986, pp. 135–67.

37 Deacon, op. cit., ch. 1; S. and B. Webb, op. cit., pp. 686–8.

38 Memo, Minister of Health (T. J. MacNamara) to Lloyd George, 3 September 1921, PRO MH 57/121C; J. L. Cohen, *Insurance by Industry Examined*, 1923, p. 45; H. L. Wittner, 'Some effects of the English Unemployment Insurance Acts on the numbers of unemployed relieved under the Poor Law', *Quarterly Journal of Economics*, xlv, 1930–1, pp. 262–88, esp. p. 266; F. Morley, *Unemployment Relief in Britain*, 1924, pp. 80–1.

39 Memo, 15 August 1921, PRO MH 57/121C.

40 Memo, 6 February 1928, PRO MH 58/242.

41 LLP, Executive Minutes, 7 September 1921, folio 714.
42 'Unemployment agitation', *Organizational Points from the London Labour Party*, no. 2, 4 November 1920.
43 W. Hannington, *Unemployed Struggles, 1919 to 1936*, 1936, pp. 13–15.
44 *Eastern Post*, 16 October 1920, 23 October 1920; Hannington, op. cit., pp. 16–18; R. Hayburn, 'The national unemployed workers' movement, 1921–1936', *International Review of Social History*, xxviii, 1983, pp. 279–95.
45 C. Key, op. cit., p. 36; Lansbury, 'Poplar and the Labour Party', *Labour Monthly*, June 1922, p. 388; P. Ryan, '"Poplarism" 1894–1930', in P. Thane (ed.), *The Origins of British Social Policy*, 1978, p. 73; Branson, op. cit., ch. 8.
46 LCC Local Government Committee, *The Metropolitan Common Poor Fund*, report by comptroller of the council, 9 October 1925.
47 J. S. Oxley, 'Report on administration of Poplar parish', 24 February 1922, PRO MH 68/214; Ryan, op. cit., pp. 74–5; Pankhurst's Unemployed Workers' Organization had most of its branches in Poplar – *Workers' Dreadnought*, 4 August 1923.
48 Metropolitan Borough of Bethnal Green, Special Committee on Unemployment, Minutes, 5 December 1921, 20 March 1924; *Eastern Post*, 26 February 1927.
49 Joe Vaughan, 'Why we failed in Bethnal Green', *The Communist*, 25 November 1922; 'The people's candidates', *Oxford House Magazine*, May 1922, p. 11.
50 Metropolitan Borough of Shoreditch, Minutes, 4 October 1921; *Hackney and Kingsland Gazette*, 13 March 1922; *Shoreditch Echo*, February 1928.
51 Councils were able to resist these tendencies by using loan funds, but all suffered severe cut-backs by the late 1920s – *Eastern Post*, 26 February 1927, 6 August 1927, 11 August 1927, 10 December 1927; Metropolitan Borough of Bethnal Green, Special Committee on Unemployment, Minutes, 21 October 1926.
52 *The Work of the London Labour Party*, 1926–7, p. 3; for attacks on the Communists from their former allies in municipal politics, see *Lansbury's Labour Weekly*, 19 December 1925, 6 December 1926; *Straight Left*, March and February 1928.
53 LCC, Public Assistance Committee, *The Reorganization of Arrangements for Public Assistance Administration in Local Areas*, report by chief officer, 18 June 1934.
54 London Labour Party, *Public Assistance Administration: A Supplementary Report of the Executive Committee*, 29 November 1930.
55 LLP, 'Public assistance policy: work, training and intelligence', memo by the hon. secretary (Herbert Morrison), 29 April 1931.
56 T. Naylor, memo, 'Work, training and instruction'; Wyndham J. Albery, 'Notes', 29 April 1931. The final view of the LLP represented a watered-down version of Morrison's memorandum, arguing for a transfer of training, as opposed to test work, from the PAC to the Education Committee of the LCC – *Work, Training and Instruction:*

Their Place in Public Assistance Administration, London Municipal Pamphlet no. 10, 1931; see also I. J. Hayward, D. H. Daines, and R. Sharp, *'What about Belmont?': The Facts about Residential Training Centres under the Labour LCC*, London Municipal Pamphlet no. 14, 1935.

57 *East London Advertiser*, 31 July 1926.
58 Symptomatic of this political failure was Scurr's response to the mooted shift to county-wide administration of the Poor Law, pointing out that this 'reform' was a response to the success of Labour control of boards of guardians, and that the 'pauper taint and stigma' were to remain. However, he was unable to go beyond this purely negative critique – J. Scurr (Labour Research Department), *The Reform (!) of the Poor Law*, Labour White Papers no. 32, January 1927.

8

The suburban nation
Politics and class in Lewisham

Tom Jeffery

Unless London Labour can solve the problem of securing the political attachment of the social strata known as the Middle Classes severe limitation will be set upon the progress of the Movement in London. In view of the character of our population it is a matter of vital importance that the problem shall be faced boldly.

Introduction to Sidney Webb, 'Labour and the middle class',
London Labour Chronicle, August 1922

To some elements of the Labour Party, particularly the trade unions, the concern of the party's 1918 constitution with the interests of workers by both hand and brain may have been little more than a disingenuous concession to the defeated middle-class socialist elements of the party. But for the London Labour Party and its secretary, Herbert Morrison, that concern expressed political necessity, the *sine qua non* of Labour progress in the capital. Webb's article, with its suggestion that London was 'probably the most extensively "middle-class" community in the world', initiated a series[1] in which Hamilton Fyfe of the *Herald*, Emile Davies of the LCC, W. J. Brown of the Civil Service Clerical Association, and Morrison himself spelt out the grounds of Labour's appeal to the middle-class vote. Throughout the 1920s London Labour Party propaganda, closely edited by Morrison, alluded at every opportunity to the common interests of Labour and the middle classes.

But while the problem may have been faced boldly from the early 1920s, in parliamentary elections it was not solved with any significant success until 1945. The general election of 1929, apparently reflecting the impact of Morrison's propaganda effort, was a false dawn. Then, and only then during the inter-war period,

189

Labour took a majority of London's sixty-one constituencies, winning for the first time such inner suburban seats as Hackney Central, Hammersmith South, Battersea South, and Fulham West. But Labour's gains resulted not only from the exhaustion of Conservatism but also from the connected revival of Liberalism: it was the spoiling effect upon the anti-socialist vote of Liberal candidacies which allowed the hope that Labour might soon break through even in outer suburban, substantially middle-class constituencies, nine of which were retained by Tories only on minority votes and sometimes by the slimmest of margins. Yet eighteen of Labour's thirty-five seats were also held on minority votes. The party was, therefore, fearfully vulnerable to the consequences of its own subsequent failure in office, to Tory revival and Liberal collapse. In 1931 Labour retained only five seats in London and was expelled even from such solidly working-class constituencies as Bermondsey and Deptford. There was no significant revival at the general election in 1935: only one of the seats gained for the first time in 1929 was regained, while Labour won none of those which the Tories had held on minority votes in 1929. Despite occasional by-election victories, always vulnerable at subsequent general elections, in terms of parliamentary representation Labour in London was little better placed in 1939 than it had been in 1924.

But notwithstanding the overwhelming victory of the national government in 1931 and its consolidation in 1935, a Tory peace did not settle over London or even over the suburbs in the 1930s. Labour won control of the LCC in 1934 and increased its majority in 1937. The London Labour Party and constituency parties grew in strength throughout the 1930s: by the close of the decade some of the largest and best-organized constituency parties in the country were to be found in London and on its outskirts, in Greenwich and West Woolwich, Hendon and Harrow, all represented by Conservative MPs. At the same time the Communist Party (CP) also gained strength in London. In 1926 London membership had stood at about 1,560, some 15 per cent of the national total; by 1937 London membership had risen to about 5,000, by 1939 to 7,100, some 40 per cent of the total.[2] Moreover, beyond the CP itself, but contributing to the rise in party membership, satellite organizations, notably the Left Book Club, flourished in London in the late 1930s. They did so in the context of a resurgent suburban radicalism and alongside a reviving Liberalism, a reinvigorated nonconformist interest in national and international affairs, and a raft of organizations raising funds for Republican Spain. London in the 1930s was alive with political activity. That activity was at least as marked in the suburbs as in

the older centre. And, in the main, it pointed leftwards. Yet until
1945 the suburbs remained beyond Labour's grasp. Then Labour
swept the board: of the 61 seats, the Conservatives retained only
11; 9 in the affluent centre, only 2, both in Wandsworth, in the
outer suburbs.

In this essay I shall look at the making and remaking of
suburban electoral majorities, taking as a case study the south-
eastern borough of Lewisham and its two constituencies, East and
West. I shall be particularly concerned with the contribution to
those majorities of the middle-class vote. I shall have in mind the
well-worn image of the suburban middle class as isolated and
reactionary and shall propose an approach which, while acknowledging such truth as lies within the image, seeks to go beyond its
potentially damaging limitations. But I shall have an eye also to
the effects of demographic change, the often unrecognized but
undoubtedly important migration of the working class to the
suburbs, and to the roles of both indigenous and immigrant
workers; for, in the suburbs as elsewhere, electoral success rested
upon the creation of cross-class coalitions. And looking at
Lewisham in the light of Morrison's strategy for Labour in London
and in the country as a whole – I shall seek to set the politics of one
particular suburb in the context of metropolitan and national
political change – arguing that, in parliamentary elections, the
politics of the suburbs, and of the metropolis to which they belonged,
were part and parcel of the politics of the nation.

Herbert Morrison had a lifelong interest in Lewisham politics,
attending the inaugural meeting of the East Lewisham Labour
Party (ELLP) in 1919 and virtually every other significant event in
the party's subsequent history, watching closely over its affairs
from his position as London County Councillor for East Woolwich
and from his home, only half a mile from the Lewisham border in
Eltham. For Lewisham presented in microcosm all Morrison's
concerns for Labour in London. It contained a substantial
working-class electorate, a large proportion of whom had only
recently moved to vast LCC cottage estates, ripe for organization.
It contained a very substantial middle-class electorate, without the
support of a significant proportion of which neither constituency
could be won for Labour. And it contained a small but vocal and
intermittently effective Communist Party, moving its attentions as
party policy shifted between working-class and middle-class
districts, and oscillating between support for and opposition to
Labour. Briefly in 1945 Lewisham represented the triumph of
Morrison's strategy for Labour in London: then, moving from
Hackney to East Lewisham, Morrison himself turned a Conserva-

tive majority of 6,000 into a Labour majority of 15,000. Thereafter, as Labour's success among the middle class proved unsustainable, Morrison retreated to the fastness of the working-class estates and eventually, in some bitterness, turned his back on the search for the middle-class vote.

To a clerk, writing for Mass Observation in 1937, the Brockley area of Lewisham in which he lived seemed

> quite pleasant, always providing you shut your eyes to the cemetery and the new council flats on the other side of the railway cutting. . . . The life of the district consists of getting out of it for most things. The men folk go out of it for their jobs and the women go away to Catford and Lewisham for their shopping. In fact they all just, and only just, live there. Nothing ever happens except for a dance each week at the Church Hall and an occasional accident on the main road. . . . Briefly Brockley is a dead and alive hole through which most people go to get somewhere else, but it is not a bad place to live just the same.[3]

This description immediately evokes the contemptuous image of the suburban middle class, eking out a dreary existence conscious of the proximity of death and the working classes. That most persistent of all social stereotypes has been remarkably consistent over time. It has equated the physical form of the suburb with the supposed moral worth of its occupants, as when one Edwardian commentator described 'the suburbans' as 'dwellers in the half-houses of the soul'.[4] It has been propagated by both working-class and *haut-bourgeois* critics but perhaps most compulsively by those born into the suburbs who have moved on to greater things. It has found favour right across the political spectrum and worked its way into academic accounts of the middle class. It has been so pervasive because it has conveyed a certain, grossly simplified truth.[5] But it has occasioned considerable damage and no more so than in discussions of middle-class politics.

For the image – or the alleged culture it encapsulates – has been accorded both predictive and explanatory capacities, summarizing apparently self-evident middle-class interests and motives and explaining their translation into political action. For observers from both right and left the natural political corollary of a beleaguered, aspirant, and anxious middle-class culture has been a reactionary politics, dormant in periods of stability, incendiary at times of crisis. Thus a middle class whose status anxieties were 'to some extent timeless' would always be predisposed towards at least Conservatism.[6] A class marked by 'an acute consciousness of social deficiency' and desperate for social validation would naturally support a Conservatism which was the institutionalized expression of the cult of gentility.[7] A class, 'extremely sensitive to any improvements below which might diminish' its status would always be 'pinching and resentful, a sullen army of the suburbs and massive supporters of right-wing and anti-labour newspapers and politicians'.[8]

There is, of course, no argument but that structural factors have had bearing upon the culture and politics of the middle class, nor that conditions of middle-class life have influenced modes of political practice. Yet when the political becomes the unmediated expression of the cultural, when an equation is enforced between a uniform and benighted culture and an equally uniform and reactionary politics, all complexity of circumstance and response is lost, and real choices, made in given situations from a limited range of options, are discounted. Moreover, explanations of political change must be sought in cultural change: short-term political developments in, periods of relative stability, such as the later 1930s – incapable of explanation in such terms – must be ignored.

To gain purchase on the politics of the suburban middle classes we must turn instead to politics as presented to and practised by the middle classes. We need to understand the ways in which the middle classes were addressed, how middle-class interests were politically constructed, and how those interpreted interests were transformed into realizable political options. In so doing we need to recognize that the middle class was rarely addressed as an independent political force but as a social group whose interests had to be concerted with those of others in a wider political framework. In the suburbs as elsewhere all political parties, none more so than Labour, if Conservative success among the suburban working class as well as in the middle class was to be challenged, needed to draw together the constructed interests of their full range of potential support and to create a wider coalition of interest. To that end all parties fashioned inclusive political rhetorics. And the most common rhetorical expression of the wider community of interest they sought to address and represent, in the inter-war period as before and since, was 'the nation'.[9]

The politics of the nation, in which the suburban middle classes were inextricably embroiled, consisted of the presentation, by political parties and the national and local press, of competing versions of the nation in which social groups, including the middle class, were assigned a place and role. In the dominant version of the nation between the wars, anti-socialist national unity, the middle classes were conceived of as essentially apolitical and quiescent, a reserve army to be electorally co-opted in opposition to socialism. For that anti-socialist nation, as presented by the great majority of suburban Conservative rhetoricians, whatever ambiguities Baldwin may have occasionally introduced, was defined by exclusion. Socialism was denied any legitimate place in the political nation. Labour was to be excluded as a sectional, class party, a threat to stability and prosperity, and the internal agent of an external enemy. To overturn the anti-socialist nation, to form a secure parliamentary majority, Labour had to create its own national coalition, winning middle-class votes in suburban constituencies. To do that, Labour had to create an alternative version of the nation in which the middle classes could be offered and could recognize a role. Labour had therefore to enter a debate whose agenda had been set by its opponents. But the party was in time capable of turning the rhetorical tables, of making the rhetoric of the nation its own. We must now turn to that debate in the suburbs, to Lewisham, to the widely differing versions of the nation presented, and, first, to the social constituents of that particular suburban community.

Lewisham's local establishment prided itself upon the borough's middle-class ethos, presenting the suburb as a haven of health and respectability. That image in some part reflected reality.[10] The readers primarily addressed by the local press were the remaining urban gentry of Sydenham, Forest Hill, and Blackheath and the clerks and shopkeepers of Catford, Lee, and Grove Park. The New Survey found that the percentage of people in middle-class circumstances was higher than in any other borough of the survey area. Of the occupied population of 78,000 in 1921, 44,000 worked outside the borough, over half travelling to work in Westminster and the City. By virtually every index – occupation, overcrowding, poverty, and infant mortality – Lewisham was one of the best-placed boroughs in London.[11]

The suburb had always, of course, contained a working-class population: there were pockets of quite stark poverty, for example in Lower Sydenham, and large numbers of skilled workers, particularly in Hither Green. But the 'indigenous' working population was vastly augmented between the wars by the building on open land in the south of two LCC cottage estates, Bellingham and Downham, in the 1920s and an estate of flats in the north-west, Honor Oak, which the Brockley clerk could see across the railway cutting, in the 1930s. Honor Oak was let on low rents to poorer tenants. Bellingham, with a population of some 10,000 by the late 1930s, housed skilled and some black-coated workers, paying particularly high rents. The tenants of Downham, with a population of some 30,000, were rather more mixed, including many transport workers as well as general labourers. The cottage estates were in some degree separate from old Lewisham. Over time newly built schools, churches, medical centres, and shops met the immediate needs of tenants, many of whom continued to work in the riverside boroughs of Bermondsey, Rotherhithe, and Deptford from whence they had come. But such huge estates could not but impinge on the respectable heart of the borough. While bringing trade they seemed also to bring crime, unruly children, unemployment, and associated charges on the rates.[12] And in the eyes of local politicians they brought too the threat or promise of political change.

Just as Lewisham's indigenous working-class population was subsumed within the middle-class ethos, so a long-standing strain of radical political dissent was hidden by a much-vaunted 'Conservative tradition'. The parliamentary constituency, divided into two in 1918, had been in Conservative hands since 1885. But ILP, SDF, and Labour Party branches had been established before the First World War,[13] and Progressives had briefly controlled the borough council and the LCC seats. After the war the Conservative hold on the West was threatened by internecine warfare at a by-election in 1921 and by a highly confident Liberal Party in 1923. In the East, the East Lewisham Labour Party (ELLP) made an immediate impact, securing 29 per cent of the vote on first standing in a general election in 1922 and steadily increasing its share thereafter. In 1929, with Liberals in the field, Conservatives retained both West and East on minority votes, with their majority cut in the latter from 10,221 in 1924 to 402. As elsewhere in the London suburbs, it seemed that one more push would bring Labour victory in Lewisham and that working-class immigration had made the crucial contribution, obviating the need for a cross-class coalition.

As early as 1925 Labour supporters had asked why the Conservatives were 'so anxious about Downham', the answer being 'because they fear that Downham is going to down 'em';[14] while Sir Assheton Pownall, the Conservative MP, speaking at Blackheath's Tranquil-vale, had warned that 'he did not encounter many Tranquil-vales when he went to Downham . . . and unless his friends played up and the Liberals decided to play for "Safety First" ', there was a danger that the seat would be lost.[15] But in fact the estates alone never made a greater impact than in 1929. Never again in the inter-war period would the Liberals split the anti-socialist vote in 'old' Lewisham. Containing only about one-quarter of East Lewisham's electorate and substantially in place by 1929, the estates could carry Labour to the edge of victory but no further even under the most favourable circumstances. The coming of the estates was therefore an important but insufficient condition of political change. But their impact on the politics of the suburb was far-reaching. Beyond boosting Labour's vote their coming created a divide in contemporary perceptions between 'old', essentially middle-class Lewisham and the 'new' working-class enclaves, thus furnishing a metaphor through which issues of class could be addressed. The estates provided a base for Labour organization and a spur to Conservative efforts, the respective success and the relative failure of the two parties contributing in some part to Labour's 1934 and 1937 LCC victories. And in parliamentary elections, so far from countermanding the coalitional imperative, the presence of the estates served to throw into relief the importance to Labour of the middle-class vote.

From the late 1920s the ELLP became the very model of a Morrisonian constituency party. Characteristically Morrison himself had orchestrated the party's disaffiliation in 1926 after the Communist take-over.[16] By 1930 membership stood at 2,500 and was heavily concentrated on the estates; even in 1946, when Labour had made significant inroads in middle-class areas, some 54 per cent of members came from the estates, constituting 7.2 per cent of their electorate. There was nothing inevitable about such progress among the suburban working class: membership in working-class districts of 'old' Lewisham accounted for only 2.2 per cent of the electorate of those areas, less than in lower middle-class areas, where 2.4 per cent of the electorate were party members.[17] Whether the estates membership was the result of patronage or of the promise of patronage is a matter for more detailed research, although of course Labour had no patronage to confer until it took control of the LCC in 1934. It is clear, however, that Labour's advance was the result of conscious and concentrated effort involving the development of local drama, choral, and sporting societies, political education, and intensive canvassing, with each road on the estates managed by a 'street captain'. Surveying marginal constituencies in 1938, the London Labour Party described the ELLP as 'a model for others'.[18]

Yet while Labour effort was, until the late 1930s, focused on the working-class electorate of the estates, it was directed by lower-middle-class leaders. The agent, Jimmy Raisin, Morrison's close friend, looked, and some said behaved, like a bank manager. Local Labour pioneers John Wilmot, Michael Stewart, and Arthur Skeffington, all later to hold government office, and prospective parliamentary candidates Freda Corbett, William Kendall, and Tom Crawford shared distinctively lower-middle-class suburban backgrounds, graduating by scholarship to secondary school and beyond, and all but Wilmot, a Dalton protégé and City figure, worked as teachers. Only the Earl of Listowel, county councillor from 1937 and later the last Secretary of State for India, broke the pattern. Labour's lack of immediate success among the middle class was not for want of showing a middle-class face to the electorate. But there was a clear progress, from middle-class candidates in the 1920s, to the involvement of a broader group of middle-class activists in the 1930s, to success among middle-class voters in 1945.

Lewisham Conservatism took its cue from the sitting MPs. Sir Philip Dawson in the West, a forceful die-hard, commanded the respect of a once strong but increasingly ossified association dominated by the upper middle classes of Sydenham and Forest Hill. Pownall in the East, while equally practised in the rhetoric of anti-socialist exclusionism, was a far weaker figure, only grudgingly accepted by a weaker association.[19] Dependent on the efforts of the women's associations and on other people's money, particularly Pownall's and the county councillors', East Lewisham's organizational effort was lacklustre and inconsistent, flowing but more often ebbing under the pull of national party morale.[20] Even a Central Office 'missioner' failed to make an impression on Downham, although a small bridgehead was eventually established and sustained on Bellingham in the 1930s. Officers chided members' apathy, seen in turn as the main cause of the greatest danger – apathy among Conservative supporters in 'old' Lewisham. But senior posts revolved among established figures, and little was done to welcome new young faces.[21] Despite the women's efforts, it was a Conservatism which reflected the national approach to the middle class, assuming loyalty but doing very little to win it, except by negative reference to the socialist threat. And it was a Conservatism quite incapable of withstanding any loss of purpose on the part of the party nationally. It was not until 1938, on Dawson's death, that Lewisham acquired, and then unwillingly, a young, dynamic figure, Henry Brooke, determined to encourage wider middle-class participation and to speak in positive terms to the middle-class electorate.

In large part, differential organization of strongholds, Labour's enthusiasm, and Conservatism's lethargy contributed to Labour's only significant breakthrough in Lewisham before 1945, the LCC victories in the East in 1934 and 1937. Of course wider factors played a part, notably the torpor and indirection affecting

Conservatism locally and centrally in 1934. But electors in 'old' Lewisham stayed at home in 1934,[22] while the estates polled heavily: no ward in 'old' Lewisham polled more than 35 per cent, while Bellingham and Downham polled 52 and 55 per cent respectively. In 1937 East Lewisham Tories employed hired men to deliver 'apathy cards'. Many went astray; two delivery men were sacked, and the foreman was described as 'incompetent'. After the election, criticism focused on 'the type of man employed'.[23]

In metropolitan elections, Labour could win East Lewisham by virtue of negative coalition: high turn-outs on the estates, abstention elsewhere. Moreover, neither in 1934 nor in 1937 could anti-socialist spokesmen, despite, for example, the labelling of Morrison as 'the little Trotsky of London',[24] succeed in regenerating the rhetoric of a threatened nation – and indeed empire – which had so marked the LCC campaign of 1931.[25] Morrison's emphasis on measured municipal improvement set against 'the dead hand of Toryism' held the campaigns within a metropolitan frame. But parliamentary elections were necessarily dominated by national and international issues, were interpreted by a national press, in turn echoed by a local press, anxious to invest suburban affairs with national significance, and were infused with national imagery. While Liberals remained in the field, negative coalition remained a feasible route to Labour victory even in parliamentary elections. In 1929 the nature of the political nation and the place of the middle classes within it were matters for open, equal debate in a three-cornered contest as both Liberal and Labour candidates addressed the electors of 'old' Lewisham on Liberal themes, notably disarmament. In 1931 the possibility of negative coalition was foreclosed as anti-socialists perfected the politics of exclusion, setting the terms of debate for the remainder of the decade. Thereafter Labour could only win by adding to the estates' votes a significant element of positive middle-class support.

For anti-socialists, in the summer crisis of 1931 and the ensuing autumn election, Lewisham epitomized the national struggle: if they were to keep 'the British flag flying', Lewisham had to be 'made safe for the nation from the socialist peril'.[26] Not without misgivings in the West, the Liberals withdrew, one declaring that he would 'consider it a duty and a privilege to vote Conservative. To do otherwise I should consider myself a traitor to my country.'[27] Across south-east London churchmen spoke at national meetings, urging 'the electors to vote like patriots'.[28] To the *Borough News* the election was 'one in which politics, class interest and all petty bickering should be subordinated to national needs'; it would be a straight fight, 'National -v- Anti-National'. To the *Mercury*, the issue was simple, 'for or against the nation'.[29]

Despite attempts to turn the tables, to ask 'whether England was to be governed by the English or foreign bankers',[30] both Stewart in the West and Wilmot in the East, the latter retreating to the estates where many meetings were 'packed and enthusiastic',[31] were pursued by unremitting exclusionist rhetoric. For the *Mercury*:

> the emergency we are facing today is the greatest since the days of the war but differs in one vital particular . . . in those perilous days the country was united against a common danger from without. Today . . . there is a powerful element within the country opposed to those measures of defence which alone can save us from disaster.[32]

For Dawson:

> the alternative to the National Government was the Anti-National Socialist Party, who were divided among themselves except when the questions of damaging the interests and welfare of their country were concerned. Shouting, hatred, malice and evil were the only things that bound them together.[33]

To a party official, the election was a 'crusade for everything that was right and decent against the enemies of this country. Those who were not with them in the fight were enemies to the country and traitors to it.'[34]

Pownall's majority leapt to 20,869, with Labour's absolute vote falling by 2,000, its share from 42 to 33 per cent. In the West Dawson's majority rose to 24,333, while Labour's share fell to 23.5 per cent. On the eve of poll the *Borough News* had obliquely identified the natural constituents and potential enemies of the anti-socialist nation, warning that 'the changed circumstances of the estates region . . . make it imperative that no lover of his country can afford to leave Sir Assheton Pownall's return to chance'.[35] But in the overpowering atmosphere of crisis, anti-socialists had no need to appeal more explicitly to the middle-class vote. Given Labour's past failures, present division, and lack of conviction as to the future, given the unanimity of the anti-socialists and the complete identification of the government with a coherent if exclusionist vision of the nation, the place of the middle class in that nation was self-evident. There was no requirement to participate, no call to action: offered only security after relatively mild sacrifice, the middle classes were asked merely to assert their loyalty at the ballot box. And that perception of loyalty seems to have been shared by many estate tenants, as suggested by the immediately subsequent borough election, which was fought wholly within the context of the general election. As the *Mercury* suggested: 'we have a National Government: a necessary corollary is National Borough Councils'.[36] Communists, a thorn in Labour's side throughout 1931, stood as Workers' Charter candidates. On Downham the Municipal Reform vote rose appreciably to well over 1,000 per candidate, while Labour held Bellingham ward by only seven votes after a recount. Combining this support on the estates with their overwhelming strength in 'old' Lewisham, it was anti-socialists, rather than Labour, who first benefited from the politics of coalition in the 1930s.

Labour's achievement in the early 1930s was to undo the damage of 1931, to regain supremacy on the estates, and thereby to break through in 1934. The anti-socialists' achievement was to weather the difficulties, electoral and organizational, of 1934, to brush aside a short-lived and weak threat from fascism[37] and, regaining unity as the general election approached in 1935,[38] to refashion the anti-socialist nation, blocking Labour progress in 'old' Lewisham. In that election, while Labour's campaign, locally as nationally, failed to impose coherence upon disparate and sometimes contradictory policies,[39] Conservatism found a more explicit place within a solid and seemingly permanent anti-socialist nation.

In the East, Pownall spoke directly to 'the large numbers of blackcoated workers' in Lewisham, resurrecting the 1931 savings scare, recalling socialist-induced privations, promising further economic recovery, pointing in particular to the restoration of teachers' salaries, and making much of the government's plans, wholly consistent with Conservative notions of a self-sufficient middle class, to extend old-age and widows' pensions on a voluntary basis to all non-manual workers.[40] This favoured but non-participative middle class had an unambiguous place in a nation now raised far above the merely political the better to protect democracy from domestic and, increasingly importantly, international danger.[41] As the *Mercury* explained, while

> politics in general are a necessary part of the life of the people
> . . . there are occasions when politics can very well be made
> subservient to the commonweal. . . . The National Government
> is the only Government likely to secure peace; the past few
> years have proved that such a Government can bring prosperity.
> . . . All voters, whilst retaining their private political opinions,

are asked once again to rise to a great national issue and place country before party for the time being.[42]

Dawson's majority was halved, Pownall's reduced to 6,449. Even so, after the triumph of 1934 and unstinting organizational efforts, the result was a disappointment for Labour. But Pownall too was unhappy. He pressed for redistribution, suggesting that the estates should be hived off, leading a delegation to the Prime Minister in 1937, pointing to the vulnerability of seats containing large LCC estates, Hendon, Romford, and Lewisham. As both Pownall and his opponents recognized, it was not the estates alone but the threat of their alliance with middle-class voters in 'old' Lewisham which challenged his tenure. For the remainder of the decade, 'old' Lewisham became the central focus of political activity in the borough.

There was a fundamental change in the approach of the left to the middle classes in the late 1930s. At the prompting of Dalton as well as Morrison, the Labour Party began to direct its propaganda effort towards the middle class. Left intellectuals and non-manual trade unions began to abandon the proletarianization thesis which had cast the middle class as mechanized automata, emphasizing instead the benefits of technical change to intellectual workers in a planned economy. The CP, taking its cue from Soviet planning and policy, began to address the middle class as leaders of scientific advance and guardians of civilized values. And, beyond the established labour movement, new radical cultural organizations began to find value in hitherto unacknowledged areas of national life, challenging the government's claim to represent the nation and the claim of the press to reproduce the voice of that nation.[43]

Those cultural organizations spoke directly to and found a ready response among a largely middle-class audience. In the crisis of the coming of war, to many, if not the majority, in the suburban middle class, particularly the lower-middle-class young, the government's assumption of their political indifference no longer seemed benign. There was no status-panic drawing these people to political action. If there was aspiration, it was aspiration to learn, to take their limited education further. And if there was anxiety, they were anxious to understand the crisis through which they were living, to make their voices heard, and to participate in its resolution. In Lewisham as across the London suburbs, many middle-class people found that sense of involvement through joining Mass Observation or the Left Book Club, raising funds for Spain, and following the affairs of other countries through Penguin

Specials and the *News Chronicle*. Though he may not have been fully conscious of it, the Brockley clerk, who elsewhere in his 'day surveys' expressed despair at the seemingly inevitable approach of war, was part of that revival of suburban radicalism.

In Lewisham, as represented by Dawson and Pownall, the government was particularly vulnerable. Dawson was a long-standing supporter of Mussolini, Pownall a member of the Council of the Anglo-German Fellowship and an enthusiastic guest at the 1937 Nuremberg rally: he reported a parade of 50,000 'political leaders, corresponding roughly to Chairmen and Ward Secretaries in our political organizations at home, all in their brown shirts'.[44] The rhetorical tables could now be turned. For Pownall, until March 1939, socialism remained 'the national menace'. But for the radical groups, the anti-socialists could now be presented as the threat to the nation, the internal agents of an external enemy.

That argument was made with increasing force through 1937 and 1938 and was addressed primarily to the middle classes of 'old' Lewisham. But while new activists were enrolled, middle-class voters did not respond in large numbers. And while a new alliance of radical forces began uncertainly to emerge, it did not coalesce as a permanent force. For the radical groups were involved in a fierce internal struggle for the leadership of suburban radicalism. Until that struggle was resolved, no lasting coalition of forces, capable of developing an electoral alliance between 'old' and 'new' Lewisham, could take shape.

By far the largest element in the vestigial alliance was, of course, the Labour Party, which began to make significant progress in 'old' Lewisham. Thoroughly organized campaigns pushed membership beyond 4,000 and 2,000 in the East and West respectively, making both among the largest constituency parties in the country by 1938. Surprisingly good results were recorded in areas such as Sydenham and Blackheath.[45] But alongside Labour, the nonconformists were once again alive; a new Liberal and Radical Association was formed; and the CP began to reach a wide audience through mass town-hall rallies addressed by Gallacher and Pollitt.[46] And beyond these established groups were organizations born of the crisis of the late 1930s.[47] The Lewisham Spanish Medical Aid Committee (SMAC) was ceaselessly active, raising money first for ambulances, then for hospital beds, co-ordinating efforts with the churches, and gaining support from the Labour parties, the trades council, co-operative guilds, and the local Left Book Club (LBC) groups. But if some CP influence in the SMAC was detectable, the LBC groups were clearly the respectable face of the Downham-based CP in 'old' Lewisham. The groups held regular meetings to discuss the monthly Club 'choice' but, beyond that, organized mass rallies, based on the Club's national campaigns and, in April 1938, promoted a 'crisis conference', calling for the formation of a 'Peace Alliance of Labour, Liberal, Communist and other Progressive bodies'. For the Lewisham LBC, thus bidding for a pivotal role in suburban radicalism, a popular front 'would not be a mere vote-catching electoral arrangement but . . . more in the nature of a nationwide crusade against war and poverty, a crusade in which all progressive people of goodwill would participate'.[48]

Nationally Labour would have no truck with such a deal; locally the reaction was more complex. The Peace Alliance was rejected outright.[49] But much depended on individuals' personal dispositions and circumstances. William Kendall, candidate in the East, temperamentally close to the ILP and sure of working-class support, warned of the dangers of meddling 'intellectuals' and 'the howlings for a fight against fascism'.[50] Listowel, on the other hand, personified the latent alliance nationally and locally. A leading member of SMAC, vice-chairman of the National Joint Council for Spanish Relief, and president of the China Campaign Committee, Listowel shared platforms in Lewisham with Cripps, Ellen Wilkinson, and Fred Copeman, a commander of the British Battalion of the International Brigades and a native of the borough.[51] Most importantly, Arthur Skeffington, candidate in the West, regularly addressed SMAC and LBC meetings and spoke to a constituency far beyond the new middle-class activists in a rhetoric of the radical nation tinged with nineteenth-century Liberalism. Pointing out that 'it was sometimes difficult to get at the non-political members of the community because, in comparison with keen politicians . . . they thought in a different vocabulary', Skeffington appealed to 'all Liberals, even Conservatives, who believe in peace'.[52]

The by-election which followed Dawson's death during the Munich Crisis illustrated both the extent and the limits of political change in the suburbs in the late 1930s.[53] First it showed that the balance of political forces was changing. Brooke, the Conservative candidate, fought alone. Skeffington, with the CP and its satellites kept in the background, was actively supported by the Liberals and local churchmen, so prominent on national platforms in 1931.[54] Second, for the first time in a decade, Labour competed on equal terms in a contest dominated by the rhetoric of the nation, Brooke resting his case on Chamberlain's defence of and socialism's threat to the nation, Skeffington arguing the contrary. For Morrison the by-election was 'about more than party politics. It is a by-election about the well-being of the nation.'[55] And third, the election was fought by two young, vigorous candidates, determined to involve the middle classes fully in democratic politics. Skeffington, 'the essence of suburban socialism',[56] had been dedicated to that task since his selection; Brooke, imposed on the association, who had preferred a local man, was determined to break the gentry's oligarchy.

But the limits of change were equally clear: neither candidate succeeded in invigorating Lewisham in 1938. On a particularly low turn-out, the Conservative majority was cut to 5,650.[57] In the *Mercury*'s view, only a 'political earthquake' could shake Lewisham.[58] Munich, at the time, with its ambiguous message, capable of interpretation as vindication or violation of the nation, was no earthquake. Skeffington had stirred activists from all parties and none but had not persuaded the less involved to vote Labour. And local Conservatism had remained lethargic and complacent.[59] But Lewisham did not drift thus towards war. The remaining months of peace saw two developments which would have a vital impact on the suburb's political future. Brooke launched a remarkable revival in local Conservatism, prefiguring the national campaign which he, among others, would lead after the war. And on the left the struggle for the leadership of the emergent alliance was resolved as the Communists first lost heart and then withdrew.

Brooke appealed over the heads of the oligarchy to those excluded by their regime, conscious that the left's challenge rested on a similarly direct approach to the middle class. He established discussion groups, reorganized the Imps, and spoke throughout the constituency to a catholic range of organizations, some far beyond the boundaries of Conservatism.[60] Above all, emphasizing an ethic of public service, Brooke called for greater middle-class involvement in a more positive Conservative nation: without such involvement, 'the quality and character of the nation would deteriorate'. He hoped that his political epitaph would read: 'he played his part in helping all sorts of people in West Lewisham take a more active interest in national affairs'.[61]

While the early months of 1939 saw a redoubling of radical effort, with impassioned pleas for aid for Spain and calls for a peace front with Russia, by June the bi-annual report of the LBC was weary and frustrated. On the estates, away from the progressive politics of 'old' Lewisham, the CP orchestrated a bitter and ultimately fruitless rent strike, vilifying the county councillors and Morrison.[62] In August, but before the Nazi–Soviet Pact, the CP abandoned the politics of alliance, reasserting an emphasis on class. Three prominent members of the ELLP resigned and openly joined the CP.[63] The pact merely ensured that the break was total.

The CP, the most insistent advocate of 'unity', had, in effect, been the major obstacle to united action.[64] With that obstacle removed, the arguments, rhetorics, and sympathies developed in the upsurge of suburban radicalism of the late 1930s could be brought fully under Labour Party control. In 1945 Labour, the sole legatee if by no means the only begetter of late-1930s radicalism, could at last secure the support of a substantial section of the suburban middle class.

The general election of 1945 was fought by reference as much to the past as to the future. It was a contest in which Pownall, resorting to calls for 'stern justice' for 'the Huns' and 'Japs' and severely embarrassed by his pre-war sympathies, could not compete.[65] But in Brooke and Morrison, though they were not pitted directly against each other, Lewisham saw, for the first time, two politicians of the first rank presenting competing versions of the nation and offering contrasting but essentially participatory roles to the middle classes. Brooke envisioned a nation of 'independent families with freedom to choose their own way of life', raising 'children who are not the playthings of bureaucrats', and 'ready to answer the country's call to service'.[66] Morrison, leading Labour's campaign nationally, argued in Lewisham for a rational and planned Britain, built by the equal efforts of all citizens, including the middle classes: the war had been 'won by organizing the talents of science, administration and labour and planning their use'.[67]

Both Morrison and Skeffington drew upon the latent coalition and developing rhetoric of the late 1930s, so powerfully reinforced by the war. Skeffington, assisted by the Common Wealth and Liberal parties, was confident that 'Labour and Progressive forces' could 'take up the fight where we left it in 1938'.[68] And once again Lewisham was seen to epitomize the national struggle. As Morrison put it, he had

> for many years counselled the Socialist Party that if it is ever to secure an independent, stable parliamentary majority, it must gain and keep the support not only of the politically conscious organized workers, but also of large numbers of professional, technical and administrative workers, of whom there are many in East Lewisham. It is because I have confidence in the reasoned appeal that the Socialist Party can make to all sections of the community – manual workers and blackcoated workers alike – that I have decided to go to East Lewisham; if I am elected, emphasizing by this action my conviction that the soundest socialist appeal is that which is most universal in its scope.[69]

Morrison appealed in the radical rhetoric of the late 1930s to 'all men and women of goodwill and intelligence and progressive outlook . . . I want them to get together on the only genuine basis of national unity which is . . . the Labour party's basis'.[70]

Skeffington took West Lewisham by a majority of 2,516, Morrison the East by 15,219. Prior to the election, the twelve inner south-east London seats had been equally divided between government and opposition; after the election none remained in Conservative hands. Freda Corbett won North-West Camberwell; John Wilmot won Deptford; across London, Michael Stewart took Wilmot's former seat, East Fulham. The election of 1945 represented a triumph not only for Labour in the suburbs but also for lower-middle-class Labour politicians trained in the Lewisham school of suburban politics.

The nature of Labour's electoral coalition in East Lewisham is revealed by detailed analyses produced by the ELLP in 1946. Those analyses set estimates of Labour's vote in each polling district alongside social descriptions of those districts. While any extrapolation from such material must be treated with caution,[71] three broad conclusions do emerge. First, demographic change during the war, the far greater fall in the electorate in middle-class districts than on the estates, could have had only a limited impact on the result. In January 1945 the estates accounted for 30 per cent of the East Lewisham electorate, compared to 25 per cent in 1939. But middle-class districts still held 37 per cent of the electorate in 1945, compared to 40 per cent in 1939. No doubt there was some subdivision of property in older middle-class areas. But the war did not proletarianize Lewisham. Second, Labour secured overwhelming working-class support in 1945. But that support was even stronger on the estates, where fully 90 per cent of voters were believed to have supported Labour, than in working-class districts of 'old' Lewisham, where Labour took some 70 per cent of the vote. And third, Labour's vote reflected very substantial, if not majority, middle-class support. Labour's total vote was 37,361, the Tories' 22,142. The party's estimates suggested that 14,360 votes came from Downham and Bellingham, a further 5,731 from working-class districts in 'old' Lewisham, and some 7,000 from polling districts with a broad mix of working-class and middle-class voters. But over 10,000 Labour votes, more than one-quarter of the total, came from solid middle-class and lower-middle-class districts: the party estimated that it secured 33 per cent of the vote in solidly middle-class areas and 45 per cent of the vote in lower-middle-class districts, figures almost identical to John Bonham's estimates of Labour's share of the national middle-class vote.[72]

The party had broken out of the estates and won support in 'old' Lewisham, the condition of success which had proved so elusive before the war.

More work is needed on the politics of the suburbs. There is scope for studies of the LCC cottage estates, looking not only at the Labour Party but also at the CP and linked organizations such as the National Unemployed Workers' Movement, which, in Downham, while always in the minority, engaged in intense rivalry with the Labour Party throughout the 1920s and 1930s. In looking at the politics of the suburban middle classes there is a need to make distinctions between, for example, professional and clerical workers; to examine the clearly significant role of women in suburban politics, both Conservative and socialist; and to adopt a wider comparative frame, looking at areas less affected by working-class immigration. And within such work, there is certainly room for analysis of the patterns of middle-class lives, of middle-class culture. But such analyses must be, at the least, wary of the dismissive image of the suburban middle class and ready to find variety and indeed some value in suburban lives and attitudes. And above all, if those analyses are to shed light on political change, they must focus upon politics as practised. There is a need to look closely at relationships between middle-class suburban radicals and their more proletarian counterparts: in Lewisham there is, for instance, some evidence that the Left Book Club organizers regarded the estates somewhat *de haut en bas* and that 'missioners' were not confined to the Conservative associations. But beyond that, if sense is to be made of suburban middle-class politics in both periods of flux and of stability, account must be taken of the place of the middle classes and of the suburbs in the politics of the nation. The politics of the suburban middle classes in the mid-century are best understood in terms of the making and remaking of versions of 'the nation'.

The politics of Lewisham fully reflected the politics of the nation: the relative confusion of the 1920s, with Liberals still in the field; the brutal simplification of 1931; the modest refashioning of the anti-socialist nation in 1935; the re-emergence of radicalism in the late 1930s; and Labour's triumph of 1945. Moreover, Lewisham politics exemplified the coalitional imperative, the necessity for Labour to create a cross-class electoral alliance and to do so by engaging fully in the politics and rhetoric of the nation. It is pointless to bemoan Labour's engagement as consensual or compromising; it was rather a condition of the party's survival and progress as a major electoral force.[73] And in time, Labour was capable of making the rhetoric of the nation its own, of casting

Conservatives as friends of the nation's enemies and of fashioning a version of the nation in which all social groups, including the middle class, were offered a place, as of right. In 1945, drawing on the rhetoric of pre-war radicalism vindicated by the war and taken fully under Labour control, Labour spoke both to the middle-class sense of service and to middle-class self-interest. Morrison's notion of a middle class central to a planned economy was but an attenuated version of early ILP ideas on the pivotal functional role of the middle classes in a socialist society. It carried, too, unforeseen consequences, as, for example, certain middle-class groups became major beneficiaries of the Welfare State, as both producers and consumers. But it was instrumental in persuading large numbers of middle-class voters, in the words of perceptive Conservative commentators, that they could, in voting Labour, 'remain middle-class but regain a sense of social purpose'.[74]

The post-war history of south-east London illustrates both the fragility of Labour's hold upon the middle classes and the importance of securing electoral alliances. Bonham showed that Labour did not lose many middle-class votes between 1945 and 1950. But by the turn of the decade the Conservatism of Brooke (by then moved to Hampstead) and Macmillan (since 1946 just across the border in Bromley) had won back abstainers and secured a much larger share of the middle-class vote. Moreover, the estates had been hived off into a separate constituency, Lewisham South, taken by Morrison: in the 1950s, adopting a much more proletarian persona, and bitter at Attlee's long-delayed departure and Gaitskell's succession, Morrison inveighed against what he saw as middle-class revisionist elements in the party.[75] In 1950, deprived of the estates and running against the political wind, Copeman (on his way from the International Brigade to Moral Rearmament)[76] lost the North, and Skeffington lost the West. Readmitted briefly in the North at a by-election in 1957, Labour did not regain control of the two constituencies until its second suburban *annus mirabilis* in 1966. In the 1980s, in a quite different anti-socialist nation, Lewisham, now again two constituencies, is in Conservative hands, despite the estates. Indeed, Downham ward is held by a new form of Alliance, as are the riverfront constituencies, the original source of the estates' tenants. In the meantime Labour in London has spoken to only a small minority in the middle class (but in a distinctively middle-class voice), has failed to speak to the self-interest of sufficient working-class voters, and has failed entirely to bind classes together in an appeal 'universal in its scope'.

Appendix: parliamentary election results, 1918–1945

Table 8.1 Lewisham East[77]

Election	Electors	Turn-out	Candidate	Party	Votes (Majority)	%
1918			A. Pownall	Co.C	Unopposed	
1922	45,377	64.0	A. Pownall	C	16,726	57.6
			E. W. Wilton	Lab	8,402	28.9
			J. C. L. Zorn	L	3,906	13.5
					(8,324)	
1923	48,812	62.6	A. Pownall	C	13,560	44.4
			E. W. Wilton	Lab	9,604	31.4
			Sir E. Penton	L	7,397	24.2
					(3,956)	
1924	50,019	74.9	A. Pownall	C	23,842	63.6
			J. C. Wilmot	Lab	13,261	36.4
					(10,581)	
1929	76,562	71.5	Sir A. Pownall	C	23,208	42.4
			J. C. Wilmot	Lab	22,806	41.7
			Sir E. Penton	L	8,729	15.9
					(402)	
1931	82,606	74.9	Sir A. Pownall	C	41,354	66.9
			J. C. Wilmot	Lab	20,485	33.1
					(20,869)	
1935	87,178	68.0	Sir A. Pownall	C	32,874	55.4
			Mrs F. K. Corbett	Lab	26,425	44.6
					(6,449)	
1945	79,318	76.2	Rt Hon. H. S. Morrison	Lab	37,361	61.9
			Sir A. Pownall	C	22,142	36.6
			F. Russell	Ind	931	1.5
					(15,219)	

Table 8.2 Lewisham West[78]

Election	Electors	Turn-out	Candidate	Party	Votes (Majority)	%
1918			Sir E. F. Coates	Co.C	Unopposed	
Death 13.9.21	40,919	59.2	Sir P. Dawson	C	9,427	39.0
			W. G. Windham	AWL	8,580	35.4
			F. W. Rafferty	L	6,211 (847)	25.6
1922	42,455	58.1	Sir P. Dawson	C	16,216	65.7
			B. L. A. O'Malley	L	8,469 (7,747)	34.3
1923	42,940	57.0	Sir P. Dawson	C	12,448	50.9
			B. L. A. O'Malley	L	12,009 (439)	49.1
1924	44,078	75.5	Sir P. Dawson	C	19,723	59.3
			Mrs B. Drake	Lab	6,781	20.4
			B. L. A. O'Malley	L	6,756 (12,942)	20.3
1929	61,191	69.3	Sir P. Dawson	C	20,830	49.1
			Mrs C. M. Wadham	Lab	10,958	25.9
			A. R. N. Roberts	L	10,590 (9,872)	25.0
1931	63,946	69.2	Sir P. Dawson	C	34,289	77.5
			R. M. M. Stewart	Lab	9,956 (24,333)	22.5
1935	65,679	63.9	Sir P. Dawson	C	27,173	64.7
			R. R. M. Stewart	Lab	14,803 (12,370)	35.3
Death 24.11.38	67,641	58.4	H. Brooke	C	22,587	57.1
			A. M. Skeffington	Lab	16,937 (5,650)	42.9
1945	59,918	73.6	A. M. Skeffington	Lab	20,008	53.4
			H. Brooke	C	17,492 (2,516)	46.6

Notes

I am grateful to Marion Sawyer, Mike Hall, and Carl Harrison and his staff at the Lewisham local history library for their help.

1 *London Labour Chronicle*, nos 82, 83, 88, 89, 91, and 95, August 1922 to September 1923.

2 Kenneth Newton, *The Sociology of British Communism*, 1969, appendix 5, pp. 175–6.

3 Mass Observation, Day Survey, no. 208, June 1937, Mass Observation Archive, University of Sussex. I am most grateful to Dorothy Sheridan and the Trustees of the Archive for their permission to quote this extract.

4 T. Crossland, *The Suburbans*, 1905, p. 141.

5 For recourse to the image by the left in the period with which we are concerned, see, for example, Allen Hutt: 'Boxed up in his little suburban house with his family, of which he still tries to play the patriarch, the middle class man presents in caricature the traditional "national" characteristics of Capitalist Britain; he sums up in himself the narrow, pettifogging outlook, the "respectability", the cant, humbug and hypocrisy, the insularity and chauvinism, the combination of practical energy and disgraceful intellectual indolence' – Allen Hutt, *The Condition of the Working Class in Britain*, 1933, p. 23. There is, of course, a certain percipience in this comment, hinting as it does of the sympathy between the middle classes and the national government in the early 1930s; but it reflects too the CP line of the time, a line which would change dramatically over the next few years. For condescension from the right, see Angus Maude and Roy Lewis, writing in pique at the lower-middle-class betrayal of Conservatism in 1945: 'To hope that members of this class will in future be able to shake off the sense of insecurity which makes them so difficult for working-class people to get on with is to hope that the leopard will change its spots. Whether they will ever get on any better with the upper middle classes may depend on whether they are able to overcome enough of their petty – but, oh, so worrying – preoccupations' – *The English Middle Classes*, 1953, pp. 243–4. For those who look back in anger at a lower-middle-class and suburban background, see John Osborne, *A Better Class of Person*, 1981; and John Fowles's comment: 'I grew up in Leigh-on-Sea which was very respectable. The repressions there seemed to be the cause of an enormous amount of evil. I have an intense suspicion of that stratum of society. It's the aping of the gentility of the class above it that I find particularly repulsive' – *New Socialist*, no. 11, 1983.

6 Richard N. Price, 'Society, status and jingoism: the social roots of lower middle class patriotism, 1870–1900', in G. Crossick (ed.), *The Lower Middle Class in Britain*, 1977, p. 100. For a valuable corrective, see, in the same volume, Hugh Macleod's 'White collar values and the role of religion'.

7 Raphael Samuel, 'Middle class between the wars', *New Socialist*, nos 9, 10, 11, January to June 1983.

8 E. J. Hobsbawm, *Industry and Empire*, 1969, p. 277. Hobsbawn has since stressed the contribution of the lower middle class to anti-fascist movements across Europe; see, for example, 'Rebuilding the left for a new Europe', *Guardian*, 27 September 1982.

9 These and other themes are dealt with in greater detail in my

forthcoming thesis, 'The lower middle class between the wars',
University of Birmingham.
10 For accounts of Lewisham childhoods, see Phyllis Willmot, *A Green
Girl* and *Growing up in a London Village*, 1979 and 1983; Leslie Paul,
Angry Young Man, 1951; and the thinly disguised autobiography of
Henry Williamson, *Donkey Boy* and *Young Phillip Maddison*, 1952
and 1953. For Lewisham before the First World War, see Hugh
Macleod, *Class and Religion in the Late Victorian City*, 1974, ch. VI.
11 H. Llewellyn Smith (ed.), *New Survey of London Life and Labour*,
vol. III, 1932, pp. 381–4.
12 Residents in an adjacent private estate in Bromley did all they could to
exclude Downham tenants, building a concrete wall, with broken glass
embedded in the top, across the connecting road. Despite considerable
controversy – with fierce debate within the middle-class community as
well as between that community and the estate – the wall was not
demolished until 1946. For a similar case in Oxford, see Peter
Collison, *The Cutteslow Walls*, 1963.
13 Paul Thompson, *Socialists, Liberals and Labour: The Struggle for
London*, 1967, p. 317.
14 *Lewisham Borough News* (*LBN*), 10 June 1925.
15 *Kentish Mercury* (*KM*), 24 May 1929.
16 For the disaffiliation, see John Attfield and John Lee, 'The General
Strike in Deptford and Lewisham', in Jeffrey Skelley (ed.), *The
General Strike, 1926*, 1976, pp. 261–80.
17 London Labour Party (LLP) Constituency Files, 1946–9, Lewisham
East and West, survey of voting strength and party membership by
polling district.
18 LLP Constituency Files, 1938, survey of marginal constituencies.
19 Membership of the West Lewisham association rose from 670 in 1922
to 3,035 in 1930, the increase being almost wholly attributable to the
one ward of Sydenham – John Ramsden, *The Age of Balfour and
Baldwin*, 1978, p. 254. Membership in the East stood at 1,900 in 1926,
with 1000 men and 900 women – Executive Committee Minutes
(ECM), 4 October 1926. Throughout the later 1920s and 1930s there
were calls for Pownall to devote more time to his constituency. I am
particularly grateful to Mrs L. Sperring, past agent, for allowing me
access to the surviving records of the East Lewisham Conservative
Association.
20 See *LBN*, 15 March 1938, 21 February 1939. Pownall contributed £300
per year by the late 1930s, the county councillors £100 each in 1934.
Lord Forster, no longer resident in the constituency but on whose land
Downham had been built, continued to contribute £50 a year, perhaps
in recompense. This dependence on large donations certainly influenced the choice of candidates.
21 See too Ramsden, op. cit., pp. 250–2.
22 For the torpor of 1934, see ibid., pp. 343–4; and Tom Stannage,
Baldwin Thwarts the Opposition: The British General Election of 1935,
1980, pp. 40–5.

23 ECM, 5 April 1937.
24 Sir Edward Pearson, MP, candidate for East Lewisham, *LBN* 2 March 1937.
25 As Sir Paul Latham, elected to the LCC for East Lewisham in 1931, had put it: 'In the days of Rome it was bread and the circus. Was it conceivable that they were equivalent to the dole and the cinema? In Poplarism there were all the signs that were found to contribute to the fall of great empires. He believed that if they got socialism in office in the County Council, they would have Poplarism spread over London, with ruinous consequences for London and the Empire. In his opinion economy was the most important issue in the election, and . . . the constitutional issue, Socialism and Anti-Socialism, came next' – *LBN*, 4 February 1931.
26 *LBN*, 30 September 1931; *KM*, 16 October 1931.
27 *LBN*, 28 October 1931.
28 *KM*, 16 October 1931.
29 *LBN*, 14 October 1931; *KM*, 16 October 1931.
30 *LBN*, 21 October 1931; *KM*, 23 October 1931.
31 *LBN*, 21 October 1931.
32 *KM*, 28 August 1931.
33 *LBN*, 14 October 1931.
34 *KM*, 16 October 1931. The Labour Party was, of course, quite aware of what was going on. The *Herald* referred to the 'insolent' device of anti-socialists 'arrogating to themselves the claim to speak for and on behalf of "the nation", to represent "the nation", to be "the nation"' – *Daily Herald*, 5 October 1931, quoted by Robert Dare in 'British labour, the national government and the "national interest", 1931', *Historical Studies*, vol. 18, no. 72, 1979.
35 *LBN*, 28 October 1931.
36 *KM*, 30 October 1931.
37 While a local office was established in 1934, the British Union of Fascists seems to have made little impression on Lewisham, such conflict as there was being confined to the correspondence columns of the press and the streets of the riverside boroughs.
38 East Lewisham Conservatism entered one of its periodical organizational revivals in the spring of 1935, reflecting renewed national vigour. The National Publicity Bureau's cinema van visited Lewisham; a registration campaign was launched; and finances, close to collapse in 1934 after the withdrawal of the defeated county councillors' subscriptions, improved, helped by the particularly successful exploitation of Jubilee Week.
39 Freda Corbett, in the East, concentrated on domestic issues; Stewart, in the West, on peace and disarmament. The truth of the *Mercury*'s jibe that Labour was 'consistent only in its inconsistencies' was illustrated by Wilmot's remark: 'if the dictatorships were to be stopped, then England had to arm' – *KM*, 18 October 1935.
40 *LBN*, 12 November 1935.
41 The government's attempt to raise itself above the political was

illustrated by the selection, at short notice, of the speed-king and national hero, Sir Malcolm Campbell, to fight the 'essentially sporting and industrial' constituency of Deptford. Campbell secured a very creditable 43 per cent of the vote.

42 *KM*, 8 November 1935.

43 For Dalton, see Ben Pimlott, *Hugh Dalton*, 1985, p. 238; for the proletarianization thesis, see Hutt, op. cit.; F. D. Klingender, *The Condition of Clerical Labour in Britain*, 1935; and Alec Brown, *The Fate of the Middle Classes*, 1936; for reaction to those theses, see Lancelot Hogben, 'Marxism and the middle classes', in *Dangerous Thoughts*, 1939; and Evan Durbin, *The Politics of Democratic Socialism*, 1940; and for the radical cultural organizations, see my *Mass-Observation: A Short History*, stencilled paper no. 55, Centre for Contemporary Cultural Studies, University of Birmingham, 1978. For a fuller treatment of these themes, see my 'A place in the nation: the lower middle class in England', in Rudy Koshar (ed.), *Splintered Classes: The European Lower Middle Class in the Age of Fascism*, New York, forthcoming.

44 For Pownall's involvement in the Anglo-German Fellowship, see Simon Haxey, *Tory MP*, 1939; for his own account of Nuremberg, *LBN*, 28 October 1937.

45 *LBN*, 22 March and 26 April 1938.

46 In the words of an *LBN* columnist, one such rally gave 'the local Colonel Blimps something to think about. There must have been a thousand people present . . . and the company were not all ignorant members of the ineptly designated "working class". There was a generous sprinkling of equally ineptly designated "intellectuals", several quiet and serious looking middle-aged men and women, one or two quite elderly people' – *LBN*, 16 February 1937.

47 It was of course pure coincidence that Mass Observation was based in Lewisham, at Blackheath.

48 *LBN*, 17 August 1937.

49 The Peace Alliance, which was formed without official Labour support soon split. See *LBN*, 29 March, 5 April, 3 May 1938.

50 *LBN*, 14 September 1937; *East Lewisham Citizen*, March 1938.

51 For Listowel's involvement in the national SMAC, see Jim Fyrth, *The Signal Was Spain*, 1986, pp. 46–7; for the National Joint Council, see ibid., p. 202; and Noreen Branson and Margot Heineman, *Britain in the 1930s*, 1971, p. 340. For the China Campaign Committee, see Ruth Dudley Edwards, *Victor Gollancz*, 1987, p. 272.

52 *LBN*, 27 July 1937; *West Lewisham Citizen*, April 1938. Skeffington was as sympathetic to the Popular Front as was possible without openly allying with the Crippsite left or courting official disfavour. While Pownall was in Germany, Skeffington had toured the Soviet Union, returning with equal enthusiasm.

53 This was one of seven by-elections, from Oxford on 27 October to Fylde on 30 November and including the victory of a Popular Front candidate, Vernon Bartlett, at Bridgwater, Somerset, which followed

the Munich Crisis. Taken as a whole the results were ambiguous. For contrasting interpretations, see Roger Eatwell, 'Munich, public opinion and the popular front', *Journal of Contemporary History*, vol. 6, no. 4, 1971; and Iain Maclean, 'Oxford and Bridgwater', in C. Cook and J. Ramsden (eds), *By-Elections in British Politics*, 1973.

54 Towards the close of the campaign Vernon Bartlett toured the constituency, speaking for Skeffington. At Bridgwater, Bartlett's campaign had been organized by the local Left Book Club and supported by a Mass Observation team.

55 *West Lewisham Citizen*, December 1938.

56 *Daily Mail*, 23 November 1938.

57 At 7.6 per cent the swing to Labour exceeded that in the three other by-elections which had been contested by Labour and National candidates in 1935 and was the largest but one at any of the thirteen by-elections between July 1938 and May 1939. The most striking feature was the fall in the Conservative vote, reflecting the very low turn-out, at 58.4 per cent the lowest of all the autumn by-elections and the third lowest in West Lewisham at the nine parliamentary elections between 1921 and 1945, indicating that Labour had taken a step towards 'negative coalition' but was still far from a positive electoral alliance.

58 *KM*, 2 December 1938.

59 By the late 1930s the East's *malaise* was reflected in the West – *LBN*, 9 February 1937. The association's annual report for 1938 was a chapter of obituaries.

60 For example, the Peace Pledge Union. Brooke's agent went further, addressing the Young Communist League.

61 *LBN*, 10 January 1939.

62 Part of a wider Communist campaign, organized nationally and in Lewisham by Jim Borders and the National Tenants' Association – Phil Piratin, *Our Flag Stays Red*, 1979 edn, pp. 41–9.

63 Again part of a wider Communist campaign. See Henry Pelling, *The British Communist Party: A Historical Profile*, 1958, p. 106.

64 For a similar argument at the national level, see Ben Pimlott, *Labour and the Left in the 1930s*, 1977, p. 202.

65 At Blackheath, his Tranquil-vale, Pownall was asked whether the detention of the German leadership would not provide 'a good opportunity for Sir Assheton to see some of his friends in the Anglo-German Fellowship' – *LBN*, 26 June 1945. Morrison did not need to name names: 'Mr Ribbentrop came over here and was very nice to our upper classes, and, believe me, our upper classes were extraordinarily nice to him' – *LBN*, 3 July 1945.

66 *LBN*, 5 June, 19 June 1945.

67 *LBN*, 3 July 1945.

68 *KM*, 15 June 1945.

69 Quoted in Bernard Donoughue and G. W. Jones, *Herbert Morrison: Portrait of a Politician*, 1973, p. 337. As his biographers point out, Morrison's move to Lewisham was a matter of pragmatism as well as

principle. He knew that his Hackney seat was likely to disappear in the post-war redistribution, while Lewisham would gain a third safe seat based on the estates. But East Lewisham could have seemed no better than marginal early in 1945, and Morrison did turn down the solid Labour seat of Deptford.

70 *KM*, 16 February 1945.
71 LLP Constituency Files, 1946–9, op. cit., fn. 18. For example, PD1 of Church Ward, Blackheath was described as a ' "superior" area. Some more or less artistic people. Remnants of pre-war cultured community'. The three such districts might be categorized as 'solid middle class'. PD26 in South Ward contained 'owner occupied houses, some in estates. Office type workers': the eight districts with similar descriptions might be categorized as 'lower middle class'. These categories are, of course, very approximate. Labour's estimates of their vote must have been the result of informed guesswork. But those estimates were no more than a division of Labour's actual vote by polling district, and as will be clear the contribution of Downham and Bellingham could hardly have been underestimated.
72 Bonham suggested that of those who voted Conservative or Labour, Labour took over 30 per cent of the middle-class vote as a whole and over 40 per cent of the lower-middle-class vote – John Bonham, *The Middle Class Vote*, 1954.
73 For an argument against Labour in its present crisis, attempting to rearticulate the symbolism of the nation in a more democratic form, see Patrick Wright, *On Living in an Old Country*, 1985, esp. pp. 5, 155–8, 186–9. Whatever its merits, that argument lacks retrospective justification. For the contention that Labour's use of the rhetoric of the nation was compromised and contaminated by Baldwin's earlier adroit manipulation of the debate, see Bill Schwartz, 'The language of constitutionalism: Baldwinite Conservatism', in *Formations of Nation and People*, 1984, pp. 1–18.
74 Lewis and Maude, op. cit., p. 85.
75 Donoughue and Jones, op. cit., p. 548.
76 Hugh Thomas, *The Spanish Civil War*, 1965, pp. 779–80.
77 Source: F. W. S. Craig, *British Parliamentary Election Results 1918–1949*, Glasgow, 1969.
78 ibid.

Identities

9

'Fierce questions and taunts'
Married life in working-class London, 1870–1914

Ellen Ross

> There he would sit by the fireside,
>   Such a chilly man was John;
> I hope and trust there's a nice warm fire
>   Where my old man's gone.
>   'He was a good kind husband', sung by Vesta Victoria,
>   1890s

> Who sits up when we're out at night?
>   Woman, lovely woman!
> Who meets us when we come home tight?
>   Woman, lovely woman!
> By who up the stairs are we carefully led,
> And when we're asleep and our senses have fled,
> Runs through our pockets, when we are in bed?
>   Woman, lovely woman!
>   'Woman, lovely woman', sung by James Fawn, late 1880s[1]

Victorian and Edwardian music-halls provide vivid commentaries on working-class London's marital and domestic lives. For every song of hopeful young romance, there were half a dozen evoking daily realities, their troubles and antagonisms. As uncovered in music-hall lyrics, in autobiographies, and in the observations of contemporary social explorers, cockney culture incorporated distinct attitudes and arrangements towards gender.[2] In the London poor, middle-class observers found an 'incomprehensible region' where many women were neither ladylike nor deferential, where men struggled to keep their authority over them, where 'sexual antagonism' was openly acknowledged.[3]

These patterns diverged strikingly from those of the British middle class. They were probably also different from those of working populations in rural or mining England, where husbands' authority was not threatened, or in pockets of textile production and of married women's well-paid employment, such as Preston, where more peaceful and co-operative marital arrangements could be found.[4] Despite their variations, though, the sexual and marriage patterns of the poor excited intense interest among middle-class policy-makers in the decades preceding the First World War, as the public prominence of such themes as wife-beating, temperance, prostitution, infant mortality, and divorce suggests.[5]

Male domination and exploitation of women do not always lead to overt antagonism between the sexes; women may exhibit proper levels of deference and submissiveness; men may be perfectly satisfied with their degree of control over women. But a number of circumstances made such unchallenged male power relatively rare in large parts of pre-First World War working-class London.

For one thing, the economic basis of men's power was highly precarious for perhaps as many as half of London's working husbands. A large portion of London jobs were in the secondary sector – undercapitalized, small scale, insecure, and not very profitable. Only about one-sixth of London's adult labour force was employed in factories through the 1890s. About 25 per cent of adult male workers were unskilled.[6] The building, garment, shoe, furniture, and dockside trades were seasonal; trade slumps, illness, or injury could leave a man dependent on his wife or children for survival. Husbands were supposed to 'keep' their families, but their failure as bread-winners, at some point, was practically inevitable. Few working men would be able to provide for their own or their wife's old age.[7] Children's wage contributions were therefore counted upon, and wives would serve as earners at some point in the life cycle of most families. At all times, wives' skill and energy were the barrier separating a decent level of comfort from mere survival.[8] A mother's aptitude for bargaining with the pawnshop assistant, the shopkeepers, and the school board visitors; her domestic arts; her friendship with the landlady – all were worth solid cash, and provided wives with some leverage against husbands. When children went to work, they viewed themselves as 'working for' their mothers; their earnings entered, and strengthened, the female part of the household exchequer.

Wives' status in London was enhanced, too, by the supportive presence of neighbours and kin (though the full extent to which matrilocal living patterns had already emerged is hard to gauge).[9] Such networks may have developed and sustained concepts of wives' material rights and prerogatives. We get a glimpse of their effect in a court-room scene in the early 1900s in which a large group of women, their prams parked outside, encourage another: 'You stick to it. Go on wiv' it. Get your separation!'[10] London mothers of this era, as they are remembered by their children or described by middle-class acquaintances, had assertive personalities and distinct opinions. 'Women have settled notions on the status of a wife and on her headship of the home,' concluded a Thames Police Court magistrate. Women's 'scolding' and 'aggravation' were cited over and over again by male defendants as mitigating factors in cases of husband–wife assault.[11] Thus despite their physical, economic, and legal disadvantages, wives were ready to stand their ground. The result was a culture where husband–wife violence was extremely frequent, where pubs were regularly invaded by angry wives, where husbands cheated wives, wives stole from husbands, and music-halls nightly unfolded new chapters in the domestic struggle for power.

This composite picture of cockney marriage best portrays life among the approximately 30 per cent of London's population who lived in 'poverty' according to Charles Booth's classification in the late 1880s (those whom he placed in Classes A to D, 'the very poor' and 'the poor'), whose means, 18 to 21 shillings a week, were just 'barely sufficient for decent independent life', and those just above them in Booth's scale. They were concentrated in London's inner ring, in Southwark, Whitechapel, Bethnal Green, Shoreditch.[12] The quiet streets of more outlying areas like Tottenham, Tooting, or Peckham, restricted by higher rents and commuting costs to better-paid or more regularly employed men, displayed somewhat less embattled marriage relationships, I suspect. Yet they too shared in the wider pattern of strict separations between male and female spheres, and developed distinct women's cultures of mutual help organized around women's common responsibilities for household subsistence.

Chronologically, this study covers the period from 1870 to the First World War, when the cultural and material boundaries shaping family life remained relatively stable for London's working poor. Migration into the metropolis reached a peak in the 1840s, and then began to slow.[13] Though there were streets where transients clustered, most of those who came to London districts like Bethnal Green, Bermondsey, or Poplar in the 1870s and after entered a relatively stable urban culture, and likely encountered families who had lived in the nearby streets for a generation or more.[14] By the 1870s, or earlier, workers lived in neighbourhoods from which the middle class had largely fled. By the last decade of the century, better-off workers like artisans, foremen, and clerks were following their social betters as they left inner London, moving to new districts supplied by commuter trains. For those who remained in the inner city, neighbourhood – even street – endogamy was the rule among the non-servant poor, and local definitions were an unspoken part of each marriage agreement, each cohabitation arrangement.[15] Compulsory education, introduced in London at the start of this period, had meant a radical reorganization of family life for Britain's poor. Families would have to do without major contributions from children under school-leaving age, which was gradually raised during this generation. Thus from the 1870s mothers with young children became more dependent on husbands' earnings, and on their own poorly paid employment. But the new school-imposed burden of keeping children clean, clothed, healthy, and punctual for class fell entirely on mothers.[16] Finally, while fertility rates were falling throughout England in the generation before the war, those of the poorest London boroughs remained high. While in 1911 there were about 226 births per thousand married women aged 15 to 49 in Bethnal Green, in middle-class Hampstead the rate was only 121. Bethnal Green's ratio of 30.7 births for each hundred wives aged under 45 in 1880–1 had, twenty years later, fallen only slightly, to 28.3; the rate in Hampstead at the turn of the century was only 18.3. Class differences in fertility were thus in fact sharpening in the decades before the First World War.[17]

Despite the ties of marriage, and their intense economic interdependence, women and men lived in quite separate material worlds organized around their responsibilities in a rigid sexual division of labour. Marriage was not viewed as creating a new social unit: the fissure between wife and children, on the one hand, and husband, on the other, was accepted as a normal part of it. The fact that children, throughout the early teens moved within 'female' space creates special problems of interpretation in the case of boys, who would have to move from the 'woman's' to the 'man's' world some time in their late teens. Cockney marriages were also posited on companionship, supervision, and material aid provided by groups outside the couple, neighbours and kin in particular. Goods, services, friendship, and certain spaces – in shops, pubs, doorways, streets – were shared with members of the same sex, and not with spouses.[18]

This sexual separation, however, should not be viewed as a contradiction in the institution of working-class marriage. For the marriage contract as it was understood did not enjoin romantic love or emotional 'intimacy' (the latter a term not appropriate until quite recently), although some couples sustained these 'unofficially', and a minority had had 'romantic' courtships.[19] Despite the dreariness, tension, and outbursts of violence that characterized much of married life, most women did not focus on the marital relationship but rather defined wages, children, and kin as more central to their happiness. 'Kindness' and efficiency in carrying out his or her appropriate responsibilities were the elements of a good spouse.

The reciprocal obligations of spouses were quite openly acknowledged. Wives' responsibility for child care and domestic labour is spelled out in numerous ballads and songs. 'They darn up all our stockings and they make our buttons fast,/ and comfort and console us throughout life,' announced the music-hall song 'Angels without wings'. An old bachelor, advertising for a wife in an earlier street ballad, complained:

> No wife have I, my bed to make,
> To wash my shirt or fry my steak;
> I am forced to dine at coffee shops,
> To scrub the room, and emp' the slops,
> O what is more than that, alack,
> No wife have I to warm my back.[20]

Ranyard nurses on their rounds in the early 1870s met a husband who starved himself rather than do his own cooking while his wife was disabled with badly burned and infected arms. When the nurses had successfully treated the long-neglected burns, the wife was intensely grateful. As she wrote: 'Now my husband likes to have something cooked for his dinner; before, he would often be content with a bit of bread and cheese, as he did not like to eat anything which I had not handled.'[21]

The failure of wives to provide meals, even for very good reason – such as a husband's refusal or inability to provide the money – was looked on by men as a major challenge to their marital claims. Those of South London pawnbroker John Small's female customers who demanded quick service because 'they had to get the old man's supper ready, or wouldn't they catch it!' were probably not exaggerating.[22] Wives' domestic lapses provide a major theme in the serious assaults that were tried at the Old Bailey, London's Central Criminal Court. Overcome with rage, Robert Plampton stabbed and killed his wife Emily Maria after a series of confrontations one afternoon in which he found, when he went to take a nap, that his blankets had been pawned. A saucepan had probably been pawned as well, much delaying the preparation of his dinner, since Emily Plampton stopped for several drinks with her neighbours as she set out to borrow another one.[23]

Husbands' primary obligations were to work, and to hand over a customary amount of their pay to their wives. A wife expected that a husband would 'work for' her, and being a husband was synonymous with providing support. A woman's court testimony suggested the close association between husband and earner: 'He has been a good father to his children, and a good husband to me as far as his means would let him.' A St Pancras woman had left her unemployed husband and children in the workhouse, and eventually found another man with whom she set up house. When told that the board of guardians would not permit visits from her children 'because she had set up a home this way', she stoutly disagreed, saying that the unemployed man 'was no husband for her, and the one that worked for her she respected'.[24] Women who were not supported by their husbands occasionally assumed that they were no longer married, and got into trouble in bigamy cases when they formed new attachments. One husband's failure to send money for many years was evidence to his wife that he was dead, and she was acquitted in her bigamy case. In another bigamy accusation, George Pitchford's second 'wife' Emily Ann Steele tried to protect him, a sailor, from the bigamy charge by asserting in court: 'You have treated me properly and you gave me half your pay' (a traditional way in which sailors indicated a serious commitment to a woman).[25]

A husband's unemployment thus generated almost intolerable domestic tensions, and seems a factor in a large minority of the Old Bailey husband–wife assault or murder cases. Unemployed men were angry and frustrated. Their wives' material deprivations could lead to taunting and reproaches, as in the assault on Emma Tritner in the late 1870s, where the husband's unemployment had structured the conflict. Because he had threatened and attacked her several times, she was living apart from William Tritner in the Mile End Road. The day of the attack, he knocked at the door. 'I opened it and said I was in hopes he had got a place, because he was out of work, and I was paying the rent,' Emma testified. The fight that sealed William Tritner's determination to 'do for' his wife had taken place a few weeks earlier. Cross-examined, Emma reported:

> You dragged me out of bed to go to work on the 28th November – you would not work, and I had to work – you slept in bed till 12 or 1 in the day – you turned the baby topsy-turvy, and it frightened me, I thought the child would go into a fit – I rushed toward the child and then you hit me – I did not throw the basin at you, I threw a cup – I said no bad word – you told people a

man at the docks cut your head – I threw the cup because that morning I had to go out to work and I had nothing to eat and nothing for the child, and I said 'Bill, you're no man, or you would not let a wife and child go out as you do', and with that you beat me and took up a lamp to throw at me, and I felt so crushed that I should have to go to work in that way, and I took up a cup and threw it at you.[26]

When men who did have employment came home with wages badly diminished – usually at the pub – their wives often attacked in sheer despair, as they thought of the week ahead. In the 1900s Margaret Loane reported that she had met a number of wives who did not hesitate to beat their husbands when they returned home missing 'an undue proportion of their week's wages'. George Acorn's Bethnal Green autobiography describes regular Saturday-afternoon quarrels between his parents, provoked by his mother's 'fierce questions and taunts' about the whereabouts of her husband's money, following which 'they would throw themselves to the floor and fight, scratching and punching like wild beasts, until the noise brought the landlady up from downstairs to separate them and enjoin peace'.[27] William Hibbard, a casually employed stevedore, who with his wife lived in Canning Town in the 1890s, was a cruel man who 'used to jeer and tantalize [his wife] very much', and apparently had beaten her regularly for years. But when he gave her only one shilling from the nine he had brought home from work on Saturday, and then treated her with contempt, she had had enough; she decided to 'do for him' and stabbed him in the street outside the pub from which he had just emerged.[28] A district nurse, whose territory included some of the poorest London courts, concluded that most of the week's domestic fighting was concentrated on Saturday afternoons and Sunday:

> From Saturday afternoon, when wages had been paid, till Monday morning the court was often a field of battle and bloodshed, and Sunday was a pitiful day. . . . When I had gone through the passage, the scene from the second archway was frightful – men kicking their wives round the court like footballs, and women fighting like wild tigers! I fixed my eyes on a bit of blue sky, and with my head held up steered my way through that raging sea.[29]

The rowing was not simply a result of weekend drinking, but also of the utterly different hopes, plans, and interests husbands and wives had for the weekly wage-packet. Women were under pressure to redeem pawned clothing for the weekend, and to present a hot Sunday meal; their husbands wanted a drink at the pub.

Household jurisdictions, and even physical spaces, were sharply divided by gender. Children's language showed their awareness of masculine and feminine household divisions. East London school-boys, asked to report on their activities one Saturday in May 1905, used wording which suggested their own place within female territory. One referred to his 'mother's fire', for which he got some wood. Another called the errands he had done 'my mother's work'.[30]

The rather extensive 'farming' carried on in East and South London basements, yards, and vacant plots of ground – raising pigeons, chickens, or rabbits, or cultivating garden allotments – was designated a male realm. Alice Linton's father in Shoreditch raised chickens and kept the proceeds of his egg sales to augment his pocket-money. A mechanic at Nicholson's gin factory in West Ham saved cash from his gardening for a holiday he took by himself, while a dock worker used his allotment to grow all the family's vegetables.[31]

Clean steps, pavements, window-sills, hearths, and so on, the work of wives or children, were physical outlines of women's space in households and streets. A young boy entrusted by his mother with domestic chores in his family's home in Wellington Place, Bethnal Green, in the early 1900s angrily noted that his father and brother repeatedly violated the household interior's feminine territory, the polished grate and swept-out hearth: 'My father used to tap his pipe and empty its contents all over it, and my step-brothers threw their cigarette ends over the hearth.' Octavia Hill reported with great satisfaction a successful lesson in cleaning as a claim of female turf in one of the 'rough' Marylebone buildings she superintended. 'One little girl was so proud of her first cleaning that she stood two hours watching her passage lest the boys, whom she considered as the natural enemies of order and cleanliness, should spoil it before I came to see it.'[32] The whitened circles, squares, or oblongs outside house doors all over working-class London before the First World War were poignant attempts of housewives to extend their turf just a bit beyond their own four walls.

Stealing routes also indicate very clearly how spheres within households were demarcated by sex. Exactly because they did not fully share their resources, theft between cohabiting spouses was quite possible. When a Cubitt Town man found he was missing a shilling he had been saving to buy leather for fixing the family boots, he suspected his wife, though she denied it vigorously. Mary Ann Ford infuriated her husband when she took his entire week's pay. 'We had a few words about money matters,' he told the court at his trial for her murder; 'I never meant to kill her, she should have kept her hand out of my pocket.'[33] In the Jasper family in Hoxton, where the husband gave his wife only 7 or 8 shillings a week, a small part of his fairly large earnings, the wife stole money regularly from her husband, and so did some of the children. As the son, A. S. Jasper, wrote in his vivid autobiography:

> I remember my father going to his own bed. As he took his trousers off, his money fell out of his pocket. He was so drunk he couldn't bend down to find it. I was going upstairs as this happened and looked in the door and saw some cash on the floor. Knowing he always kept Mum short, I dived under the bed and picked up a two-shilling piece. . . . I slid out, found Mum and gave her the two shillings I managed to pick up. She asked me how I came by it, and I explained what had happened. 'Good boy,' she says, and upstairs she went. Dad was now out to the world, so she had all the silver and left him the coppers.[34]

Of the hundreds of East London theft cases I have examined in newspapers and court records, covering the years 1869 to 1889, none involved a child stealing from a mother, though adult siblings robbed each other regularly, and fathers were robbed by sons – in one case by a daughter – with some frequency also.[35]

The internal 'wage' system accentuated and dramatized the sexual separation within families. The custom of paying wives 'wages' for housekeeping expenses, from which the wage-earner's 'pocket-money' was reserved, was widespread throughout England and Wales by the mid-nineteenth century.[36] Its size was determined in part by husbands' tastes and habits (teetotallers often gave their wives a few more shillings each week than did moderate drinkers).[37] Power relations within the couple and neighbourhood custom also bore on the size of her payment. Wives' wages declined with husbands' underemployment, and disappeared altogether with their unemployment, but many arrangements were so formalized that they remained unchanged throughout the wage-earning years, without regard to inflation, the birth of additional children, or special emergencies.[38] George Acorn's father gave his wife 18 shillings a week 'when he first married, and never increased it', despite the arrival of about half a dozen children, all housed in the family's single room. When Alice Linton's father took a high-paying job, he 'still didn't give mother much share of his extra money, and she still needed to go to work'.[39] Many men maintained control over their wages by being secretive about what they earned, and wives used a variety of ways of penetrating the secret, such as listening attentively to street orators during strikes.[40]

Actual household spending was entirely in wives' domain. 'The custom of leaving the spending of money to the wife', reported Margaret Loane,

> is so deeply-rooted that children always speak of the family income as belonging entirely to her, and will constantly tell you, 'Mother has to pay so and so for rent', 'Mother is going to afford father this or that', 'Mother isn't going to let father work for Mr — any more, she says the wages isn't worth the hours.'[41]

'Family socialism', the term Loane used to describe the working-class family economy, applied rightly only to the wife/children part of the household. For husbands, even if kindly and well loved, lived on budgets separate from wives. A Hoxton girl showed her tact, and her grasp of these separate budgetary streams, when she won £3 in a dancing contest and gave each parent 30 shillings (each of whom returned 2s 6d to her).[42] Husbands often organized at least some meals and the shopping for them on their own, sending children out, for example, to buy haddock and rewarding them with the head and tail. Jasper's father was not unusual in agreeing to pay his wife for preparing his lunches at home after he took a job at a lumber yard in his own neighbourhood.[43] Many husbands bought clothing for themselves out of their pocket-money, or provided special items for the household out of their separate funds.

The lower nutritional and caloric levels of wives' and children's diets throughout the pre-First-World-War period are well documented. The disparity tended to go on outside of the notice of husbands, who exhibited remarkably little curiosity about where, and how, their own meals had been procured – an indifference that is surprising in a period when about two-thirds of workers' earnings were spent on food.[44] Acorn's father, to his son's disgust, 'took all the meals we had so anxiously provided without the slightest thought or consideration'.[45] In Alice Linton's Shoreditch household, the father ate butter while the rest of the family had margarine. Another East London father ate bacon regularly, 'a sign that you was well off' (his daughter observed much later), but the rest of the family went without; another had bacon and eggs for Sunday breakfast while his family ate fried bread at the same table.[46] Women generally accepted this 'auto-starvation', as one observer termed it, and were often discreet about their poor food. A Poplar woman was in the habit of dining on a 'kettle bender', 'a cup of crusts with hot water, pepper and salt, and a knob of margarine'. 'She always had this meal', her daughter remembers, 'just before father came in for his.' That fear of husbands' reprisals was not entirely what motivated women to go without food is illustrated by a dockside widow's habit of refusing meals, instead 'quite cheerfully' putting balls of dry bread in her mouth while her children ate. Her son, Joe Williamson, later a slum priest, always thought of these one-sided meals and the mystery of his mother's survival when he encountered the biblical passage, 'I have meat ye know not of.'[47]

Much of the praise of good husbands Anna Martin heard from South London women presupposed a hunger gap as the norm: 'All his thought is for his little children'; 'It's his rule never to eat a mouthful unless I share it'; 'He would never touch a bit if I and the children were without.'[48]

The events surrounding the hardships of the 1889 dock strike suggest that the disjunction between the budgets of male workers and those of their wives and children was an accepted fact of East London culture. The meagre 'dockers' dinner', a common piece of iconography in the strike's daily parades and processions,[49] was most likely meant to represent the meal of the dockers themselves. The strike fund was used to provide (very inadequate) meals only for the men, leaving their families to forage for themselves. The union's policy was never criticized, but East London newspapers were full of reports of starving women and children, and of the efforts of charitable groups to feed them.[50] For the charities too accepted the division of households by gender (and in any case most were unwilling to support the dockers directly). On the other side, 'The general rule among men', according to Anna Martin's observations of the 1911 dock strike, 'was to touch no food indoors. What the wife manages to secure is held sacred for her use and the children's.'[51]

Neighbourhood-based 'charitable' exchange was organized predominantly by women, whose friendship and gossip networks implicitly accepted the need for mutual aid. Contemporary observers familiar with London's neighbourhood life, like George Sims in the 1880s and, later, Margaret Loane and Maud Pember Reeves, understood its vital significance to family survival. Neighbours sustained each other through periods of illness, desertion, and unemployment; they contributed to the maintenance of the sick, the old, and women giving birth. Shopkeepers provided credit when unemployment was scarce.[52]

The complexity, and significance to survival, of the neighbourhood economy emerges clearly in autobiographies and oral histories, where the tracing of a mother's activities is likely to unwind a long series of connections, both material and personal. Mary Barnes Waters gives a detailed account of her mother's movements in a Hoxton neighbourhood off Curtain Road in the early 1900s. Her second 'husband' providing her only 10 shillings a week, Mrs Barnes took to selling offal from a basket in the gutter in front of Reid's Butchers near her home. With the butcher's help, Barnes eventually began to sell cooked sheep's heads and pigs' feet at a stall outside the Britannia Theatre. Her economies included selling rabbit skins and the remains of the sheep's heads to Ward's, a nearby shop, while her daughter sold rags and jamjars to ragmen. Mrs Barnes, meanwhile, was giving needy neighbours free meals from her stall: 'When they were out of work and told her the tale, she couldn't refuse it,' said her daughter years later. On Saturday evenings she regularly distributed her left-overs to those she knew needed extra food, and the odours of the meat stewing for Sunday dinner registered her distinct contribution to the neighbourhood economy.[53]

Mrs Barnes's systematic distribution of her left-overs is a reminder of the connections which daily borrowing and lending, gossiping, quarrelling, and caring established between neighbourhood women. Elsewhere I have tried to show how these actually created and perpetuated neighbourhoods as major working-class institutions in London, despite the regularity of household removals and migrations. Many London neighbourhoods not only defined appropriate standards for children's dress and supervision, and set protocols for caring for the bereaved, the sick, and those giving birth, but also pronounced on the acceptability of church attendance, routines for sheltering those wanted by the police, and degrees of hospitality with which such figures as church visitors, the public vaccinator, visiting nurses, and school-meals and summer-holiday investigators were to be treated. Neighbourhood conventions determined the success or failure of many government policies from compulsory education itself to the anti-infant-mortality campaigns of the 1900s and the old age pension of 1909, and gave these policies new meanings and consequences. Most (but by no means all) neighbourhood conventions were maintained by women, especially mothers of families, for neighbourhood sociability as well as the upholding of local 'standards' and the assertion of individual and collective rights were extensions of the mothering function as it was defined in this London world.

Pawning, a crucial link between household and neighbourhood

economy, was a regular feature of London life. In 1902 the figure was six annual pledges per capita, and London children were regularly seen doing their own make-believe pawning. Pawning was a female domain all over Britain by the 1870s at least, when a parliamentary investigation uncovered and worried over this fact.[54] Women accumulated stacks of pawn tickets and fretted about losing them. Women giving depositions at London's Worship Street Police Court often reported thefts of pawn tickets, and they also appear to have stolen them more than did men. Lent, stolen, or honestly obtained pledge tickets were transferred and traded in complex patterns between groups of women, the court cases show.[55] It required skill and experience to know which shops paid best for pledges of different categories, and how to package them to get maximum value,[56] and women were far more likely than men to have cultivated this skill. The rings of thieves who used women to pawn their stolen goods paid homage to this expertise.[57] Indeed, it was the recognition of the significance of pawning for women as organizers of weekly household survival in poor districts that prompted the Women's Co-operative Guild to propose that the Co-op open its own pawnshops (to be called a 'loan department'), a plan rejected by the movement's male leadership.[58]

A great deal of domestic pawning went on outside the knowledge of men. A boy growing up in Bromley-by-Bow before the First World War remembers running errands and taking items to the pawnshop for a neighbour who often urged him to hurry ''fore the old man comes in'. Dorothy Scannell recalls that in her Poplar household in the 1900s extensive pawning was carried on by mother and children without the father's knowledge, and 'no other fathers seemed to know of their wives' and children's visits to this establishment'. A family friend pawned her father's watch every Monday in winter, 'for then her father arose in the dark and went to bed in the dark so he didn't see that the watch was missing'.[59] John Small, a South London pawnbroker whose clientele was very poor, told reporter James Greenwood about a woman who had for eleven years daily pawned her husband's razor for threepence after he had used it and gone off to work for a clothier. Each morning the woman got herself a glass of gin with the money. In the evening when the husband brought home his wages, the wife went out to buy his dinner and redeem the razor. Small had made £3 17s over the years through this transaction.[60]

Because of their potential as pawnable goods, most family possessions were seen as a part of the mother's jurisdiction. When John Blake's father wore his good suit to the pub near their Poplar house, he was sharply instructed by his wife to avoid spilling beer on it, which would lower its value at the counter. Indeed, men's clothing was prime material for the pawnshop, as it was better made than women's and did not go out of style. A music-hall song, parodying 'After the ball', ruefully acknowledged these virtues:

After the shawl went over,
After she got 9d,
She pulled out another bundle,
That bundle belonged to me!
'Twas a pair of my best Sunday trousers:
'Five bob' I heard her call;
I then saw my best Sunday trousers
Go after the shawl.[61]

Both the magnitude and the female gender of pawning in the poorest quarters are vividly illustrated by a Friday-night fire at a large St Giles pawnshop in the 1870s. Neighbourhood women by the hundreds had regularly resorted there, many without informing their husbands, and pledging was at its most intense on weekends. The women turned out *en masse* to help and treat the firemen with beer, remaining with them throughout the night as the fire continued to burn. Their lack of success led to an epidemic of wife-beatings. As the former shop apprentice recalled:

There were more station-house cases that Saturday night than had been known for years, and come Monday morning, if you walked through some of the low streets and alleys you might have thought that the fashion amongst women was to wear the eyes blackened and streaks of surgical tape fancifully arranged about the face.

First World War air raids raised a similar spectre for London women.[62]

As the St Giles episode shows, husband–wife violence was indeed a 'privileged' form in a culture which permitted a wide range of physical expressions of anger, and where violence was a special prerogative of those in authority. Children were slapped and spanked by police, neighbours, and teachers as well as by parents; families feuded violently; fights broke out in pubs and streets not only between men but sometimes between women. Nancy Tomes's rough estimate for London in a slightly earlier period, the 1850s and 1860s, was that in any neighbourhood of two to four hundred houses, ten to twenty men would be convicted of common assaults on women during any year. On a street off Brick Lane in the 1870s, where a coster had attempted to murder his mother-in-law, a slipper-maker told a court that he 'heard cries of murder, but that being such a common occurrence in that neighbourhood I took no notice of it'. Cross-examined, he explained that he heard such cries three or four times a week.[63] The vast majority of wife-beating incidents, leaving 'not one case in a hundred' in Anna Martin's view, were never reported to the police. While figures for all kinds of violent crimes, including assaults, had declined in London by the end of the nineteenth century, there is no evidence that the proportion involving husbands beating wives had similarly declined. Mrs C—, one of Anna Martin's informants just before the war, estimated: 'I should say seven out of ten of the wives down my way feel their husbands' fists at times, and lots of 'em are used shocking.'[64] Police court magistrates before and after the First World War were overwhelmed by the problem. Their waiting-rooms each morning were filled with injured women, who after 1878 could seek separations if badly enough assaulted. 'If I were to sit here from Monday morning till Saturday to protect women that had got drunken and brutal husbands, I should not get through half of them,' exclaimed the experienced magistrate Montague Williams.[65]

Community behaviour in wife-beating incidents certainly acknowledged the inevitability of violence between spouses, and the 'right' of husbands to beat up wives. Outsiders were considerably more likely to intervene when men attacked women with whom they were not living or married. Neighbours in the same house or street were acutely aware of conflict going on near by, often because they could easily hear or see it. The sound of shouting and blows would cause them to collect on stairs and landings, and at windows, but fights would normally be allowed to continue. Only the presence of a really dangerous weapon, the sight of a lot of blood, or sounds of real terror would get them to intervene.[66] William Hancock's murder of Elizabeth Glover, whom he had probably just met, outside the Black Swan Tavern in Bow Road in January 1879, serves as a dramatic case in point. Hancock threw Glover to the ground repeatedly as a crowd of six or seven gathered. He kept them from interfering by saying: 'It's my wife, and I want to take her home, she is drunk' (which Glover was meanwhile loudly denying). Both a waiter from the tavern and a policeman who had been spectators testified in court that they had avoided interfering 'because I thought [said the policeman] they were man and wife'.[67]

Fighting between men, or between women, was usually public and ritualized. Both parties had to agree on the match; coats were removed; seconds were chosen; a place 'to spar' was found.[68]

Domestic collisions were far less orderly, and more dangerous as a result, especially to women who were usually, though not always, the weaker fighters. The fights normally took place at home. Couples did not decorously exchange punches, but wrestled, slapped, kicked, bit, and threw household objects, while terrified children looked on or tried to intervene. Injuries could be severe. While a few shootings were the result of premeditation, most assaults were products of uncontrollable rage. Both women and men in their court testimony commented on their inability to cope with it. 'I got into that way I did not know what I was doing,' said one woman who had knifed her husband.[69] The image of wives as delicate and passive, immobile victims of brutal husbands, which dominated nineteenth-century campaigns against wife-beating, and still prevails in today's literature, was probably inaccurate. Cockney men were small and wiry (East London boxing was welterweight and lightweight), while married women tended to be stout, and their very heavy domestic labour developed their shoulders and biceps. Religious visitors' lessons in female patience and meekness did not always fall on receptive ears.

Violence itself would not bring wives to the 'threshold' of tolerance for marriage or husbands. What did cause women to seek legal separations, or to leave their husbands informally, were threats of murder, physical attacks on the children (very rare according to all observers), refusal to provide income, and sexual insults. 'I would forgive anything', a woman told William Fitzsimmons, a police missionary, 'but the filthy names he calls me.' At age 23, she had been deafened in one ear and had her nose broken in a long series of attacks by her husband.[70] Wives hated and feared the injuries they received, some of which did indeed leave scars or disabilities. But all the evidence we have on domestic violence in this era suggests that its social meaning was different from today's. If marriage did not enjoin trust, sharing, and partnership, then it was far less surprising that conflict should frequently erupt there. Since men's desire for domination in marriage and women's to undermine it were an openly acknowledged part of their culture, it was not unexpected that men might use violent means to obtain wives' obedience. Marriage created no sacred or separate space; there was nothing secret or shameful about a Saturday-night fight. Wives' black eyes were one material, and predictable, result of sexual antagonism.

While wife-beating is easily comprehensible in the atmosphere of male–female struggle I have sketched out, sexuality, which today is associated with emotional intimacy and reciprocity, is far more problematic. Working-class London was considerably more open about sex than was genteel culture, but sexuality none the less remained a private and largely invisible realm. As a result, women's rights and privileges were neither defined nor asserted, and, in the realm of sex, male domination remained mostly unchallenged.

The sexual practices of the Victorian working classes are well hidden from view; in the later decades of the century, the sexual taboos of contemporary middle-class observers of the poor nearly coincided with those of their subjects. Poor women were not likely to talk about sex to outsiders, female or male. The vague and euphemistic statements of the pre-First-World-War generations are difficult to interpret today. Even Anna Martin, an outspoken suffragist and birth-control advocate, only hinted that wives were 'subjected, and sometimes deliberately, to injuries of a far worse kind [than wife-beating], as doctors in the leading hospitals can testify'.[71] Sexual silence and ignorance provided the backdrop against which the slightly naughty songs of Marie Lloyd ('Please, Mr Porter', 'A little of what you fancy does you good') could be richly appreciated. Colin MacInnis is impressed, indeed, with the almost complete absence of sexual passion as a theme in British music-hall lyrics, a strong contrast with contemporary French, German, and Spanish popular music.[72] Prostitutes lived among the poor, every neighbourhood had someone who served as an abortionist, and children could see smutty acts at penny gaffs, but sexual ignorance was somehow maintained. Adults were careful to avoid sexual subjects in front of children, and children were always sent out during childbirth. Grace Foakes, whose mother had fourteen births, was, she claimed, surprised by each of them. A Hoxton woman 'knew nothing' about sex at her marriage after the war; a woman from Lewisham recently recalled her astonishment at her first childbirth in 1911 when she realized that the baby was not born through her navel as she had supposed. Thus the 17-year-old Whitechapel girl whose new-born was found dead in a pile of rubbish had some credibility when she told the magistrate that she had had no idea that she was 'in the family way'.[73]

The public and private silence about sex made this arena one in which it was impossible for wives to develop a collective sense of where their 'rights' lay, and what their interests were. Women who would fight furiously over a husband's sixpence spent on drink would yield regretfully to an unwanted sexual advance. As one Rotherhithe woman, then several months pregnant, told Martin in about 1911:

> I dreaded your finding out, for I knew how upset you would be; of course it's only bringing poverty and misery into the world,

but what is a woman to do when a man's got a drop of drink in him, and she's all alone?

Court missionary William Fitzsimmons implied that wives of men who had contracted venereal diseases feared the infection but had no choice but to submit to their husbands, so long as they lived together.[74] To judge from the letters published by the Women's Co-operative Guild under the title *Maternity* from correspondents all over England, sexual intercourse indeed usually took place without emotional intimacy. By and large women seem to have viewed sex as an unpleasant duty which was none the less a fact of daily life. Wrote one woman: 'I could quote several instances where a mother's life has become intolerable through a husband's lack of control.' Another wrote revealingly: 'I felt my health giving way, and being in a weak condition, I became an easy prey to sexual intercourse, and thus once more I became a mother in fourteen months.'[75]

Pregnancy was assigned squarely to 'women's sphere'; it was vaguely blamed on women, though biological fatherhood was surely understood. Music-hall songs like 'I'm very unkind to my wife' jocularly view the arrival of a pack of children as one of the many annoyances which a wife brings to a man. Lilly Morris sang 'Don't have any more, Missus Moore', holding the mother solely responsible it seems for the Moores' twenty children.[76] A Poplar man was overheard by his young daughter complaining to his wife: 'I can't hang me trousers on the end of the bed . . . that you're not like that [pregnant].'[77] The fissures present in the family thus encouraged husbands in their failure to consider sex, or its products – children – a joint responsibility. Another child was generally not 'another mouth to feed' for the father, but only for the mother. For most couples, there is certainly no evidence during the pre-First-World-War era that sex provided occasions in which tensions between women and men were resolved. It had simply remained an area in which male dominance was still unchallenged.

It is not my purpose to buttress the now sagging 'Whig' theory of family history according to which the antagonisms of Victorian marriage have today been eradicated, replaced by intimate, 'companionate' relationships which guarantee equality and minimize hostility between the sexes. Young and Willmott's Bethnal Green study of the children and grandchildren of 'outcast London' in the 1950s reveals few 'symmetrical' couples. Most had worked out complex compromises between the demands of spouse and of neighbours, kin, and workmates; between wives' claims and husbands' wages; between public and domestic spaces. Ann Whitehead's 1967 ethnography of a small Herefordshire community describes a system of gender relationships both harsher and more mystified than that of pre-war proletarian London.[78] Looking closely at male pub culture, Whitehead was struck by the degree to which hostility towards women, their sexual objectification, and a preoccupation with controlling them shaped relations between the men, as well as with women. 'Sexual antagonism' in Herefordshire was a relatively one-sided affair; male contempt for women was publicly expressed both verbally and non-verbally, but women were isolated from each other, and their own hostility to men was hidden, cautious.

London's pub culture in the generations before the First World War strikes one as less poisonously misogynous. Male anger and humour were mainly directed at wives' endless clamouring for control over potential drinking-money. Sexuality was not yet the domestic battleground nor the locus of the belligerent assertion of collective male power which it had become by the mid-twentieth century. Silence about sex prevailed even in the roughest criminal culture – to judge from Old Nichol racketeer Arthur Harding's chivalrous attitudes[79] – and the vast majority of working-class men were cut off from some of the rich veins of misogynist pornography available to their social betters.[80] Cockney women could voice their own antagonisms: many had access to pubs; they formulated their thoughts in regular doorstep gossip, and could count on support for their claims from their neighbours, kin, and children. No expectations about 'privacy' or marital 'unity' clouded their thinking about their stark differences with husbands.

Gender relationships are malleable, and the forces shaping them in Victorian London were as complex as that society itself: the size and regularity of male and female wages; the activities of the state and voluntary institutions; patterns of housing and residence; sexual knowledge and attitudes; hopes for social mobility; and so on. The depressed, sweated, and casualized labour market described in such detail in *Outcast London* and Schmiechen's *Sweated Industries and Sweated Labour*[81] thus provided the external boundaries for London's distinct domestic arrangements. Working-class London's marriages furnish a close look at the domestic side of gender in a single time and place, as well as a lesson in the intertwining of gender with the other major sources of social power and resources.

Notes

This is a revised version of a paper originally published in *Feminist Studies*, vol. 8, no. 3, 1982. If I were to start this piece from scratch today, it would surely be different – more attentive to contradictions and crossings of sexual boundaries. The research on which this study is based was supported by grants from the National Endowment for the Humanities, the American Council of Learned Societies, and Ramapo College, to whom I am very grateful. This paper also very much benefited from the suggestions of Sally Alexander, Anna Davin, John Gillis, Raphael Samuel, Judith Walkowitz, and the editors of *Feminist Studies*.

Abbreviations used in the notes:
Sessions Papers, Central Criminal Court of London (Old Bailey): OB.
Greater London Record Office, Clerkenwell: GLRO.
Depositions, Worship Street Police Court, (GLRO, MS/CD): Worship St.
Parliamentary Papers: PP.
Family Life and Work Experience Archive, collected by Paul Thompson and Thea Vigne, housed at the University of Essex: Family Life Archive.
Journal of the Royal Statistical Society: JRSS.

1 Christopher Pulling, *They Were Singing*, 1952, pp. 70–1. Throughout the paper I use the late-Victorian and Edwardian music-hall as a genuine, if attenuated, expression of London working-class culture, a position convincingly presented in Jacqueline S. Bratton, *The Victorian Popular Ballad*, Totowa, NJ, 1975; and Martha Vicinus, *The Industrial Muse*, 1974, ch. 6.
2 'Cockney' is used here to refer to working-class London.
3 C. F. G. Masterman, *The Heart of the Empire*, 1901, quoted in Gareth Stedman Jones, *Outcast London: A Study in the Relationship between Classes in Victorian Society*, Harmondsworth, 1976, p. 326. The term 'sexual antagonism' is introduced and illustrated in Marilyn Strathern, *Women in Between*, London and New York, 1972, esp. pp. 296–314; and Ann Whitehead, 'Sexual antagonism in Herefordshire', in D. L. Barker and S. Allen (eds), *Dependence and Exploitation in Work and Marriage*, 1976.
4 On family and marriage in other parts of contemporaneous Britain, see: Elizabeth Roberts, *A Woman's Place: An Oral History of Working-Class Women 1890–1940*, Oxford, 1984; Paul Thompson with Tony Wailey and Trevor Lummis, *Living the Fishing*, 1983, III; John Gillis, *For Better, for Worse: British Marriages, 1600 to the Present*, New York, 1985, III; Trevor Lummis, 'The historical dimensions of fatherhood: a case study 1890–1914', in Margaret O'Brien and Lorna McKee (eds), *The Father Figure*, 1982; and Jan Lambertz and Pat Ayers, 'Marriage relations, money and domestic

violence in working-class Liverpool, 1919–39', in Jane Lewis (ed.), *Labour and Love: Women's Experience of Home and Family 1850–1940*, Oxford, 1986.

5 For some recent discussions of nineteenth-century domestic violence, see Jan Lambertz, 'Male–female violence in late Victorian and Edwardian England', unpublished BA thesis, Department of History, Harvard University, 1979; Margaret May, 'Violence in the family: an historical perspective', in John Powell Martin (ed.), *Violence and the Family*, New York, 1978; and Nancy Tomes, ' "A torrent of abuse": crimes of violence between working-class men and women in London, 1840–1875', *Journal of Social History*, vol. 11, no. 3, 1978, pp. 329–45. Also, Lambertz and Ayers, 'Marriage relations'.

6 Stedman Jones, *Outcast London*, pt I and appendix 2, p. 386 (1891 figures).

7 See Michèle Barrett and Mary McIntosh, in 'The family wage: some problems for socialists and feminists', *Capital and Class*, vol. 11, 1980, pp. 51–72. On poverty in old age, see, among the large body of literature produced by pension advocates in the 1890s, Charles Booth, *The Aged Poor in England and Wales*, 1894, pp. 14–15.

8 Demonstrated in, for example, Ada Heather-Bigg, 'The wife's contribution to the family income', *Economic Journal*, vol. 4, 1894, pp. 51–8; and Henry Higgs, 'Workmen's budgets', *JRSS*, vol. 66, 1893, pp. 255–85.

9 In the Katharine Buildings, model dwellings near Tower Bridge opened in 1885, 13 per cent of the adult women and 6 per cent of the men had kin living in the buildings, according to my rough count of the building records kept by Beatrice Webb and Ella Pycroft for five years after 1885 ('Received of the inhabitants', unpublished MS, London School of Economics, Coll. Misc. 43). See also Raphael Samuel, *East End Underworld: Chapters in the Life of Arthur Harding*, 1981, ch. 8; and Hugh McLeod, *Class and Religion in the Late Victorian City*, 1974, p. 10.

10 John Hasloch Potter, *Inasmuch: The Story of the Police Court Mission 1876–1926*, 1927, pp. 67–8.

11 J. A. R. Cairns, *Drab Street Glory: Impressions of Life in the Slums*, 1934, p. 125; Tomes, ' "Torrent of abuse" ', p. 332.

12 Charles Booth, *Life and Labour of the People in London*, first series: *Poverty*, 5 vols, repr. of the 1902 edn, New York, 1969, vol. 2, p. 21.

13 Eric E. Lampard, 'The urbanizing world', in H. J. Dyos and Michael Wolff (eds), *The Victorian City: Images and Realities*, 2 vols, London and Boston, 1973, vol. 1, p. 13; H. A. Shannon, 'Migration and the growth of London, 1841–91; a statistical note', *Economic History Review*, vol. 5, no. 2, 1935, pp. 79–86.

14 H. J. Dyos, 'The slums of Victorian London', *Victorian Studies*, vol. 11, no. 1, 1967, pp. 5–40.

15 On street and neighbourhood endogamy in some selected working-class districts, see McLeod, *Class and Religion*, table 4, pp. 296–7; Stedman Jones, *Outcast London*, p. 322, ch. 18.

16 This position is stated very forcefully, in a variety of different ways, in the writing of Rotherhithe settlement worker Anna Martin. See 'The mother and social reform', *The Nineteenth Century and After*, vol. 73, May and June 1913, pp. 1060–79, and 1235–55.

17 John W. Innes, *Class Fertility Trends in England and Wales 1876–1934*, Princeton, 1938, appendix II, p. 134; T. A. Welton, 'A study of some portions of the census of London for 1901', *JRSS*, vol. 65, 1902, pp. 470–3; T. H. C. Stevenson, 'The fertility of various social classes in England and Wales from the middle of the nineteenth century to 1911', *JRSS*, vol. 83, 1920, p. 431.

18 Women's neighbourhood ties, and their mutual aid, are the subject of E. Ross, 'Survival networks', *History Workshop*, no. 15, 1983, pp. 4–27.

19 Crimes of passion and sexual jealousy were of course not unknown in London, and male and female suicides were also sometimes attributed to romantic heartbreak. I am still working out the relationship of love to marriage for these populations. For a sensitive study of this issue, see Gillis, *For Better, for Worse*.

20 'Angels without wings', in John M. Garrett (ed.), *Sixty Years of British Music Hall*, 1976; 'The bachelor of sixty-two', in W. Henderson (ed.), *Victorian Street Ballads*, 1938, pp. 133–4.

21 Ellen Ranyard, *Nurses for the Needy, or Bible Women Nurses in the Homes of the London Poor*, 1875, p. 24.

22 James Greenwood, 'Pawnbrokery in London', *Hours at Home*, vol. 7, 1868, p. 116, cited in Lambertz, 'Male–female violence'.

23 OB, Plampton, vol. 99, 1883–4, p. 533.

24 ibid., Gardner, vol. 80, 1874, p. 207; Clara Grant, *Farthing Bundles*, 2nd edn, 1931, p. 113; PP, 1912–13, vol. XIX, q. 20, 120 (testimony of Miss Elizabeth Lidgett).

25 OB, Creighton, vol. 120, 1894, p. 1196; ibid., Pitchford, vol. 100, 1884, p. 115.

26 ibid., Tritner, vol. 89, 1878–9, p. 279.

27 Margaret Loane, 'Husband and wife among the poor', *Contemporary Review*, vol. 87, 1905, p. 222; George Acorn (pseud.), *One of the Multitude: An Autobiography by a Resident of Bethnal Green*, 1911, p. 2.

28 OB, Hibbard, vol. 120, 1894, p. 1084.

29 Agnes Stafford, 'Experiences of a district nurse, VII', *The Co-operative News*, 9 October 1886, quoted in Lambertz, 'Male–female violence', p. 75.

30 T. E. Harvey, *A London Boy's Saturday*, Birmingham, 1906, p. 12. Reference courtesy of Anna Davin and Jerry White.

31 Alice Linton, *Not Expecting Miracles*, 1982, pp. 5–6; Lillian Hine, 'A Poplar childhood', *East London Record*, vol. 3, 1980, pp. 32–43; and oral history of a woman born in 1901 in Bromley-by-Bow, daughter of a lighterman who kept chickens in the family yard at Custom House, Family Life Archive, no. 333, p. 18. A man born in 1899 remembers his father's vegetable garden in West Ham as a big help to the family during the 1911 dock strikes; a woman, born in Bow in 1897, recalls

her grandfather's private use of cash proceeds from his garden allotment – ibid., nos 70, 92.

32 George Rushbrook, Memories, typescript, Tower Hamlets Local History Library, p. 4; Octavia Hill, *Homes of the London Poor*, New York, 1873, p. 41.

33 A woman born in Crew Street near Milwall Bridge in the early 1900s, typescript of an interview by Raphael Samuel, in the interviewer's possession, London; cited in Tomes, 'Torrent of abuse', p. 32.

34 A. S. Jasper, *A Hoxton Childhood*, repr. edn, 1974, p. 31; see also pp. 40, 51.

35 This may be the result of the court reporters' assumption that all family property is the husband's. But from the context it is usually possible to judge which family member is being robbed, as when a 14-year-old girl stole a watch, obviously her father's – *East London Observer*, 14 June 1870, p. 7.

36 On the use of the term 'wages' for wives, see Laura Oren, 'The welfare of women in labouring families: England 1860–1950', *Feminist Studies*, vol. 1, nos. 3–4, 1973, pp. 112–13; Family Life Archive, no. 368 (a man born in Wapping in 1897 whose father was a docker); Elizabeth Roberts, 'Working class women in the north-west', *Oral History*, vol. 5, no. 2, 1977, p. 13; E. Robinson, 'I remember', 1960–1970, typescript, Brunel University Library, p. 7. For another arrangement for the distribution of household income, see Patricia E. Malcolmson, *English Laundresses: A Social History 1850–1930*, Urbana, Ill., 1986, p. 40.

37 Charles Booth Manuscripts, London School of Economics, series B, vol. 352 (George Duckworth's discussion with Constable W. R. Ryland, Hoxton Subdivision of the G Division of the Metropolitan Police, 23 May 1898).

38 Oren, 'Welfare of women in labouring families', pp. 111–12; Peter N. Stearns, 'Working class women in Britain, 1890–1914', in Martha Vicinus (ed.), *Suffer and Be Still*, Bloomington, Ind., 1972, p. 116; Meacham, *A Life Apart*, ch. 3.

39 Acorn, *One of the Multitude*, p. 5; Linton, *Not Expecting Miracles*, p. 6.

40 H. A. Mess, *Casual Labour at the Docks*, 1916, p. 35; Henry Iselin, 'The story of a children's care committee', *Economic Review*, vol. 22, no. 1, 1912, p. 46. In Middlesbrough over a third of wives did not know how much their husbands earned – Lady Florence Bell, *At the Works*, 1907, repr. edn 1985, p. 78. For a more recent study, see Michael Young and Peter Willmott, *Family and Kinship in East London*, Harmondsworth, 1962, pp. 18, 26–7.

41 Loane, 'Husband and wife', p. 226.

42 Margaret Loane, *The Common Growth*, 1911, p. 278; Mrs Benjamin, untitled MS autobiography, Hackney People's Autobiography, London, p. 3.

43 Samuel, *East End Underworld*, pp. 28–9; a man born in 1884, son of a cabinet-maker who eventually moved to Battersea, Family Life

Archive, no. 225; Hine, 'Poplar childhood', p. 35; Jasper, *Hoxton Childhood*, p. 57.

44 PP, 1905, vol. LXXXIV, pp. 6, 8 (pt II of Board of Trade survey of British workers' family budgets). See also D. J. Oddy, 'A nutritional analysis of historical evidence: the working-class diet, 1880–1914', in Derek Oddy and Derek Miller (eds), *The Making of the Modern British Diet*, 1976.

45 Acorn, *One of the Multitude*, p. 6.

46 Linton, *Not Expecting Miracles*, p. 6; interview by Raphael Samuel with a daughter of a railway employee who grew up in Fulbourne Street in Whitechapel; another interview by Raphael Samuel with a daughter of a Trueman's Brewery worker, p. 28.

47 PP, 1904, vol. XXXII, q. 12970 (testimony of Dr Lewis Hawkes); Dorothy Scannell, *Mother Knew Best: An East End Childhood*, New York, 1974, p. 37; *Father Joe: The Autobiography of Joseph Williamson of Poplar and Stepney*, 1963, p. 22.

48 Martin, 'Mother and social reform', p. 1079.

49 Children playing 'dock strike': *East London Observer*, 31 August 1889, p. 5. On the use of the 'docker's dinner', see ibid., 24 August 1889, p. 5; and the *Star*, 19 August 1889, p. 3.

50 London Cottage Mission provided separate meals for women and children, the *Star*, 27 August 1889, p. 2; Charrington collects money to feed 'a thousand wives and children a day', ibid., 28 August p. 2; a comment on 'thousands of destitute women and children', ibid., 12 September p. 2; free breakfasts during the 1911 dock strike, see Mrs Benjamin's autobiography, p. 44.

51 Martin, 'Mother and social reform', p. 1079.

52 Loane, *Common Growth*, p. 104; id., *An Englishman's Castle*, 2nd imp., 1909, p. 298; George Sims, *How the Poor Live and Horrible London*, combined edn, 1889, p. 127; Pember Reeves, *Round About a Pound*, p. 39. For some other descriptions of survival programmes, successful and unsuccessful, see: Acorn, *One of the Multitude*, pp. 4–5; E. Collet and M. Robertson, *Family Budgets: Being the Income and Expenses of 28 British Households 1891–94*, 1896, families 1, 2, 3, 7; Poplar Union, records of applications for out-relief, GLRO, PO BG 132/1–4 (1893).

53 Mary Barnes Waters (pseud. for a woman born in the notorious Norfolk Gardens, off Curtain Road in Hoxton, in 1904), Hackney People's Autobiography, typescript.

54 C. R. Cuthbert Keeson, 'Pawnbroking London', in George R. Sims (ed.), *Living London*, 1902, vol. 2, p. 37; Grant, *Farthing Bundles*, p. 98; Melanie Tebbutt, *Making Ends Meet: Pawnbroking and Working-Class Credit*, 1983, p. 42; ch. 2, 'The housewife's saviour', is a wonderful discussion of pawning as a female resort, with a slightly different reading of its significance from the one I have given here.

55 *London City Mission Magazine*, October 1864, p. 206 (women at police court because of lost pawn tickets); Mary Blaney, Worship St 'May 1874' bundle (a servant who stole three pawn tickets from her

landlady and sold two of them to another woman); Sophia Cooper got twenty-one days for stealing three sheets from her landlady, and selling their pawn tickets – Worship St 'Feb–March 1874' bundle. Police court depositions from 1855 to 1889 are at the GLRO. My thanks to the staff of the old Middlesex Record Office, who helped me locate them in 1979. (They may have been recatalogued since then.)

56 (Thomas Wright), *The Pinch of Poverty: Sufferings and Heroism of the London Poor*, 1892, p. 301.

57 Jasper, *Hoxton Childhood*, pp. 22–3; OB, Perry, Hollingsworth, and Black, vol. 110, 1889, p. 849 (a Barking case in which a man asked a neighbourhood woman to pawn boots he had stolen); Thames Police Court 'Feb–March 1873' bundle (a mixed-sex group of thieves, in which the women did the group's pawning).

58 Pat Thane, 'The working class and state "welfare" in Britain, 1880–1914', *Historical Journal*, vol. 27, no. 4, 1984, p. 891; Catherine Webb, *The Woman with the Basket: The Story of the Women's Co-operative Guild 1883–1927*, Manchester, 1927, p. 89.

59 A man born in 1891, Donald Street, Bromley-by-Bow, typescript interview with Raphael Samuel; Dorothy Scannell, *Mother Knew Best: An East End Childhood*, 1974, p. 42.

60 Greenwood, 'Pawnbrokery in London', p. 114.

61 John C. Blake, *Memories of Old Poplar*, 1977, p. 11; Arthur Hadley, 'Penny plain: autobiography of a Bethnal Green boy', 1947, typescript, Tower Hamlets Local History Library.

62 Greenwood, 'Pawnbrokery in London', pp. 114–15; Grant, *Farthing Bundles*, p. 117.

63 Tomes, 'Torrent of abuse', p. 330; OB, French, vol. 79, 1874, pp. 389–90.

64 Tomes, 'Torrent of abuse', p. 330; Martin, 'Mother and social reform', pp. 1071–2.

65 Quoted in Thomas Holmes, *Pictures and Problems from London Police Courts*, 1900, p. 62. See also R. C. Corder, *Tales Told to a Magistrate*, 1925, pp. 205–6.

66 Tomes, 'Torrent of abuse', pp. 336–8; on similar patterns in New York City in earlier decades, see Christine Stansell, *City of Women: Sex and Class in New York 1789–1860*, New York, 1986, pp. 76–83.

67 OB, Hancock, vol. 89, 1879, p. 321; also Holmes, *Pictures and Problems*, pp. 62–3.

68 Some examples of ritualized fights between men are: *Bethnal Green News*, 7 September 1895, p. 6; and OB, Onion, vol. 80, 1874, p. 209.

69 OB, Palmer, vol. 69, 1869, p. 267.

70 The term 'threshold' describing wives' tolerance for domestic violence is developed by Lambertz, in 'Male–female violence', PP, 1912–13, vol. XIX, qq. 19,473 f. (testimony of William Fitzsimmons).

71 Martin, 'Mother and social reform', p. 1077.

72 Colin MacInnes, *Sweet Saturday Night: Songs of the 1890's*, 1967, p. 39.

73 Grace Foakes, *Between High Walls: A London Childhood*, 1972, p. 11; interview with a married couple both born in East London, the

wife in 1905, the husband in 1894, by Raphael Samuel, typescript, Family Life Archive, no. 333, p. 26; 'Mrs N., born 1884, childbirth at home – Lewisham, 1911', dittoed excerpts from an interview by Frances Widdowson, Goldsmith's College, University of London, n.d.; *Bethnal Green News*, 16 March 1895, p. 6. I have discussed this further in Ross, ' "Not the sort that would sit on the doorstep": respectability in pre-World War I London neighborhoods', *International Labor and Working Class History*, no. 27, 1985, pp. 49–51.

74 Martin, 'Mother and social reform', p. 1061; PP, 1912–13, vol. XIX, q. 19,522.

75 Margaret Llewelyn Davies (ed.), *Maternity: Letters from Working Women*, repr. edn, New York, 1978, pp. 65–6, 99.

76 Pulling, *They Were Singing*, pp. 70–1; MacInnis, *Sweet Saturday Night*, p. 5.

77 A woman born in Canning Town, 1895, Family Life Archive, no. 126, p. 25. Her mother had 19 children of whom only 7 survived.

78 Michael Young and Peter Willmott, *The Symmetrical Family*, 1973; and id., *Family and Kinship in East London*; Whitehead, 'Sexual antagonism in Herefordshire'.

79 Samuel, *East End Underworld*.

80 But see Judith Walkowitz, 'Jack the Ripper and the myth of male violence', *Feminist Studies*, vol. 8, no. 3, 1982, pp. 543–74, for the use of the Jack the Ripper story by working-class boys and men in London in the decades that followed the murders.

81 James A. Schmiechen, *Sweated Industries and Sweated Labor: The London Clothing Trades, 1860–1914*, Urbana, Ill., 1983.

10

Becoming a woman in London in the 1920s and 1930s

Sally Alexander

Introduction

Two visual images of the working class vie for attention in the popular memory of the inter-war years: the cloth cap and spare frame of the unemployed man whose wasted face and staring eyes still wrench pity from the onlooker; and the young working girl – lipsticked, silk-stockinged, and dressed, in the phrase of novelist, playwright, and broadcaster J. B. Priestley, 'like an actress'. The juxtaposition pierced contemporary consciousness. The two figures represented, on the one hand, the means test, hunger marches, and Orwell's 'twenty million inadequately fed'; and, on the other,

the England of arterial and by-pass roads, of filling stations, factories that look like exhibition buildings, of giant cinema and dance-halls and cafes, bungalows with tiny garages, cocktail bars, Woolworths, motor-coaches, wireless, hiking . . . greyhound racing and dirt tracks, swimming pools and everything given away for cigarette coupons.[1]

This was the north/south divide. It was also a sexual division. Priestley was lamenting the changing industrial structure of Britain, or rather the effects of this change on the people. Nineteenth-century industrial power had been built on the blast furnace, coal-mines, and textile mills of the north and west; labour was manly and strong, its output substantial. Priestley lists twentieth-century industries in contrast: the tea-shops, corsetries, and hairdressers of the south-eastern suburbs and East Anglian small towns; the potato crisps, scent, toothpaste, bathing costumes, and fire extinguishers of West London. Priestley's lament is partly the recoil of the middle-brow man of letters from the influence of the United States – in particular California – on English people's wants and needs: the new forms of mass entertainment, the glare of advertisements, and ephemera of the new consumerism.[2] But there is also the fear that England and the English are in danger of being feminized by their wirelesses, movie-star worship, silk stockings, and hire-purchase: not only is the new working class in these new industries female, but the wants and needs which the new industries supply are feminine.

Priestley's sense that some vital energy in English life was being sapped by the new industries and suburban sprawls in which they were situated or which swiftly surrounded them (like the north of Notting Hill, described by Rebecca West in the 1930s as 'hacked out of the countryside and still bleeding')[3] was echoed by Orwell, the Coles, and other contemporaries, and has been reiterated by historians.[4] Feminists too eyed the new young woman warily. 'Clothes, hat, shoes, stockings, furs, bag, scarf – all are standardized,' wrote Mary Agnes Hamilton, novelist and labour organizer in 1936, noting also her make-up and lissom boyish figure. This young woman smoked, she went on; she spoke with confidence, and was no longer interested in feminism. She 'took her freedom for granted'.[5] Most agreed with Ellen Wilkinson, MP for Jarrow, that 'the real difficulty' caused by industrial decline in Britain's staple industries 'is that of the adult male'.[6] Unable to find work, he lost status in his family and community through the indignities of negotiating with the Unemployed Assistance Board. The new jobs of the trading estates trailing the northern towns were, like those in the south-east, principally for young women and youths. Skilled and unskilled men feared the changes in industrial structure and process which made their work redundant and new industries open to women. The stark misery of Max Cohen's *I Was One of the Unemployed*, for example, documents the physical and mental suffering wrought by unemployment. Fear broke into hostility and contempt in some accounts. Those 'silly girls', wrote the socialist novelist John Sommerfield in *MayDay*, published in 1936, 'in their synthetic Hollywood dreams, their pathetic silk stockings and lipsticks, their foolish strivings'[7] – dismissing at once both them and their dreams.

The following essay reconsiders some of those dreams and the young women who dreamt them. I want to query the use of the epithet 'feminine' to denigrate both the new consumer industries and the human needs they evoke.[8] Part of the explanation for this denigration lies with the habits of mind of the socialist and labour movements (to which Priestley, Orwell, Wilkinson, and the Coles, cited above, all belong). Both movements – in spite of resolute attempts of feminists – were organized around notions of class whose formation and destinies vary, but in which the individual subject was masculine and founded on the notion of independence

246

through, and property in, labour. Femininity and women themselves, outside of the category 'wife and mother', were a problem associated with either their 'sex' or, worse, the threat of 'cheap labour'. Fear of cheap labour was the rational kernel in the labour movement's antagonism towards the female worker, but the denigration of the feminine should alert us to deeper levels of unease. Since it is through the division into masculinity and femininity that human identity is formed, and sexual desire and reproduction organized, any disturbance of that division will provoke anxiety, and labour is one element in the division of women and men more unstable than popular belief would like. Though the structure of the sexual division of labour in modern industry was set down during the Industrial Revolution – 'women's work' was designated unskilled, low paid, and unorganized – its boundaries constantly shift. The social relations of labour, in other words, are central not simply to the historical understanding of class, but also to the relation of sexual difference.[9]

In the 1920s and 1930s the sexual division of labour and women's sense of themselves – indeed what it meant to be a woman – were changing in significant ways, and the changes were nowhere more apparent than in London. Families were smaller, the working day shorter, wages (for those in work) were higher, and the numbers living below the poverty line fewer than before the First World War.[10] Aspirations too were changing. Women in trade unions, education, local government, and feminist groups, as well as writers of fiction, were articulating women's wants and trying to persuade authorities to consider them, even if they refused to embody them.[11] But most strikingly, advertising and the cinema, playing on fantasy and desire, enabled women to *imagine* an end to domestic drudgery and chronic want. Images of streamlined kitchens, effective cleaning equipment, cheap and pretty clothes and make-up, on hoardings and cinema screens and in the new women's magazines, added a new dimension to romance – a source of narrative pleasure to women since the eighteenth century at least, the scourge alike of puritan and feminist critics of femininity.[12] Few women replaced the copper with the washing-machine or the outside lavatory with the bathroom during the 1930s. But houses were built with these amenities, and by the end of the decade families were moving into them – apprehensive often of the costs of this new life, but moving in nevertheless.[13]

Women were moving into new areas of work too, in offices, shops, and office cleaning (domestic service was notoriously unpopular with London girls). Their numbers in the new and

247

expanding industries – glass, chemicals, light metals, commerce, the manufacture of food and drink, for instance, all of which were growth industries in Greater London – were increasing. But the 'general tendency observed by the *General Report* of the 1931 Census towards the gradual weakening of the influences that restricted an occupation to the members of one sex, especially the male sex', was simply an acceleration in the development of mass production: the division of labour into short repetitive tasks, and the introduction of machinery and cheap labour.[14] This tendency, uneven, local, specific, was shifting the allocation of jobs among women and men, but not undermining the designations women's and men's work. The content of 'women's work' remained in colloquial speech what it had been since the beginning of waged labour: 'Men done the hard work, the good work,' was how one Woolwich factory worker put it, 'and women done the light work.' And the vital distinction remained what it had always been – pay. 'They'd be out on strike at the drop of a reel of cotton,' Lily, an East London clothing worker, told me, if men had been paid women's rates. 'A man could have done it,' a clerical worker said of her job, 'but they would have had to pay them more.' When women were employed on men's work they were paid less.[15] And employ them they did. The location of the new industries was deliberate: close to their markets and within easy reach of cheap ununionized labour.[16] In the 1920s and 1930s office cleaners, packers, shop assistants, typists became the unlikely and suddenly visible shock troops of industrial restructuring.

Who were these women, and what did they want? Women's political and industrial organization, the vote, and changes in education, publishing, purchasing power, and with them habits of reading, writing, and even remembering have deepened individual subjectivity. And in the past twenty years the voices of some women may be heard through autobiography and oral history. Listening to, or reading, women's own descriptions of their growing up places women's subjectivity, their own sense of themselves, at the centre of historical change. Women's subjectivity is only one element in the relation of sexual difference, but one fraught with difficulties of interpretation because it opens up not only behaviour, thought, opinion, and family stories to historical enquiry, but also the unconscious mental processes. That is, we listen to fantasies of desire and loss, the compelling inner directives of the structure of sexual difference. Sceptics wonder whether there can be a *history* of subjectivity which borrows its understanding of that precarious process from psychoanalysis. But fantasy draws on the immediate and historical for aspects of its content, form, and context, and the conditions of these are always changing. This essay is a part of a longer study. Here I only touch on women's first jobs, and their changing appearance: the one a condition of femininity, the other a symbol. Its polemical purpose, of course, is to counter the repudiation of femininity which underlines the visions of England and the English described by Orwell and Priestley in the 1930s.[17]

Becoming a woman: the first job

For each young girl reaching her fourteenth birthday, the step from school to work was a step towards adulthood. 'There was nothing gradual about growing up,' wrote Rose Gamble in *Chelsea Child*:[18]

> As long as you were at school you looked like a child in short trousers and frocks, and you were treated like one, but when you left school at the end of the term after your fourteenth birthday, childhood ended. It was abrupt and final and your life changed overnight.

But the end of childhood was not so absolute. The end of schooling meant the end of lessons and children's play but not the end of obligations to the family nor yet the achievement of full adult identity. For a woman, that came with marriage and motherhood; few young women in London in the 1920s and 1930s escaped this destiny. But first there was adolescence – the transition between child and woman when identity itself is in flux and when the wage, new clothes, and the tangle of emotions associated with those years seem to promise the transformation of the self and relations with others. Memories of adolescence are vivid, perhaps because they still carry the weight of possibility – the intense wondering what one might become.

Rose Gamble, one of five children growing up in Chelsea in the 1920s, looked forward to the change from child to woman with excitement and hope. They lived in two rooms in the streets and courts behind Chelsea Town Hall, moving often; their mother earned sixpence an hour charring until she took a job in a mothers' clinic for 25 shillings (£1.25) a week; their father – a feared and intermittent presence – described himself once as 'a wharfinger', though he was mostly unemployed. Dodie, the eldest, 'plunged' from the top to the bottom of the class in 1928 when she saw a job for a greengrocer's cashier advertised in the local tobacconist. Fiercely insistent on her qualifications in spite of her childlike appearance, she got the job, and the whole family celebrated her achievement. She plaited her hair; her mum showed her how to put it up; and without a backward glance at her abandoned education, she flung herself heart and soul into her job. She was quick and obliging, polite and smiling with both customers and staff. It was not enough to sit behind the cash register. She mastered the books, learned to serve, and began to do small jobs in the florist's department. She made wreaths, and was trusted to collect the rents on her employers' properties. Every penny of her 10 shilling wage (50p) (for a 56-hour week) was handed over to her mother. Dodie's delight and satisfaction were in pleasing her mother – relieving her of some of the financial burden for the family. Her sole personal ambition was to own a bicycle; an ambition not realized until some years later when, still at the greengrocer's, still handing over her full wage-packet – 18s 6d (92½p) by this time – to her mother, she heard of another job in a 'posh' shop off Sloane Street. The errand boy at the greengrocer's, whose gran cleaned for them, told her about it one day as they commiserated over their static status. The posh shop was called the Little Gallery and it not only took her on with an advance in wages of 9 shillings (45p) but also employed the second sister, Luli. Both girls learned about fine arts and handicrafts; their young brother and sister also became familiar with the pottery and paintings and quilts on sale in the shop. Rose herself hand-decorated cellophane boxes and cards for sale while still at school. The Little Gallery was owned by two sisters, whose empathy with their young employees prompted them to finance their first ever trip to the seaside and a weekend in France. Dodie and Luli were lucky. Their new jobs opened up physical and intellectual landscapes, extended their knowledge and understanding.

Luli was two years younger than Dodie. Her first venture into employment had been less auspicious. She too had wanted to go straight into a shop and ''ave a black frock an' wavy hair', and had scoured the district around her home in Chelsea to no avail. Hearing from Lily Browning that 'there was a job goin' in 'aberdashery' over in Clapham Junction, she traipsed over there (a distance of several miles) only to be turned down because of the state of her hands; they were ingrained with dirt. Dirt – the mark of poverty and domestic labour – was incompatible with the aura of ladylike respectability which a salesgirl in a large departmental store should exude. These gradations of status were quickly learned. On her disappointed return from Clapham, Luli's mother seized the opportunity. Tactfully, she suggested that, just to begin with, while looking for further employment in a shop, Luli should 'work up' a few cleaning jobs at fourpence an hour, and she could be home to see to her younger brothers and sisters after school. Luli, in despair at the prospect of more cleaning – 'Please, Mum, I don't want to be a char' and 'Oh no, Mum, I done with that' – reluctantly acquiesced, and within a couple of days had fifteen different jobs each week 'worked up' through her mother's contacts at the clinic: a few private homes, a doctor's surgery, scrubbing the stairs in a block of service flats in Fulham, and so on. She walked, like Dodie, from Fulham to Earls Court and Knightsbridge and back each and every day. She was dressed appropriately: 'Dodie made her a sacking apron for scrubbing and Mum cut down a cross-over pinny to wear under her coat.'

Luli was not released from these charring labours until her mother, after an illness, gave up her job at the mother-and-child clinic in Chelsea, and went to work in a factory canteen with 'a nice bit of easy office cleaning in the evening with no scrubbing'. She told Lu about a vacancy at the factory, and after frantic preparations to hair and underclothing Lu went after the job, was taken on, and gave up cleaning. 'With her bosum high up on her chest and her hair done, she was a lady,' remembered Rose, 'and I couldn't understand where the old Lu had gone.'

The story of Luli and Dodie's first steps into employment was the story of many London girls. The labour market was, to begin with, local and specific – 'You all worked in the nearest factory job to your home,' as I was told, or shop, office, workshop, wherever employment could be found.[19] Resistance to domestic service was strong and persistent among London girls. Each factory listed the jobs available on boards outside the factory gates or advertised for 'hands' – 'the only part of my body they was interested in!' – in the local paper.[20] But word of mouth and 'working-in' were the more vital labour exchange, and a mother's occupation and contacts usually more important than the father's, though the father's status if skilled could be decisive.

Jane Smith, for instance, came from a family of artisans on her father's side, while her mother's family were small tradespeople. The youngest of five children (her brothers were all in apprenticed trades; one sister was a tailoress, the other a high-class private domestic servant), she was kept at home in the first year after leaving school to keep house for her father and brothers in Pimlico:[21]

My father came from people where they were proud of their occupation; where they trained. They were artisans. Daughters were expected to stay at home unless they were able to train, perhaps as a schoolteacher, or train as a ladies' maid where you met a better class of man.

Not until she 'kicked up a fuss' and provoked a 'family conference' could she persuade her father (her mother was dead) to allow her to search for an apprenticeship in her older sister's trade, West End tailoring.

Celia Wilmot, who became a Fleet Street secretary during the 1930s, was the daughter of a printworker killed during the First World War. His widow, Celia's mother, besides a small pension from the printworkers' union, worked as an early-morning cleaner in Fleet Street (and was one of the organizers of the General Strike there). Celia took a job as a clerical assistant to Pitman the printers straight from school. She learned shorthand at evening classes, and taught herself typing in the office, but it was her contact with the print union through their mother by virtue of her father's trade which provided the opening in Fleet Street.[22]

'Skill' was picked up haphazardly – or not at all. Apprenticeships were rare and, because low paid, often impatiently worked.[23] Lily Van Duren's first job when she left the Jewish orphanage in 1929, aged 15, was with a court dressmaker in Conduit Street, W1 – 'The clothing trade was the thing for poor Jewish children to do.' Her pay was 10 shillings (50p) a week. Hurt and angry when she overheard a conversation in which she and the other learners were described by the proprietor as 'cheap little girls',[24] she

> immediately decided to find my own job – which meant I had to root around and I found a job in the East End on the more popular, lower-priced clothing. I discovered that I was no good and I just had to poke around from job to job until I got the experience. . . . I trained myself by watching what other girls did, and they would help me as much as possible, and I gradually picked it up until I became an experienced [hand] finisher and I was able to find work during the busy periods.

Soon Lily moved from hand finishing to machining. Machinists (men were called machiners) were paid more than finishers (the difference between 30s (£1.50) and £2 10s (£2.50) in the early 1930s) because it was a much more skilled job. When Lily switched to the machine:

> I'd go into a factory, and say I was a machinist, get half a day's experience and get the sack because I couldn't do it. Maybe a couple of days later I'd get another job as a machinist and last a day, and so on until I became an experienced machinist and was able to claim I was an able machinist.

Jane Smith, daughter of the Pimlico engineer described above, was equally impatient. She earned 8 shillings (40p) a week as a learner to a waistcoat maker in Soho, a situation which she regarded, in the same way as Lily, as a 'waste of time':[25]

And I was taught, I had no papers of apprenticeship. . . . I was paid a poor wage in order to learn the trade, that's what it amounted to. My father didn't find the job, my sister found the job . . . she worked in a little workshop in Marshall Street, Soho, and they used to let out sittings for tailors. There'd be a big room and there'd be tables, half a dozen tables, and each tailor had a table with his goose iron (have you even seen a goose iron? It was a large chunk of iron with a handle which was put into a gas heater, and it was . . . used for pressing, shrinking work. It was recognized that women weren't capable of handling this huge iron) and his equipment, and his sewing-machine, and he had what is called his 'hand', that is, a female to help him. . . . And he was called a journeyman tailor. . . . And we made clothes for gentlemen, in inverted commas if you like! . . . And my sister knew a number of tailors because she'd worked there for some years, and she said to one of them, 'I've got a sister who wants to learn the trade, who we think we ought to teach the trade', and somebody said to her, 'Well, I can do with a girl.' And I remember very well I was paid 8 shillings a week. I remember the amount of money. I was paid 8 shillings a week by virtue of the fact that I was learning a trade. . . . Well, now, they estimated that it would take me five or six years. But I learnt it in little over a year, and I branched out on my own. . . . it wasn't going to take me six years.

Having grasped the essentials of the work, as well as the nicer distinctions between women's and men's skills (women did not become journeymen tailors unless the widow of a tailor, and even then they probably made only the 'smaller garments'), Jane left, and found herself employment as a tailoress to an Irish waistcoat maker for 30 shillings (£1.50) a week. She was determined to set up on her own: 'I was a bit rebellious . . . I wasn't the kind of person that was going to be satisfied with anything less than getting what I wanted to get.' When I asked her later what she meant by rebellious, Jane replied that she 'didn't take things for granted. I had my own views.'[26] Presumably it was to protect themselves from the competition of young women like Jane that the West End branch of the Tailors and Garment Workers' Union excluded women from membership.[27] Undeterred by mere custom, Jane began touting for work and joined the union. She paid her subs regularly, had a strong sense of skill learned from her father, and had read widely the labour papers and the books on her father's shelves which included, apart from *The Ragged Trousered Philanthropist*, Jack London, William Morris, and Upton Sinclair.[28] But, as every woman knows, knowledge and skill in themselves are not always enough to overcome male prejudice:

> I canvassed the shops, and I went in and said, 'Do you want a good waistcoat maker in this shop?' And, if you'll forgive me for saying this, I was ginger-haired and freckle-faced and quite a lively youngster, probably a bit unusual, not beautiful or anything like that, but I had this pale skin that you do have, and this ginger hair . . . and I was something of a rebel, a red from an early age. So it may have been that they were attracted to me. But I did manage to get work, and I did manage to make waistcoats.

So a father's trade could impart confidence and raise expectations as well as provide access to skilled work; wider kin were influential in a city of small trades and diverse industry and with a huge service sector; but a mother's word was usually final. She was in charge of the family budget and, for the first years of earning at least, took most of the young woman's wage:[29]

> You'd walk home, like the men had done in the past, with your wage packet. She'd open it and give you back your five or ten shillings. It was a hangover from the Victorian days, and you were equivalent of the man in the family.

For most young women their first jobs were a compromise between the rude structure of the local labour market, family need, and their own hopes. Surprisingly, what emerged in conversation was the extent to which the women felt they had chosen their occupation. 'I *wanted* to go on a machine,' said Margaret Payne, the ninth of eleven children in Bermondsey. She was restless until she found her niche in a leather factory, in which industry she remained, always working in South London, refusing promotion (she did not want to be in authority over the other women and girls) even though she designed for the firms and trained the younger women. When I met her in the late 1970s, she was an outworker, respected and still designing. 'I wanted factory work,' said another who became a coil-winder in Woolwich; 'I couldn't stand an office.'[30]

Recognition of social divisions and inequalities slip into speech unobtrusively, and they mediated choice: girls who went into office jobs were 'well-to-do' or 'well spoken'; others were the 'commonest of the common'. The girl who won a coveted scholarship to elementary school was the 'daughter of a professional man, the local detective'; in private domestic service, or higher-class restaurants and shops, you 'met a better class of person'. Most women and men from the London poor still situated themselves within a hierarchy from 'respectable' to 'rough' which covered the uneven terrain of different religions ('We went to church three times on Sunday,' May Jones told me; 'we were a cut above'), degrees of 'slovenliness', book-learning, and levels of skill too.[31] I say 'still' because this is a hierarchy familiar to all students of late-nineteenth-century London and one which reproduces itself tenaciously in popular memory. Divisions within the working class, or among the poor, are remembered in detail – which is partly the inevitable perspective of the child whose vista is immediate: the family, street, and school. But the young women born into those families and streets remembered them so intensely partly because they wanted to escape from them. A good job and, later, marriage seemed to be the way out.[32]

The exception to this general, albeit attenuated, sense of choice were those girls who had wanted to continue in education. They felt disappointed and sometimes angry that they had been forced to leave school at 14. Even if they had won a rare and coveted scholarship to trade or secondary school the cost of school uniform and the family's need for money prevented them from taking it up. Among the very poor, even a learnership was beyond their grasp; it was too low paid for too many years. 'My mother wanted my dibs from work,' was a mild reproof. 'I wasn't dumb. I passed a preliminary trade scholarship at 14; but she had to have the money come in,' was another.[33] This sense of disappointment never left the women. It had different effects. It left powerful feelings of ambivalence towards both their mothers and the homes they did not want to reproduce (notwithstanding the equally ubiquitous memory of community as a child: 'No one ever locked their door'; 'Everyone was in and out of each other's houses'). In some it contributed to a fine sense of social injustice which led to trade union or political work with the unemployed, against fascism, or for the working class (there was no feminist consciousness *then* among the women I interviewed).[34] But, sadly, the sense of disappointment also contributed to the low self-esteem to which many of the women of that generation fell prey. Education was longed for by more than were permitted to have it, and those who 'spoke well' and 'knew a lot' were admired and often envied by others deprived of an education. These young women strove to improve themselves, attending evening classes, acquiring skills in the ways described above, and attending to their appearance and social life.

Lives were narrowed by the lack of education and by family poverty, but this narrowing was not always immediately clear to the young women themselves. All the women I spoke to felt themselves then, they said, lucky to be in work when brothers and fathers were often unemployed.[35] And there was also the immediate excitement of leaving school and earning a wage, and of long skirts and new hair-styles which seemed to anticipate a new independence, a new self.

Becoming a woman: dress

A child's appearance changed when she took her first job. Dodie was scarcely tall enough to reach the cashier's desk when she started work at the greengrocer's; nevertheless her hair was up. Younger brothers and sisters were left behind with the schoolroom, learning by rote, the Saturday job, and street games, as the need to earn a living propelled the child into the adult world of work with new preoccupations and responsibilities. The transition was keenly felt. Rose (Dodie and Luli's younger sister) had won a place at a private school when she was 13. She was able to attend because the earnings of older children relieved financial pressure on the family; and while she remained in a drill-slip until matriculation at 16, her friends from the old elementary school 'had perms and handbags and ear-rings'. Boys as well as girls underwent this transformation. They appeared immediately after their fourteenth birthday in long trousers:[36]

> If their mothers belonged to a clothing club there was a fair chance of a new pair ready and waiting, but more often their first pair were cut-downs, the slack folded into a belt, and the crotch halfway down their thighs. They slicked their hair with water into a quiff above their foreheads, and half a comb stuck out of the top pocket of every jacket.

Dress not only marked the transition from child into adult, it also carried the visual weight of sexual difference, and held too the promise of daydreams and drama. Images and identifications acquired and rehearsed in play as she was growing up were elaborated and sustained in the imagination of the young woman with every new pair of shoes or special outfit. For, paradoxically, if the changed appearance was the most immediate outward sign of the 'abrupt and final' end of childhood, then as a form of self-imagining it also signified one of the continuities between child and woman. Most little girls (and little boys) loved to dress up. Rose Gamble's description of Lu's love-affair with 'a disastrous black-and-yellow dance dress, the skirt heavily encrusted with jet beads' that she wore to school every day, for instance, recaptures the occasional bliss experienced by a child normally clothed – as so many children of the poor were – by the ingenuity of mothers and sisters putting together bits and pieces brought home from work, or gleaned from jumble sales, or charitable cast-offs.[37] Others remember the white frock worn for coveted ballet lessons, the red tapshoes, 'sexy' black silk knickers under black wool tights for gymnastics in a Holborn trade school, a flowered straw hat, white socks and embroidered frock for Sunday school in Hackney, and so on. Every such memory enclosed an imaginary identification with a graceful or beautiful self which both anticipated the woman she would like to become, and transcended the hard work and poverty around her. And when later on she squeezed into stays and embroidered white cotton knickers, or into brassières and liberty bodices under synthetic silk frocks with perhaps high heels and a piece of fur, she felt herself someone new and different.

English historians often attribute the relative affluence of the young working girl, and her new self-image, to the growth of individualism, the absorption of middle-class values, and the beginnings of the consumerism of the 1950s.[38] These are partial truths but they miss the dynamic of sexual difference. Looks figure in a woman's psyche on the whole more than in a man's. Dress both declares a woman's femininity to the outside world and is one measure of her own self-esteem. Few women neglect to describe their appearance, or forget what they were wearing at vital moments in their lives. Anyway, clothing factories producing cheap frocks and skirts in Tottenham and Edmonton, make-up, cinema, and dance halls were not part of a middle-class culture *before* they were used by working-class girls and boys. Cinema was always a cheap urban entertainment, which had to be cleaned up before the respectable or polite would attend.[39] And although individuality could be accentuated by the new pleasures – if only by lifting each person momentarily out of the uniform drabness of poverty – the process was under way long before the advent of cheap consumer goods in the 1930s.

When I first spoke to women I asked about their first job. I was interested in their work. Only later, when transcribing, did I notice the insistent presence of dress, romance, and leisure. In speech (as in life), work, love, family, and politics have trouble keeping to separate compartments of the mind. Day-dreams and reverie impose continuities across different sorts of activity as well as past and present. Day-dreams – a blend of inner imago or memory-trace with everyday life – gives fantasy its repetitive pull, and gives each of us our sense of self as surely as class position, relation of kin, ethnic identity, or religious or political affiliation. And although the joy of a new frock, the memory of violence, or separation make full sense in their particularity only in the context of an individual life history, they also can outline the contours of a shared emotional economy.[40]

Memories of authority: deprivation and separation

Clothing children and keeping the family clean were time-consuming and laborious. One woman's memory of her appearance in school commemorates for many the time and effort put into school 'outfits' by mothers and the way in which the teacher used to single her out from the other girls:[41]

> We were very well-dressed in these pieces of material that my mother used to knock up, or have over. Bits from jumble sales and that. 'Cause my mother made everything. I didn't have anything from a shop until I was 16. We were always brought up in front of the class to show how we looked, with a piece of rag machined round for a hankey, and a pin, and all that sort of thing. That was before the secondary school. But we was always that little bit – spotless clean, of course, you know, and always had the shoes for Sunday. We were never allowed to wear the shoes in the week, or the socks, or the rig-out for church, you know, it was death if you ever asked to put it on in the week, because they used to be put away for the weekend. . . . You just had them for Sunday, and let me say, it gave you a sense of values that sticks with my sister and I, for ever and a day. Not my brother, he was a spendthrift.

In May's account we glimpse something of the tempo and discipline of the domestic routine of their home in Stepney. May's mother lived with her three children, their grandfather (her father, 'whose word was law . . . everything that was said or done was referred to him. He was the head of the household'), and 'any available cousin' that her mother took into the grandfather's four-roomed house in Stepney. Her husband had been an oyster-sorter on the London docks. He died of pneumonia when May was six weeks old. May's mother worked through the nights making shirt-blouses with leg-o'mutton sleeves by machine and hand-sewing at sixpence a time; she cleaned in the early mornings and evenings and waitressed over the weekends. She dressed their grandfather (who always looked 'very smart, he drove a hearse') and her son in the same way she did her daughters, and took pride in her own appearance. She was, in May's description, 'fantastic! A handsome woman'. May's mother was not exceptional. The working week for mothers was one of ceaseless activity – its rhythm broken only by the Sunday rituals.[42]

The singling out of the respectably dressed child was not an unusual experience either. School was substantially about ordering through example, exhortation, praise, and punishment. Just as children learned by rote, and were lined up by teachers in silent single file in corridor and playground, so too they were regularly inspected for nits and ringworm, their heads shaved if either were discovered. Apart from the damage to the child's self-regard, this could bring painful ostracism from peers. Rules of health, cleanliness, and appearance were imprinted in the child's mind for another reason too. Childhood fears of abandonment and separation, of spectral figures threatening severance from loved ones, are probably universal; and in the 1920s and 1930s poverty or illness could make them real. Scarlet fever, for instance, meant having your head shaved, being removed from home and sent to isolation hospital for perhaps six weeks. For May Jones the experience was traumatic. She wore a 'sassafras' cap of carbolic soap on her shorn head, and was sent to the 'depths of Kent':[43]

> You never saw your parents or anything like that. . . . If you were unfortunate enough to have kidney trouble it was three months before you ever saw your parents. There was no question of them ever coming to see you. You're in tin huts – oh shocking . . . there used to be such terrible, terrible loneliness.

May's horror of scarlet fever fused with stories she had heard from mother, grandfather, and sister – 'family stories' – about 'Dr Barnardo's coming with the van' to take three children away after her father had died of pneumonia. Her mother had sent them packing, but no one explained to May why they had come or who had sent them.

The London poor had a long memory reaching back into the nineteenth century of arbitrary intervention into their homes and families. Family stories told of interference from city missionary or charity visitor, and these then reinforced suspicion, alienation, and powerlessness when faced with the relieving officer, teacher, or anyone well dressed and well spoken in authority. (Educated speech was as important a social distinction as occupation or income and gave content to the division between 'them' and 'us'. Rose Gamble's description of the ladies who ran the mother-and-child clinic in Chelsea where her mother worked – for instance, they 'knew exactly what they were going to say before they said it' – is as succinct a description of what class difference could *feel* like as Beatrice Webb's 'I belonged to a class of persons who habitually gave orders.')[44] But from the child's perspective, the public humiliation that the school or official from another world meted out was often less distressing emotionally than the effect of such discoveries on their mother when they returned home. The condition of her children's health, hair, and dress was one measure of a mother's self-respect and status in her neighbourhood. The child's fall from grace was a reproach to the mother's capabilities, a sign to the neighbours or street that she had been momentarily defeated in the battle against bugs, infection, and ill health, which, although the product of bad housing and lack of amenities, was a constant challenge to a mother's skills, and was understood as such by herself as well as others. 'What will your father say? . . . What will the neighbours think?' sprang to the lips of so many mothers faced with disaster.

A mother's disappointment or disapproval was often reprimand enough to keep a child in line. Most remember themselves – especially in conversation rather than written autobiography, and probably inaccurately – as obedient. Anger might provoke a smack, or clip round the head, or, in some families, a beating with brush or belt from either parent. Some children feared their fathers. Doris Bailey's father (a french polisher; they lived in Bethnal Green), though kind, generous, and good to the children when sober, became violent and terrifying after drinking:

> Many a night, my young sister and I lay in bed petrified, listening to the almighty din downstairs when someone or something had crossed his path and made him angry. Sometimes Mum came running up the stairs and came in and sat quietly crying on the end of our bed. He would come belting up after her. He would open the bedroom door and point down the stairs. 'Come down and take your medicine,' he would say in a queer and level voice, and she would go sobbing down the stairs, and the thumping began again.

Violence was not part of every child's family life, but it was present in most overcrowded neighbourhoods, as much as poverty and drink. Both were associated with men rather than women. 'Drinking and pubs went with manhood,' Doris Bailey wrote, 'and I knew no different.'[45]

For a whole generation of children raised in an atmosphere of constant anxiety about inadequate clothing – inadequate for warmth or comfort, inadequate to meet the teacher's approved standards of decency and respectability, and inadequate to ward off ridicule from one's peers – the first items of clothing bought with the wage-packet are remembered with undimmed pleasure. Mrs Murphy, a wire-winder from Woolwich, sitting in her daughter's South London council flat fifty years later, gestured with her slender ankle and foot as she recalled the penny-three-farthing pairs of stockings that she and her friends used to buy:[46]

> and, you know, buy myself a 4s 11d [25p] pair of shoes perhaps. The best shoes you could buy was only 6s 11d. Beautiful shoes we used to buy for 6s 11d. They used to be flat heeled, two-inch heels. The best ones were black patent with a lovely silver buckle.

It was as though those shoes eradicated the memory of men's boots, patched and restored, of huge slopping grown-ups' thrown-aways, or stiff heavy uncomfortable new boots that were worn through schooldays and form part of every child's memory of the 1920s and 1930s. Every reminiscence describes the misery and discomfort of leaky boots, chilblains, or shoeless feet of the very poor during their schooldays in the inter-war years. No one I spoke to ever went without shoes themselves, but all remember other children barefoot. Shoeless children, like 'nitty nora', bugs, the pawnshop, guardians, and relieving officer are part of a shared memory of poverty.

Rebellion and glamour

The new consumerism may be charted in reminiscence. Detonated by mass production, its growth was uneven and rooted in local traditions of distribution and desire. Until the late 1920s, for instance, make-up was primitive, though improvised with inspiration:[47]

> Of course, we were particularly heavily made up in those days. Make-up was, what shall I say, a tin of erasmic, twopence. No such thing as eye-black, we didn't know. We used to stick a matchstick up the chimney and ruin your eyes once and for all. Make a ring around your eyes and cut your eyebrows with a pair of scissors. There were no tweezers or anything like that.

Those who did wear make-up – still quite rare in the mid-1930s – were in the avant-garde of young womanhood. Would-be heroines have pinched their cheeks and bitten their lips to bring colour to their faces since time immemorial. But until the First World War in London, make-up was the mark of the prostitute, the fast woman. Vera Brittain, herself no amateur in the art of self-adornment, dismissed a maid in the summer of 1918 because she was 'clearly an amateur prostitute who painted her face ten years before lipstick began to acquire its present fashionable respectability'.

(She also smoked 'pungent cigarettes,' another sign of the modern young woman.)[48]

Dress or self-presentation was in this sense a symbol of defiance, a gesture of independence often combined with risqué friendships or love-affairs, each a statement of individuality, of distance from siblings and parents. 'We were living with my father as a family,' the daughter of the Pimlico engineer confided:[49]

> and we were very hard up. We both of us smoked – in defiance as far as I was concerned. I mean . . . I started to smoke when I was something of a bloomer girl, suffragette. Defiance. Had my hair cropped, and I was, you know, childishly to some extent, asserting myself.

Cropped hair and cigarettes, bloomer girl and suffragette: Jane's rebellion, we have seen, took the form of defying her father and learning a trade.

May Jones chose romance for her rebellion. She went dancing at the People's Palace in the Mile End Road with[50]

> particular girlfriends that hadn't had a disciplined upbringing. You sort of got more saucy and more cheeky in their company, you know. . . . You went and had a port at the Three Nuns – that was a regular outing, without my mother knowing. This girl and I, we used to get ourselves three penn'orth of port to get ourselves in the mood, so we'd float away in the tango and goodness knows what.

Later, May defied her carefully protective mother by marrying the manager of a public house whom she had met in secret. Theirs was a 'romantic marriage', a deliberate breaking from mother, sister, and the environs of the East End. It did not last long and brought much unhappiness, but in her mind it was associated with romance and everything that her mother's life was not.[51]

Young women growing up in streets and houses overcrowded with dirt and noise, as well as people, watched their mothers and fathers and learned what it meant to be a woman. 'I was never told to do the housework,' May Jones remarked; 'I just saw it done.' 'I want to grow up to be a man,' Rose Gamble had declared. Looking at their mothers, they saw economic hardship, hard work, and neglect from husbands who were often unemployed, who drank, or who abandoned them (a recurring image in reminiscence and autobiography is of mothers waiting for their husbands to return, or watching them leave).[52] They experienced want as girls and young women and heard their mothers talk of it. Overhearing women talking, in the streets or in their kitchens, was a vital source of knowledge. Stories were of childbirth, abortion, death, sex, and money, and listening to them was usually forbidden.

What was allowed to be heard and spoken was surrounded by as much taboo and prohibition as what was, and was not, allowed to be seen. No speaking at mealtimes, no speaking out of turn, no answering back. May Jones remembers standing in the window of their front room in Stepney and seeing a woman with a fat belly walk past. 'What's she got in her tummy?' she asked her mother, and received in reply a hit across her face. The silence surrounding sexuality, particularly female sexuality (there was no word for 'pregnant'; the term for 'menstruation' was 'the curse'; when Angela Rodway tried to describe what she knew about sexual intercourse she found she had 'no words to say what I meant'), underlined women's lack of self-esteem.[53]

Most young women expected to marry. This 'expectation', reiterated in official sources, denied them training and economic equality, and made them, it was alleged, difficult to organize, preoccupied with romance, and so on. Yet knowledge of sex, reproduction, and their own bodies was random, haphazardly learned, and often wrong. 'We learned the dirty way', was a phrase often heard; or from peers, or sisters, or 'in the playground', but seldom from mothers. Time and again I was told that women went to childbirth 'completely ignorant'.

By the end of the 1930s more and more young women were able to refuse their mothers' lives, not because they had new jobs, and cheap clothes, but because they could have fewer children. Everyone I asked said they had had fewer children deliberately. Several had been thus urged by their mothers, like Jean Moremont: 'The only thing my mum ever said to me was, "Don't have a load of kids."'[54]

This wanting to live lives different from their mothers had – if education failed them – enormous impetus from the cinema. By the mid-1930s the department store, Oxford Street, and its local equivalents had begun their reign as the Mecca of fashion for the working girl, site of her much-vaunted new affluence. Court dressmakers continued to turn out stiffened satins and brocades, and shop windows still displayed their clothes draped decorously on plaster busts. But high fashion failed to capture the imagination of the young. Mimetic images of Harlow, Garbo, and Crawford paraded the high street, as they glowed across the cinema screen. Few, in the 1930s, could afford the new clothes in the shops. Mothers, sisters, and friends hastily put together copies of their clothes with material a few pence a yard from market or cheap department stores.

'I had girlfriends who worked in dressmaking and millinery,' Celia Wilmost explained:[55]

We'd get them to make us a hat, and it was really something unusual, or they would make our dresses for us, and they could make the dresses for a mere 10 shillings [50p]. . . . Oh, I was keen on clothes, very, very keen on dresses. . . . As a young girl, basically, one considers one ought to be smart. One would buy a black suit with a check colour, and then you would get a white flat hat with a black-and-white ribbon round it, match it all up. And you'd have your white gloves and your black-and-white shoes, or your black shoes, but you would, on occasions, you would be smart. But you only wore them on Sundays to start off with . . . and you only went out shopping just before Whitsun and just before Christmas – twice a year. . . . I even changed my bag to make the colours correct.

Shopping was a ritual, a tribute to a special occasion, and one willingly saved up for. Window-shopping, on the other hand, was a more regular enjoyment, like the cinema or dancing. Helena Rubinstein claimed to have democratized glamour, but the sewing-machine, mass-produced in the early twentieth century, often inherited from mother or mother-in-law, bought on hire-purchase, played its part. In this way, via the high street or the sewing-machine, the mantle of glamour passed from the aristocrat and courtesan to the shop, office, or factory girl via the film star.

There is no doubt that the film star transformed popular identities of femininity. Not all women identified with film stars or wanted to be like them. It all depended on what sort of woman you wanted to become. Angela Rodway, for instance, who discovered ecstasy for the first time when her writing was praised at school, and who like Jean-Paul Sartre took an almost physical pleasure in words and poetic feeling, wore open-necked shirts in imitation of Shelley, and developed a limp in sympathy with Lord Byron.[56] Rose, we have seen, wanted to become a man when she grew up. Jane, though aware of the appeal of her curly hair and bright blue eyes, had her heart set on a proper trade and socialism. Only some drew a sharpened sense of self from the images on the screen and the stories they acted out (it was extraordinary the number and versions of 'rags-to-riches', and how rarely the heroines were shown anywhere near domesticity). May Jones spoke for many when she described going to the cinema once a week or more, and then 'You acted out what you saw the rest of the week.' The high heels and tilt of the hat gave the illusion for a moment of wealth, of abundance, of being like Greta Garbo or Ginger Rodgers:[57] 'You probably saw the film round two or three times for sixpence, so you got the proper gist of it . . . and you used to walk along the road imbued with it, caught up with it.' The cinema offered to millions *en masse* an alternative to their mothers, schoolteachers ('flat-chested, hair scraped off their faces, tortoiseshell glasses', was one description), and the actual upper classes. The vamps of the 1920s, Garbo, Dietrich, Carole Lombard, and Mae West, were a long way too from the familiar and colloquial sensibilities of Marie Lloyd and her contemporaries, with whom perhaps their mothers had identified.[58]

But these new images of glamour were fitted over old. 'The East End has a long tradition of glamour,' I was told by a friend, born and brought up in Stepney. Most reminiscences include someone like Celia's aunt, a cleaner all her life in Covent Garden, who 'loved it' and was[59]

> very pretty, lovely curly hair, and she dressed well. My impression of her is with a satin hat wrapped like a turban round her head with a rose underneath. That was gay, exciting. She was a very lovely woman, and very exciting in her dress.

Arthur Harding, East End villain and autobiographer extra-ordinary, dates the passion for fur coats among the women of Bethnal Green from the beginning of the First World War.[60] Allowing for masculine contempt, his explanation for the phenom-enon is probably accurate: it was a time of unexpected affluence, when the men were away, and women 'went mad on furs and pianos'. The point was that furs could be bought cheap. Pieces of fur, like everything else enjoyed by the poor, could be bought in weekly instalments. May told me:[61]

> lots of furs we used to have then. We used to buy them on the weekly . . . it was the local coalman used to sell them, you see. He used to sell shoes as well. Coal and shoes always went together, 'cause you used to pay sixpence a week for your coal, and he always used to chip in with the shoes. He was an executive, not the coalman actually who brought round the coal; and you used to pay him, and that used to be your shoe bill and your coal bill. . . . He used to bring half a dozen pairs for you to try on.

Celia recalls wearing a fur she bought at a jumble sale, cut down and altered to the latest fashion. She wore it on a demonstration against unemployment, with a hat and veil, as they shouted, 'We want bread!' By then she was earning the high wage of £4 a week, and the fur coat had cost her £5.[62] Poverty and unemployment did not preclude small luxuries; nor, in spite of Orwell's famous equation between cheap luxuries and political palliatives, did they necessarily inhibit political consciousness.[63] The unemployed in London in the 1930s did not belong to a separate culture from the young who wore the lipstick and went to the cinema.

The cheap trappings of glamour were seized on by many young women in the 1920s and 1930s, frustrated in their wish for further education, yearning to escape the domestic treadmill of their mothers' lives, haunted by the fantasy, not of the prostitute as in the nineteenth century, but of the glamorous screen heroine who paradoxically could be you, the girl next door. But if adolescence is when everything seems possible and identity is in flux, when the imagination yields to convention and restraint only with difficulty, economic conditions in the inter-war years ensured that the flamboyance and flourish of most working girls symbolized by their dress were brief. The discipline of the production line or typing pool, prefigured as they were by school, public authorities, and parents, curtailed, if it did not entirely repress, high spirits as the young entered the labour force. Speed-up and the piecework system were blamed for illness and breakdown; supervision was strict, and the hours of work long. Unemployment, of course, was the most severe disciplinarian:[64]

> All I can think of is, you could never be out of work – you could never, ever be out of work. . . . You left on a Friday to go somewhere else on the Monday . . . you dared not be out of work because there wasn't any work, you see. And now, even after all these years, even now, as you say, I've just practically left at 65, quite candidly, you never lifted your head. It's a remarkable thing, but you don't. You do everything precisely and correctly because you dared not lift your head in those days. There'd have to be a complete revolution for you to leave. You were never out of work. You went sort of from one job to another.

And later, marriage and motherhood produced different aspirations and responsibilities. The self-assertion indicated by the silk stockings or piece of fur were replaced, though not forgotten, by children's needs and the demands of husband and household. Dress for most mothers became a symbol of lack not excess. At least that's how some remember their mothers in the 1920s and 1930s. 'She had no vanities,' Rose Gamble wrote of her mother:[65]

> But now and again a pretty pattern would catch her eye, perhaps on a scrap of cloth in Dodie's bucket, or on a roll of lino

standing outside the ironmonger's. 'I'd like a frock of that,' she would say, showing just for a moment that she still had an occasional thought for herself.

Notes

Thanks to Catherine Hall and Gareth Stedman Jones.

1 J. B. Priestley, *English Journey*, 1934, p. 401; George Orwell, *The Road to Wigan Pier*, 1937, p. 76.
2 Significantly, Priestley wrote the screenplay for the 1934 Gracie Fields film, *Sing As We Go*, in which as an unemployed Lancashire millworker Gracie succeeds in reversing the fortunes of both her boss and her workmates. She sets off for Blackpool, metaphor for the bits of the new, cheap, democratic England that Priestley liked: the north, shades of music-hall and English landladies, devoted to immediate fantastic and sensual pleasures, the product of industrial democracy, not the USA.
3 Rebecca West, *Family Memories*, 1987, p. 15.
4 G. D. H. and M. I. Cole, *The Condition of Britain*, 1937, p. 25; Sidney Pollard, *The Development of the British Economy 1914–1967*, 1973 edn, ch. 5; Keith Middlemas, *Politics in Industrial Society: The Experience of the British System since 1911*, 1979, p. 17, which describes the 'middle-class growth . . . and derelict north'; John Stevenson, *Social Conditions in Britain between the Wars*, Harmondsworth, 1977, p. 39, asks which mattered more in the 1930s, one million unemployed or one million cars?
5 Mary Agnes Hamilton, 'Changes in social life', in Ray Strachey (ed.), *Our Freedom and its Results, by Five Women*, 1936, pp. 234–9. See also Winifred Holtby, *Women*, 1934, 1941 edn, introductory.
6 Ellen Wilkinson, *The Town That Was Murdered: The Life-Story of Jarrow*, 1939, pp. 262–3.
7 John Sommerfield, *MayDay*, 1936, p. 30; Max Cohen, *I Was One of the Unemployed*, 1945, p. 40.
8 Priestley's anti-feminism is relatively benign, Orwell's is more virulent. He scarcely writes of a woman except to reduce her to physical or mental caricature. Women of the middle class are especially despised in his documentary and fiction alike for being strike-breakers and materialists. See, for instance, *Keep the Aspidistra Flying*, Harmondsworth, 1936, 1963 edn, where the anti-hero Gordon argues sourly: 'it's the women who really believe in the money-code. The men obey it; they have to, but they don't believe in it. It's the women who keep it going. The women and their Putney villas and their fur coats and their babies and their aspidistras.' John Sommerfield's heroes echo these sentiments, op. cit., pp. 12, 24, 27, etc.
9 For further discussion of these themes, S. Alexander, 'Women, class and sexual difference in the 1830s and 1840s', *History Workshop Journal*, 17, spring 1984, esp. pp. 126–35.

10 H. Llewellyn Smith, *The New Survey of London Life and Labour* (*NSL* hereafter), vol. 1, 1930, ch. 1.

11 Feminists in the 1920s and 1930s campaigned for equal pay, endowment of motherhood, birth control, custody of children, education and training for women, peace, housing, and health.

12 See, for example, Mary Wollstonecraft, *A Vindication of the Rights of Women*, 1965 edn, pp. 37, 67–8. For women's addiction to romance in the 1930s, Q. D. Leavis, *Fiction and the Reading Public*, 1965, pp. 27, 54–60.

13 Doris M. Bailey, *Children of the Green*, 1981, p. 121. Only the 'really respectable' moved from Drury Lane to Becontree, according to Celia Wilmot, 2nd interview, p. 1. The Ministry of Labour memo to the Barlow Royal Commission on the Geographical Distribution of the Industrial Population, *Minutes of Evidence*, 1937–9, p. 251, confirmed that the 'better type of person' from the slum areas was rehoused in the 1930s by the LCC.

14 Census, *General Report*, 1931, p. 111. For London, *NSL*, vol. II, 1931, p. 19, and vol. 8, 1934, p. 34; Barlow, *Report*, 1939–40, IV, pp. 88–9. For the concentration of new industries in London, Barlow, *Report*, op. cit., pp. 37–40; and Board of Trade's evidence, Barlow, *Minutes of Evidence*, op. cit., BS/23/48, p. 50. See also note 16 below. The most recent study of women's work in this period is Miriam Glucksmann, 'In a class of their own', *Feminist Review*, no. 24, autumn 1986.

15 Mrs Murphy (electrical engineering), p. 9; L. Van Duren (women's clothing), 1st interview, p. 19; Miss Tugwell (office), Women's Co-operative Guild interview, p. 6; Mrs Payne (leather), 2nd interview, p. 1. In 1919 the War Cabinet Committee Report on *Women in Industry* found that women 'have habitually been paid at lower rates than men for equivalent work, on the pretence that women are a class apart, with no family obligations, smaller needs, less capacity, and a lower level of intelligence' – 1919, vol. 31, p. 254.

16 Between 1932–7 five-sixths of Great Britain's new factories were built in Greater London, and one-third of the extensions to existing ones. They were built on the outer ring of London, in the east, north-east, and west, where land, transport, and power were relatively cheap, and close to consumers and to supplies of unskilled and 'adaptable' labour, especially females and juveniles. See, for instance, Barlow, *Report*, op. cit., pp. 46, 88–9, 166–7. Employers' evidence to Barlow reiterated the search for flexible supplies of semi-skilled machine-minders and process workers, away from the organized labour of the north of England, and the preference for female and juvenile labour – Barlow, *Minutes of Evidence*, op. cit., pp. 491–504, and memo from Mr Noel Hobbs, Chairman, Slough Estates Ltd, pp. 336–49.

In 1931 approximately 1.4 million women over 14 years were occupied in industry (compared with 1.1 million in 1921) in Greater London (and 2.7 million men out of a total population of 8.2 million). These included (to nearest thousand): 20,000 in chemicals, etc.; 64,000 in metals, jewellery, etc. (45,000 in 1921); 167,000 in clothing (137,000 in 1921); 67,000 in food, drink, tobacco; 59,000 in papermaking, stationery, etc.; 36,000 in other manufacturing industries; 263,000 in commerce and finance (213,000 in 1921); 98,000 in public administration and defence; 86,000 in professions (65,000 in 1921); 21,000 in entertainment and sport; 448,000 in personal service (334,000 in 1921) – Census, *Industry Tables*, 1931, table C, p. 730.

17 I have interviewed twenty-one women, most more than once, and in five cases several times. I have drawn on interviews from other sources, oral histories, and autobiographies (of men as well as women). All my subjects except one were born in the first twenty years of this century, were brought up in London except for the domestic servants, one of whom came from South Wales, the other from the Isle of Wight), and worked through the 1920s and 1930s, having left school at 14.

18 Rose Gamble, *Chelsea Child*, 1979, p. 122; the following pages are drawn from her autobiography.

19 Mrs Payne, 1st interview, p. 1. In fact, people travelled long distances to work. Workers were bussed to new factories in the west from East London, for instance, in the 1930s – Barlow, *Minutes of Evidence*, op. cit., p. 174.

20 Lily Van Duren, 1st interview, p. 3. Almost everyone I interviewed mentioned the reluctance of London girls to become domestic servants. They came from Wales, Scotland, the rural districts, and unemployed towns, I was told, and the girls were very homesick. 'I did my share of crying,' said Miss Sutton, WCG, p. 1. Homesickness becomes 'hysteria', said Ellen Wilkinson, op. cit., p. 268. Munitions had led the exodus of girls in London away from service.

21 Jane Smith, 2nd interview, p. 2.

22 Celia Wilmot, 1st interview, p. 11.

23 Formal apprenticeships for girls were non-existent. Dressmaking, millinery, tailoring, embroidery, and some large shops offered to pay girls a low wage while they 'learned' the trade – Ray Strachey, *Careers and Openings for Women*, 1935, pp. 98–9. She lists 150 technical schools for girls provided by the LCC, pp. 99–100. Dressmaking, for example, put girls through a four-year 'learnership' in factory or workshop – *NSL*, vol. 11, p. 13. *NSL*, vol. 5, p. 15, adds bookbinding to list above.

24 Lily Van Duren, 1st interview, pp. 2, 3, 7. In 1926 the factory inspectors found that most women learned their skill by watching – *Annual Report of the Chief Inspector of Factories and Workshops*, 1927, vol. 9, p. 63.

25 Jane Smith, 1st interview, pp. 9–15.

26 Jane Smith, 1st interview, p. 15.

27 Jane Smith, 1st interview, p. 15. (The Tailors and Garment Workers' Union absorbed the handicrafts union, the Tailors and Tailoresses, in 1932.)

28 Jane Smith, 1st interview, pp. 16, 19.

29 C. Wilmot, 1st interview, p. 23.

30 Mrs Payne; Mrs Murphy. Employers wanted their workers young; they were easier to train – S. R. Dennison, *The Location of Industry and the Depressed Areas*, 1939, p. 78.

31 May Jones, 1st interview, p. 3.

32 Jerry White argued in a recent seminar (June 1988) that women were the 'vectors of change' in London in the inter-war years; and see his *Campbell Bunk, the Worst Street in North London*, History Workshop Series, autumn 1979.

33 Mary Welch, leather worker, *Working Lives*, vol. 1, 1905–45, *A People's Autobiography of Hackney*, n.d., p. 52; May Jones, 1st interview, p. 3.

34 See note 11 above.

35 Barlow, *Minutes of Evidence*, Ministry of Labour memo, p. 322, stated that in central London employment exchanges (City, Gt Marlborough Street, and Westminster) there were 9.5 vacancies for each boy, and 33.3 for each girl.

36 Rose Gamble, op. cit., pp. 186, 122.

37 ibid., p. 61.

38 Jeffrey Richards, *The Age of the Dream Palace*, 1984, pp. 208–10, 224, 323–4, where he argues that English films of the 1930s perpetuate ruling-class hegemony and the political consensus and conservatism of that decade. Cynthia L. White, *Women's Magazines, 1693–1968*, 1970, ch. 8, traces the uneven relationship between class identities and aspirations, new affluence, and domestic consumerism.

39 Robert Murphy, 'Fantasy worlds: British cinema between the wars', *Screen*, vol. 26, no. 1, January–February, 1985, pp. 10–20, points out that cinema needed its mass appeal to rake in the profits, so it combined with the plebeian entertainments of showmanship and variety in the 1930s to secure them. Interestingly, Elizabeth Bowen, in *The Death of the Heart*, 1938, has her elegant, upper-middle-class hero and heroines transform into 'workers' when they visit the cinema in London in the 1930s, Harmondsworth, 1984 edn, p. 43.

40 For my understanding of fantasy, I draw on J. Laplanche and J. B. Pontalis, 'Fantasy and the origins of sexuality', *International Journal of Psycho-Analysis*, vol. 49, 1968, pt 1. See also Elizabeth Cowie, 'Fantasia', *m/f*, no. 9, 1984, pp. 71–104, for a reading of some of the connections between femininity, fantasy, and film.

41 May Jones, 1st interview, pp. 8, 13.

42 Margery Spring Rice, *Working Class Wives*, 1939, 2nd edn 1981, ch. 5.

43 May Jones, 1st interview, p. 10.

44 Gamble, op. cit., p. 48; Beatrice Webb, *My Apprenticeship*, 1926, p. 43.

45 Bailey, op. cit., p. 18. See also Ellen Ross, ' "Fierce questions and taunts" ', this volume, for violence within marriage in late-nineteenth-century London.

46 Mrs Murphy, 1st interview, p. 4. Frances Partridge, the daughter of an architect, discovered that one pair of shoes cost her 45s (£2.25) in 1918) – *Memories*, 1981, p. 58.

47 May Jones, 1st interview, p. 61; *Women's Magazines*, op. cit., p. 114: only 20 per cent of women wore lipstick in 1930.
48 Vera Brittain, *Testament of Youth*, 1948 edn, p. 304.
49 Jane Smith, 1st interview, p. 19.
50 May Jones, 2nd interview, p. 7; 3rd interview, p. 5.
51 May Jones, 2nd and 3rd interviews, *passim*.
52 May Jones, 1st interview, p. 16; Gamble, op. cit., p. 11. For a woman waiting, see, for example, Doris Knight, *Millfield Memories*, 1976, p. 8.
53 May Jones, 3rd interview, p. 3; Angela Rodway, *A London Childhood*, 1960, 1985 edn, p. 52; Marie Stopes, *Married Love*, 1918, broke the silence according to herself, and this is confirmed by Robert Roberts, *The Classic Slum: Salford Life in the First Quarter of the Century*, Harmondsworth, 1973, pp. 231–2.
54 Jean Moremont, ed. Jean McCrindle and Sheila Rowbotham, *Dutiful Daughters*, 1977, p. 149. Diana Gittins, *Fair Sex, Family Size and Structure, 1900–39*, 1982, argues that women altered family size according to changing socio-economic circumstances, in particular their work outside the home and their degree of knowledge concerning sexuality and birth control; see esp. pp. 19, 25, chs 5, 6. Eva M. Hubback, *The Population of Britain*, Harmondsworth, 1947, ch. 4, argues that higher standard of living and aspiration reduced the birth rate.
55 Celia Wilmot, 1st interview, p. 22.
56 Rodway, op. cit., p. 82; Margaret Cole, *Growing Up in a Revolution*, London, 1949, p. 22, one of the many who wanted to be a boy.
57 May Jones, 2nd interview, p. 15. For women's cinema attendance, *NSL*, vol. 9, p. 40. Memoirs reveal that men too dressed up, but drink, gambling, boxing, and the possibility of sex with a woman rather than romance were their (sometimes transgressive) pleasures.
58 Violet Boulton, 2nd interview, p. 10. For the impact of music-hall on a preceding generation, see G. S. Jones's essay in this volume. Marie Lloyd sang about London, love, drink, and husbands and wives; she was like her audiences; for a description of her, M. Storm Jameson, *No Time Like the Present*, 1933, pp. 73–4. Jessie Matthews, the second most popular English music-hall star in the 1930s (Gracie Fields was the first) was also closer to London than Hollywood.
59 Ann Mitchell, in conversation; Celia Wilmot, 4th interview, p. 2.
60 Raphael Samuel (ed.), *East End Underworld: Chapters in the Life of Arthur Harding*, History Workshop Series, 1981, p. 237.
61 May Jones, 1st interview, p. 8.
62 Celia Wilmot, 1st interview, p. 22.
63 George Orwell, *Road to Wigan Pier*, 1937, p. 90.
64 May Jones, 1st interview, p. 4; 2nd interview, p. 15.
65 Gamble, op. cit., p. 33.

11

The 'cockney' and the nation, 1780–1988

Gareth Stedman Jones

Introduction: the death of the 'cockney'?

Of all the symbols which conjure up London, none is more obvious and yet more elusive than that of the 'cockney'. 'Cockney' may refer to the true Londoner born within the sound of Bow Bells, to a metropolitan pattern of speech, to a species of humour and repartee associated with street markets or East End pubs, or, more grandly, to a whole attitude to life thought to be implicit in the speech and behaviour of ordinary Londoners. Everyone has some notion of the 'cockney', but few have pondered its significance, and no one has made a serious attempt to decode it. The subject seems too trivial to merit sustained attention and certainly not worth the effort of sorting through acres of archival litter to discover meaningful clues. Writing about the 'cockney' has therefore been confined to amateur enthusiasts and connoisseurs of London life.

But 'cockney' is more important than it might at first seem. Once decoded, it opens up important questions, both historical and political: questions which are of particular relevance now. In the 1980s the 'cockney' is both archaic, yet furtively actual, a presence, yet a presence which can no longer be named.

As a word, 'cockney' is certainly not current in a way in which it was thirty or forty years ago. The 'cockney' is now a somewhat ghostly figure, usually summoned up in nostalgic or sentimental memories of a London past. An evocation of the 'cockney' is likely to bring to mind odd snatches of forgotten music-hall songs, recollections of the Blitz, minor characters in Ealing comedies, whelks, old-fashioned bank holidays on Hampstead Heath, Eliza Doolittle in *My Fair Lady*, the laughing pearlies in *Mary Poppins*. It suggests a past world in which the pleasures and pastimes of the common people were quite distinct from those of their rulers, and also one in which the common people were white and predominantly

Anglo-Saxon.[1] Maybe this is why the word cannot now be employed without embarrassment or anxiety. The 'cockney' has no legitimate place in the declassed and multiracial society that post-imperial Britain has officially become. The epoch of the 'cockney' is over.

But if 'cockneys' can no longer be named and pointed to, the contemporary potency of 'cockney' as an unnamed presence can scarcely be denied. Whether it is Derek Jameson, *EastEnders*, the insignia of the skinhead, or the slogans of the Millwall football crowd, traces of the 'cockney' abound. No doubt many different meanings can be attached to this phenomenon. It may even be that a new 'cockney' stereotype is about to crystallize, concocted out of the brave new world of bucket-shops and City upstarts – Jameson's breezy populism points in this direction. But it seems more likely that its predominant appeal is to a form of atavism, whether sentimental or rancorous, and that at its core lies a powerful yearning for the lost verities of family, neighbourhood, class, and national community of a not quite admissible kind.

Particularly indicative of this current desire to sweeten the present with an unacknowledged recourse to the past is the phenomenal success of *EastEnders*, a television soap opera often celebrated for its 'realism'. *EastEnders* depicts the 'cockney' street market and pub community at precisely the moment when City expansion, 'yuppy' invasion, the disappearance of the docks, and racist hostilities have turned its location into a historical make-believe. In itself, this may not be extraordinary. In the 1950s *Coronation Street* was also invented just when the Manchester street life it portrayed was being bulldozed into rubble. But the anachronism of *EastEnders* runs deeper than this. For Albert Square seems even to predate the masses of tower blocks and council estates which spread across the East End in the 1960s and 1970s. For all its determined topicality, the physical setting and some of the central families in this drama hark back to a mythical time in the 1950s just before the traditional 'cockney' neighbourhood supposedly slid into terminal decline.

If the significance of the 'cockney' is to be understood, it has to be placed in a far larger historical perspective. But, as the example of *EastEnders* suggests, 'cockney' cannot be understood as a straightforward expression of London life, nor could a history of the 'cockney' be written in these terms. The real and the imaginary are, and always have been, closely intertwined in the depiction of the 'cockney'. Both have been subject to historical change and both relate to the history of London, if in quite different ways.

It is simplest to begin with the more realistic components of the 'cockney's' make-up. For beneath the layers of imaginative construction, it is possible to detect a number of elementary and unremarked features which have identified the 'cockney' as a product of London.

First, as an emblem of London life, the 'cockney' has highlighted what has been considered to distinguish London from other regions of the country, both rural and industrial. The 'cockney' has connoted that difference in one form or another since the beginning of the seventeenth century. Thus the historian is offered changing representations of London's peculiarity over an exceptionally long time span. Recent work in economic history underlines the value of this record. For it has emphasized, not only the distinctiveness of London as a political and economic region, but also the basic continuities in its form of development from the seventeenth to twentieth centuries.[2] What these continuities indicate is that London has always been first and foremost a commercial city, both in fact and in imagination. Of course, London had its industrial workers and employers – by the end of the nineteenth century, probably enough to fill a large town. But their presence was inconspicuous in a city far more renowned for its armies of office workers, cleaners, domestic servants, *rentiers*, public employees, sellers of professional services, porters, day-labourers, and traders at every level from Petticoat Lane to Threadneedle Street. It is noteworthy, as this essay will suggest, that the 'cockney' has been represented in a succession of different occupational guises, but rarely if ever as a maker or producer of things.

Second, London and its environs seem always to have remained the most powerful and most prosperous region of the country. This relative opulence was not confined to its millionaires or even to its disproportionately large numbers of middle-class inhabitants. It also extended down to legions of clerks, artisans, and minor functionaries. For those whose skill, knowledge, or special qualities were in demand, metropolitan wage rates were higher and opportunities for employment wider than elsewhere. Of course, London also possessed the largest concentration of the casual poor. But if revelations of the scale of London's underside periodically provoked tremors of anxiety, that was in part because they clashed so radically with the dominant myth. In common parlance, London's streets were 'paved with gold'. This had been a commonplace ever since the legend of Dick Whittington had first become part of London folklore in the early seventeenth century and it helps to illuminate one persistent theme in successive representations of the 'cockney': the emphasis on consumption and display.[3] The 'cockney' could be presented as heroic, but more usually belonged to a comedy of manners – characteristically complacent, parvenu, and intent upon cutting a dash, or young, rakish, swell, and full of pretension. Even in its humblest manifestations, 'cockney' went together with holidays, windfalls, courtship, and 'having a good time'. This could be seen as a joke or regarded as a threat. But whatever the attitude, 'cockney' in this sense again pointed to something specific about London: not only to the buoyancy and variety of demand for the labour of young persons of both sexes, but also to the proximity to high fashion and conspicuous consumption, imitated and disseminated all the way downwards through London's innumerable places of pleasure and entertainment.

So far the argument has stuck to the familiar territory of the social and economic historian. A particular type of economy produces a particular type of culture; the one refers back to the other and vice versa. At a certain level of generality, these affinities, correspondences, expressions, or reflections – however we choose to characterize them – are undeniable. But they do not begin to explain the historical shifts in the meaning of the 'cockney': what changed and how, and for what reason, why the 'cockney' assumed great importance in some periods, little or none in others, or why the 'cockney' should be regarded with nostalgia now.

Any attempt to answer these questions will require a different approach. Since the 'cockney' was an emblem of London life, it is self-evident that London should have provided the raw materials from which the 'cockney' was shaped. But the turning-points in the story of the 'cockney' are to be found in the shaping process itself rather than in the history of what was shaped. For this reason, the subject-matter of this essay is a sequence of representations rather than a history of what was purportedly represented. Its assumption is that the 'cockney' is a figure successively constructed and reconstructed by different types of discourse. It is only under this assumption that the changing historical meaning of the 'cockney' makes any sense.

The reasons for adopting this approach will become clearer once the familiar twentieth-century depiction of the 'cockney' is examined in a little more detail. First, here are some sample pictures.

In a guidebook to London in 1903, Mrs E. T. Cook attributed to the London poor 'a certain rude, Dickensian, good nature' reminiscent of 'that incorrigible Cockney, Sam Weller'. The 'raciest cockney' she went on, was spoken by factory girls, flower girls, and costermongers.[4] An inter-war description filled out this picture. According to H. J. Massingham, Surveying the *London Scene* in 1933:

> In Farringdon Road, you will run across the more traditional Cockney, whose astuteness, nonchalance, easy indifferent fellowship, tolerance, casual endurance, grumbling gusto, shallowness, unconcern for anything but the passing moment, jackdaw love of glitter, picaresque adaptability and jesting spirit make up a unique individual.[5]

By this time, the 'cockney' seems to have been primarily associated with street markets. The author of *London's Eight Millions*, writing in 1937, agreed that the markets were 'the strongholds of the cockney', adding that 'In them you will always find the bubbling humour and cynical wisdom which are the undying London . . . the cockney is the same yesterday, today and for ever.'[6] But along with other authors writing at the time, he also described 'the cockney charwoman'. In an account of the early-morning 'charwomen's express' taking office cleaners from Camberwell to the City, he stated: 'The women were irrepressibly Cockney. Their voices were as shrill as schoolgirls' and their humour as boisterous as George Robey's.'[7]

After the Second World War, the topography of the 'cockney' shifted. Pre-war 'cockneys' were mainly to be encountered in street markets, city offices, the surviving music-halls, dancing on Hampstead Heath, or 'doing the Lambeth Walk'. Now 'cockneys' were firmly located in the dockland areas and the East End; their culture and humour best savoured in pubs or boxing gyms or in television sit-coms like *Till Death Do Us Part*. It was in reference to the East End that Robert Clayton could still write as late as 1980: 'the caricature cockney of today is a tough, resilient and "knees-up Mother Brown" exuberant'.[8]

What emerges from these accounts is that while the salient characteristics of the 'cockney' have not changed much since the beginning of the century, 'cockneys' themselves have become increasingly elusive. This has indeed been a consistent feature of the literature. The 'cockney' always belongs to yesterday. Since the end of the First World War, the 'cockney' has been part of a vanishing species, an intermittently renewed metaphor for the corrosive character of modernity. 'Alas, for the colour and character of modern life,' wrote Arthur Roberts in 1927:

> Even the pearlies and the ostrich feathers have gone now. The donah and the duchess share the same tastes in fox-trots, in

clothes and cinemas. As for 'Arry, when he is not on duty, he will pass muster as a city clerk any time. He has not a pearlie on him.[9]

In 1933 'the vivid quality of London's humour' was already 'degenerating' due to 'the dulling forces continually at work on the public mentality', 'the more than daily press, the talkies, the gramophone and the radio'.[10] In 1951 the decline was as inexorable as ever: 'cockney's decay has robbed the common tongue of vitality. American slang with all its vigour, has a juke-box rattle compared with the earthy freshness of the catchwords of the street boy of old.'[11] By the 1970s it was television, tower blocks, and cars which were pitted against the 'cockney'.[12] By that time, but for the interlude of the Second World War, the 'cockney' had been hovering on the threshold of extinction for over fifty years.

'Cockneys', as this literature makes clear, have been at best ill at ease in the present, and doomed in the future. Conversely, their past has become rich and concrete. Already deemed 'traditional' by the 1930s, by the 1950s the 'cockney' had become heir to a long and continuous history. In the two most ambitious attempts to depict that history, that of Julian Franklyn in 1953 begins in the twelfth century with Fitzstephen's *Descriptio Nobilissimae Civitatis Londoniae*,[13] while that of William Matthews in 1938 starts more modestly with Beaumont and Fletcher's *Knight of the Burning Pestle* and Shakespeare's Mistress Quickly – 'a supreme portrayal of a character which has since become one of the puppets in the dramatist's cupboard, the cockney charwoman'.[14] The pearly, the most dramatic visual embodiment of the twentieth-century 'cockney', has been given an equally ancient lineage. The unmysterious purpose for which pearlies assume their extraordinary costume is the collection of charity, and their history does not go back beyond the 1880s. The 'original pearly king', Henry Croft, was born in 1862 and was a St Pancras road-sweeper, not a costermonger. But in popular histories of the pearlies, not only was the costume the remnant of a once-widespread cockney fashion, but pearly kings themselves were heirs to a medieval tradition of 'cockney-coster royalty'. This tradition, according to political taste, had been either transformed or betrayed. In the radical version of the story, medieval pearly kings had been 'lords of misrule' and had been closely associated with the costers who had been 'a thorn in the side of authority since the end of the 12th century'.[15] But they had fallen victim to the interference of Lord Shaftesbury and Victorian philanthropy:

hangers-on at the Coster's Mission were encouraged to steal the

thunder of the pearly kings by wearing suits of pearls themselves
and collecting money, not for the greater glory of the Lords of
Misrule, but for the benefit of the City Hospitals.[16]

In the conservative version of the story, on the other hand, the
pearly king descended from the 'tough, but natural leaders in an
earlier London when market squabbles were a daily scene. Such
costers were in effect the uncrowned Kings of their respective
communities, when Croft recruited them for his novel fund-raising
scheme.'[17]

This brief survey of the descriptive literature on the modern
'cockney' could be treated as the raw material of a social history.
But that would be to miss the main point. The recurrent theme of
this writing is decline. But *what* is it that has declined? It is true
that part of the social and cultural milieu of the 'cockney' has
disappeared. The music-hall has vanished, and the old slums have
been cleared away. But ordinary Londoners still have a distinctive
pattern of speech, they still sing in pubs and dance halls, and there
are still children's games, street markets, and office cleaners. What
has declined or disappeared is something else, a particular form
into which these elements were combined and shaped, a particular
representation of an archetypal 'cockney', whose distinguishing
features recur from one evocation to the next. These features
include a picturesque cheerfulness and wit embedded in characteristic turns of phrase, a mildly irreverent attitude to law and
authority, a comic particularism, a stubborn and often illogical
ethical code, combined with a good-hearted patriotism. To invoke
this 'cockney' is also to invoke a particular notion of an urban
community: a community of the poor, but of a distinctly
conservative and indigenous kind. There is no place in a 'cockney'
typology for the spiv, the teddy boy, the punk, or any of the other
more provocative or disruptive manifestations of London street
life in the last fifty years. Nor is it easy to imagine a place within
this community for the West Indian, the Bangladeshi, or the
Cypriot.[18] The 'cockney' is 'traditional' and 'English', and the
community is of a *Fings Ain't What They Used to Be* world, of the
singsong and the knees-up, of an old-fashioned Saturday night, or
of the atmosphere conjured up in faded photographs of street
parties festooned with Union Jacks.

But as this essay will argue, this age-old 'traditional' 'cockney'
community dates back scarcely beyond the turn of the century.
The 'cockney' whom the twentieth century invokes was an
invention of the 1890s.[19] Most of the history which has been
constructed around this 'cockney' is fictive, and in the case of the

pearlies, blatantly so. Indeed, far from being the heir to an ancient lineage, the 'traditional cockney' was the successor to a number of other eighteenth- and nineteenth-century cockney stereotypes, whose features were quite different. By charting these previous incarnations of the 'cockney', it will be possible not only to suggest why the twentieth-century 'cockney' arose when it did, but also what links these successive incarnations, and, finally, why it is that the 'cockney' now possesses only a posthumous existence.

The history of 'the cockney' denotes something specific about the political and cultural complexion of London. But for much of the modern period, it has also stood for something more universal and in this sense suggests how representations emanating from London might have coloured representations of the nation as a whole. The identity of the 'cockney' shifted considerably in the last two hundred years, as we shall see. But what the 'cockney' signified shifted much less. Throughout all its successive personifications, 'cockney' never shook itself free from its association with the low, the ridiculous, or the grotesque. Such an association could be summoned up simply by means of a magnification of the peculiarities of cockney speech. In the modern period, the 'cockney' was one who could not wield political authority, above all because he or she could not *speak* with authority. He or she was thus always *other*, whether this *other* was to be repulsed and excluded, taught and improved, or celebrated, encompassed, and led. Because peculiarity of speech was the badge of the 'cockney', and yet at the same time the most immediate and universal code by which differences of power and status were registered in English society between the early nineteenth century and the 1960s, an investigation of the 'cockney' is more important than it might at first appear. In the nineteenth and twentieth centuries, this essay will suggest, the 'cockney' was in turn a signifier of the disputed boundaries of the political nation, a clue to the riddle of the marriage between democracy and inequality, a portent of the destiny of empire, an emblem of Englishness in the face of twentieth-century American culture, and finally, in the Second World War, the unlikely embodiment of the spirit of national defence. The 'cockney' marked the difference between the rulers and the ruled in a way which has now ceased to be culturally recognizable in its original sense. Hence the penumbra of nostalgia which surrounds the term. To trace the story of the 'cockney' is an unfamiliar way of illuminating wider cultural and aesthetic notions of inclusion and exclusion which underpinned the discussion of citizenship in the age of reform and of patriotism in the age of empire.

'A native of London, by way of contempt'

Two assumptions seem to underlie twentieth-century evocations of the 'cockney'. The first is that 'cockney' is a pattern of speech characteristic of ordinary, lower- or working-class Londoners, and the second is that an equation can be made between this pattern of speech and a putative cluster of attitudes, both private and public, towards life in general. So the first point worth establishing is that the identification of 'cockney' with a pattern of speech is comparatively recent. There was no reference to 'cockney' as a form of speech in the early editions of Johnson's *Dictionary*, and it was not until the late eighteenth century that any systematic attention was paid to the characteristics of 'cockney' diction. Moreover, the terms in which it was classified were geographical rather than social. 'Cockney' referred to the speech habits of Londoners. According to John Walker in his *Critical Pronouncing Dictionary* of 1791, in some introductory remarks addressed to his 'countrymen the cockneys', they were

> with all their faults . . . still upon the whole the best pronouncers of the English language. For though the pronunciation of London is certainly erroneous in many words, yet upon being compared with that of any other place, it is undoubtedly the best.[20]

Among the errors he mentioned were the famous switching of the 'v' for the 'w' and the dropping of the 'h'. But it is interesting that, of the four main mistakes which Walker considered to characterize London speech, only one he particularly associated with 'the lower orders'. The main problem, as Walker saw it, was this:

> The grand difference between the metropolis and the provinces is that people of education in London are free from all the vices of the vulgar; but the best educated people in the provinces, if constantly resident there, are sure to be strongly tinctured with the dialect of the country in which they live. Hence it is, that the vulgar pronunciation of London though not half so erroneous as that of Scotland, Ireland or any of the provinces, is, to a person of correct taste, a thousand times more offensive and disgusting.[21]

This points to what perhaps was the major difference between late-eighteenth-century and late-nineteenth-century connotations of the word 'cockney'. The distinction between 'vulgar' and 'educated' referred, to a difference not between middle and lower, let alone working, class, but between the citizen and the courtier, the plebeian and the patrician, the vulgar and the genteel. It is in this way that the definitions in Dr Johnson's *Dictionary* should be understood.

Johnson defined 'cockney', first, as 'a native of London, by way of contempt' and, second, as 'any effeminate, ignorant, low, mean, despicable citizen'.[22] Interestingly, while not wholly committing himself Johnson also suggests that the etymology of the word 'cockney' was connected with the notion of cockagne, 'a country of dainties', and goes on to cite 'an old Normano-Saxon poem': 'Far in see by west Spayng,/ is a lond yhoze cocayng.' There seems to be no basis for this association. Modern scholarship argues that the land referred to in the poem is Ireland, not England, and the setting of the poem is a monastery, not a town.[23] What is interesting is what it tells us about country and genteel attitudes towards towns in the seventeenth and eighteenth centuries. Cockneys had been identified with the Elizabethan word 'cocker'. Thus a 'cockered child' was a 'child tenderly brought up, a dearling'. If this explained the notion of effeminacy, it also suggested a further connotation of consumption without production. The 1819 edition of the *Dictionary* added a citation from Hobbes, 'the land of Cockany, where fowls ready roasted cry, come and eat me', and speculated further on its possible connection with the barbarous Neapolitan practice of Cocagna.[24]

Such a set of associations could easily connect with various stories about the townsman's profound ignorance of the country-side, including the first citation connecting the 'cockney' with Bow Bells, that of Minsheu in 1617. Minsheu had also provided a story of the origins of the cockney, to be repeated again and again in eighteenth- and nineteenth-century accounts:

> That a cittizen's sonne riding with his father . . . into the country . . . asked, when he heard a horse neigh, what the horse did, his father answered, the horse doth neigh; riding farther he heard a cock crow and said, doth the cock neigh too?[25]

This sense of the cockney's complete ignorance of anything beyond his immediate surroundings – a clear sign of vulgarity in eighteenth-century theories of language, like those of Harris, Monboddo, or Johnson himself – is also suggested by the inclusion in some dictionaries of a citation from Whitlocke's *Zootomania* of 1654: 'that Synod's Geography was as ridiculous as a Cockney's (to whom all is Barbary beyond Brainford and Christendome endethe at Greenwitch)'.[26]

The political significance of what was at stake in these definitions becomes clearer in a book written in defence of London linguistic usages against Dr Johnson's strictures on cant: Samuel Pegge's *Anecdotes of the English Language – chiefly regarding the local dialect of London and its Environs – whence it will appear that the Natives of the Metropolis have not corrupted the Language of their Ancestors*. Pegge objected that

> Dr Johnson was scarcely at all aware of the authenticity of antient dialectical words, and therefore seldom gives them any place in his *Dictionary*. He seems not to consider them as *freeborn* or even as denizens; but rather treats them as outlaws, who have lost the protection of the Commonwealth.[27]

As a reviewer in the *Monthly Review* noted in 1805: 'The sneering *Courtier* is reminded that the dialect in use among the citizens within the sound of Bow-Bells is that of Antiquity.'[28] Pegge attacked the genteel derivation of English words from Greek; and in his hands the defence of cockney became analogous to a Norman-yoke theory of language. For while conceding that in London 'every language will be found incorporated', that 'of the true Cockney is for the most part, composed of Saxonisms'.[29]

But perhaps the sharpest sense of what might have been at issue in the antagonism between cockney and genteel appeared from the conservative side. The reactionary *Blackwood's Magazine* opened a vitriolic attack upon Leigh Hunt and his collaborators in the *Examiner* in 1817 under the title 'The cockney school of poetry'. No doubt, Hunt's fundamental faults were 'a want of respect for the Christian religion . . . a contempt for Kingly power and an indecent mode of attacking the government'.[30] But the form that the attack took was to accentuate to the maximum the distinction inscribed in eighteenth-century aesthetics between the vulgar and the genteel. Hunt was accused of being 'a man of little education. He knows absolutely nothing of Greek, almost nothing of Latin.' And, the *Magazine* went on:

> Everything is pretence, affectation, finery and gaudiness. The beaux are attorney's apprentices, with chapeaux bras and Limerick gloves – fiddlers, harp teachers and clerks of genius: the belles are faded fan-twinkling spinsters, prurient vulgar misses from school and enormous citizen's wives. The company are entertained with luke warm negus and the sounds of a paltry pianoforte.

'All the great poets of our country', *Blackwood's* alleged, 'have been men of some rank in society and there is no vulgarity in any of their writings.' But, it continued:

Mr Hunt cannot alter a dedication or even a note without betraying the shibboleth of low birth and low habits. He is the ideal of a cockney poet. He raves perpetually about 'green fields', 'jaunty streams' and 'o'er-arching leafiness' exactly as a Cheapside shop-keeper does about the beauties of his box on the Camberwell Road. . . . He has never seen a mountain higher than Highgate Hill, nor reclined by any stream more pastoral than the Serpentine river. . . . His books are indeed not known in the Country; his fame as a poet (and I might say, as a politician too) is entirely confined to the young attorneys and embryo barristers about town. In the opinion of these competent judges, London is the world and Hunt is Homer.[31]

As this passage suggests, the lowness of the cockney in this period was not restricted to 'the lower orders'. Embryo barristers hardly fit that description. It encompassed all those without landed connection, including the 'vulgar' apothecary, Keats. Nine years later, *Blackwood's* remained unrepentant. Keats 'was a cockney and the cockneys claimed him for their own'.[32] As for Leigh Hunt, he argued in his *Autobiography* that 'the jests about Londoners and Cockneys did not affect me in the least, as far as my faith was concerned' and that 'the cockney school of poetry was the most illustrious in England', including as it might Pope, Gray, Milton, Chaucer, and Spenser. Nevertheless, he admitted that 'the charge of cockneyism frightened the booksellers' and that his career as a writer was in effect blighted for the following twenty years.[33]

Certainly the idea of an antinomy between cockneyism and literature remained more potent than Hunt cared to avow. Thirty years later, in Charles Kingsley's novel, *Alton Locke, Tailor and Poet*, it was not the incongruity between tailor and poet which established the pathos of its first chapter, but that between poet and cockney. The book begins:

I am a Cockney born among Cockneys. Italy and the Tropics, the Highlands and Devonshire, I know only in dreams. Even the Surrey Hills, of whose loveliness I have heard so much, are to me a distant fairy-land, whose gleaming ridges I am worthy only to behold from afar.[34]

Even thirty years after *Alton Locke* this form of juxtaposition had not wholly disappeared. At the beginning of the 1880s a late continuation of the *Blackwood's* theme was to be found in John Ruskin's 'Fiction fair and foul'. In this text, an argument for the nobility of Scott's novels was established by counterposing them to the 'ordinariness' of 'essentially Cockney literature – developed only in the London suburbs, and feeding the demands of the rows of similar brick houses, which branch in devouring cancer round every manufacturing town'. In the 'English Cockney School', 'the personages are picked up from behind the counter and out of the gutter; and the landscape, by excursion train to Gravesend, with return ticket for the City-Road'.[35] The consummation of this 'cockney school' was, for Ruskin, George Eliot's *Mill on the Floss*!

'Cockney' in this predominantly Tory tradition was a term mediating between the aesthetic and the political. The vulgar spoke 'cant' because they thought 'cant' and they thought 'cant', not least because they possessed no yardstick of comparison. They were hence incapable of art and not fit members of the political nation. True art like political judgement meant the ability to abstract from particulars. Vulgar language, according to Monboddo, was 'degraded and debased by its necessary connection with flesh and blood'.[36] It was unable to transcend the present, the particular, the material, the emotional. A refined language was a language of reason and abstraction created by philosophers to express perfect ideas and divested of time and place. It is therefore not difficult to see how the recurrent emphasis upon the spatial limitations of the cockneys' world was an excluding device designed to place them beyond the pale. It is partly as a response to this equation between smallness of horizons and smallness of judgement that the 'cockney' genre of novels in the early-Victorian period can be understood.

'The Cockney Quixote' – the London burgher as comic hero

One of the confusing legacies of the twentieth-century invented tradition of the 'cockney' is the assumption that 'cockney' was always identified with low-life slang or cant. Thus, William Matthews claims that the literary depiction of 'cockney' began in 1821 with Pierce Egan's *Life in London*, even though, according to the 1819 edition of Johnson's *Dictionary*, the term was 'now falling into little use'.[37] Egan was certainly interested in dramatizing low-life and underworld cant and slang, much of which he derived from Francis Grose's *Classical Dictionary of the Vulgar Tongue* of 1785.[38] Indeed, Egan conceived the city primarily as a collection of different forms of cant:

> A kind of *cant* phraseology is current from one end of the metropolis to the other. Indeed, even in the time of Lord Chesterfield, he complained of it. In some females of the highest rank it is as strongly marked as in dingy draggled-tail Sall, who is compelled to dispose of a few sprats to turn an honest penny.[39]

But Egan does not identify this low-life cant with the 'cockney'. The twentieth-century view is a retrospective projection. Egan's actual picture of the 'cockney' is to be found in his novel, *Pilgrims of the Thames*, published in 1839.

The hero of this novel, Peter Makemoney,

> was a thorough cockney, to the utmost extent of the phrase – except knocking about the vs and ws. The sound of Bow Bells, to his ears, was delightful music and the sight of 'Old Best' (as he termed St Paul's) the delight of his eyes; in fact, he had seen nothing else but *London* and he thought there was no place like London; and excepting Highgate and Hampstead (the cockney's round), the Metropolis was the only place he called his home.

Makemoney had risen to become not only a City alderman, but Lord Mayor of London. Nevertheless, his tastes remained simple and unpretentious:

> He despised anything like ostentation; and self-importance he was equally disgusted with; but his home and fireside were great objects to his mind: he was also fond of a game of whist or cribbage. . . . He was an excellent companion – a social fellow – and he had no objection to a pipe and a glass in their proper place and was particularly fond of a good song . . . the Italian Opera House might be fine as to music, but the best of them, said he, 'were a hundred miles behind our English ballad singer'.[40]

The humour of *Pilgrims of the Thames* suggests a strong discontinuity between the early and late nineteenth-century stereotypes and emphasizes the longevity of the eighteenth-century picture of the cockney. *The town as the world* is exemplified by the anxieties of the cockneys at the prospect of the great river voyage to Gravesend and the perilous whipping up of a storm in the 'Cocknies' Sea': Chelsea Reach. The antagonism between vulgar and genteel is mildly evoked in a rowing-boat excursion at Windsor, in which Makemoney is spotted as a tradesman by some Etonians and turned out into the water. Makemoney recognizably shares some of the same cockney features so harshly attacked by *Blackwood's*. But he is not a ridiculous figure. Rather, he is the representative of plain London burgher virtues: a disdain for finery and show, honesty in his transactions, respect for civic customs, and an unashamed London pride.

A not dissimilar portrayal is to be found around the same time in Surtees's *Jorrocks* novels. Mr Jorrocks, the son of a washerwoman and 'a great city grocer of the old school',[41] was, if anything, more emphatically 'cockney' than Makemoney, and his tradesman's care with money is similarly stressed. Surtees exploits to the full the comic incongruity of a cockney master of fox-hounds and the later cockney squire of Hillingdon Hall. This incongruity was both political and aesthetic. In contrast to the genteel idea of beauty, for example, Surtees's cockneys were always too thin or too fat. Mrs Jorrocks had once 'been reckoned a beauty in Tooting'.[42] But now she, like her husband and most older cockneys in the literature of the period, was unashamedly corpulent: 'We've got here at last, and precious glad I was on it', observes Mr Jorrocks, 'two fat women and one's fat self.'[43] On the other hand, Jorrocks's manservant, Binjimin, prefigured the 'little, puny, pale faced' cockney stereotype of the early twentieth century.[44]

But, like Makemoney, Jorrocks is not simply a figure of fun. Ultimately, it is he rather than county society who embodies true nobility. Jorrocks stands for the uprightness and shrewdness of plain virtues in the face of wily and effeminate genteel snares. Throughout the novels, there are echoes of latent burgher–patrician antagonism, reminiscent of the epoch of Wilkes in the 1760s. As Jorrocks tells a servant of the greedy aristocrat, Sir Archey Depecarde of Pluckwell:

> But arter all's said and done there are but two sorts o' folks i' the world, Peerage folks, and Post Hoffice Directory folks, Peerage folks, wot think it's right and proper to do their tailors, and Post Hoffice Directory folks wot think it's the greatest sin under the sun not to pay twenty shillings i' the pund.[45]

In *Hillington Hall*, a comedy of political reversal, it is precisely because of these old-fashioned civic virtues that the 'whig', Jorrocks, finds himself standing for the farmers against the Anti-Corn Law League, while the effete aristocrat comes to represent the cause of total repeal. For, as Jorrocks observes to an old London friend, 'a swell of slender means' now turned Anti-Corn Law League Lecturer:

> It arn't a bad dodge, but I don't think it will do. There is no elbow room for the imagination, and the purposes o' the promoters is too apparent on the face of it. . . . If I was to adwise the workin' classes, I'd say, 'don't you sign no petition for nothin' o' the sort, unless your masters will hire you for siv'n years sartin at present wages'.[46]

Surtees's and Egan's characters found no place in the late-Victorian representation of the cockney. The idea of a cockney Lord Mayor or of there being real tensions between city and county society would by that time have been unthinkable. By contrast, Dickens's *Pickwick Papers* lent itself easily to such an incorporation. The link, however, was not through Pickwick but Weller, and by the end of the century, Weller was being presented as the ur-type of cockney legend, endlessly depicted in prints and ornamental plates hung on pub walls or celebrated in comic recitals and theatrical sketches.

The original intention behind *Pickwick*, evident both in the artist's frontispiece and in the publisher's agreement, was to exploit the genre of cockney sportsman, so successfully pioneered by Surtees.[47] But Dickens deviated from this model from the beginning, not only by downplaying the sporting theme, but more crucially by not associating the Pickwick Club with cockney speech. By identifying this diction unilaterally with Weller, he left the way open to later equations between cockneyism and specifically lower-class patterns of speech and wit. Whatever the reasons for this innovation, a concern for sociological exactitude was clearly not uppermost. According to B. H. Smart in his 1846 updated edition of Walker's *Pronouncing Dictionary*:

> The diffusion of literature among even the lowest classes of the metropolis, renders it almost unnecessary to speak now of such extreme vulgarisms as the substitution of v for w, or w for v. Few persons under forty years of age with such a predilection for literary nicety as will lead them to these pages can be in much danger of saying that they like 'weal and winegar wery well' or that they are going to 'Vest Vickham in a po shay', and with regard to men who, in spite of their intelligence and information, retain the habits of a more distant generation of cocknies, it is doubtful whether at their age, a reformation could be promised without an expense of time and labour they would be unwilling to bestow.[48]

It is clear that Dickens did change the literary convention in a way that accentuated social distinctions. For on age grounds, if Smart was right, it should have been Pickwick reversing his *v*s and *w*s rather than Weller. Nevertheless if Dickens was incorporated into the later cockney myth, he did not himself create it. Dickens never described Weller as a cockney; he was presented instead as 'the specimen of London life'.[49] For the readers of the 1830s, it was Pickwick who represented the embodiment of cockney virtues. As the *Metropolitan* put it in 1837:

> Sam Weller improves upon acquaintance. The world never saw drollery and wit offered to them before in a form so singular.

The renowned Mr Pickwick is himself the legitimate successor to Don Quixote; indeed, he is the cockney Quixote of the 19th century, and instead of an armour of iron, he is encased in a good coating of aldermanic fur.[50]

From 'London pride' to 'sham gentility'

Undoubtedly, from this period on, the 'cockney' seems to have begun his or her social descent; but not at this stage to the level evoked by the later cockney tradition. Twentieth-century guides take as axiomatic, for instance, the association between cockney and costermonger and therefore devote much time to a résumé of Mayhew's depiction of the costers.[51] But Mayhew made no such association. Costers in *London Labour and the London Poor* belong to a quite different taxonomy, that between 'settled' and 'wandering tribes'.[52] They are treated by him, largely if not exclusively, as members of the 'dangerous classes' with no more than a predatory respect for property, unsentimental relations with their animals, and a sturdy hostility to Christianity and marriage.

Like Dickens, Mayhew also tended to avoid using the term 'cockney', but so far as he implied the idea, it was precisely in the same sense as Egan and Surtees. 'The characteristic dialect of Bow-Bells has almost become obsolete; and aldermen now-a-days, rarely transpose the vs and ws.' But, he went on, though this form had passed away, 'there are many other modes of speech still peculiar to Metropolitan people', and he proceeded to list 'the London exquisite', 'the affected Metropolitan miss', 'the fast young gentleman', 'the cadger's (beggar's) cant', 'the coster slang (backslang)', and lastly 'the veritable slang, or English argot', the secret language of London thieves.[53] Clearly, the equation between cockney and coster or broader patterns of lower-class metropolitan speech had not yet been made.

If there was an attempt to create a stereotype cockney in the middle decades of the century, it was focused, not upon the low life of the streets, but upon the plebeian smartness of the young journeyman, shop assistant, or lawyer's clerk. It is to be found, for instance, in Renton Nicholson's *Cockney Adventures and Tales of London Life* of 1838. While these stories played up the comic possibilities of the 'coarse manners and broad humour of the London mechanic',[54] they also played upon the conventions of melodrama, mixing burlesque with the assertion of plebeian heroism. In one story, Jem Piper, the lawyer's clerk, asserts himself over the 'swell squire' only to find that the lady was not worth the contest: 'her mother vos er hard vorkin voman and used to cry cat's meat about Shoreditch . . . but Bet was always a thief and fond ov the men'.[55] Similarly, Ned Sharkey, 'yclept butcher and likewise one of the most slap up of his craft', with 'top boots, white corderoy smalls, a white hat turned up with green, red neckerchief, green coat, and likewise the owner of a fast-trotter',[56] finds a rival in his affection for Miss Jemima Fubsby, daughter of a retired butcher of West Ham. He is the sham gentleman soldier, Captain Fitzwaddle. Sharkey eventually challenges the captain to a duel and, since only one sword is available, offers to make do with Mr Fubsby's 'bull-hanker'. Fitzwaddle duly goes into 'a funk' and is revealed as 'a linen-draper's shopman' – 'a counter-jumper'. The recurrence of the theme of 'cockney hero versus wicked or sham-genteel' suggests that these stories still belong to the older cockney genre. But other elements in the narratives and descriptions look forward to what was to become predominant in cockney representation from the 1860s to the 1880s – the lower-class 'swell':

> Ben Plank was a young gentleman of surprising neatness of appearance. He was that description of young fellow often denominated by invidious and vulgar critics as a Sunday swell. He paid very great attention to the arrangement of his hair. . . . On the sabbath-day, Ben invariably adonised his person to an alarming degree. . . . As we profess to be true and honest in our narrative, we feel bound to inform our readers of the humble station in society of the subject of it. Mr Benjamin Plank was skilled in the mysterious ramifications of the trade or business of a carpenter; he was an assistant artisan – in common parlance, a journeyman.[57]

Between the 1840s and the late 1860s the representation of the 'cockney' underwent a major change from solid London burgher to sham-genteel swell. The swell himself had been around for a long time as a minor character of London life, but it was the events of the 1860s which turned him into the new epitome of the 'cockney':[58] two events in particular – first, the extension of the franchise in 1867 and, second, the emergence of new patterns of mass consumption and popular entertainment among the better-paid youth of London's working population. In the eyes of pessimistic contemporaries, these two developments were of a piece. For if 1867 represented the first instalment of the triumph of democracy and equality over culture and refinement, that fear seemed confirmed by the adoption of new styles of dress and behaviour by the metropolitan masses. The newly established

music-halls not only provided congenial rendezvous for London's
burgeoning population of socially indeterminate single young men
– 'linen drapers' assistants', 'counter-jumpers', 'city clerks', or
'penniless swells'. They also actively celebrated the 'sham-genteel'
pattern of conspicuous consumption with which they had become
associated. Leading performers, like Alfred Vance ('The Great
Vance'), not only extolled the 'swell' clothing in which they
performed, but even incorporated into their songs advertisements
for tailors from whom cheap-cut fashionable imitations could be
purchased.[59] 'We do not hesitate', wrote one outraged observer in
1869,

> to lay upon the music-halls the parentage of that sham-gentility
> which has become so abnormally prominent among the striplings
> of the uneducated classes during the past few years. Nowadays,
> your attorney's clerk – apparently struck by some 'levelling up'
> theory of democracy – is dissatisfied unless he can dress as well
> as the son of a duke.[60]

Equally offensive, whether to the church, the theatre, the
educated, or the serious, was the fake equality encouraged by the
new palaces of consumption. Vance had addressed his audience as
'jolly dogs', and twenty years later instant familiarity was still the
dominant note:

> At the music-hall, everything is tinselled over; and we find a
> kind of racy gin-born affection to be the mode; everyone being a
> 'dear boy' or a 'pal'. There is a frank, cordial bearing, a
> familiarity which stands for candour and open-heartedness.[61]

The 'new 'Arry-stockracy'

It was out of this mixture of derision, apprehension, and mistrust
that a new cockney archetype was created – *'Arry*, the invention of
E. J. Milliken in a series of *Punch* sketches which ran from 1877 to
the 1890s. 'Arry, according to his creator, was 'a cockney cad',
'loud, slangy and vulgar', with a taste for 'smart patter and snide
phrases'.[62] He was 'a city product' – 'wot the crokerdile is to the
Nile, 'Arry is to the Thames' – and was no more at home in the
country than his cockney predecessors.[63] But not because he was
plebeian, rather because he was a 'vulgarian': 'no lamps arter
dark, no gay shops. No whelk stalls to light up the corners, no
paper boys, cabbies or cops . . . green fields with nothink to
slorter, no pubs, no theaytres, no gas.'[64] On such excursions he
blew his post-horn in a shay, had loud singsongs in third-class
railway carriages, or carved his initials on Stonehenge.

'Arry was a commercial clerk earning around £2 a week and could expect a fortnight's annual holiday together with whatever windfalls came his way from the turf:

> Last year I done Jersey, old pal, and I 'ardly know where to go next. I should very much like to try Monte Carlo, and 'ave a fair flutter for once. But I fear it won't run to it, pardner; my boss is the dashdest old dunce. Won't rise me to three quid a week, the old skinflint.[65]

Sartorially, he was a 'swell' or in more hostile accounts 'a feeble copy of the swell who is otherwise familiar to Londoners as the irrepressible 'Arry'.[66] He was able to spend £2 10s on his check suit 'in yaller and green' and, though he could not 'run to the Gaiety stalls',[67] he could drink bitter, smoke 2d cigars, and have the run of 'the 'Alls'.

Politically, the joint product of the music-halls and the 1867 Reform Act, 'Arry was flattered to think that 'politics isn't no longer a species of upper class sport' and that 'a toff *is* a man and a brother; it's merely a matter of dress'.[68] United with those above him in the belief that 'the petticoats want keepin' down, like niggers and radicals',[69] 'Arry sensed 'a drorin' the clarses together'. His proudest hour came in the war fever of 1878, the founding moment of 'jingoism':

> I say we're the new 'Arry-stockracy! Not arf a dusty one, hay?
> We're quite 'and-in-glove with the nobs on the leadin' ideas of the day;
> Our manners they take for their model, our argyments too, they support,
> And our misic-'all patriot war-song is patternized even at court![70]

Wallowing in the new-found patronage of Tory democracy, in 1883 he was even to be found at a Royal Evening Fête: 'ten bob and snap togs took me in, and I chummed with the very eleet'.[71] In the following years, he developed strong views on the Irish, joined the Primrose League, and canvassed the 'working man's vote' – though he was also to be found at disorders in Trafalgar Square in 1887: 'wen a spree's on, 'Arry's there'.[72] But at the same time, growing competition in white-collar employment emphasized his marginality. Already in 1879 he had been snubbed by a girl because 'I was not educated enough, but too much of the loud cockney cad.'[73] In 1886 he got the sack 'all along of a dashed German sossidge'. 'The sossidge as collared my crib . . . reads

Shakespeare instead of the Pink 'un.'[74] Embittered by the thought
that 'the furriner's mucking our market and histing us out of our
stools', it was not surprising that 'Arry should become even more
xenophobic and turn to 'fair trade'.

'Arry's fame spread far beyond the pages of *Punch*. His
plausibility as cockney stereotype was not challenged. In 1881
music-hall directly replied to Milliken with one of the best-
remembered hit songs of the period, ''Arry', composed by E. V.
Page and sung by its greatest female star of the 1870s and 1880s,
Jenny Hill. The song did not attempt to deny *Punch*'s portrait, but
treated 'Arry's faults with no more than an affectionate tut-tut:

> 'Arry smokes a twopenny smoke,
> Oh! poor 'Arry.
> 'Arry's pipe's enough to choke,
> Bad boy,'Arry.
> 'Arry thinks it jolly good form,
> To puff his cheap cigar,
> Into the faces of everyone
> While doing the la-di-da.

And it ended by defending his behaviour as a hard-earned right to
do as he pleased:

> 'Arry likes a jolly good joke
> Quite right, 'Arry.
> 'Arry won't mind the fun that I spoke,
> What say, 'Arry?
> The 'Upper ten' may jeer and say
> What 'cads' the 'Arries are,
> But the 'Arries *work*, and *pay their way*
> While doing the la-di-da.[75]

For more than a decade, 'Arry remained the symbolic point of
tension between civilization and the masses. When in 1886 Gissing
published his disenchanted novel, *Demos: A Story of English
Socialism*, it was 'Arry once again who was chosen to represent the
unacceptable face of the people. In *Demos*, the dismal reality
behind socialism and the unfitness of 'the uncultured classes' to
rule was unfolded through the story of a Hoxton working-class
family, the Mutimers, in particular of the two brothers, Richard
and 'Arry: the one, a humourless socialist autodidact artisan, 'a
mechanical engineer'; the other, a shiftless clerk in a drainpipe
factory, a denizen of the pub and the music-hall, an 'aristocrat of
rowdyism' and eventually a petty thief:

His attire was such as the cheap tailors turn out in imitation of extreme fashions: trousers closely moulded upon the leg, a buff waistcoat, a short coat with pockets everywhere. A very high collar kept his head up against his will; his necktie was crimson, and passed through a brass ring; he wore a silver watch-chain, or what seemed to be such. One hand was gloved, and a cane lay across his knees. His attitude was one of relaxed muscles, his legs very far apart, his body not quite straight.[76]

If Richard represented 'Demos grasping the sceptre',[77] 'Arry represented the Mr Hyde-like *alter ego*, who would share in that triumph:

the shape of his head, which was covered with hair of the lightest hue, did not encourage hope of mental or moral qualities. It was not quite fair to judge his face as seen at present; the vacant grin of half timid, half insolent, resentment made him considerably more simian of visage than was the case under ordinary circumstances. But the features were unpleasant to look upon; it was Richard's face, distorted and enfeebled with the impress of sensual instincts.[78]

As Gissing saw the problem:

'Arry represented a very large section of Demos, alike in his natural characteristics and in the circumstances of his position. 'Arry, being 'Arry, was on the threshold of emancipation, and without the smallest likelihood that the event would change his nature.[79]

Barely acceptable, an affront as much to the principles of hierarchy as to the ideal of self-improvement or the dignity of labour, alternatively flattered and kicked by those above him, a dubious and embarrassing asset to Conservatives, half grotesque, half sinister, in the eyes of Liberals, 'Arry was the clownish Frankenstein unleashed by Disraeli's 'leap in the dark' – a rogue signifier uncoupled from the rhetorical chain, an untidy smudge on the political and cultural map. An invention of anti-Tory malice, he was hardly what Lord Salisbury had in mind when he pointed to the potentialities of 'villa Toryism', or even – though here there is the shadow of a doubt – what Lord Randolph Churchill envisaged, when he conjured up 'Tory democracy'. The salience of 'Arry as stage Londoner could be taken as a sign that conservatism had still to come to terms with the masses of the capital city.

Yet only ten years after *Demos*, the 'cockney cad' had disappeared. 'Arry was still there, but in name only: he had undergone an extraordinary transformation. He was now a reformed character, a reassuring rather than disturbing figure, occupying a humble yet colourful place in the metropolitan galaxy. He had also changed his occupation. He had lost his position as a clerk to the gently spoken 'Mr Pooter'. He himself had become a costermonger and was fast on his way to becoming the new, yet timelessly old, embodiment of cockneydom. This involved a number of shifts and displacements. For, before the late-Victorian cockney archetype could begin to take shape, not only did 'Arry have to be transformed into a coster, but the coster himself had to be refashioned in a manner scarcely less radical than 'Arry himself.

The advent of the twentieth-century cockney: the transformation of the coster

We have already argued that the twentieth-century equation between the cockney and Mayhew's costers is a retrospective projection. In the mid-nineteenth century, coster connoted a particular type of 'cant' and a liminal form of London 'low life' in which roughness shaded into criminality. According to *A Dictionary of Modern Slang, Cant and Vulgar Words*, compiled a few years after Mayhew:

> Costermongers form a distinct class occupying whole neighbourhoods, and are cut off from the rest of metropolitan society by their low habits, general improvidence, pugnacity, love of gambling, total want of education, disregard for lawful marriage ceremonies, *and their use of a cant* (or so-called *back-slang*) *language.*[80]

This was the image of the coster taken up by the music-hall in the 1860s. The first star to make the coster song a stock part of the music-hall repertoire was 'The Great Vance'. In two of these songs, for which Vance was famous, 'The chickaleary cove' and 'Costermonger Joe', the criminal connotations were undisguised. According to the reminiscences of another performer, the 'chickaleary cove' was the eldest son of Bill Sikes. He dressed very like Sikes, wore a beaver hat, a belcher handkerchief, and very often corderoy shorts';[81] he also used backslang and reversed his *v*s and *w*s in Sam Weller Fashion. As for 'Costermonger Joe', according to one report at the time:

> on the night we were present, he was recalled in a tumult of applause and requested by some bold individual to give us 'Costermonger Joe'. Mr Vance told his 'old pal', who had just

spoken, that the respected Joseph had retired to the penitentiary for a time, but was ultimately prevailed upon to sing the song desired.[82]

The flashiness of Vance's coster was not that of the 'swell', real or sham, but that of 'the dandy crook dressed up fit to kill and certainly to paralyse his donah'.[83] Indeed, it was the contrast between the coster and the swell that formed the mainstay of Vance's act. According to Arthur Roberts: 'It was wonderful to see him change rapidly from the brutal denizen of Whitechapel to the immaculate "swell" – a type of character in which he was second only in success to that of George Leybourne.'[84]

Vance's success paved the way for a series of specialist 'coster carollers' in the 1870s and 1880s – J. W. Rowley, 'Teddy' Mosedale, Hyram Travers, Walter Laburnum, and others. They were, according to Chance Newton, 'comics of the rorty or slangster type'.[85] The most salient features of such acts seem either to have been the use of backslang and 'patter', or dance and physical dexterity. Mosedale was a 'slang-singer' and 'step-dancer', Travers, 'the limit in coster, hawker and crook slang'. Rowley was known as 'Over' Rowley because of 'his wonderful somersault dance'; he was also renowned for his 'physical force rendering' of Vance's coster song, 'Going to the Derby'. The emphasis on crime seems to have receded, but the association of costers with drink, violence, horseplay, and comic coarseness remained. Charles Coburn remarked of his first successful coster song, 'the typsy impersonation was almost a triumphant success',[86] while the only reference made to a coster in Andrew Tuer's pioneering transcription of modern cockney speech was to a 'kaukneigh costermonger' who 'sowld 'is wife for eyeteen pence en' a pot uv beer'.[87] Certainly there were no signs of hesitation or ambivalence in polite society's depiction of the coster. In 1888 Frederick Anstey included in his *Burglar Bill and Other Pieces for the Use of the Young Reciter* a sketch entitled 'A coster's conversion: style, low-life realistic'. In his instructions to the performer, he remarked: 'The compiler is not greatly troubled by the fear that its diction and sentiments will be condemned on the grounds of coarseness. Coarse they undoubtedly are – but then the nature of the subject renders that inevitable.'[88] The theme of the sketch is sufficiently indicated by the following lines:

> I'm a rough kind o' cove, but it's bin my pride as I've led a regular life.
> Bein' niver too tight of a Saturday night but what I kin wallop the wife.

> In liquor I'm allus light'arted, and fling things about pretty
> free;
> For a 'ardworkin man at the end o' the week – well, he must
> 'ave a bit of a spree.[89]

We are now in a better position to appreciate the novelty and apparent suddenness of the emergence of a new cockney archetype in the early 1890s. The shift was complex, but it was crystallized by one particular event to which contemporaries attached a quite extraordinary importance. This was the appearance in the halls of the stage actor Albert Chevalier, who first sang and acted his coster songs publicly at the London Pavillion on 5 February 1891. Some impression of Chevalier's impact was given by the *Star*:

> All of a sudden the house wakes up with a start. The buzz is hushed, there is a rustle of expectant attention, and a cry of sit down in front. Number thirteen has gone up at the wings – the number, says the programme, of Mr Albert Chevalier, comedian. A queer little figure bounces on the stage, and is received with a storm of hand-clapping. It is not a figure of ideal beauty. Phidias would hardly have chosen it for a model. A puny, crouching, angular figure – a sort of human ferret. A peaked cap over a close-cropped poll; a rag of coloured cloth where the rest of us wear a collar; a check-patterned jacket on the meagre body turned up with velveteen; trousers trumpet-shaped, like those of a Mexican vaquero. 'Et puis, des boutons, des boutons, des boutons', as the husband in 'Frou-Frou' says about the costume of the débardeur. It is all very ugly, very quaint – and very interesting. For you, at once feel yourself in the presence of one of Mr Zola's 'human documents'. It is a genuine type: the East-End Costermonger in his habits as he lives. After the fantastic idealism of the earlier part of the performance, boneless gentleman simulating serpent, and ladies in crimson Mephistophelian doublet and hose – this figure of uncompromising realism is a welcome relief.[90]

Chevalier's programme included a number of his most famous songs, including 'Knocked 'em in the Old Kent Road', 'The future Mrs 'Awkins', and 'My old Dutch'. But the song which seems to have made the most immediate impression on contemporaries was his opening number, 'The coster's serenade':

> You ain't forgotten yet that night in May,
> Dahn at the Welsh 'Arp, which is 'Endon way?
> You fancied winkles and a pot of tea,
> 'Four'alf', I murmured, ''s good enough for me.'

'Give me a word of 'ope that I may win' –
You prods me gently with the winkle pin.
We was as 'appy as could be that day
Dahn at the Welsh 'Arp, which is 'Endon way.

Oh, 'Arriet, I'm waiting, waiting for you, my dear,
Oh, 'Arriet, I'm waiting alone out here.
When that moon shall cease to shine,
False will be this 'eart of mine;
I'm bound to go on lovin' yer, my dear; d'ye 'ear?

You ain't forgotten how we drove that day
Dahn to the Welsh 'Arp, in my donkey shay;
Folks with a 'chy-ike' shouted, 'Ain't they smart?'
You looked like a queen, me every inch a Bart.
Seemed that the moke was saying, 'Do me proud;
Mine is the nobbiest turn-out in the crowd.'
Me in my 'pearlies' felt a toff that day,
Dahn at the Welsh 'Arp, which is 'Endon way.

Oh, 'Arriet, etc.[91]

'That memorable night at the London Pavilion', wrote Arthur Symmons, 'was at once the statement and the achievement of a new art.' Chevalier was hailed as the 'Werther of the donkey cart', 'the coster laureate', 'the coster Burns'. 'Mr Chevalier', wrote the *Morning Leader*, 'is the Kipling of the music-hall, for he takes the common clay of Whitechapel, and fashions it into real works of art. He is an epoch-maker entitled to a lasting memory as a latter day Monteverdi or Wagner.'[92] Not only were his songs taken up in the plebeian halls, they were also extolled in high society. 'Last night I saw more grave legislators than one, hereditary and elected, listening to them enraptured.' Offers for private engagements poured in 'from Princess Louise, Dowager Lady Vernon, Lady Jeune, Lady Osborne Morgan, Mrs Asquith, Mrs Labouchere, the Duke of Westminster. . . . Every club and coulisse knew in Albert Chevalier the man of the moment.'[93] Even that formidable censor of the music-hall Mrs Ormiston Chant was alleged to have been impressed.[94]

No doubt some of this could be put down to the sort of hyperbole which attends unusual dramatic successes. But its historical significance should not be underestimated. However momentarily, Chevalier was the first London artist since Dickens to straddle the chasm between high and popular culture, to capture the enthusiasm both of the drawing-rooms and of the streets. To what can his success be attributed?

The claim of 'uncompromising realism' will not bear much scrutiny. 'What of the coster's love story?' wrote one informed observer a few years later. 'It is a very brief and unromantic one. The coster does all his courting in the gutter with one eye on his "filly" and the other on his stall.'[95] The same writer also noted that 'not one coster in a hundred' possessed a donkey. Where these animals were used, it was on the basis of weekly hire. If 'Arry and 'Arriet had driven to the Welsh Harp in a shay, it is more likely they would have gone there to sell winkles rather than to eat them.

The distinctiveness of Chevalier's performance derived from art, not life, and the art was that of the traditional actor, not the music-hall artiste. As Harold Scott later observed: 'Chevalier's habit of mind was that of an actor; all his songs became in his hands elaborately built up impersonations; the style was broad, but on it was superimposed a minute attention to detailed effect.'[96] Chevalier had not originally written his songs for the halls; he had performed them among friends in clubs like the Savage and the Green Room, had sold some to other artists, and had included them in recital tours he had made in the provinces.[97] It was the financial failure of these ventures together with a theatrical flop which drove him to the halls. This crossing of the social divide between theatre and music-hall was itself part of the novelty and drama of Chevalier's appearance at the Pavillion. It would be 'social suicide', the dramatist Pinero had assured him. Friends in clubland, wrote Chevalier, 'imagined that I was going to challenge the lions comiques – to adopt their methods'.[98]

This, however, was to mistake the entrepreneurial calculation which lay behind Chevalier's engagement. It was Newsom Smith who encouraged Chevalier into the Pavillion and it was he who assiduously promoted Chevalier's stardom at the newly built Tivoli. While the early music-hall had largely been run by publicans, Newsom Smith was a new-style theatrical manager who in the early 1890s set up the first West End music-hall 'syndicate'.[99] The intention was to place less emphasis upon the sale of drink and more upon the drawing power of the performer. By a policy of exclusive contracts and high salaries, the new cartel monopolized the services of a small number of star performers, widening the gulf between them and the rest of the profession. The aim was also to attract a socially and generationally more varied audience, to minister, as Chevalier boasted, 'to the healthy amusement of both sexes'.[100] In this sense, Chevalier's début formed part of a larger turning-point in the history of the music-hall.

It was ironic that an actor as prickly about his professional reputation as Chevalier should finally have attained 'legendary' success and access to the drawing-rooms of the great through the music-hall and an impersonation of the low-born coster. But in many ways, his perception of the coster mirrored that of his new audience. His was a coster seen and heard from afar. This emerges clearly enough in his answer to an interviewer who enquired how 'he came to think of presenting the coster in the sentimental mood':

> I can remember quite distinctly . . . it was one summer evening at Hammersmith when I was walking on the towpath . . . some distance in front of me, were the coster and his girl. His arm was around her shoulder and hers around his waist, and they kissed one another now and again. Presently they became playful and he made a grab at her hat, dragged it off and ran with it. . . . Well – I thought – these people will marry some day; and they must make love somehow or other. I wonder what they do say. And this wonder it was which first gave me the idea for my 'coster songs'.[101]

'What they do say' was the product of Chevalier's introspection, and the sources of that introspection were literary and theatrical – the melodrama, the burlesque, the Dickensian set-piece: an enactment of his aesthetic credo, 'always keep to that little bit of human nature in your work. Aim at depicting true comedy, in which there is not only laughter but tears.'[102] Thus, if there was a sense in which the post-1890 cockney archetype appeared new, but also timelessly old, or in some sense a Sam Weller redivivus, here was one of its sources.

But it was not simply what they said. How they said it was equally important. Chevalier was saluted by Shaw as one of the first to recognize 'the obsolescence of the Dickens dialect' and to capture the cadences of modern cockney.[103] Yet here again Chevalier's success was established not through proximity but through distance. Before Chevalier, the stage coster did not speak a generalized cockney. He spoke the particular backslang or rhyming slang which had been associated with him since the time of Mayhew. It was this type of speech that was employed by 'coster carollers' like Travers and Mosedale. Chevalier, on the other hand, made no effort to capture the particular speech pattern of the costers. As he told his interviewer: 'It's a great mistake to suppose there is any one cockney dialect. There are half a dozen. The "coster song", as people will call the things I sing, is a kind of embodiment of several; and it isn't necessarily coster at all.'[104] No doubt, part of the reason why Chevalier did not employ coster patter was that, had he done so, his club and West End audiences would not have understood him. But whatever the reasons, its effect was to enhance the new association between the coster and the universal cockney.

The 'cockney' as part of the 'English nation'

If Chevalier's depiction of the coster was formative, it was in large part because it was enacted at the point at which polite, bohemian, and popular culture now intersected – in the music-hall. Part of the reason why the new representations of the cockney were to become so powerful and alluring was that they were both taken up in literary culture and the arts, and, in some sense, acted out in the streets. The visible manifestation of the cockney at the street level, the pearly, will be discussed presently. But first it is necessary to mention the spectrum of representations of the cockney in literature and the arts.

It was to be found in painting, cartoon, music, fiction, travelogue, and drama ranging from Sickert's portrayal of music-hall audiences to Shaw's *Pygmalion*, from Kipling's *Barrack Room Ballads* to Clarence Rook's *Hooligan Nights*, from Elgar's chirpy cockney theme in his *Cockaigne* Ouverture to Phil May's celebration of cockney wit in *Punch* – 'the great cockney joke of being alive', as James Douglas termed it.[105] The effort was imaginative rather than investigative, and the ambition was to create a gallery of cockney character, a typology rather than a sociology of London life. What was aimed at was not an extension of the statistical enquiries such as those of Booth, but a counterpoint to them. 'Yes, the existence of the "unemployed" may be "due to economic causes",' wrote the reverend James Adderly in 1897, 'but there are human hearts beating beneath their seedy waistcoats.'[106] The point of departure was not the cockneys' economic condition, but their speech patterns, their physiognomy, their dress, their gestures, their milieu, and the mysterious codes which governed their attitudes towards each other and towards the world. 'The speech of the folk stimulates observations,' wrote Pett Ridge; 'it provides a clue that would otherwise be absent; it furnishes a welcome riot of individuality. Kept within reasonable bounds, the cockney accent is a signal that the owner belongs to a great and good humoured town.'[107]

As will already be evident, the prevailing tone of this new depiction and exploration of the cockney was conservative rather than reformist, and populist and celebratory rather than elitist and moralistic. Cockneys were not shams, usurpers, or outcasts, they were part of the nation. As Edwin Pugh wrote in 1912:

The cockney, you see, in his bright moods as well as in his dark, is the supreme type of Englishman: in his sturdy optimism, in his unwavering determination not only to make the best of things as they are, but to make them seem actually better than they are by adapting his mood to the exigencies of the occasion, and in his supreme disdain of all outside influences.[108]

In place of the anonymous metropolitan masses represented by the brazen *lion comique*, the sinister socialist demagogue, and the vulgar and presumptuous 'Arry of the 1870s and 1880s, music-hall had created a variety of strongly delineated and highly individualized types. The unknown back-street city dwellers were given faces and names. At last there was a city, with whose masses a new kind of conservatism could feel at home; and in embryo at least there could come into a being a kind of conservative language of class, not hierarchical in the traditional sense, but domesticating and enshrining social difference within a larger framework of national and imperial unity; a novel celebration and valuing of the popular *in its place*; or, as T. S. Eliot put it in his salute to the popularity of the music-hall artiste Marie Lloyd: 'It is evidence of the extent to which she represented and expressed that part of the English nation which has perhaps the greatest vitality and interest.'[109]

The recurrent point of interrogation within this novel exploration of the 'cockney' was a question about identity and difference. In what sense were cockneys of 'our own flesh and blood'? In what sense were their language and behaviour those of a quite different 'breed'? In what sense could diversity exist within unity? The answer might lie, as it did in Chevalier, in emphasizing the unity which underlay difference, in focusing on the universal and incarnating it in the hopes and fears of the humble coster. As one of his admirers wrote in 1909: 'We are what he sings and what he says, and as we are transfigured into the common life of common humanity, we find ourselves melting into a passionate sympathy of human smiles and human tears.'[110] But the answer might lie in the opposite direction, as it did in Kipling. Difference was not to be dissolved into an underlying unity. On the contrary, unity was constructed out of complementarity and the mutual acceptance of irreducible and unavoidable difference. The codes which governed the behaviour of the common soldier or the slumland street were not the same as those of the officer or the missionary. They were not even comprehensible to them. But they had to be respected, rather than ignored or trampled upon, because they possessed their own inner logic and – however opaque that might be to the outer world – made their own contribution to a larger whole.

Kipling's position was important, not only because of its impact upon the subsequent depiction of the slumland cockney, but also because it forged out of the cockney the indispensable plebeian component in Britain's imperial mission. The empire's reliance upon Tommy Atkins, the cockney common soldier, was established with shattering effect in *Barrack Room Ballads* in 1892,[111] but it was followed up with an analogous parable about the London slums in his innovative short story 'The record of Badalia Herodsfoot' in 1893. Badalia, 'the costermonger's girl', lived in Gunniston Street, and 'the customs of Gunniston Street . . . do not differ from those of the Barralong'.[112] The story which followed was one of unrelieved brutality on the part of the man, 'following the law of his kind', verbal abuse mixed with an incomprehensible submissiveness on the part of the woman, petty calculation on the part of the other slum dwellers, and an uncomprehending and unworldly well-meaningness on the part of the missionaries serving the street. As P. J. Keating has pointed out, Kipling's story established an association between violence and the slum, which left a trail through the London literature of the 1890s and reached extremes in some of the stories of Arthur Morrison and Somerset Maugham.[113]

But the real innovation of the story was not its detailing of male violence towards women – this had in some sense been familiar ever since Bill Sikes. What was really new was to locate heroism, not in the missions, but in the unchristian slums. The heroine was Badalia herself; and, just as Tommy was no 'plaster saint',[114] so Badalia remained a denizen of the slum and a partaker in its customs. After her husband's desertion and the loss of her child, she became the mediator between the unreality of the missions and the real needs of the slum's inhabitants. Just as Tommy had little respect for the competence of his officers, so Badalia saw full well the limitations of their home-front counterparts. For the fact was that the army could not function without Tommy Atkins, any more than charity and philanthropy could work without Badalia. It was only on the basis of their largely unseen support, which had to be accepted and respected in its own terms, that empire and civilization could survive.

Between the universalist sentimentalism of Chevalier and the stark naturalism of Kipling, much of the cockney literature of the period veered incoherently, producing incongruous mixtures of harmlessness and brutality, coarseness and nobility of soul. Characteristic in this respect was Richard Whiteing's best-selling novel, *No. 5 John Street*, set in the year of the Diamond Jubilee. Whiteing started in the manner of Kipling. From St James's to

John Street was 'less than a mile', 'yet in the reckoning of life and habits and ways of thought it was as remote . . . as Africa'.[115] Thus the novel duly has its set-piece fight between a sturdy flower-girl and a drunken man with a knife, witnessed phlegmatically by the slum-dwelling crowd. Nevertheless, by the end of the book we are closer to Chevalier's Tivoli than to the recesses of Africa. The flower-girl's sick friend, whom she vainly tried to nurse back to health, was 'the gentlest and most thoughtful of hostesses. And, ah, how little separates her in essentials from the smartest and the best bred: – the Cockney aspirate, the Cockney vowel, a tendency to eat jam with a knife.'[116]

But the main message that developed through the literature was that the slums might be different, they might be violent, but they did not constitute a threat. Indeed, treated aright, they had a valuable contribution to make to the nation. Cockneys were, it was true, constitutionally indisposed to accept arbitrarily imposed authority. They were often at odds with policemen and uncomfortable in genteel surroundings. In one of the first novels to establish this convention, *Mord Em'ly*, the heroine escapes her position as a domestic servant in a stuffy Peckham household out of a yearning to return to the freedom, warmth, and cheerfulness of the Walworth streets.[117] But such cheerful anarchism was conservative rather than radical. In Pett Ridge's view, 'a revolution organized during August would never stand a chance of success, especially if Surrey happened to be doing well at the Oval'.[118] Not only were Londoners lazy and lacking in ambition, but the requisite class feeling was absent:

> Canrobert Street, Bethnal Green E, may experience something like jealousy in contemplating Cambridge Road, E, and the small shops in that modest thoroughfare, but it has no sensation of the kind in regard to Park Lane, W; indeed Canrobert Street is rather sorry for the very wealthy.[119]

Similar views were reiterated by Edwin Pugh in his search for the 'cockney' in 1913. There was no typical cockney, he concluded, but there were an array of character types who partially fitted the designation. Among them was the diminutive 'Arry: 'he is quite harmless, quite honest, not at all vicious, very good natured, more intelligent than he seems and inveterately plucky';[120] or 'Bill the Yahoo', his bigger and rougher counterpart. His type were 'just big boys overflowing with animal spirits'. Despite his rowdyism, Bill was a conservative romantic: 'There are some nobles with Liberal leanings, but every costermonger is a conservative in grain. There are socialistic Countesses, but never a flower-girl, that is not an individualist.' [121]

Even violence itself had come to have its natural and appropriate place in this order of things. In Clarence Rook's description of Lambeth Walk in 1899:

> Small and compact, the colony is easily organized; and here, as in all turbulent communities, such as an English public school, the leader gains his place by sheer force of personality. The boy who has kicked in a door can crow over the boy who has merely smashed a window. If you hve knocked-out your adversary at the little boxing place off the Walk, you will have proved that your friendship is desirable. [122]

In other circumstances, Rook's hero, the hooligan Alf, might have provided just the sort of material from which moral panics are concocted:

> You have an enemy, we will say, whom you wish to mark, but for one reason and another, you do not wish to appear in the matter. Young Alf will take on the job. Indicate to him your enemy; hand him . . . five shillings . . . and he will make all the necessary arrangements. [123]

Yet Jane Findlater, in a survey of slumland literature in 1904, saluted Alf's honesty and claimed: 'we certainly would meet him quite unconcernedly at dead of night'. [124] Similarly, to Pett Ridge, writing in 1908 of imprisoned London juveniles, it seemed that 'most of them are not bad nuts; they are only marred by a small speck' and that 'if justice were always justice, they would be playing at football in the fields close by, and going home later to the suppers their mothers had prepared'. [125] Pugh repeated this litany in 1913. He considered hooligans 'a much maligned class':

> Boys more fortunately circumstanced may satisfy this desire on the clean greensward, but the hooligan has only the dreary streets in which to disport himself . . . how else is he to rid himself of his surplus energy, but by senseless horseplay and unprofitable violence? [126]

It is tempting to believe that this literature in some sense prefigured the demands of war: there was nothing wrong with the aggressive instincts of male youth, it was simply a question of directing them into more appropriate channels. As Kipling had written:

> For it's Tommy this, an' Tommy that, an'
> 'Chuck him out, the brute!'

But it's 'Saviour of 'is country', when the guns begin to shoot.[127]

The 'cockney' on the streets

Asked in 1892 about the reasons for his success, Chevalier put it down to timing: 'if I had sung the same things ten years ago, people wouldn't have listened to them'.[128] Between the early 1880s and the early 1890s London had undergone some large and obvious changes. The fear of an outcast who might overrun civilization had been dispelled by the dock strike. The orderly character of the dock labourers quietened anxieties about mob violence. The modest aims of the strike suggested that distinctions could be made between the revolutionary rhetoric of socialist orators and the 'legitimate demands' of labour. Such discriminations were reinforced by Charles Booth's investigation of East London. However poor the generality of London workers might be, the criminal and vicious formed but an insignificant fraction of the toiling masses.[129] The great trade union upsurge of 1889–91 had demonstrated the potential of labour, and the new franchise in local government suggested that the working classes could no longer be left to the ministrations of the charitable and the religious, but had to be addressed as a prospective citizenry. All this, together with a growing preoccupation with London's imperial role, helps to explain why, for propertied and middle-class London, Chevalier's cheerful cockney should so successfully displace 'the cockney cad' and dark fears about the residuum.

But what of the London poor themselves? How far did the inhabitants of slumland accept or adopt the new cockney identity? Without more detailed research, it is difficult to give more than a very preliminary answer. The available evidence suggests that, to the extent that they did so, it was not simply as consumers of a representation bestowed upon them, but at least as much on their own terms. The 'cockney' was no doubt a very partial representation of their lives, as indeed were the music-hall songs which they sang. But in as far as they lived out this representation, it was as much their own creation as Chevalier's and shaped to their own purposes. How many did so, and who in particular, is far from clear. The great popularity of Chevalier's songs in the plebeian halls suggests widespread endorsement at some level. But the emergence of the 'pearlies' – the one unambiguous instance of the adoption of the 'cockney' identity at a popular level – suggests that the idea of the cockney appealed most strongly to a particular type of London worker rather than randomly across the working classes as a whole.

Just as the success of the new cockney stereotype among the genteel was in part dependent upon the fading away of the more lurid visions of the outcast, so, at a popular level, its success was connected with equally important, if more gradual, changes in the habits and expectations of the poor in the last third of the nineteenth century: in particular, a subtle shift in the terms of the relationship between the inhabitants of the slums and the hospitals, charities, churches, and settlements which ministered to them. The appearance of the pearly at some point in the 1880s was an instance of this. It was related to the growth of pageants and carnivals in aid of the London hospitals in the post-1870 period.[130] It was for such an occasion that Henry Croft, the first pearly king, is first said to have worn his pearly suit; and by the end of the century such pageants and carnivals had become a frequent occurrence in London streets. On these fancy-dress occasions the pearly king became a standard participant, alongside medical students, nurses, and junior doctors in their respective uniforms, and a colourful array of red Indians, clowns, comic policemen, and Buffalo Bills.[131]

Who were the pearlies? Contrary to the suggestion of Chevalier's song, they were not costermongers in their bank-holiday best.[132] The association of costers with pearlies, like most other components of Chevalier's portrait, was a fiction. According to the survey of 'Costerland' in *Living London* a few years later: 'we laugh at "the pearliers", but there is little laughter in the coster's life. Nor are there any "pearlies", for the true London coster would never dream of sporting such buttons.'[133] In fact, pearly dress appears to have been the invention of the music-hall. Chevalier's friend and fellow music-hall performer Charles Coburn claimed that pearlies were originally invented by the coster-slang singer Hiram Travers,[134] and the contention is supported by one first-hand reminiscence of Henry Croft, in which he is said to have taken the idea 'from a local music-hall entertainer of the time who wore a stage costume entirely covered with brass buttons'.[135]

Nevertheless, if art did not imitate life, life imitated art. If few costers were pearlies, most pearlies seem to have aspired to become costers. Accounts of pearly families in the twentieth century suggest that they were mainly drawn, like Croft himself, from the lower ranks of manual workers. Their numbers included road-sweepers, bookie's runners, Civil Service messengers, Covent Garden lorry drivers, rat-catchers, chimney sweeps, dockers, and so on.[136] But in nearly every case their ambition at some point was to become a coster and drive a 'moke and shay'. A characteristic example was Fred Tinsley. He was born in 1890, the son of a Lancashire weaver come south to find employment. When very young, he sold watercress and lettuce from a stall in a London street market. His first philanthropic efforts were with the Jolly Boys' Club, a hospital charity, for which he collected in a clown disguise. After becoming secretary of the club, he was admitted into the pearlies in 1911, becoming pearly king of Southwark. His first pearly outfit was a 'skeleton style' which he copied from Albert Chevalier. He was a coster until 1914, but was wounded in the war and thereafter worked as a chimney sweep. He stayed in this job until he retired, but was still collecting for charities until the beginning of the 1960s.[137]

In many ways, the pearlies were the perfect embodiment of the new idea of the 'cockney'. Their clownish folk-dress did not challenge social boundaries, but reinforced them. They were enthusiastic monarchists, achieving royal patronage from Princess Marie Louise in 1927, and by 1953, official representation at the coronation. They were wholeheartedly patriotic. Full pearly dress, at least from 1918, included military decorations, and nearly every pearly family lost husbands and sons in the two world wars. They were also for the most part Anglicans, though their religion seems to have been as much folkloric as Christian.[138] Finally, their official stance was apolitical. Their commitment was not to political change, but to philanthropy. The motto of their association, founded in 1911, was, 'One never knows'.[139]

But if the outlook of the pearly was in the most general sense patriotic and particularistic, it is also important to note that the cluster of attitudes associated with the pearly, and more generally the cockney, was not in any simple sense the triumph of traditional conservatism. Its peculiar brand of populism was rather the outcome of a compromise between the political and ideological forces contending in the late-Victorian city. Pearlies may not have seen themselves as political, but neither were they in any straightforward sense conservative working men. They were closely associated with working-class friendly societies, and their association employed trade union forms of address. It is said that early Labour marchers always gave generously to their collecting boxes and they themselves collected for striking miners in 1926.[140]

Nor were their charitable activities as reassuringly traditional as might at first seem. The association of the poor with the collection of charity was not uncontentious. It disrupted the object of the gift relationship, as mid-Victorian charity organizers had conceived it,[141] and it challenged the status of metropolitan hospitals by placing them under a new form of collective pressure. The most controversial of these new charities, the Hospital Saturday Fund, established in 1874, was founded with the aim of making hospitals available to all working men, and not merely the destitute poor.[142] The money was collected on a Saturday – pay day – both in the workshops and on the streets, and the money went towards the purchase of free treatment. As Geoffrey Rivett has demonstrated, the assumptions behind this fund were quite different from those informing more conventional forms of charity:

> The Saturday Fund expected to have a voice in the management of the hospitals it supported and to receive a fair share of governor's letters. If a working man with one of these letters was refused treatment, the Fund would want to know why, as the Hospital Saturday Fund worked on the assumption that by purchasing letters or contributing to hospital funds, it had bought the right to treatment.[143]

Moreover, it was not only the aims but also the methods of collection of such charities that incurred disapproval. Carnivals and street collections aroused popular excitement and might easily degenerate into disorder. 'Bands of music and street processions are very good,' the *Lancet* noted nervously, 'but they do not produce as much money as might be expected from the sensation they excite.'[144] 'One part of the proceedings of the day did seem rather objectionable,' wrote the *Camden Gazette* in 1881; 'boys with banners ran about in some of the thoroughfares, shaking their boxes before passengers and plaguing them for pence.'[145] It was perhaps for these sorts of reasons that in 1913 Edwin Pugh could associate the pearly with the hooliganism of 'Bill the Yahoo'[146] and that in 1928 hospital processions were banned by the police. Such processions, accompanied by pearlies, were, according to one account, 'noisy and unruly' and 'dominated by undesirable elements'.[147]

The example of the pearlies indicates the existence of a type of London working man, whose numbers were quite considerable (very roughly corresponding to Charles Booth's Classes C and D)[148] but whose lives and aspirations have more or less escaped the attention of historians. These were people who were beneath the journeyman, but who were just above the ranks of irregular casual labour: the poor, rather than the very poor. They did not possess skills, but retained positions through a reputation for 'steadiness', reliability, honesty, and good character. They were, as often as not, heavily dependent upon the good offices of employers or customers, and 'cheeriness' might have been a necessary stock-in-trade. They were not hostile to trade unions, but did not belong to them, either because of the vulnerability and indeterminate nature of their occupations, or else because the level of their earnings was too low to sustain a regular trade union subscription. But they were not for that reason beyond the sphere of associational life. These were the members of the humbler friendly societies, of the militias, and of the clubs operating under the aegis of the churches, the missions, and the university or public-school settlements.[149] Unlike the skilled and the better paid, they could not afford the luxury of rejecting the patronage of those above them and probably did not see the point of doing so. By the 1890s these forms of patronized club life were extensive in the poorer areas. Over a large part of Hackney, according to Booth:

> It seems to be regarded as part of the duty of the Church to supply decent amusements, and the entertainments in winter time are described as 'incessant'; consisting of dances, balls, concerts, plays, and, in two of the parishes, culminating in an annual pantomime. These entertainments often pay for themselves. . . . In the summer there are excursions without end, and the cricket clubs are extremely numerous. Every permitted pitch in Victoria Park and every other available place is appropriated, and mostly by clubs with Apostolic names.[150]

These were also the people whose sporting or pugilistic skills might have been encouraged by the sporting gentry from the City, the public schools, and the National Sporting Club.[151] They were certainly the people whom writers on the 'cockney' were most likely to encounter in the settlement halls, the cadet corps, the amateur entertainments, and the boxing gyms. Not tradesmen and not in a position to share in the ethos of independence associated with radical working men's clubs, they were nevertheless not without judgements of their own, as the pearlies or Kipling's trooper indicate. They nursed their own modest dreams of a self-sufficient position in the world – perhaps to become a publican or, in the pearlies' case, to become a coster with moke and shay – and they did manage to hold on to a status removed from that of the really dependent poor. Finally, some at least were able to carve a space for meaningful activity beyond work. For this sort of working man, it may be suggested, the notion of the 'cockney' offered an attractive identity and one which enabled them to make their presence visible in the city.[152]

From the cockney to the 'traditional' cockney

In high culture, the heyday of the 'cockney' was relatively short. It was already being undermined before 1914 and occupied a far more subordinate position until the mid-1930s.

After the Wilde scandal, a new generation of poets rejected the city as a symbol of decadence and rediscovered the spirit of England in the countryman of the home counties. Not only the Georgian poets but Kipling himself abandoned metropolitan imagery for the folkways of Sussex.[153] The enthusiasm for the soldier was dented by the final phase of the Boer War and all but obliterated by the Great War of 1914. Moreover, even in its time, the 'cockney' genre did not pass without criticism. Bernard Shaw's *Pygmalion* was in part a satire upon the supposed identity between speech, character, and class associated with the 'cockney' stereotype. As Professor Higgins told his mother:

> You have no idea how frightfully interesting it is to take a human being and change her into a quite different human being by creating a new speech for her. It's filling up the deepest gulf that separates class from class and soul from soul.[154]

To construct a whole way of life out of one or two music-hall songs and an assortment of cockney turns of phrase was to confine the outlook and behaviour of ordinary Londoners within a grotesquely restricted emotional register. As G. K. Chesterton protested against the pseudo-ethnography of the slums, 'a poor man is a man who has not got much money':

> The religious teacher is at least supposed to be interested in the costermonger because he is a man; the politician is in some dim and perverted sense interested in the costermonger because he is a citizen; it is only the wretched writer who is interested in the costermonger merely because he is a costermonger . . . when he endeavours to represent that he is describing the spiritual core of the costermonger, his dim vices and delicate virtues, then we must object that his claim is preposterous.[155]

Finally, the indigenous character of 'cockney' culture was itself beginning to come under threat. Not only were the moke and shay becoming an anachronism with the arrival of motorized transport, but so were the halls after the arrival of ragtime and moving pictures from America after 1906. Even the songs themselves were no longer quite what they seemed. The 'cockney' favourite, 'Down at the Old Bull and Bush' was a product of Tin Pan Alley and written in New York.[156] This was to prefigure an important inter-war theme: dwelling upon the cockney was one way of registering a protest against the American cultural threat.

Between the wars, London doubled yet again in population from four to eight million. The economic and cultural impact of the United States, already discernible before 1914, was by the 1930s visually overwhelming – American department stores, American tubes, American films, and Californian-style arterial motorways. It was summed up in J. B. Priestley's famous evocation of 1934: 'cocktail bars, motor coaches, wireless, hiking, factory girls looking like actresses, grey-hound racing and dirt-tracks, swimming pools, and everything given away for cigarette coupons'.[157] What captured the imagination was Greater London, rather than its Victorian core; Park Royal Station and the Great West Road, rather than Bethnal Green and the Strand. Even the old centres of Edwardian high life – Piccadilly and Leicester Square – were scarcely recognizable with their bright neon lights and shiny black marble cinemas. Moreover, after 1934 London government was in Labour hands. The metropolitan region, as the Barlow Commission and other inquiries complained, seemed like a gigantic, futuristic, and cosmopolitan magnet drawing talent and energy away from the depressed and traditional regions.

This was no longer a city in which a nationalist Conservatism felt at ease. Thus London found no place in Stanley Baldwin's *England* in which 'England is the country and the country is England.'[158] Nor did it play any positive role in the prolific writings of the Dean of St Paul's, W. R. Inge, who endorsed the notion that the comradeship of the trenches had been that between 'the aristocrat' and the 'ploughman' and who considered that the 'people who know London and do not like it are a very large proportion of Londoners', since 'we are all countrymen at heart'.[159] London played a distinctly modest part in Sir Winston Churchill's story of *The Island Race*. Nor, apparently, did it make any contribution to the formation of 'national character'. For, as Arthur Bryant explained, after noting that Samuel Pepys though born within the sound of Bow Bells nevertheless regarded himself as a Cambridgeshire man:

All this is important if we are to understand ourselves. Because, having country roots, we are constantly haunted by needs and cravings whose purpose is no longer clear to us. Our culture – to use a terrifying and much misused word – is a country culture: that is, such of it as is still left for us, for, though we have, since our emigration to the towns, lost and destroyed much of our

own country culture, we have not as yet built up a civil structure
to take its place.[160]

Even in the supposedly revamped Conservatism which followed
the Second World War, Quintin Hogg could still state in his *Case
for Conservatism* that farming was essential to the community, not
only as a business, but as a way of life, since 'the Conservative
believes – and so far science has borne him out – that a purely
urban community tends to die out'.[161]

If the 'cockney' played a muted part in the imagery of
Conservative England between the wars, it was because the
'national spirit' was now so firmly located in the shires.[162] Why the
Conservatives turned their backs so peremptorily upon 'the
cockney' as 'the supreme type of Englishman', and how far they
did so, needs further investigation. But what is clear is that, in
doing so, they were to isolate themselves from a potentially
powerful repertoire of patriotic sentiment. Before the First World
War, the inner East End had been a Conservative bastion.
Moreover, during the war itself, it seems probable that music-hall
song and humour through the medium of camp entertainments did
much more to sustain the morale of the troops than the official
hand-outs evoking Hodge and the Thatched Cottage. But the
combination of Labour's capture of the East End in 1919 and the
increasingly Americanized image of London high society may have
combined to reinforce the marked Conservative identification with
the timeless rural. Left to his own devices, the now 'traditional
cockney', encased in his pre-1914 mould, became a minor
character, a hardy perennial of bank holidays and affectionate
renderings of London life, a dwindling remnant of a vanishing
race.

From the 'Lambeth Walk' to the 'carry-on spirit'

But the latent power still locked within this frozen cockney
imagery was dramatically revealed in the astonishing national and
international success of *Me and My Girl* which opened at the
Victoria Theatre, Westminster, at the end of 1937 and was to play
continuously for a further four years. It was this musical that was
to launch the 'Lambeth Walk', a dance which became so famous
that even Mussolini was reported to have learnt its steps in 1938.
In Britain itself, the dance became a national craze; and according
to Mass Observation's book on Britain in 1938: 'you can find them
doing the Lambeth Walk in Mayfair ball-rooms, suburban dance-
halls, cockney parties and village hops'.[163]

The plot of *Me and My Girl* was traditional music-hall fare. Bill, the Lambeth coster, becomes heir to a country estate. The 'walk' may have gone back to an imitation of Charlie Chaplin in 1915, and the words of the song were those of a hit of 1903. Nor was there anything especially innovative in its politics. Its contrast between the cheerful community life of the Lambeth slums and the stuffy etiquette of Hareford Hall descends in a straight line from the turn-of-the-century cockney tales of Pett Ridge. If the working class was valorized, it was in the words of Mass Observation because it was 'the class who knew how to have a good time'.[164]

One of the most intriguing aspects of the success of the Lambeth Walk was the way in which it set the agenda of the official attempt to invoke a spirit of popular and plebeian national resistance in the early years of the war. Ironically, in so far as the 'walk' contained a moment of national assertion, it had been conceived as an answer to Americanism rather than Fascism. According to Mass-Observation, its composer, Noel Gay, believed, 'and all our evidence entirely supports him – that ordinary working folk are not satisfied with the endless American heaven in your arms and moonlight on silent waters'.[165] While one hostile contemporary witness considered:

it might possibly have originated as a facet of *almost* deliberate propaganda of the 'See Britain First' variety (and-to-hell-with-all-this-Yankee-stuff-and-why-should-England-be-run-by-America-anyhow) plus a vague kind of patronizing attitude *on behalf of* 'Our Betters' towards the ordinary working class cockney, such cockney being pictured as of the pearly-king coster variety *only* (of 1888 at that!) such picture being the inevitable product of complete class-ignorance.[166]

The phenomenal success of *Me and My Girl* was followed by the revival of cockney songs, like 'Knees up, Mother Brown', now transmitted to millions by the radio. When the war began, it was this archaic and nostalgic notion of the 'cockney' spirit which was enlisted by the Ministry of Information, with its emphasis on 'cheerfulness' and the 'carry-on spirit', as the dominant motif in its attempt to sustain morale during the Blitz. Indeed, if the Conservative press was to be believed, the 'cheerfulness' of the bombed-out East Enders bordered on imbecility:

The East End loved it. They settled themselves down each night, on rugs and cushions and blankets, along the corridors; in the day-time they sat in the tip-up seats and sent their children to play in a disused ice-rink at the back of the stage . . . and wasn't it a lovely bright place, almost like a palace? So they told each other.[167]

Actually, when the Blitz began in the autumn of 1940, the reaction of the 'cockney' was anything but cheerful. As Harold Nicolson noted in his diary on 17 September: 'everybody is worried about the feeling in the East End. . . . There is much bitterness. It is said that even the King and Queen were booed the other day when they visited the destroyed areas.' [168] It was only in the subsequent months that a more realistic and socially conscious style of reporting emerged, led by the *Mirror*, the *Herald*, and the *Picture Post*.[169]

With the onset of the Blitz, it could scarcely be denied that London was once more at the heart of the nation. But the shire-bound imagery of inter-war Conservatism – a successful formula of the Baldwin years – left the party ill prepared for this change of focus. The terms in which the iconography of the 'cheerful cockney' were resurrected by the Conservative press betrayed its ignorance and lack of intimacy with the world of the back streets. As one official at the Ministry of Information commented:

> The superficial observation of journalists who are not of the working classes and who have little economic or personal experience of the masses have produced a picture of complete courage, determination, carry-onism, a vast propaganda of 'everything is ok with the civilians'. . . . The working masses are almost a race apart, the primitively simple and heroic poor, admired from a distance. They, the people, are admired by we, the leaders and those above.[170]

The late-Victorian cockney archetype had gathered together many of the ingredients of a populist and city-based conception of the nation and had projected the fantasy of a metropolitan community grounded in the good-humoured, if sometimes ironic, acceptance of social difference and subordination. During the Second World War, it was Labour which proved to possess a more certain sense of the patriotism of the urban nation. The Labour press did not turn its back upon the 'cockney' stereotype, but subtly transformed it.

Much of the Labour rhetoric also contained an implicit 'us and them'. It came out clearly, for example, in an unguarded remark of Harold Laski, in which he stated that he could share in 'the pride every citizen of this country is bound to have in the amazing heroism and endurance of the common people'.[171] But unlike the 'us and them' embedded in Conservative rhetoric, that of 'the common people' was not burdened with anti-urban prejudice and could more easily be turned in a democratic direction. Nor was it saddled with the lumber of 1890s jingoism. As George Orwell put it: 'In England all the boasting and flag-wagging, the rule Britannia stuff, is done by small minorities. The patriotism of the common people is not vocal or even conscious.'[172] In the notion of 'the common people', images of nation, class, and democracy, in both town and country, could be made to coincide, and through the medium of the 'cockney' strands of popular and patriotic sentiment, which possessed little or no historic or intrinsic connection with socialism, were in 1945 harnessed to the language of Labour.

Conclusion

The rest of the story can only be sketched. In the ten years or so which followed the war, the 'cockney' enjoyed an Indian summer. It provided the repertoire of radio entertainment (Mrs Mop and her successors) and an assortment of London characters to populate Ealing comedies. Its notions of class and authority were drawn upon to provide set-piece exchanges between officers and men in British war films. Its pathetic features were also rehearsed in poignant press stories of stubborn slum dwellers reluctantly moved into the sunlit world of garden cities and new towns. Its wit and wartime heroism were lovingly described in Julian Franklyn's 1953 depiction of *The Cockney*, its old-world nostalgia beautifully evoked in Chaplin's *Limelight*.

But in 1959 the last donkey stables of the pearlies were pulled down in Camden, and within a year Macmillan's 'wind of change' speech effectively wound up the British Empire. It was perhaps fitting that both should have ended around the same time, just as both should have enjoyed their heyday in the 1890s. It was not that the 'cockneys' – let alone the poor Londoners who were its referent – were intrinsically jingoistic. But what was true was that as a form of representation, whether brutal, comic, or sentimental, the cockney archetype was intrinsically connected with the attempt to discover and embody a form of national spirit in the city dweller, to break down the anonymous and shabby crowds into a catalogue of particular types, and to incorporate them into a national community. If the temporality of the last cockney archetype was imperial rather than merely national or municipal, it was because the problems of defining English nationhood in the first half of the twentieth century were so intimately tied to assumptions of imperial heritage or destiny. The salient questions were not those of religious conformity, of thrift and prudence, of domestic morality, of deference in a traditional sense, or of efficiency and productivity. Such questions belonged to the past or the future. In the epoch of the 'cockney', the predominant questions were rather those concerned with the maintenance of political rule and authority at home and abroad, with the preservation of Britain's status as a world imperial power, and with the forging of an inclusive sense of nationhood appropriate to that calling. It was this cluster of concerns which created 'a British way of life', part of whose genius was to blunt the threat of mass democracy and to fragment it into a mosaic of colourful idiosyncrasy. In this endeavour, 1956 was the moment of truth. The archaism of the project was highlighted, not only by the Suez expedition, but also by Osborne's *Entertainer*.

In fact, from start to finish, the question of the 'cockney' had always been political. From the eighteenth century to the 1950s the question of the 'cockney' was always a question about who did and who did not belong to the political nation and on what terms. The story of the social descent of the 'cockney' through the nineteenth century was the story of the extension of the political nation; in the twentieth century, the terms of his or her belonging to 'the national community'. The chronological sequence was punctuated by alternating phases, of exclusion and assimilation, of fear followed by reassurance. Thus, Dr Johnson and *Blackwood's* were followed by Surtees, Egan, and Dickens; Milliken and Gissing by Kipling and Chevalier. The significant turning-points were also political: the Reform Acts of 1832, 1867, and 1884, the redistribution Act of the 1880s and the reforms of the local government franchise in the late 1880s and the 1890s. From the First World War, on the other hand, the story was one of transition from Labour as threat to the nation to Labour as the embodiment of nation, and thus the shift from the Tory 'cockney' of Edwardian England to the Labour 'cockney' of the 1940s.

With the construction of the Welfare State, the historical functions of the 'cockney' were already slipping away. In the new society to be built upon the National Health Service and full employment, there was no longer a sanctioned place for the subordination that the 'cockney' represented. Finally, with the ending of empire, the proliferation of new commodities, and the aspiration towards more classless styles of consumption promoted by television and the 'affluent society', interest in the 'cockney' would seem to have reached its historical terminus. In terms of the content and supposed subjects of successive discourses about the 'cockney', this was obviously true. Church, army, and public school were no longer especially interested in 'cockneys'; their posthumous existence was largely sponsored by the London Chamber of Commerce and the London Tourist Board.

But if we were to focus upon the form, rather than upon the

content, of those preoccupations, such a conclusion is not so clear cut. A year before the demolition of the pearly stables, in 1958, London posed a new problem in the demarcation of nationality, citizenship, and difference. This was the year of the Notting Hill race riots. The history of the 'cockney' is thus not as remote as it might appear. For, in more ways than one, it would seem that the debate about race, citizenship, and the inner city – with its conflicting impulses towards exclusion, suppression, domestication, and integration – began precisely at the point where the debate about the 'cockney' left off.

Notes

An early version of this essay was given as the Alderman Sydney Smith Lecture at the University of Hull in October 1986.

1 This essay, it should be emphasized, is a very preliminary survey. I am well aware of its incompleteness. For instance, one important historical question which I do not discuss is the extent to which London's Irish and Jewish populations were incorporated within notions of the 'cockney' or excluded from them.

2 See, for instance, A. L. Beier and R. Finlay (eds), *London 1500–1700: The Making of the Metropolis*, 1986; C. H. Lee, 'Regional growth and structural change in Victorian Britain', *Economic History Review*, 2nd series, 33, 1981, pp. 438–52.

3 See C. M. Barron, 'Richard Whittington: the man behind the myth', in A. E. Hollaender and W. Kellaway (eds), *Studies in London History*, 1969.

4 Mrs E. T. Cook, *Highways and Byeways in London*, 1903, p. 437.

5 H. J. Massingham, *London Scene*, 1933, p. 89.

6 James A. Jones, *London's Eight Millions*, Plymouth, 1937, p. 89.

7 ibid., p. 144; on the 'cockney charwoman' cf. J. and C. Gordon, *London Roundabout*, 1933, p. 159: 'Sturdy Briton that she was, Mrs Harris naturally hated all official control. This characteristic both unites and severs the served and the working classes; they are both fundamentally contemptuous of the law, and a full third of the bitterness daily growing in England today is due to the fact that the law is lenient to breaches committed from above and harsh to similar misdemeanours committed from below.'

8 R. Clayton, *Portrait of London*, 1980, p. 188.

9 Arthur Roberts, *Fifty Years of Spoof*, 1927, p. 163.

10 J. and C. Gordon, op. cit., p. 152.

11 R. J. Cruikshank, *The Moods of London*, 1951, p. 54.

12 W. Matthews, *The Cockney Past and Present*, 1938, 1972 edn, p. ix.

13 J. Franklyn, *The Cockney: A Survey of London Life and Language*, 1953, p. 3.

14 Matthews, op. cit., pp. 3–4.

15 Adam Joseph, *King of the Pearlies, the Story of Henry Croft*, n.d., p. 7; more generally on the origins of the pearlies, see P. Binder, *The Pearlies: A Social Record*, 1975; R. Samuel and G. Stedman Jones, 'Pearly kings and queens', in R. Samuel (ed.), *Patriotism and the Making of British National Identities*, vol. 3, London, 1989.

16 'The rise and fall of the pearly king', *Picture Post*, vol. 36, no. 5, 2 August 1947, p. 14.

17 R. Hudson, 'The first king of the pearlies', *Lady*, 17 July 1980, p. 104.

18 For confirmation, see the Reggae song 'Cockney translation', cited in Dick Hebdige, *Cut 'N' Mix*, 1987, pp. 149–50.

19 The invention of this age-old cockney bears some resemblance to the invention of other traditions in the same period; see Eric Hobsbawm and Terence Ranger (eds), *The Invention of Tradition*, Cambridge, 1983.

20 John Walker, *A Critical Pronouncing Dictionary*, 1791, p. xiii.

21 ibid., p. xiv.

22 Dr Johnson, *Dictionary*, 1785 edn.

23 See 'The land of Cokaygne', in J. A. Bennett and G. V. Smithers (eds), *Early Middle English Verse and Prose*, Oxford, 1968, pp. 137–44.

24 *Johnson's Dictionary*, ed. Todd, 1819, vol. 1, p. 48; see also J. O. Halliwell, *A Dictionary of Archaic and Provincial Words*, 1846, vol. 1, p. 261; on the *cuccagna* in Naples, see Harold Acton, *The Bourbons of Naples (1734–1825)*, 1956, pp. 42–4.

25 *Murray's New English Dictionary*, Oxford, 1893, vol. 2, p. 576; and see also F. Grose, *A Classical Dictionary of the Vulgar Tongue*, 1785, p. 247.

26 *Johnson's Dictionary*, op. cit., p. 48; on the relevance of eighteenth-century theories of language to this definition, see Olivia Smith, *The Politics of Language 1791–1819*, Oxford, 1984, pp. 1–35.

27 S. Pegge, *Anecdotes of the English Language . . .*, 2nd edn, 1814, p. 4.

28 ibid., p. vi.

29 ibid., p. 5.

30 'On the cockney school of poetry', *Blackwood's Edinburgh Magasine*, vol. ii, October 1817, p. 415.

31 ibid., pp. 38–9.

32 *Blackwood's Edinburgh Magasine*, vol. xix, January–June 1826, p. xxvi.

33 R. Ingpen (ed.), *The Autobiography of Leigh Hunt*, 1903, vol. 2, p. 197; for analogous uses of 'cockney' during this period, cf. University College, London, as 'the cockney university', S. Maccoby (ed.), *English Radicalism 1760–1832*, 1952, p. 461; or Macaulay: '[These writers] conceived of liberty as monks conceive of love, as cockneys conceive of the happiness and innocence of rural life' – T. Macaulay, *Miscellaneous Writings and Speeches*, 1913, p. 143.

34 C. Kingsley, *Alton Locke: Tailor and Poet*, 1850.

35 John Ruskin, 'Fiction, fair and foul', *Works*, vol. xxxiv, p. 277.

36 Cited in Smith, op. cit., p. 24; cf. James Harris: '*By a more refin'd operation of our Mind alone, we abstract any Attribute from its*

necessary subject, and consider it *apart*, devoid of its dependence' – ibid., p. 23.

37 Matthews, op. cit., p. 42; *Johnson's Dictionary*, op. cit., p. 48.

38 Grose, op. cit. Egan produced a new edition of this dictionary in 1823, expunging 'coarse and broad expressions'.

39 P. Egan, *Life in London*, 1821, pp. 84–5.

40 P. Egan, *The Pilgrims of the Thames in Search of the National*, 1839, pp. 7–8.

41 (R. S. Surtees), *Handley Cross or Mr Jorrocks' Hunt*, 1854 edn, p. 56.

42 ibid.

43 (R. S. Surtees), *Hillingdon Hall or the Cockney Squire*, 1888 edn, p. 31; for a pictorial representation of the cockney in this period, see John Wardroper, *The Caricatures of George Cruikshank*, 1977, p. 73.

44 *Handley Cross*, op. cit., p. 109.

45 ibid., p. 123. On the significance of credit as an issue in the radicalism of the Wilkes era, see J. Brewer, 'English radicalism in the age of George III', in J. G. A. Pocock (ed.), *Three British Revolutions*, Princeton, NJ, 1890. How far back the traits of this positive depiction of London burgher virtue go is unclear. Laura Stephenson argues that it does not go back further than Daniel Defoe's *The Complete English Tradesman* at the end of the seventeenth century. Elizabethan literature in praise of London merchants stressed their knightly rather than their bourgeois characteristics. See Laura Stephenson, *Praise and Paradox: Merchants and Craftsmen in Elizabethan Popular Literature*, Cambridge, 1984, pp. 196–7 and *passim*.

46 *Hillingdon Hall*, op. cit., p. 35.

47 James Kinsley (ed.), C. Dickens, *The Pickwick Papers*, Oxford, 1986, editor's introduction, pp. xvii–xviii, xxii–xxiii.

48 B. H. Smart, *Walker's Pronouncing Dictionary of the English Language Adapted to the Present State of Literature and Science*, 1846, p. 179.

49 Kinsley, op. cit., p. xxxviii.

50 ibid., p. lvii.

51 See, for instance, Binder, op. cit., pp. 11–77.

52 H. Mayhew, *London Labour and the London Poor*, 1861, vol. 1, pp. 1–2.

53 (H. Mayhew), *The Great World of London*, 1857, pp. 5–6.

54 Renton Nicholson, *Cockney Adventures and Tales of London Life*, 1838, p. iv.

55 ibid., p. 5.

56 ibid., p. 42.

57 ibid., p. 106.

58 On the various connotations of the 'swell', see P. Bailey, 'Champagne Charlie: performance and ideology in the music-hall swell song', in J. S. Bratton (ed.), *Music Hall: Performance and Style*, Milton Keynes, 1986, pp. 54–5 and *passim*.

59 Bailey, op. cit., p. 60; H. Chance Newton, *Idols of the Halls*, 1928, p. 24.

60 'Our music-halls', *Tinsley's Magasine*, April 1869, p. 216.
61 P. Fitzgerald, *Music-Hall Land*, 1890, p. 4.
62 E. J. Milliken, *From Punch 'Arry Ballads*, 1892, p. 1. For a detailed analysis of 'Arry's language, see C. Stoffel, *Studies in English Written and Spoken for the Use of the Continental Student*, 1894, pp. 170 ff. Stoffel thought 'Arry, 'the young British philistine of low life: in him we find all the weaknesses, follies, perversities, imperfections and vices of the average middle class Cockney divested of all the honourable and redeeming qualities of heart and mind that in the Englishman of the better class, go far to make up his short-comings' – ibid., p. 170. Gissing, on the other hand, represented 'Arry as part of the working classes. In part, this was because the social identity of the clerk was changing. The main point about the liberal representation of 'Arry, however, was not his precise socio-economic status, but rather his lack of education. It was class in the sense of Arnold rather than Marx.
63 *Punch*, 17 December 1887, p. 280.
64 Milliken, op. cit., p. 3.
65 ibid., p. 5.
66 T. Hopkins, 'Music halls', *University Magasine, Dublin*, NS, vol. ii, no. viii, August 1878, p. 194.
67 *Punch*, 10 September 1881, p. 110.
68 *Punch*, 11 May 1878, p. 2.
69 *Punch*, 2 April 1881, p. 156.
70 *Punch*, 11 May 1878, p. 205.
71 *Punch*, 28 July 1883, p. 38.
72 *Punch*, 26 November, p. 249.
73 *Punch*, 5 April 1879, p. 145.
74 *Punch*, 25 September 1886, p. 145.
75 E. V. Page, *'Arry*, 1881. The cover drawing by Concannen shows Jenny Hill in red tail-coat, small straw hat with red ribbon, blue striped trousers, white waistcoat, buttonhole and watch-chain. I can find no grounds for accepting the suggestion (Bratton, op. cit., p. 66) that this was a 'coster song'. On Jenny Hill, see J. S. Bratton, 'Jenny Hill: sex and sexism in Victorian music-hall', in Bratton, op. cit., pp. 92–111.
76 George Gissing, *Demos: A Study of English Socialism*, 1886, Brighton, 1982 edn, p. 4.
77 ibid., p. 77.
78 ibid., p. 40.
79 ibid., p. 104.
80 (J. C. Hotten), *A Dictionary of Modern Slang, Cant and Vulgar Words*, 2nd edn, 1860, p. 122.
81 Roberts, op. cit., p. 163.
82 *Era*, 15 April 1866, p. 11.
83 H. Chance Newton, *Idols of the 'Halls'*, 1928, p. 24.
84 Roberts, op. cit., p. 164.
85 Newton, op. cit., p. 118.
86 Coburn, op. cit., p. 111.

87 (A. Tuer), *The Kaukneigh Alminek edited by 'Enery 'Arris, down't-tcher-now*, 1883, p. 15.
88 F. Anstey, *Burglar Bill and Other Pieces for the Use of the Young Reciter*, 1888, p. 36.
89 ibid., p. 37.
90 A. Chevalier, *A Record by Himself*, 1895, p. 116.
91 ibid., p. 118.
92 ibid., p. 121.
93 ibid.
94 ibid., p. 128.
95 C. Duncan Lucas, 'Costerland in London', in G. R. Sims (ed.), *Living London*, 1892, vol. 2, p. 77.
96 Harold Scott, *Early Doors*, 1946, p. 179.
97 A. Chevalier, *Before I Forget – the Autobiography of a Chevalier d'Industrie*, 1903, pp. 26–7, 32–3.
98 ibid., p. 45; Roberts, op. cit., p. 28. Chevalier's fears must have been particularly acute since he was the son-in-law of George Leybourne, 'Champagne Charlie', the most celebrated *lion comique* of the 1860s and 1870s. On the *lion comique*, see P. Bailey, 'Champagne Charlie', op. cit.
99 See Scott, op. cit., pp. 179–80.
100 Chevalier, *Before I Forget*, pp. 179–80.
101 *Graphic*, 29 October 1892, p. 521.
102 It is significant that the mainstay of his provincial tours, before turning to the halls, were sketches (together with John Beauchamp) of Sam and Tony Weller, Betsy Prigg and Sairey Gamp, Sikes and Fagin – *Before I Forget*, op. cit., p. 32.
103 G. B. Shaw, 'Notes to *Captain Brassbound's Conversion*', in *Collected Plays*, vol. 2, 1971, pp. 424–5.
104 *Graphic*, 29 October 1892, p. 521.
105 James Douglas, *Adventures in London*, 1909, p. 17.
106 Rev. J. Adderly, 'Introduction', to A. St John Adcock, *East End Idylls*, 1897, p. 1.
107 W. Pett Ridge, *A Story Teller, Forty Years in London*, 1923, p. 78.
108 E. Pugh, *The City of the World*, 1912, p. 315.
109 T. S. Eliot, *Selected Essays*, 1969, p. 456.
110 Douglas, op. cit., p. 143.
111 For an important analysis of Kipling's relationship with the 'cockney' and his impact upon the subsequent 'cockney school' of literature, see P. J. Keating, *The Working Classes in Victorian Fiction*, 1971, chs 6, 7, 8.
112 R. Kipling, 'The record of Badalia Herodsfoot', in *Many Inventions*, 1922, p. 296.
113 Keating, op. cit., pp. 170 ff.
114 R. Kipling, *Barrack Room Ballads and Other Verses*, 1921, p. 8.
115 R. Whiteing, *No. 5 John Street*, 1899, p. 13.
116 ibid., p. 291.
117 W. Pett Ridge, *Mord Em'ly*, 1898.

118 W. Pett Ridge, *Speaking Rather Seriously*, 1908, p. 186.
119 ibid., p. 227.
120 Pugh, op. cit., p. 41.
121 ibid., p. 44.
122 Clarence Rook, *The Hooligan Nights*, 1899, Oxford, 1979 edn, p. 16.
123 ibid., p. 17.
124 Jane H. Findlater, *Stones from a Glass House*, 1904, p. 87.
125 Pett Ridge, *Speaking Seriously*, op. cit., p. 192.
126 Pugh, op. cit., pp. 45, 46.
127 Kipling, *Barrack Room Ballads*, op. cit., p. 9.
128 *Graphic*, 29 October 1892, p. 521.
129 See G. Stedman Jones, *Outcast London*, 1971, chs 17, 18.
130 See Samuel and Stedman Jones, op. cit.
131 Peter F. Brooks, *Pearly Kings and Queens in Britain*, n.d., p. 35;
     Joseph, op. cit., p. 10.
132 According to Chevalier's 'The coster's serenade', 'Me in my
     "pearlies" felt a toff that day.'
133 Duncan Lucas, op. cit., p. 77.
134 'I think he should be really regarded as the original representative of
     the coster type. . . . Undoubtedly he was the first to bring the
     "pearly" button into great prominence and nobody before *his* time
     could boast of a coat covered with "pearlies" and weighing thirteen
     pounds. . . . Travers was for many years known and advertised as the
     "Pearly King" ' – Coburn, op. cit., p. 107.
135 Binder, op. cit., p. 154.
136 See the biographies of pearly families contained in ibid., pp. 115–56.
137 ibid., pp. 147–50.
138 ibid., p. 96; Hudon, op. cit., p. 104.
139 Binder, op. cit., p. 97.
140 ibid., pp. 126, 148.
141 Stedman Jones, op. cit., pp. 241–62.
142 Geoffrey Rivett, *The Development of the London Hospital System
     1823–1982*, 1986, p. 122.
143 ibid.
144 *Lancet*, 25 July 1885, p. 187.
145 *Camden and Kentish Towns, Hampstead, Highgate, Holloway and St
     Pancras Gazette*, 10 September 1881. According to pearly legend
     (e.g. Hudson, op. cit., p. 104; Joseph, op. cit., p. 10), Henry Croft
     first wore a pearly suit in Somers Town market 'on carnival day 1880'.
     The costers were so impressed that they elected him 'pearly king of
     Somerstown'. If such an event did occur, there is no record of it in the
     local press. But there was an active costermongers' evangelical
     mission, founded in 1873 (see *Camden Gazette*, 4 January 1879, 30
     August 1879, 10 January 1880, 1 January 1881), and there is also
     evidence of attempts by the churches to attract costers by staging
     elaborate harvest thanksgiving services (*Camden Gazette*, 6 Novem-
     ber 1880). The siting of this mission in Somers Town is significant
     since this market had been the object of aggressive sabbatarian

campaigns against Sunday trading in the 1850s and 1860s. On the evangelical missions to the costers under the patronage of Lord Shaftesbury, see G. Holden Pike, *Golden Lane, Quaint Adventures and Life Pictures*, London, 1876.

146 Pugh, op. cit., pp. 191–2.
147 Brooks, op. cit., p. 35.
148 Charles Booth, *Life and Labour of the People of London*, 17 vols, 1902, 1st series, vol. 2, p. 21.
149 On the relevance of these types of friendly societies to the pearlies, see Binder, op. cit., pp. 77, 121, 147–8.
150 Booth, op. cit., 3rd series, vol. 1, p. 102.
151 For an account which touches upon this milieu, see Stan Shipley, 'Tom Causer of Bermondsey: a boxer hero of the 1890s', *History Workshop*, 15, spring 1983, pp. 28–60; see also the reminiscences collected by Mass Observation in 1938: 'there used to be private gymnasiums in the West End where the gents used to watch us' – Charles Madge and Tom Harrison, *Britain by Mass Observation*, 1939, pp. 154–5; on gentlemanly interest in cadet corps in the 1890s, see H. W. Nevinson, *Changes and Chances*, 1923, pp. 90–5.
152 Cf. this hostile account from the 1930s: 'The cockney has been to a certain extent ruined by the knowledge that people have heard a lot about him and are interested in him. . . . He knows now that he is expected to be witty, having read his *Evening News* and borrowed *Punch*, or seen it at his barber's. If he is a bus conductor, he is always, painfully and obviously, trying to live up to the idea of a stage cockney' – G. Roberts, *I Take This City*, 1933, p. 117.
153 See Holbrook Jackson, *The Eighteen Nineties*, 1913, p. 62; M. Wiener, *English Culture and the Decline of the Industrial Spirit 1850–1980*, Cambridge, 1981, pp. 56–8; Alun Howkins, 'The discovery of rural England', in R. Colls and P. Dodd (eds), *Englishness: Politics and Culture, 1880–1920*, 1986, pp. 62–88.
154 G. B. Shaw, *Pygmalion*, Harmondsworth, 1986, pp. 81–2.
155 G. K. Chesterton, 'Slum novelists and the slums', in *Heretics*, 1906, p. 277.
156 G. Weightman and S. Humphries, *The Making of Modern London 1914–1939*, 1984, p. 9.
157 J. B. Priestley, *English Journey*, 1934, p. 401.
158 S. Baldwin, *On England*, 1926, p. 6.
159 W. R. Inge, *A Rustic Moralist*, 1937, p. 334.
160 A. Bryant, *The National Character*, 1934, p. 24.
161 Q. Hogg, *The Case for Conservatism*, Harmondsworth, 1947. Cited in M. Wiener, op. cit., p. 110.
162 On this, see especially Wiener, op. cit., pp. 100–2.
163 Mass Observation, op. cit., p. 139; and see also Alison Light and Raphael Samuel, 'Pantomimes of class', *New Society*, 19–26 December 1986, pp. 14–18.
164 Mass Observation, op. cit., p. 174.
165 ibid., p. 162.

166 ibid., p. 170.
167 Cited in Kingsley Martin, 'Reflections on air-raids', *Political Quarterly*, 12, 1941, p. 78; cf. the distinctly infantilizing treatment of the working classes in *Me and My Girl*: 'the point comes out quite clearly that the working class characters are "nearer to nature" than the upper class ones: George Groves, who takes the part of a whisky-drinking but benevolent member of the aristocracy, says to Sally the Lambeth girl: "I like you and I like your Bill. You're two little simple children of nature"' – Mass Observation, op. cit., p. 158.
168 Harold Nicolson, *Diaries and Letters 1939–1945*, 1967, p. 114; for an account of the Blitz, see Angus Calder, *The People's War: Britain 1939–1945*, 1969, ch. 4.
169 See L. Budrass, 'British home front propaganda in World War II and the bombing of Coventry', unpublished MA dissertation, Centre for the Study of Social History, University of Warwick, 1986, ch. 2.
170 Cited in Budrass, op. cit., p. 52.
171 Cited in P. Addison, *The Road to 1945*, 1977, p. 184.
172 G. Orwell, *The Lion and the Unicorn*, Harmondsworth, 1986, p. 42.

Index

327